D1000101

JEWISH LAW
IN
GENTILE CHURCHES

JEWISH LAW
IN
GENTILE CHURCHES

Halakhah and the Beginning of Christian Public Ethics

Markus Bockmuehl

T&T CLARK
EDINBURGH

T&T CLARK LTD
59 GEORGE STREET
EDINBURGH EH2 2LQ
SCOTLAND

www.tandtclark.co.uk

First published 2000

ISBN 0 567 08734 4

British Library Cataloguing-in-Publication Data
A catalogue record for this book is available
from the British Library

Typeset by Fakenham Photosetting Limited, Fakenham, Norfolk
Printed and bound in Great Britain by Bookcraft Ltd, Avon

CONTENTS

PREFACE

Two subjects have especially captured my attention in the course of recent research.[1] The first is the prominent role of Jewish law and legal tradition in the ethics of Jesus and the early church, while the second concerns the principles and criteria by which Christians moved from this highly particular Jewish moral discourse to the problem of formulating an ethic for Gentiles. The guiding question shaping the present book is that of the early Christian reception and articulation of normative criteria for ethics. There has long been a popular antinomian point of view in mainstream Protestant thought, which denies that New Testament faith could involve binding moral norms of any kind. On this view, aside from the general exhortation to 'love', any 'imposition'[2] of substantive and non-negotiable moral warrants must be a legalistic distortion of the gospel of grace.

Much as this sort of interpretation may be rooted in historically understandable Reformational debates, as an interpretation of the New Testament it now seems seriously misguided. Paul's influential theological rhetoric about the law in Romans and especially in Galatians arose in a highly charged, sensitive historical context. A close reading shows that alongside this rhetoric the early Christians, and Paul prominently among them, continued in practice to operate with a clear and common canon of basic moral principles affecting a wide range of human behaviour. Similarly, the New Testament's effective history confirms that the Jewish tradition of moral teaching for Gentiles, rooted ultimately in the Torah, consistently determined much of the substance of ethics in the mainstream of emerging Christian orthodoxy.[3] It is the shared concern of these studies to examine something of the moral logic of early Christian ethics. If there were binding norms, what made them so, and on what basis were they articulated?

This book divides into three interrelated parts, roughly concerned in turn with Jewish law, ideas of universal or 'natural' law, and public ethics. Part One, comprising the first three chapters, addresses the moral rationale of Jesus and its reception in Palestinian Jewish

---

[1] Several chapters have been revised from previously published essays; see the list on p. 281 below. They are re-issued here with the publishers' permission.

[2] Why are they typically said to be 'imposed', as if by a tyrant, rather than 'heard' or 'received' as a gracious gift of life? The very choice of terminology suggests a Promethean perspective alien to the biblical context of divine revelation, where Israel's response of Exod 24.7 came to be famously celebrated by the rabbis.

Christianity. The four chapters of Part Two deal with the application of this Jewish moral heritage to the context of the Gentile mission – the resources that Jews and Christians employed in articulating universally binding moral norms that might apply even to Gentiles. And finally, Part Three turns more specifically to aspects of the emerging Christian interest in a 'public' formulation of ethics – first in a detailed study of two second-century writers and then in a more broadly based comparison with the problem of 'public ethics' in analogous Jewish texts.

There are of course a number of highly contested problems of definition and terminology to be tackled along the way. How legitimate is it to speak of 'halakhah' in relation to pre-rabbinic Judaism, let alone Christianity? A number of both Jewish and Christian writers have begun to engage constructively with this issue, which clearly remains a 'live' one for the purposes of this book.[4] Similarly, the use of terms like 'Noachide law' or 'natural law' remains highly contested in this connection, and we will need to bear this in mind as the argument progresses.

Part One

The first four chapters, then, address some of the substantive principles and criteria of ethics in the Jesus tradition and its Palestinian setting. Since the earliest days (Matt 5.17, Marcion, Origen) it has often been assumed that a basic tenet of Jesus' teaching was the effective abolition of all or at least part of the Jewish law in favour of distinctively Christian concerns of faith, hope and love. Jesus' view of Sabbath, food and purity laws would indeed have seemed objectionably lax and liberal to some of his more conservative contemporaries. Nevertheless, closer examination at least of the synoptic tradition produces little evidence that Jesus deliberately contravened the Torah in any substantive point. Instead, virtually every one of his ethical teachings can be shown to be conversant with contemporary Jewish legal debate and readily accommodated on the spectrum of 'mainstream' first-century Jewish

---

[3]This is true even where in due course that derivation was no longer fully understood, or even denied. Jürgen Wehnert (1997:174–208 and *passim*) has shown that the explicit rationale for this Jewish moral tradition came in time to be attached to the Apostolic Decree as recorded in Acts 15.

[4]See e.g. Neusner 1998; Tomson 1990; Doering 1999. The legitimacy of using the term for Second-Temple Judaism seems to be establishing itself especially in light of recent work on the halakhah at Qumran: following Schiffman 1975, see Qimron 1994 and Sussmann 1994; cf. also Brin 1994; Hempel 1998.

opinion. It is immediately worth asking, therefore, to what extent the Torah and a Jewish, halakhic mode of moral reasoning continue to shape the teaching of the Jesus movement. Four contributions to this inquiry are here presented:

1. *Ethics and Halakhah in the Jesus Tradition*

First, a general introduction and overview attempts to examine the balance between halakhic and more broadly moral concerns in Jesus' teaching. A good many of the concrete ethical questions in the gospel tradition can be usefully understood against the background of contemporary Jewish halakhic debate, even if that is interpreted in light of overriding emphases such as the love command and the eschatological urgency of the kingdom of God.

Out of the host of texts and issues arising out of this first chapter, two are then singled out for further attention: Jesus' logia on divorce, especially as received in Matthew, and Jesus' enigmatic advice to an inquirer to 'let the dead bury their dead'. Both have often been supposed in different ways to be highly revealing of early Christian attitudes to Jesus' teaching on the law.

2. *Matthew's Divorce Texts in the Light of Pre-Rabbinic Jewish Law*

Chapter 2 constitutes both the shortest and the earliest of the studies included in this volume, originally published over ten years ago. The original article was meant as a modest contribution to the problem of Matthew's insertion of 'exception clauses' into Jesus' prohibition of divorce (5.32; 19.9). The argument was that Matthew's redaction is guided by well-established biblical and post-biblical halakhah that saw the marriage bond as (i) intrinsically dependent on sexual fidelity, and (ii) irreversibly annulled by sexual union with a third party.

Needless to say, the intervening years have seen a good many relevant publications on the same subject. Nevertheless, I include this study here virtually without revisions. This is not of course to deny that more could be said on the topic. It is simply that my straightforward but pointed observation about the halakhic setting and significance of Matthew's exception clauses still seems sufficiently self-contained to stand on its own. What is more, the original short article has had the good fortune of being noted and endorsed in the secondary literature,[5] so that it seems best simply to reproduce it here as a point of reference.

3. 'Let the Dead Bury their Dead': Jesus and the Law Revisited

The next chapter offers a more extended discussion of a passage that has frequently been regarded as the *pièce de résistance* of the old Christian argument that Jesus either 'abolished' the Mosaic Law or at any rate claimed for himself the ('messianic' or 'charismatic') authority to bypass or supersede it at will. That argument itself, which is also touched upon in Chapter 1, would certainly merit a full-scale re-assessment on its own. In this chapter, however, my primary aim is to show that Jesus' instruction to a (potential) disciple to forgo burying his father (Matt 8.22; Luke 9.62) *cannot* be used to illustrate a supposedly liberal or casual attitude to the Law. A further, more tentative suggestion is that the passage might make sense if understood to define discipleship in analogy to widespread Nazirite practices in first-century Palestine. Whether or not that suggestion is correct, even this supposedly most 'law-free' of Jesus' sayings turns out to have its original *setting* in a legally and halakhically alert environment.

4. James, Israel and Antioch

The last chapter of Part One illustrates the application of Palestinian Christian halakhah to a new Christian community that turned out to be a boundary situation in more ways than one. St Paul's famous dispute with St Peter in Antioch has exercised scholars for many centuries; and Protestant biblical scholarship has usually interpreted it from the Pauline perspective of Galatians 2. Interlopers sent by James, the Lord's brother, set out to disrupt the fledgling mission to the Gentiles in Antioch, the place where it had begun. All the Jewish members of the church there, including even Peter and Barnabas, withdrew from eating with Gentiles, but only Paul resisted.

The interpretation of this episode is of course one of the most sensitive questions of New Testament scholarship; and it is clear that on issues such as the Gentile mission the earliest church's identity and self-understanding came to be tested to the breaking point. In this chapter, I propose to investigate the question from the perspective of James rather than that of Paul. What might have caused the leader of the Palestinian Jesus movement to intervene in this fashion in Jewish-Gentile relations at Antioch, a city on the boundary of the biblical Holy Land – but never to our knowledge in the other major cities of the Gentile mission? To answer this question, the chapter begins by

[5]See e.g. Allison 1993:3; Luz 1997:3.98n.52; Davies & Allison 1997:3.16–17.

considering the place of Antioch from a Palestinian Jewish perspective. As a result of this survey, it becomes clear that James's motivation is best understood in primarily ideological rather than pragmatic terms: political pressures on the church in Jerusalem can account for only part of the rationale behind the appeal to the Jewish Christians at Antioch. The early Jesus movement evidently continued to focus upon the restoration of Israel's twelve tribes in a new messianic kingdom, whose promised biblical boundaries extended to all the 'lost sheep of the house of Israel'. Within this, the role of Gentiles was ambivalent – and as the apostolic conference of Acts 15 and Galatians 2 shows, even among those who accepted that Gentile believers need not convert to Judaism there was no easy agreement as to whether this meant a fully integrated church of Jews and Gentiles or two socially distinct and parallel movements. Considerable light can be shed on James's action if it is understood to reflect this concern for the renewal of the twelve tribes within the boundaries of the Promised Land.

Part Two

The four chapters of Part Two turn from here to the next logical question: once a 'non-proselytizing' (i.e. non-Judaizing) mission to Gentiles was affirmed, how could the Jewish Christian moral and legal presuppositions of the Jesus movement be brought to bear on the complex issues arising from such a mission? The problem raised both in Acts 15 and in the Pauline letters is that of validating a distinctly Gentile Christian *modus vivendi*. Given the *theory* that Gentiles could be adherents of a Jewish Messiah, what for them would be the moral *practice* of their new faith and discipleship? The answer, as Part Two suggests, lies in the Christian appropriation of an ancient Jewish tradition that regarded Gentiles to be under obligation only to those laws which the Torah itself in fact applies to them. These laws were already part of a long interpretative tradition of universal ethics.

5. *Natural Law in Second Temple Judaism*

Two studies on 'natural law' lead the way. That terminology is not of course native to Scripture or to Palestinian Judaism. And yet the issue itself has in recent years increasingly come to be recognized as foundational not only to Hellenistic Jewish discourse with outsiders, but also to important strands of Scripture and tradition (see e.g. Barr 1990, 1993; Barton 1998:58–76; Novak 1992, 1998). David Novak has advanced a controversial but compelling argument that the very notion of a covenant inherently presupposes both natural law and freedom of choice, and therefore that a natural law theory must be the necessary basis for a conceptual understanding even of halakhah.[6] The subordination and yet compatibility of 'natural' to 'revealed' law is certainly part of the conceptual dynamic which this chapter uncovers. Despite their sometimes deep mistrust of 'natural' morality, Jewish writers especially in the diaspora went out of their way to affirm, not so much that the Torah is according to nature, but rather that nature works according to the Torah.

6. Natural Law in the New Testament?

The obvious complement to the previous chapter is a study of the same topic as it is developd in the New Testament. What we find makes for relatively slim pickings; indeed one might argue that in significant respects the New Testament writers share some of the reservations of Qumran and rabbinic literature. In particular, the few arguments from nature tend not to be deductive but analogical; and they are complemented by a keen sense of creation's fallenness and need for revelation and redemption. Still, a number of important texts do surface and the profile of the New Testament evidence shows that Christian writers, too, remained aware of the 'universal' relevance and compatibility of divinely revealed morality to the created order.

7. The Noachide Commandments and New Testament Ethics

On what basis, then, did Jews address the problem of a 'public' or universal ethics for dealings with Gentiles? This concluding chapter of Part Two now approaches that question from the perspective not of 'natural' but of positive law. Beginning with an examination of the Torah's application of certain laws to Gentiles, this and related themes are traced, via the prophets and post-biblical interpretation in *Jubilees* and other texts, to the second-century rabbinic doctrines of the three cardinal sins and of the 'Noachide Commandments'. The formal doctrine of the Noachide Commandments is a second-century rabbinic development. Nevertheless, its antecedents were

---

[6]Novak 1998:22–44, esp. p. 24. He shows that this is a point which, despite their reservations, even the rabbis seem to acknowledge in their doctrine that the 'positive' divine commandments of Torah have their underlying reasons – the *ta'amê ha-miṣvot* (ibid., p. 37 with reference to Heinemann 1959, who demonstrates this concern not just for the medieval period but in Scripture (pp. 11–18), rabbinic (18–29) and Hellenistic Judaism (30–8) as well).

very clearly in place in the first century and can be shown to influence the way in which the New Testament authors, especially Luke and Paul, articulate the specific substance of Christian moral teaching. Jewish law for Gentiles has become one of the pillars of ethics for Christians, fully integrated with its christological foundation.

Part Three

The last two chapters take one further logical step in this progression from Jewish halakhah to universal ethics. If Jewish principles of 'natural' and 'international' law aided in the formulation of an ethic for Gentile Christians, how did these Christians in turn develop their own public moral discourse in the Graeco-Roman context?

8. The Beginning of Christian Public Ethics

The first of these two chapters traces the origin of a 'public' Christian moral discourse from Luke to the later second century. The increasingly obvious emergence of a distinct Christian public identity engendered the need for a new apologetic to explain this self-styled 'third race' apart from Jews and Gentiles – not least in its moral profile. Among New Testament writers, it is Luke above all who stands out as anticipating many of these questions. Having surveyed his interest in a publicly defensible account of Christian faith and practice, the remainder of the chapter examines the historical development of these ideas to the third quarter of the second century, i.e. prior to the first serious reflection about the challenges posed by pagan critics like Fronto and Celsus. In particular, Aristides and the *Epistle to Diognetus* serve as two test cases of such 'pre-critical' public moral discourse; strengths and contributions as well as notable weaknesses of their approach are explored.

9. Public Ethics in Judaism and Christianity

After the more detailed historical study of Chapter 8, the final chapter offers a concluding synthesis of the main topics and approaches that Jews and Christians employed in the articulation of ethics in a public forum. In its original form, this study was prepared for a conference concerned with the limits of tolerance and intolerance in early Christianity and ancient Judaism. Within that context, it also attempts to reflect on the strengths as well as the obvious limits of a 'public' discourse about ethics that is perforce conducted against the horizon of martyrdom.

Conclusion

Given the preliminary nature of this collection of studies, there are inevitable weaknesses and lacunae that remain to be addressed in future work. Reviewers, one suspects, will not be slow in coming up with suggestions for improvement. Doubtless, too, I have not read some things I ought to have read, and perhaps read some things I ought not to have read. To elicit such suggestions, indeed, is partly my hope in publishing a preliminary work of this kind.

Since Part One in particular offers specialized historical case studies rather than synthetic statements, there is obviously a good deal to be done before one could begin to paint 'the big picture' in a way that would be desirable. Open questions include the extent to which the Christian appropriation of Jewish halakhah for Gentiles can be said to be truly *representative* of mainstream Christian opinion in the period under investigation, and in important respects *theologically* integral to Christian faith. Some might be inclined to argue along the lines of F. C. Baur, that the original Pauline 'freedom' in this regard came in time to be sedated or suppressed by the progress of 'early catholic' and anti-Marcionite concerns. The evidence adduced in this book leads me to doubt that such an argument could carry the day, but it is obviously a debate worth having.

By taking the problem of a halakhah for Gentiles to its logical extension in the realm of public ethics, this volume also raises the question of the genesis of Christian political thought. This correlation is deliberate: it points to an area that remains not only wide open for fruitful research, but has considerable bearing for the church's contemporary situation. In particular, 'modernist' and 'post-modern' challenges have left the church's political context in both East and West more reminiscent of its first three centuries than of the last three. Even where it still enjoys the right to speak, it must now earn the right to be heard; and even then it can only hope to persuade by the Spirit's witness in argument and example. Among the richest resources for this task may well turn out to be the Christian writings of the pre-Constantinian period.

The cumulative result of the studies in this book, then, seems to be the remarkable extent to which early Christianity adopted the Jewish tradition of a 'public' or 'international' morality, which alone renders ethical dialogue possible. As Parts Two and Three show, examples of this tradition include the Pentateuchal laws for resident aliens and the rabbinical idea of universal laws for the descendants of Noah. Without requiring any formal sanction, such principles could be translated and expressed in terms of publicly recognizable principles of 'best practice', all the while carefully guarding the distinctive substance of the biblical revelation. The balance, one might say, lies in the symmetry of law and wisdom. Ironically, it seems to have been precisely the application of Jewish law to the Gentile mission that allowed Christianity to blossom into a faith for the world, with a clear and distinctive yet truly universal ethic.

Christian approaches to public ethics have always ranged from mystical withdrawal to active engagement of the pagan world on its own terms. The 'take it or leave it' perspective of Christian pietists and mystics bears powerful witness to the fact that God's truth is of another world, which cannot be fathomed by pragmatic political wisdom. Apologists and philosophers, on the other hand, are convinced that the gospel is both profoundly reasonable and profoundly good for humanity. On this account, all truth is God's truth, and every act of virtue mirrors something of the mercy and justice of Christ.

Paradoxically, both withdrawal and engagement signify something of the essence of the gospel. Both, too, can exact a steep personal and political cost. And, throughout Christian history, *both* have variously contributed to the articulation of a Christian public moral and political witness. The more interesting, and nowadays largely forgotten, illustrations of this fact include obscure Syrian stylites on their pillars[7] as well as medieval manuals for the Christian conduct of political office.[8] There is much room here for fruitful historical research and theological reflection.

Acknowledgements

It remains for me to thank some of the many friends and institutions without whose counsel and support this work could not have taken shape. Here at Cambridge, both the Faculty of Divinity and Fitzwilliam College have provided financial assistance for repeated and generous periods of research leave. Several stints in Tübingen, made possible in part by an Alexander von Humboldt fellowship, were the more fruitful for the warm hospitality and critical

---

[7]See e.g. Kötting 1953; Drijvers 1984; also Spidlík 1990.
[8]See e.g. Hadot 1972; Blum 1981, especially pp. 1–23; Singer 1983; also Gail 1968:9–37 on Erasmus.

encouragement extended by Albrecht Haizmann, Martin Hengel, Werner Neuer, Rainer Riesner, Peter Stuhlmacher and their families. Over the years, many others have offered invaluable criticisms and suggestions on various parts of this work. Among them are Richard Beaton, Pierre-Antoine Bernheim, Marc Bregman, Christoph Bultmann, James Carleton Paget, Peter Head, Morna Hooker, William Horbury, Michael Lloyd, Winrich Löhr, David Novak, Brian Rosner, Paul Spilsbury, Guy Stroumsa, Justin Taylor, Michael Thompson, Peter Tomson, Ben Viviano, Francis Watson and Hugh Williamson. What merit this book may have owes much to the kindness and patience of friends and colleagues like these. Its faults, of course, are all my own.

We alluded earlier to the correspondence between the law of God and the wisdom of God, a symmetry that is fundamental to both the Jewish and the early Christian moral vision. While writing this preface, I discovered these two divine gifts movingly encapsulated in the church's ancient Advent Antiphons for December 17 and 18, the first of a series of seven daily prayers for the coming of Emmanuel:

O *Wisdom* who came from the mouth of the Most High,
reaching from end to end
and ordering all things mightily and sweetly:
Come, and teach us the way of prudence.

O *Adonai* and ruler of the House of Israel,
who appeared to Moses in the flame of the burning bush
and gave him the law on Sinai:
Come, and redeem us with outstretched arms.

M. B.
May 2000

ABBREVIATIONS

With a few self-explanatory exceptions, the system of abbreviations is mainly that of *The SBL Handbook of Style*, ed. P. H. Alexander (Peabody: Hendrickson, 1999), soon to be available online at *www.sbl-site.org*. Note the following additions:

DSSSE   *The Dead Sea Scrolls Study Edition*, ed. F. García Martínez & J. C. Tigchelaar, 2 vols (Leiden etc.: Brill, 1997).

JBT   *Jahrbuch für biblische Theologie*

LACL²   *Lexikon der antiken christlichen Literatur*, second edn. Freiburg: Herder, 1999.

SCE   *Studies in Christian Ethics*

PART ONE

Christianity in the Land of Israel

HALAKHAH AND ETHICS IN THE JESUS TRADITION

Previous generations of scholars frequently approached the ethics of Jesus from a naïvely Christian perspective, by categorically asserting the superiority of his love command and the Sermon on the Mount to the supposed 'legalism' and hide-bound casuistry of his Jewish contemporaries. More recently, however, the blossoming study of ancient Judaism has enabled us, perhaps for the first time since the first century, to explore Jesus' moral teaching meaningfully in its original setting.

All the main features of Jesus' ethics are deeply conversant with Jewish moral presuppositions. God is one and he is supreme. Ethics is therefore inalienably theonomous rather than autonomous: both the substance and authority of right behaviour have their source in the God of Israel. 'Why do you call me good?' Jesus asks. 'No one is good but God alone' (Mark 10.18 par.). The commandment to love God in the *Shema' Israel*, along with the love of one's neighbour, is for Jesus the heart of the Torah – as it was for some of his contemporaries (see Deut 6.4–5; Mark 12.29; cf. *Test. Iss.* 5.2; *t. Peah* 4.19; R. Aqiba in *y. Ned.* 9.4, 41c36–7; Philo, *Spec. Leg.* 1.299–300).

To this day, textbooks continue to make much of the fact that explicit use of the Torah plays only a very minor role for the Gospel writers. This in itself might seem to cast doubt on Jesus' indebtedness to Jewish moral teaching. Three points, however, must be raised in defence of our proposition. First, many other Jewish ethical texts also make only limited explicit use of the Torah (see Niebuhr 1987; also cf. the Mishnah), and one must not extrapolate from the specialized exegetical discourse of certain sages and Dead Sea Scrolls to the whole of pre-70 Judaism, as is still so often recklessly done. Secondly, we are dealing with Gospels written in Greek for a Gentile or mixed audience outside Palestine; and that in itself will have a great deal to say about the shape in which the gospel material has been transmitted. But thirdly and most importantly, to understand the Jewishness of Jesus' morality it is in any case far less appropriate to theologize abstractly about what he said (or indeed did *not* say) about the Torah in general than to examine the verbal and practical clues as to how and why he acted as he did. In other words, it is impossible to judge the supposed 'uniqueness' or otherwise of Jesus' moral teaching without an adequate assessment of his practical ethics and his *halakhah*. It is to this subject, therefore, that we must now turn.

We shall consider four main halakhic principles that arise out of a large number of pertinent cases, and all of which in my view have a relatively strong claim to an authentic setting at least within the earliest Palestinian Jewish Christian circles.[1] A fifth principle will be examined and then set aside, as probably not of the same relevance.

The Precedence of Written Torah

The Mishnah commends that the good interpreter should 'make a fence' for the Torah, i.e. interpret in keeping with tradition (*m. 'Abot* 1.1; cf. 3.17). Pharisaic halakhah, and later normative rabbinic halakhah, was a way of giving increasingly definitive traditional shape to the practice of Judaism. Whether or not the Pharisaic respect for oral tradition had already crystallized into a formal doctrine of oral *law*, Jesus' legal disputes with the Pharisees represent a clash between different conceptions of halakhah, different ways of building that protective hermeneutical fence.

That Jesus, too, was engaged in the erection of an interpretative fence cannot be in doubt, even if his overall concern had a different focus. Several emphases of Jesus' teaching demonstrate this quite clearly. First, and most strongly attested, is his opposition to halakhic arguments that restrict or suspend the plain meaning of the written Torah.

The key illustration here must be the dispute about handwashing in Mark 7.1–13 par. The argument concerns the authoritative place of Pharisaic tradition in a matter of purity not explicitly legislated in the Torah, viz. that of ritual handwashing to cleanse any acquired contamination before each meal. Jesus' interlocutors appeal to a well-known Pharisaic principle of halakhah that is not based on the Torah (and is apparently not attested at Qumran): food is rendered unclean even at second remove, by *derived* impurity of the hands (cf. e.g. *m. Zab.* 5.12; *m. Yad.* 3.1–2; *m. Tohar.* 2.2; NB impurity of 'hands' as distinct from the body). Biblical law, by contrast, recognizes only *direct* sources of impurity, which affect the body as a whole (e.g. Lev 11.31–35).[2]

Jesus' reply, as recorded somewhat differently in Mark and Matthew, consists of two parts. First, he insists on the distinction between the authority of Torah, which he accepts, and that of the

---

[1] For our purposes it will suffice to distinguish between the redaction of the Gospels for Hellenistic readers and the understanding of Jesus' sayings in the original Jewish Christian communities. To go from there to a plausible link with the historical Jesus is always difficult, but only rarely impossible.

[2] See Tomson 1988:63–5 and nn. 39–40, citing Ḥ. Albeck.

ascendant Pharisaic halakhah, which he rejects (Mark 7.8–9 with reference to Isa 29.13). This insistence on the halakhic primacy of Scripture over against Pharisaic tradition was also shared by the Sadducees and the sectarian Dead Sea Scrolls.

The second part of the argument in Mark 7, equally rooted in a Palestinian Jewish *Sitz im Leben* well before AD 70, illustrates Jesus' charge that the Pharisees in practice assign a higher authority to their tradition than to Scripture. He does so by drawing on the familiar halakhic topic of vows (cf. also Matt 5.33–37; 23.16–22), to which the Mishnah later devotes an entire tractate and which was also of interest to the Essenes.[3] The halakhah of Jesus' opponents apparently did not allow them to release a person from a vow to make an offering in the Temple, even in the case where the designated resources were needed to support one's parents. There is clearly a conflict of commandments here, between the duty to keep one's vows (Num 30.2; cf. Deut 23.21, 23) and that of honouring one's parents (Exod 20.12; Deut 5.16). The tradition of Jesus' opponents, perhaps holding all *mitzvot* to be of equally binding force (cf. e.g. 4 Macc 5.20; Josephus *Ag. Ap.* 2.17 §173), had led them to a legal rigorism that made the mitigation or suspension of a lesser commandment in favour of a more important one very difficult to achieve.

It is of course true that the opponents in this story represent at best a particular faction of Pharisees, rather than Pharisaism as a whole. A far more pragmatic position is often taken by Hillel, who is credited with the institution of the *prosbul* (a legal document facilitating suspension of the mandatory cancellation of loans in a Sabbath year (Deut 15.1–3), which in the increasingly capital-oriented Graeco-Roman economy made it difficult for the poor to obtain credit).[4]

What is more, Jesus' view in Mark 7 relates easily to the range of mainstream Jewish positions, as is clear from a late first-century debate recorded in the Mishnah (*m. Ned.* 9.1; cf. already Philo, *Hyp.* 7.5). There, a position not dissimilar from that of Jesus is taken by the late first-century R. Eliezer ben Hyrcanus (who is elsewhere reported to have been sympathetic to an apocryphal halakhah of Jesus: *t. Ḥul.* 2.24; *b. 'Abod. Zar.* 16b–17a (*baraita*)): the explicit Scriptural commandment to honour one's parents can take

---

[3]Josephus, *War* 2.8.6–7 §135–9 suggests that the Essenes refuse to take vows altogether. Although vows are envisaged in CD (9.9–12; 16.7–12), the document nevertheless criticizes the conditional hedging of vows in terms reminiscent of Matt 5.34–36; 23.16–22: CD 15.3–5.

[4]M. *Šebi.* 10.3–4; *m. Giṭ.* 4.3; *Sifre Deut.* 113 (ed. Finkelstein, p. 173).

precedence over the secondary and merely traditional rules about the cancellation of vows.

For Jesus, therefore, the 'fence' around the Torah is itself rigorously scriptural: in case of conflict, the Decalogue's commandment to honour one's parents takes precedence over the laws about vows, which are in any case voluntary. Jesus refuses to subordinate one written commandment to the oral tradition pertaining to another (a distinction recognized in the rabbinic doctrine of *gufê Torah*, e.g. *m. Ḥag.* 1.8).[5]

In the first instance, then, Torah serves as its own interpretative fence.

'The Weightier Things of the Torah'

All three Synoptic Gospels provide evidence that in legal disputes with his opponents Jesus quite often appeals to 'higher principles' *within the Torah* (cf. the rabbinic *kelal gadol ba-Torah*, e.g. R. Aqiba in *y. Ned.* 9.4, 41c36–7; *Sifra* Qedoshim 4 on Lev 19.18, §200.3.7) in prioritizing the regulations pertaining to the particular point at issue. One might argue this even for the case of Mark 7, as we have just seen. Other, clearer examples of this include his appeal to the original divine intention for marriage in Mark 10.2–12 par. While Deut 24.1 amounts to a concession (v. 5) regulating an existing practice of divorce, Jesus rejects the Pharisees' suggestion that this constitutes a divine sanction of divorce. Instead, he asserts the priority of a more foundational practice based on an earlier, positive principle within the Torah, namely the Creator's intention for the permanence of marriage (Mark 10.6–9 par., citing Gen 1.27; 2.24). This approach resonates strikingly with the contemporary halakhic debate: while the Pharisaic schools of Hillel and Shammai disputed whether the grounds for divorce in Deuteronomy 24.1 (*'erwat dabar* = 'something objectionable') should be interpreted loosely or stringently,[6] the Qumran sectarians rejected divorce altogether – on precisely the same scriptural grounds as are cited by Jesus (CD 4.20–21; cf. CD 5.8–11; 11QT 57.11–19).[7] A more fundamental principle within the Torah is preferred over a later and primarily concessionary statement.[8]

---

[5]Different but related is the concern for the moral 'rationale' behind the commandments, the *ta'ⁿmê ha-miṣvot*; cf. Novak 1998:37 and Heinemann 1959:11–38 and *passim*.

[6]*M. Git.* 9.10; *b. Git.* 90a. Matthew seems more clearly aware of this debate: the Pharisees in 19.3 ask, 'Is it lawful for a man to divorce his wife *for any cause*?' See further Chapter 2 below.

[7]Dissent from this consensus view is, however, voiced by Brin 1997.

[8]Cf. e.g. Deut 23.22 on vows; in the case of Hillel's *prosbul*, the general command Deut 15.7–11 overrides Deut 15.1–3.

In a dispute about healing on the Sabbath, Jesus appeals to the halakhic principle of the priority of saving a life (*pikkuaḥ nefesh*) in justifying his healing of a man whose withered hand arguably prevented him from supporting himself and his family (Mark 3.4 par.).[9] In the Mishnah, the work of midwives on the Sabbath is permitted on this account, as is lighting a fire and boiling water (*m. Šab.* 18.3). While minor cures are on the whole forbidden,[10] medicine may be administered to someone in pain, since 'whenever there is doubt whether life is in danger this overrides the Sabbath.'[11]

The contemporary halakhic debate on this matter shows that a range of interpretations was possible. This is further illustrated by Matthew's inclusion of an *a fortiori* (*qal waḥomer*) argument from the example of a sheep falling into a pit on the Sabbath (Matt 12.11–12; cf. Luke 13.15–16). To a Galilean farmer the answer probably seemed obvious, and the early rabbis would agree with Jesus (*t. Šab.* 14.3). Scribes at Qumran, however, refused to recognize the principle of *pikkuaḥ nefesh*, allowing only cultic requirements to supersede the Sabbath; they argued that neither animal nor human may in such circumstances be pulled out![12] Jesus apparently endorses a broad application, extending the halakhic principle of life-saving on the Sabbath to any act of restoring people from affliction to wholeness.[13]

A number of other instances could be cited. Jesus assigns pride of place among the commandments to the 'entrance requirements' to the Kingdom, taken from the Decalogue (Mark 10.19 par.). Like Hillel, but unlike Shammai, before him (*b. Šab.* 31a, *baraita*), Jesus

[9]Luke 6.6 poignantly makes it his *right* hand. Jerome on Matt 12.13 cites the *Gospel of the Nazaraeans* (frg.10) in suggesting that the man was a mason. See the commentaries.

[10]M. Šab. 14.3–4; t. Šab. 12.8–14; cf. similarly CD 11.10.

[11]M. Yoma 8.6 (R. Mattyah b. Ḥeresh, late 1st cent.). B. Yoma 35b (*baraita*) attributes the principle to Shemaya and Abtalion (1st cent. BC).

[12]CD 11.13–17; see Sigal 1986:145–6, 149–52. Note further the Hasmonean acceptance of *pikkuaḥ nefesh* in regard to Sabbath warfare (1 Macc 2.40–41; cf. Shammai in *b. Šab.* 19a *baraita*), in contrast to the conservative position also reflected in 2 Macc 5.25–26; 15.1–5. See also *Jub.* 50.12; Josephus, *Ant.* 13.12.4 §337; *War* 7.8.7 §362–3; and cf. Sigal 1986:120. E. P. Sanders 1990a:7–8 does not make this distinction.

[13]Note, however, that both Mark and Matthew have Jesus healing only by word and not by laying on of hands (Luke 13.10–13), preparing medication (John 9.6), or encouraging a man to carry his pallet (John 5.8–10, 18). Such actions were widely viewed as forbidden on the Sabbath except to save life. Cf. E. P. Sanders 1990a:20; Doering 1999:468–76.

A more difficult case is the question of the disciples' plucking (and/or rubbing, Luke 6.1) of grain on the Sabbath, Mark 2.23 par., which in Mark is justified on the basis of hunger and human need (see below on 2.27–28). Tannaitic literature confirms that rubbing or crushing grain to eat it came to be permitted (cf. Sigal 1986:128–36; Casey 1988, 1998:138–92 *pace* Doering 1999:429). Thus, Jesus may only be in breach of his opponents' more stringent halakhah – even if in Matthew and Luke, the story assumes a more christological focus.

is also happy to summarize the substance of the Torah in the Golden Rule (Matt 7.12; cf. Luke 6.31). It is especially Matthew's Jesus who repeatedly exalts justice, mercy and faith above the detailed regulations about tithes and purity. He calls the former the 'weightier matters of the law' (Matt 23.23; cf. 9.13; 12.7), thereby clearly confirming a distinction between central and peripheral commandments.[14]

Nevertheless, it is worth noting that Jesus himself probably remained quite deliberate in his observance of the Torah. Even Matt 23.23b suggests that he approved of tithing. He clearly endorsed sacrifice and voluntary gifts to the Temple (Mark 12.41–44 par.). He said grace before meals (Mark 6.41 par.; 14.22 par.) and apparently wore tassels on his garments (compare Matt 9.20 par.; 14.36 with 23.5 and Num 15.37–39). With regard to the Sabbath, the very argument of Mark 3.4 par., discussed above, must be ample indication that Jesus *affirmed* the sanctity of the Sabbath.[15] Despite his dispute in Mark 7.1–23 par. he continued to appeal to biblical purity laws (e.g. Mark 1.44 par.; Luke 11.44; Matt 7.6; 23.27; also Mark 5.11–13 par.). He tended to avoid contact with Gentiles (Matt 10.6; cf. Mark 7.27 par.); the exceptions are rare enough to be specially highlighted in the Gospels.

While this evidence is relatively limited in scope, it runs counter to the largely pro-Gentile redaction of the Gospels (except, arguably, in Luke: cf. 2.22; 23.56, etc.) and thus carries a strong claim to authenticity. For Jesus, the 'weighty' matters of the Torah do not suspend the other commandments.

Act and Motive

An equally significant, if somewhat less well attested, moral concern in the teaching of Jesus is the considerable halakhic emphasis placed on *motive and intention*, an issue related to the 'weightier' moral concerns discussed in the previous section. This is perhaps clearest in the so-called Antitheses of the Matthean Sermon on the Mount (5.21–48). Here, in near-rabbinic style (cf. Daube 1956:55–62; E. P. Sanders 1990a:93), a formula like 'You have heard that it was said' introduces the citation of an interpretative tradition with which Jesus takes issue; with his own 'But I say to you' he then proposes his own

[14]Note that the first-century R. Yoḥanan b. Zakkai uses the same Old Testament verse (Hosea 6.6) to argue that deeds of kindness are more important than Temple sacrifice: *'Abot R. Nat. A 4 / B 8* (ed. Schechter, p. 21). Cf. also Alexander 1997 on the Golden Rule.

[15]See further Mark 2.27; Matt 24.20 and note Luke 23.56. Cf. *Gospel of Thomas 27*.

line of interpretation. The opposed interpretation in each scenario appears to restrict moral responsibility to the mere performance or omission of a particular act (5.21 murder, 5.27 adultery, 5.31 divorce certificates, 5.33 vows, 5.38 retaliation, 5.43 love for one's fellow citizen). In several of these cases, Jesus re-interprets the issue from the perspective of relational moral intention (anger or insult, the adulterous glance, a frivolous attitude to divorce, insincere speech, vengefulness, hatred of outsiders), on that basis equating the gravity of a seemingly innocent or lesser offence with the one that tradition itself condemns.

This principle of moral intention is familiar from the prophets (e.g. in the passage from Isa 29.13 cited in Mark 7.8), but it is not in fact alien even to the Mosaic legislation (Exod 20.17; Deut 5.21; also Lev 19.17). The idea can also be variously documented in post-biblical Jewish thought, not least in rabbinic discussion.[16] In particular, one can often observe that Tannaitic traditions about the houses of Shammai and of Hillel reveal distinct halakhic emphases on the external act and on moral intention, respectively.[17]

Various other examples of a prior emphasis on moral intention could be cited from all four Gospels – although in many of these cases this principle serves less specifically halakhic and legal than moral and spiritual concerns. For Mark, examples may be said to include Jesus' anointing in Bethany (14.3–9) and possibly the story of the widow's mite (12.41–44 par.); in Matthew, we find the priority of reconciliation over sacrifice (5.23–24) and the passage about fasting, alms and prayer in secret (6.1–18). The story of Jesus' anointing is differently developed in both Luke (7.36–50) and John (12.1–8); Luke's parable of the Pharisee and the tax collector (18.9–14) and the Fourth Gospel's account of Jesus' conversation with the Samaritan woman (note John 4.9, 27) are also worth mentioning. In each case, the agent's intention qualifies the moral assessment of an act which, aside from that factor, might be subject to a rather different appraisal.

Without needing to argue the authenticity of every one of these traditions, certain clear principles of differentiation within the Torah emerge. Generally speaking, in case of conflict between command-ments, those governing relationality and intentionality in one's actions towards God and fellow human beings are of greater importance than the rules governing correct formality of ritual

---

[16]For examples cf. Schrage 1988:97–8; Tomson 1990:208–16; and see pp. 158, 168 and *passim* in Chapter 7 below.

[17]Thus e.g. Stemberger 1996:66.

observance. These principles have a demonstrable Jewish setting and can be illustrated by case studies.

Purity and Integrity

A number of studies in recent years have considered Jesus' attitude to Jewish purity laws, and several scholars have argued that it shows signs of a distinctive reinterpretation. We have already noted the relative emphasis on the agent's moral intention rather than formal observance. An obvious corollary of this is Jesus' tendency, similarly evident in a variety of Jewish writings and especially in Paul, to stress the need for a moral complement of religious purity. It is clear that, for all his participation in contemporary debate, Jesus' interests perhaps extend not primarily to the halakhic and legal realm but rather, or at least equally, to that of the moral and spiritual realm.

A note of caution is in order, however. Before speaking of Jesus' 'transformation' of purity laws, it is important to avoid the spiritualizing short-cut so common in much Christian exegesis. We must note that Jesus participated in the Temple cult apparently without questioning the need for ritual purity; he approved of the need for priestly purification after leprosy (Mark 1.42 par.; Luke 17.14). Although he often scathingly criticizes Pharisaic halakhah (but note Matt 23.2–3, 23), the distinction between clean and unclean is clearly not abolished. Leprosy is still unclean, as are evil spirits (e.g. Mark 1.23 par.) and, apparently, dogs and swine (Mark 5.13 par.; 7.27 par.; Matt 7.6; Luke 16.21) as well as camels and gnats (Matt 23.24). Probably for similar reasons, Jesus is not entirely at ease with Gentiles and Samaritans (Matt 10.5; 18.17; Mark 7.26–27 par.), even if these boundaries are on occasion signally transcended.

Jesus, therefore, does *not* abolish the purity laws – an observation which is all the more weighty in that it contradicts the redactional interests of the later Hellenistic churches, as the famous editorial aside in Mark 7.19c plainly shows (cf. John 13.10?; Acts 10.15; Rom 14.14).

Nevertheless, it is also clear that Jesus does promote a significant spiritual (hasidic) *reorientation* of the halakhic concept of purity, calling for a balance of moral and ceremonial responsibility (note Matt 23.25 par.). Ritual and moral purity must go in tandem, as Qumran and other Jewish renewal movements insisted at this time (e.g. 1QS 3.2–12; *As. Mos.* 7.7–9). It is not the attention to ritual observance which Jesus prophetically denounces, but the blatant spiritual discrepancy between words and deeds – for which he so frequently uses the term 'hypocrite', borrowed from the theatre (e.g. Mark 7.6 par.; 12.15).

In some cases, it is true, Jesus' attitude to the purity laws does point towards a more thorough-going transformation of priorities. As we have seen, it is probably not correct to infer an outright abolition of purity laws from the context-specific statement that it is not what enters a person that defiles (Mark 7.15, 18).[18] Nevertheless, if interpreted at face value (though it may of course be hyperbolical), Jesus' reported explanation in that context almost appears to subsume the halakhic issue of acquired impurity (NB *toharot*, 7.2 par. – never *kashrut*, despite Mark's redactional interpretation in 7.19c[19]) under the larger topic of sin and immorality (7.21–22).

Other passages confirm this impression. Jesus' free association with tax gatherers and 'sinners' is a constant goad to his opponents, and the general likelihood of defilement by those who are less than careful about purity makes Jesus' behaviour objectionable to a stricter brand of Pharisee concerned to maintain the state of Temple purity at all times.[20]

Jesus' behaviour *vis-à-vis* other kinds of impurity is still more intriguing. The Gospel accounts show him exhibiting remarkably few scruples in touching the dead (e.g. Mark 5.41 par.; Luke 7.14), lepers (Mark 1.41 par.) or a haemorrhaging woman (5.27). In each case the understanding seems to be that *toharot* concerns are suspended when it is *purity* rather than impurity that is transferred by touch, from the pure to the impure (note Mark 1.41; 5.30).[21] This does not actually conflict with later rabbinic halakhah, but it differs from the primary interest in the reverse contact that governs much discussion in rabbinic literature and the Dead Sea Scrolls.[22]

[18]Citing *Ep. Arist.* 234, E. P. Sanders 1990a:28 argues plausibly that Mark 7.15 quite likely means 'not only this but much more that'. Cf. similarly Booth 1986:219, 206. Räisänen 1992:127–48 also doubts that Jesus held radical views on the food laws, but somewhat hastily dismisses Mark 7.15 as an inauthentic reflection of Pauline missionary practice.

[19]Food (kosher) laws, unlike purity regulations (*toharot*), had undergone very little development from their relatively clear biblical origins, and were (at least in Palestinian Judaism) far less disputed in either theory or practice. Cf. E. P. Sanders 1985:264.

[20]Cf. e.g. Saldarini 1992:289–91; de Lacey 1992.

[21]See similarly Evans 1997:368, who is right to suggest that 'the healing of the woman with the hemorrhage is as much a purity miracle as it is anything else'. Unfortunately he does not explore the implications in halakhic terms, especially the potential parallels with texts like those cited in n. 22 below.

[22]Note, however, texts like Exod 29.37 (the altar in the Tabernacle conveys purity to unclean vessels); 1QapGen 20.28–29 (Abraham's laying on of hands exorcises an evil spirit). Cf. further the various Hillelite views about the purity of bathhouses (e.g. famously *m. 'Abod. Zar.* 3.4 (Rabban Gamaliel II in Acco; cf. also Chilton 1997b:306 on the later text about Hillel in *Lev. Rab.* 34.4 [on 25.25]).

It may well be, then, that in this respect Jesus operated with the characteristic *chutzpah* of a wandering charismatic, almost claiming in the divine presence to be the conveyor of purity and holiness in his very person, assuming and asserting the purity of the people of God.[23] But did his eschatological self-consciousness lead him to side-step the Torah altogether? For an answer to this question we must turn to our fifth and final point.

Antinomian Eschatology?

In spite of the clear halakhic categories outlined above, an analysis of Jesus' teaching simply along these lines may run into difficulty in a few significant cases. A number of Gospel passages suggest that Jesus' moral teaching claimed to be doing rather more than simply to stake his place on the existing spectrum of contemporary Jewish halakhah. Instead, as in the case of some other Messianic movements (cf. Scholem 1971:21–2 and *passim*), the greater urgency implied in his Kingdom ministry also seems to have required the breach of conventional forms of Torah observance in a number of cases.

Key examples of this include the call to the young man to forgo burying his father in order to follow Jesus (Matt 8.22 par. – somewhat overrated in recent scholarship[24]), and probably Jesus' reluctance to acknowledge his biological family (Mark 3.32–35 par.) along with a requirement of the same from his disciples (Luke 14.26 par.). His disciples' failure to fast may also fall into this category (Mark 2.18–20 par.). Some would wish to include the Matthean antitheses, but we have seen above that they should be interpreted differently. Jesus repeatedly justifies apparently offensive aspects of his teaching and behaviour on the grounds that his ministry represents something greater than the Temple (Matt 12.6), Jonah and Solomon (12.41–42 par.). The fact that the Fourth Gospel makes Jesus greater even than Abraham (John 8.58) suggests something of the influence which the development of an exalted christology may have had on the transmission of such sayings. Nevertheless, there can be little doubt that the eschatological character of Jesus' ministry engendered certain claims and actions which, probably cumulatively rather than individually, incurred the ire and determined opposition of his Pharisaic (and later Sadducean) detractors. His demonstration in the Temple (Mark 11.15–17 par.) was only the most blatant and decisive of these cases, although his socializing in dubious company

---

[23]Cf. also Chilton 1997b:306–8, 316.
[24]See the fuller discussion in Chapter 3 below.

(note Matt 11.19 par.) and his seemingly cavalier attitude to matters of purity and the Sabbath will have contributed to a general image of lawlessness in Pharisaic eyes.

Nevertheless, we cannot be sure to what extent this eschatological mind-set practically governed Jesus' day to day actions, not to mention his teaching on ethics. We must turn for a moment to Mark 2.27–28 par., a saying that is still very commonly cited in support of the claim that Jesus consciously and deliberately superseded the Torah and placed himself above it: 'The Sabbath was made for humankind, and not humankind for the Sabbath; so the son of man is lord even of the Sabbath.'

The first half of this couplet declares that the Sabbath was made for humankind – a quasi-proverbial statement with explicit parallels in Tannaitic sources.[25] In the second half, the use of the pregnant term 'son of man' might seem to invite a christological reading, especially on the redactional level of the Gospel as a whole. This is indeed how Matthew 12.8 and Luke 6.5 understand the saying, taking 2.28 in isolation to denote the authority of Jesus. Read in an original Palestinian setting, however, verses 27–28 may be seen to belong together. Balancing the twin occurrences of ἄνθρωπος ('humankind') in v. 27, the term 'son of man' in v. 28 stands in a typically Hebraic parallelism with 'humankind' (as also in Ps 8.4; 90.3; Job 25.6; 35.8). Because the Sabbath was made for human need and enjoyment, therefore and in that sense humanity has greater authority even than the Sabbath.[26]

It is at least possible that the plainly christological reading of 2.28 may not do justice to the primary meaning even on the level of Marcan composition: of fourteen uses of the term 'son of man' in Mark, twelve occur in or after the first passion prediction in 8.31 and deal with the suffering Messiah theme. The only two in the first half of the Gospel (2.10, 28) arguably carry none of this meaning but should be taken as a reference to humankind in general (as is the case for the plural υἱοῖς τῶν ἀνθρώπων in 3.28). Mark is undoubtedly conscious of the christological Son of Man throughout. But the literary function of these two references in the early chapters may well retain an element of deliberate *double entendre*.

At the end of the day, the evidence for a substantive antinomian

---

[25]R. Simeon ben Menasyah, *Mek.* Shabbata 1 (Exod 31.14; ed. Lauterbach, 3.198); cf. also R. Jonathan ben Joseph, *b. Yoma* 85b.

[26]So e.g. R. Bultmann 1963:16–17, 155 (both also for 2.10); Jeremias 1967:165; Lindars 1983:44–7; Vermes 1983:180–1; Dunn 1990:26, 33; Sigal 1986:132; Doering 1999:422–3. I reluctantly disagree here with Hooker 1967:93–102 and 1993 *ad loc.*, who does not consider the 'man'/'Son of Man' parallels cited.

tendency in Jesus' halakhah turns out to be rather thin and speculative. In this light, we should also finally lay to rest the idea of Jesus'
affirmation of a supposed eschatological or 'Zion' Torah in place of
that of Mt. Sinai.[27] Indeed the popular notion that Jesus abrogated
the Torah, though dating back at least to Origen,[28] has little evidence
to support it and all too often serves to conceal quasi-Marcionite
presuppositions. Jesus' God is the covenantal God of Israel, and his
message of the Kingdom is rooted in the Torah.[29]

Conclusion

Recent scholarship underscores the fact that the early church
operated with a fundamentally Jewish notion of sin and morality.[30]
In view of Christianity's origins, this should hardly be surprising, but
the roots and branches of this Jewish moral heritage are in need of
much further exploration. In these pages, we have seen how a
reading of the Jesus tradition in deliberately Jewish halakhic terms
can help to highlight some of his key moral concerns in terms that
make sense of the situation he addressed: his strongly scriptural
interpretation of Judaism, the need for complementarity between
formal observance and the 'weightier commandments' about love for
God and neighbour; his stress on moral intention, and so on.

To note these observations, of course, is merely the beginning of
our task. As we have seen, all three synoptic evangelists have
adapted and developed the 'Jesus halakhah' with a view to the
validity of Jewish calendar, food and purity laws. They have done so
both to enhance the questions of christological authority already

[27]See, above all, Gese 1977 and the critique of Räisänen 1992:225–51; note futher W. D.
Davies 1952. E. P. Sanders 1990b allows that Jesus (like Paul) did act as an eschatologically
motivated giver of radical new rules for a new age, even if these were not presented as new
laws. Nevertheless, Jesus' halakhic innovations can be well understood in terms of his vision
for an eschatologically revitalized Torah.

[28]Cf. Diestel 1869:45–6 and see p. 147 and n. 5 below.

[29]Cf. Fiedler 1986:78, 85; also Broer 1986:131–3 (regarding the Matthean antitheses), cf.
1992. Like other textbooks of NT ethics, Hays 1996:158–68 and Matera 1996 fail to grasp
the implications of this point for the gospel tradition.

[30]So also Meeks 1993:121–6. It is a matter of regret that while Meeks's work has provided much vital background information, its direct relevance for the present study has
remained somewhat marginal. In part perhaps this is due to his methodological preference for
'ethnography of early Christian morality' (see his p. 10) rather than an analysis of early
Christian reflection on moral and legal principles. Doubtless both concerns are vital to any
understanding of early Christianity. Nevertheless, it is worth noting that the 'origin of
Christian morality' is for Meeks construed predominantly in social-anthropological terms,
whereas the present study concentrates (rightly or wrongly) on the question of the outworking
and re-appropriation of principles that were held to be divinely revealed.

inherent in the story and to tailor pertinent sayings to the emerging halakhic concerns of their Gentile churches – although their eloquent silence on circumcision and mixed marriages suggests a notable reluctance to import later debates entirely without historical warrant (cf. Lemcio 1991). Despite this relatively conservative appearance of the Jesus tradition itself, both Paul and the Gospels present us with clear signs of a distinctive moral and halakhic point of view.

At the same time, this new perspective is inevitably related to the old. Any study of the origin of early Christian ethics must begin with the observation that Jesus was a Jew teaching Jews exclusively, but that the moral heritage of the Jesus tradition in the New Testament is written by Jews *for Gentiles*. That is to say, the Jewish background of early Christian halakhah and ethics may well be illuminated not only by the Jesus tradition itself, but also by a careful reassessment of Jewish halakhah for Gentiles. It is that topic to which we will turn our attention in Parts Two and Three of this book.[31]

---

[31]See below, especially Chapters 7–9.

2

MATTHEW'S DIVORCE TEXTS IN THE LIGHT OF PRE-RABBINIC JEWISH LAW

In his major commentary on Matthew, U. Luz estimates the number of recent scholarly publications on the Matthean divorce texts to be around sixty;[1] secondary literature especially on the 'exception clauses' (παρεκτὸς λόγου πορνείας, 5.32; μὴ ἐπὶ πορνεία, 19.9) is 'unübersehbar'.[2] With so much scholarship on these passages already in print, what can possibly be the justification of yet another attempt at explanation? In this brief note I propose to appeal to a neglected text from Qumran in suggesting one possible answer to the often-underrated question, Why were the Matthean exception clauses felt to be necessary?

Let us suppose for the moment that the exception clauses stem from the redactional activity of the evangelist Matthew. Are they really intended merely to ameliorate a practically 'unworkable' rule of conduct? Is it really just a matter of Matthew's church being less 'radical' than Jesus,[3] and therefore requiring a more 'realistic' view of divorce? Although this possibility certainly cannot be rejected out of hand, it is nevertheless curious to note how few writers of this opinion have made any effort to ground these phrases in *existing halakhah*.

Where scholars do try to provide such an explanation, they often associate Matthew's position with the Shammaite view that divorce is permissible only on the grounds of immorality (Deut 24.1 as interpreted by Shammai, according to *m. Git. 9.10; b. Git.* 90a–b). It is, however, difficult to know to what extent the accounts of the famous debate between Hillel and Shammai and their schools on this matter can safely be assumed to reflect the real halakhic *status quaestionis* before 70. The other problem with this view, seldom recognized, is that its modern exponents tend to take for granted an easy shift in Matthew's church from one clear halakhic position (no divorce and remarriage; cf. also CD 4.19; 11QT 57.17–18) which had the authority of Jesus behind it to a different one (divorce in case of unchastity; thus Shammai) which at least prima facie did not.

A more promising track would appear to be followed by those

---

[1] Luz 1985:270.
[2] Luz 1985:273.
[3] Thus Bornkamm 1968:57; Goulder 1974:290–1; Green 1975:250.

who refer to rabbinic injunctions prescribing divorce in case of infidelity.[4] An adulterous wife must be divorced and is forbidden to her husband;[5] *t. Sot.* 5.9 even considers it a *commandment* (מצוה) to divorce a wife who bathes with the men (cf. *b. Git* 90a–b). This idea of a required divorce, which also occurs in Gentile law,[6] has in its favour a considerable amount of rabbinic evidence, and it finds probable support in Prov 18.22a LXX ('he who holds on to an adulteress is foolish and godless [ἀσεβής]') as well as in Matt 1.19 ('Joseph, being righteous, wanted to divorce her [ἀπολῦσαι: NB cf. 5.32, 19.9]'). A not dissimilar position (requiring separation, though not divorce) is found e.g. in Tertullian, Origen, Ephrem and other church fathers, often with reference to Matt 1.19.[7]

A plausible biblical point of departure for this halakhah is Deut 24.1–4: a divorcee, if divorced a second time, may not return to her first husband. Of particular importance for our purpose is v. 4, giving what could be taken as the reason for this prohibition: אחרי אשר הטמאה 'after she has been made unclean'. Significantly, *Tg. Neof.* Deut 24.4 renders, 'after she has been defiled *by another* man' [מן בתר דאסתאבת לגבר אחרן], thus suggesting more clearly that it is in fact the woman's sexual union with another man that makes her impure (and thus ineligible) to her first husband (cf. *m. Sot.* 5.1, citing Num 5.13–14; also Philo, *Spec. Leg.* 3.30–31). In this regard it may be relevant that the term טמא, which in Deut 24.4 describes the remarried woman's state in relation to her first husband, is in Lev 18.20 and Num 5.13, 14, 20 applied to the case of adultery (cf. also the use of חלל in Gen 49.4; 1 Chr 5.1; Lev 21.15). The seriousness of the prohibition of remarrying a first husband was already expressed in Deut 24.4b: contravening it is an abomination (תועבה) before the Lord and brings sin on[8] the land itself.[9] Other Old Testament passages suggesting the impossibility of restoring a disrupted first union include Jer 3.1; Ezek 16.38, 40; as well as Lev 21.7, 13–15 (stricter regulations for priests, but reflecting the cognate principle that marriage to a wife who had previous relations with another man would cause the priest to 'defile his seed': ולא יחלל זרעו, v. 15). *Tg. Ps.-J.* Deut 22.26 prescribes divorce even where a betrothed girl was

[4]Cf e.g. Luz 1985:275 et al.; also Nembach 1970. See already Abrahams 1917:1.72–5.

[5]E.g. *m. Ned.* 11.12; cf. *m. Sot.* 5.1; *y. Sot.* 1.1, 16b27; *b. Sanh.* 41a; also Rashi on Deut 24.1.

[6]See especially the Roman *Lex Julia de adulteriis* of 18 BC: cf e.g. Balsdon 1962:218–19, citing P. E. Corbett; Crouzel 1971:38–9.

[7]See Crouzel 1971:47–51; Luz 1985:275 n. 47.

[8]*Tg. Neof.* (gloss) and LXX: 'defiles' (סאב/μιαίνω); cf. Jer 3.1.

[9]For this idea cf. e.g. W. D. Davies 1982:20–1.

raped. On a more general note, the prescribed (though apparently rarely enforced) death penalty for adultery (Lev 20.10; Deut 22.22; cf. Ezek 16.38, 40; John 8.5) also suggests that a marriage in this case could not continue.

The rabbinic, liturgical and biblical material just cited suggests an established exegetical tradition that extended the prohibition of Deut 24.1–4 by *gezerah shawah* to the cases of impurity incurred by adultery. But clearly the case would be strengthened significantly by the existence of more explicit pre-rabbinic evidence. Is there any early attestation of such a tradition?

It is in answer to this question that I would adduce 1QapGen 20.15 for our discussion. In this text, Abraham in Egypt entreats God, in bitter tears and lamentation, that Pharaoh may not be able to violate Sarah whom he has taken away from her husband:

ואל ישלט בליליא דן לטמיא אנתתי מני

May he not be able to defile my wife away from me tonight.

It would seem natural in context to read this prayer as Abraham's desperate plea for God to save his marriage at the eleventh hour. Although Pharaoh has already taken Sarah for himself as a wife (20.9 ונסבהא לה לאנתא), there is still a possibility of receiving her back. Pharaoh's sexual union with Sarah, however would 'make her unclean from me', i.e. make further sexual intercourse between her and Abraham impossible.

As early as 1959, F. Rosenthal hinted at the possible significance of Deut 24.4 for the understanding of this passage in his review of the *editio princeps*.[10] More recently, J. C. Greenfield has argued that 'once a woman had relations with another man, even licit sexual relations, she was טמאה "defiled" as far as her first husband was concerned'.[11] Although he concedes that in later sources this rule applies only to priests, Greenfield sees the 'earlier', inclusive halakhah represented here[12] as well as in Philo, *Abr.* 98 (Sarah's purity [ἁγνεία] was preserved; Abraham's endangered marriage saved unharmed [ἀσινῆ καὶ ἀνύβριστον]) and *Jub.* 33.7–8 (Bilhah was unclean for intercourse with Jacob after being defiled by Reuben[13]).

---

[10]Rosenthal 1959:83.

[11]Greenfield 1980:xxxv.

[12]*Pace* Rosenthal 1959:83. Finkelstein 1923:55–6, is miscited by Rosenthal and in fact supports the position advocated by Greenfield and the present writer: Jacob is not viewed as a priest.

[13]Gen 35. 22 (a passage too offensive to be translated in the synagogue: *m. Meg.* 4.10; see *Tg. Ps.-J.*); cf. Gen 49.4 and LXX [ἐμίανας]; 1 Chr 5.1.

It does indeed seem plausible to read the reference in Philo as Greenfield does, viz. in implicit agreement with 1QapGen 20.15. However, the comparison with Jacob's separation from Bilhah is perhaps less than straightforward. In *Jub.* 33.2–8, the description of the incident is clearly concerned not with adultery in general but with the biblical *incest* laws in particular: Reuben has uncovered his father's shame (33.8–10; cf. Gen 35.22 and see Lev 20.11; Deut 27.20). Nevertheless, the notion that even in this case the sexual union cannot be restored is new. In *Test. Reub.* 3.10–15, on the other hand, the context does address adultery in general; here, too, Jacob 'had no further relations with her' (v. 15).

A similar but much earlier example, not mentioned by Greenfield, might be David's removal of the ten royal concubines with whom Absalom had had intercourse during his brief spell in control of Jerusalem: 'he did not go in to them' and they became 'living widows' (2 Sam 20.3 [אלמנות חיות: LXX χῆραι ζῶσαι]; cf. 15.16; 16.21–22). Here, too, the legal infraction in question is ostensibly incest as defined in Mosaic law, but once again there appears to be the additional understanding that David cannot take back his concubines.[14]

We have seen, then, that 1QapGen 20.15 in particular provides a clear pre-rabbinic attestation for the halakhic idea that any sexual interference with an existing marriage bond produces a state of impurity, which precludes a resumption of that marriage. The concurrence of Philo and the *Testament of Reuben* suggests that this may well have been a relatively widespread view; it could at any rate lay claim to definite roots in the Old Testament.

As for Matthew, his apparent approval in principle of Joseph's reasoning in 1.19 suggests that the exception clauses of 5.32 and 19.9 are to him the necessary corollary to Jesus' teaching on divorce. Jesus, although he may hold to uncommon exegetical distinctions and priorities (see 19.8; cf. 23.23), does not abrogate the Torah (5.17–18). It is no offence if Jesus (e.g. in the antitheses) interprets the Torah more strictly than is required; indeed it could conceivably be regarded as 'making a fence for the Torah' (cf. *m.'Abot* 1.1). But to deny a commandment (viz., Deut 24.4 as understood in Judaism and evidently in Matthew's church) would be entirely another matter. Thus, since in halakhic terms a second union precludes resumption of the first, it was essential for Matthew's partly Jewish Christian community to affirm that their otherwise strict divorce

---

[14]Finkelstein 1923:56 and n. 78 further points out that this incident agrees with later Karaite halakhah, while in rabbinic discussion the principle was thought to apply only to royalty.

halakhah did not at this point contravene the Torah. Otherwise, Jesus' teaching could have incurred the charge of condoning sexual misdemeanour under the universal umbrella of an indissoluble marriage bond: a Gentile who knew only Luke 16.18 might well have been less clear than Paul in dealing with issues like those underlying 1 Cor 5.1–11 or 6.15–20. Matthew prevents this by excepting the case of πορνεία – presumably meaning neither specifically adultery nor illicit degrees of kinship,[15] but (like זנות) any kind of unlawful sexual relationship.[16]

The exception clauses need not of course settle the problem of how adultery was in fact dealt with in Matthew's church: the choice of language does not specify whether divorce may or must take place in case of πορνεία.[17] This problem is not ours to solve: suffice it here to commend Wenham's intriguing analysis of Matt 19.10–12 and 5.32b/19.9[18] as supporting a divorce only *a mensa et thoro*, i.e. without remarriage; this (and the hope for repentance and reconciliation) is also the preferred reading of the Fathers, beginning with Justin (2 *Apol.* 2) and Hermas (*Mand.* 4.1.6).[19]

For present purposes, my conclusion may be simply summarized: 1QapGen 20.15, seconded by references like Philo, *Abr.* 98; Matt 1.19; etc., clearly establishes a pre-rabbinic exegetical tradition (based on Deut 24.4 and Lev 18.20; Num 5.13–14, 20) to the effect that adultery (and rape) requires divorce. Matthew's Gospel is indebted to this tradition and therefore teaches that πορνεία makes husband and wife unfit for continued conjugal union.

---

[15]Thus most recently Fitzmyer 1981a:97.

[16]So e.g. Green 1975:84; Patte 1987:108n.27.

[17]Cf Luz 1985:275.

[18]Wenham 1984:98–100 and 102–5, respectively. Cf. further idem 1986.

[19]The patristic trend against second marriages in general (even after the death of the spouse) is possibly a related matter. It is present in Origen, Tertullian and others (see e.g. Kötting 1957, 1988), and may be implied, at least for church officers, in 1 Tim 3.2, 12; 5.9–12 (widows); Tit 1.6. See Lev 21.13–15 (but cf. Ezek 44.22); for widows cf. perhaps Jdt 8.4–8; 16.22; Luke 2.36–37.

3

'LET THE DEAD BURY THEIR DEAD'

JESUS AND THE LAW REVISITED

Jesus' challenge in Matthew 8.22 (par. Luke 9.62) to 'let the dead bury their own dead' has in recent years attracted a good deal of attention, not least for what it has been thought to reveal about Jesus' attitude to the Jewish Law. Indeed, it is perhaps no exaggeration to claim that this logion has become a kind of shibboleth for the assessment of Jesus' whole relationship with Judaism. The last two or three decades have of course witnessed a gradual rekindling of interest in the first-century Judaean and Galilean setting of Jesus' ministry. Nevertheless, scholars from a wide range of perspectives have continued to regard this saying as evidence that Jesus departed from conventional Jewish Torah piety in significant ways.

My purpose in this chapter is neither to question that view of Jesus nor to propose a significant reinterpretation of his handling of the Torah. All I expect to do here is to give a brief review of what appears to me a somewhat unsatisfactory state of discussion, and to plead for a more careful debate of the basic issues. I shall leave aside questions of authenticity and redactional analysis, on which I have few quarrels with the major published treatments. My primary conclusion is fairly modest and simple: whatever this logion means, it cannot mean what the current scholarly consensus assumes it to mean. Further study is needed.

The Prevailing Consensus

Martin Hengel

Although he follows in the footsteps of other writers like Adolf Schlatter,[1] Martin Hengel may be said to have kicked off the current debate about Matthew 8.22 par. It was in 1968 that he first published a learned study expanded from his original *Probevorlesung* at Tübingen. In their printed form, his remarks on this subject formed the first chapter of his widely admired book, *The Charismatic Leader and His Followers*, published in German in 1968 and later in two English editions in 1981 and 1996.

---

[1]See Klemm 1969 for the history of earlier interpretation.

In brief, Hengel's argument is as follows. An opening assessment of the logion's form and redaction history within and beyond the Q tradition suggests that it has been influenced by prophetic call narratives and by a desire to highlight Jesus' imperative command to follow him. In his further analysis, Hengel shows the substantial authenticity of both the logion and its necessary narrative frame in the prospective disciple's request to bury his father. With or without this context, however, it is indeed unlikely that the saying would have been invented in either a Jewish or a Gentile Christian setting. Hengel compares it to similarly drastic and shocking sayings among the Cynics, some of which were previously discussed by H. D. Betz and A. T. Ehrhardt.[2] His conclusion, however, is that one finds here nothing of the didactic polemicism against inherited taboos and conventions that characterizes the supposed Cynic parallels. Instead, our saying shows all the marks of being formulated as an 'ad hoc maxim' (p. 7) comparable to others both in the immediate context (Luke 9.58 par.; 9.62) and in the Jewish sapiential tradition. Hengel also dismisses attempts to re-translate the saying into Aramaic, and it must be conceded that subsequent efforts to do so have failed to be any more persuasive than the ones he commented on in 1968 (see below).

Instead, Hengel's own interpretation moves in a different direction. He asserts quite baldly that our logion 'derives its unique sharpness' from the fact that it encourages 'not only an attack on the respect for parents that is demanded in the fourth commandment but also at the same time it disregarded ... *works of love*, which according to Ab[oth] 1.2 had an independent place alongside Torah and cultus and yet at the same time had their basis in the Torah'.[3] The argument in support of this assertion is that both pre-rabbinic and rabbinic sources take for granted a halakhic duty to bury the dead, and one's parents *a fortiori*. He cites a wide range of evidence to document the fact that both Judaism and the wider Hellenistic world placed considerable stress on one's obligation to bury the dead.

Hengel concedes that the Torah itself prescribes two exceptions to this command to bury one's parents. Neither High Priests (Lev 21.11–12) nor Nazirites (Num 6.6) were allowed to contract corpse impurity even in the case of close relatives, although ordinary priests were permitted this. However, Hengel argues that even the requirements relating to High Priests and Nazirites had become

[2]Cited in Hengel 1996:6n. 11.
[3]Hengel 1996:8.

considerably relaxed and relativized by the Tannaitic period, so that 'the interment of a dead person without relatives, enjoined by the commandment (מת מצוה) cancelled even the prohibition on pollution of the high priests and Nazarites [sic] by a corpse'.[4] The evidence for this relaxation is drawn largely from rabbinic sources quoted in Strack-Billerbeck.

Professor Hengel's conclusion seems to follow along familiar supersessionist lines of a law–gospel polarity. By his drastic departure from Jewish law and tradition, Jesus 'expresses his sovereign freedom in respect of the Law of Moses and of custom in general' (p. 11); the present passage is 'a paradigm for all the others' on the Law (p. 3). It shows Jesus' 'rejection of ritualism' (p. 11 n. 27) and his 'annulment of the Fourth Commandment' (p. 13 n. 31). Any cultic or ritual considerations are 'in any case far from his thoughts' (p. 11); instead, 'Jesus ... is in sovereign fashion breaking down the barrier of respect for the dead and of custom' (p. 12). In short, 'There is hardly one logion of Jesus which more sharply runs counter to law, piety and custom' (p. 14).

E. P. Sanders

Martin Hengel's assessment of this issue has dominated the discussion over the last thirty years. It is indicative of the state of play that even E. P. Sanders, by no means uncritical of Hengel in other respects, readily accepts his verdict on this issue. Sanders, is in general far more reluctant to assert a Jesus at odds with Judaism. In the case of this particular logion, however, he defers entirely to Hengel's argument and agrees that on this occasion Jesus deliberately steps outside contemporary Jewish practice. Sanders' closely follows Hengel's presentation of the Hellenistic and Jewish sources and concludes that this is 'the most revealing passage in the synoptics for penetrating to Jesus' view of the law'.[5] Its implication is that 'Jesus *consciously* requires disobedience of a commandment understood by all Jews to have been given by God'.[6] Sanders allows that one might want to hesitate about a maximalist extrapolation regarding Jesus' antinomian attitude to the law. Nevertheless, he

---

[4]Hengel 1996:9.

[5]E. P. Sanders 1985:252. Note, however, his somewhat more moderate tone in 1993:224–6.

[6]E. P. Sanders 1985:254. Cf. in this regard the intriguing (if somewhat overstated) analysis of Chilton 1997a:223, 229–30, who suggests that a 'driving force' of Sanders' work is the consistent interest in a Jesus who trivializes ritual and accepts into his fellowship, not merely the impure, but the unrepentantly 'wicked'.

goes on to conclude unequivocally that 'Jesus was prepared, if necessary, to challenge the adequacy of the Mosaic dispensation' (1985:255).

Other Writers

Hengel and Sanders have between them contributed to a consensus to which a very wide range of scholars now subscribe, including both those adhering to conventional views of Jesus and those who view Jesus more deliberately within the context of first-century Judaism. To cite just a smattering of the many recent commentators, one might mention Blomberg, Gnilka and Luz on Matthew and Bovon, Nolland and Schürmann on Luke.[7] Relevant monograph literature follows along similar lines.[8]

For all these and others, it seems true despite occasional differences in detail that *Hengel locutus est; causa finita est*. Even those few who question the scope of Professor Hengel's conclusion tend nevertheless to take his rabbinic background work for granted, citing Hengel and Strack-Billerbeck.[9]

Assessment of the Case for the Prevailing Consensus

What might be said by way of evaluation? In a good many respects, Professor Hengel has clearly advanced the discussion considerably, and his learned treatment justly occupies a prominent position in the secondary literature. His impressively wide-ranging survey of the relevant background material serves to demonstrate the fundamentally Jewish setting of the logion, and he confirms the long-standing claim that this saying would indeed have been unusually demanding and shocking in a first-century Palestinian setting. His comments on the likely authenticity and redaction of the saying also seem to me largely on target,[10] as does his argument that on balance 'the dead' to whom the burial is left should be seen as the metaphorically

---

[7]Blomberg 1992:148; Gnilka 1986:1.312–13; Luz 1990:2.24–5; Bovon 1996:2.36; Nolland 1993:2.342; Schürmann 1994:2.40–1.

[8]Cf. e.g. Charlesworth 1988:154–5 and nn. 59–60; Merkel 1984:134, 138; Meyer 1979:153 and n. 79; Wright 1996:401 and (somewhat more moderately) S. C. Barton 1994:149–50. Contrast the more circumspect comments of Bernheim 1997:88–91.

[9]E.g. Davies & Allison 1991:2.57–8; Fitzmyer 1981b:1.835.

[10]But see e.g. Davies & Allison 1991:2.53–4 for a critique of Hengel's assumption that Matthew's arrangement of the Q logion is closer to the original.

dead.[11] Hengel and the commentators who cite him also seem justified in resisting interpretations designed to domesticate what is on any reckoning one of the 'hard sayings' of the Jesus tradition.

In this connection Professor Hengel may even be right to reject Aramaic retroversion attempts, though perhaps he does so a little too hastily. It is an unfortunate fact that most of the twentieth-century proposals seem to have been motivated less by linguistic and exegetical concerns than by a desire to show that the logion must mean something other than what it seems to mean.[12] As a result, one encounters a good deal of wishful and anachronistic linguistics. As David Goldenberg (1996:74) rightly points out in his recent reply to Herbert Basser's (1993) contribution on the subject, 'The major problem in retroverting to Jesus' original speech lies in proving that the targeted vocabulary was part of the spoken lexical base of the time.' This is not of course to assert that an Aramaic original never existed, merely that it is in many cases impossible to offer a confident and reliable reconstruction. At the same time, and *pace* Hengel, it still seems to me worth noting the linguistically neutral and elegant solution proposed by Dalman and later picked up by Jeremias[13]: שבוק מיתייא קברין מיתיהון. This may not bear a great deal of exegetical fruit, but it does at least acknowledge the legitimacy of asking about an Aramaic substratum.

My main argument here, however, is that the evidence cited by Professors Hengel, Sanders and others does not support their conclusions. The two main points of my critique will address their dating and interpretation of rabbinic sources. No one would deny that burial of the dead was in the first century viewed as a universal duty

[11]Hengel 1996:8 (following A. Schlatter and R. Bultmann); cf. e.g. Fitzmyer 1981b:1.836. For a recent view to the contrary, see e.g. Luz 1990:2.25–6; cf. Nolland 1993:2.543. However, it is not necessary to assume that the metaphor is here best understood in a heightened spiritual sense (e.g. 'dead to the things of God'). Instead, it might just as well denote a more direct and 'gnomic' notion either of futile mortality (e.g. 'earth-bound mortals') or even of the impurity of death (e.g. 'those who busy themselves with corpses'), as Professors W. Horbury and B. Chilton have independently suggested to me.

The meaning of 'the dead' here is admittedly difficult to determine with precision. The relative indeterminacy of this word-play may well be intentional; and in any case it derives in part from the saying's tersely gnomic and *ad hoc* formulation. It should be noted, however, that this difficulty is necessarily faced by *all* interpretations, and that the particular argument here presented is not dependent on finding an unequivocal resolution.

[12]E.g. Perles 1919–20; Black 1973:207–8; also Basser 1993. Note also the comments of Fitzmyer 1981b:1.836.

[13]Dalman 1924:163; Jeremias 1971:22 (without acknowledgement). Note, however, that Dalman himself had earlier offered a different version in 1922:210 (ET 1929:232): ארפא למיתייא דיקברון מיתיהון; and although he alludes to the other version in 1922:iv n. 1, there is no acknowledgement of this difference.

and an important act of kindness, and that not to be buried was widely considered the ultimate disgrace.[14] It is plausible, too, that the duty of burial would be particularly invoked where the commandment to honour one's parents was at stake.

Two problems arise, however, in the documentation of the claim that this requirement was viewed as being of such paramount importance that even the Torah's prohibitions for High Priests and Nazirites had been relaxed.

Dating the Evidence

All the sources Professor Hengel adduces are Tannaitic at the earliest, and so cannot be dated with confidence before the beginning of the third century. It will not do to cite references to Yose ben Yoezer in the Mishnah ('*Ed.* 8.4) and Talmud (*b.* '*Abod. Zar.* 37b) as 'attesting'[15] the actual state of halakhah in the early Maccabean period. This is especially true in view of the notoriously enigmatic tenor of Yose ben Yoezer's evidently liberalising original statement, 'He that touches a corpse becomes unclean' (*m.* '*Ed.* 8.4). That saying was probably intended to limit corpse contamination to direct contact, but in any case it originally had nothing to do with a relaxation in requirements pertaining to the High Priest or to Nazirites.

The problem of dating rabbinic traditions need not ordinarily be an insurmountable problem, as long as one can establish a credible continuum of tradition that links the later with demonstrably earlier evidence. Precisely such a link, however, is not to my knowledge extant in this case. And this lacuna is all the more significant in that it relates to two institutions – the (temporary) Nazirate and the High Priesthood – which abruptly ceased to operate with the destruction of the Temple.[16] In the absence of more specific early evidence, we cannot simply assume second- or third-century rabbinic halakhah to have been in force in the first century.

Interpreting the Evidence

Secondly, however, and contrary to Hengel's assertion, even the Tannaitic evidence he cites does not in fact amount to a relaxation of the Pentateuchal law. Instead, it merely affirms a halakhic *priority*

---

[14]See e.g. Deut 28.26; Jer 7.33; 8.1–2; Ezek 6.5; 29.5; 39.17; *Pss. Sol.* 4.19; cf. Christian texts like Rev 11.9; 4 Ezra 2.23.

[15]So Hengel 1996:9.

[16]See e.g. *m. Naz.* 5.4 on the problem of what to do after AD 70 with Nazirites whose vows had been taken before the Temple's destruction.

within the Torah, in keeping with a general Hillelite tendency to stress core commandments and the agent's moral intention. Where there are no other relatives and the dead person would otherwise remain unburied, the written requirement of burial (e.g. Deut 21.23; cf. Gen 23.4–20; 47.29–30; 49.29–30; Sir 38.16; Eccl 6.3)[17] takes precedence over the demands both of a High Priest's duty (note *Sifra Emor* 2 on Lev 21.11 (§213.1.7); *b. Naz.* 47b) and of a Nazirite's optional vow (*m. Naz.* 6.5; *Sifre Num.* 6.6 (§26)).

Significantly, not one of the rabbinic sources cited by Professor Hengel and Strack-Billerbeck makes an allowance for High Priests or Nazirites specifically in order to bury *parents*.[18] Most of them deal either with the *general* duty of burial or with the specific case of *ordinary* priests, of whom the law does of course in any case require the burial of close relatives.[19] The cited exemptions for High Priests and Nazirites apply only to the very specific case of the מת מצוה, i.e. the burial of those with no-one else to bury them.[20] The biblical prohibition of burying parents, by contrast, is explicitly and repeatedly *re-affirmed* in Philo,[21] Josephus[22] and in every one of the relevant rabbinic discussions.[23] And the Nazirite rules about corpse defilement are broadly in keeping with those spelled out in the tractates *Ohalot* and *Kelim*, which would in practice rule out not only direct contact but also, for example, joining the mourners in the house of the deceased.[24]

The Dead Sea Scrolls appear to lack any direct discussions of Lev 21.11 or Num 6.6, although two biblical MSS containing Lev 21.11 survive[25] and there are Aramaic fragments of several relevant passages in Tobit.[26] It may be that the sectarian boycott of the

[17]Cf. also the Tannaitic derivation of the duty of burial from Exod 18.20 (*Mek., Yitro* 4 on 18.20 (ed. Lauterbach 2.182) (R. Eleazar of Modiim T2), par. *b. B.Qam.* 99b) and Mic 6.8 (*b. Suk.* 49b, R. Elazar b. Pedat A3).

[18]Even someone of Joseph Fitzmyer's astuteness can assert quite categorically that 'According to later rabbinic tradition, the obligation of burying the dead parents fell even on Nazirites, priests, and the high priest himself' (1981b:1.835).

[19]Lev 21.2–3; cf. *Sifra Emor* 1 *ad loc.* (§211.1.5–20); *Sifre Num.* 26 on 6.7. Hengel's specific appeal to *Sifra* on Num [*sic:* read Lev] 21.3, par. *b. Zeb.* 100a, deals precisely with the case of an *ordinary* priest urged to forgo Passover purity for the sake of burying his wife.

[20]Note the Tannaitic definition כל שאין לו קוברין 'everyone who has none to bury him': *b. 'Erub.* 17b; *b. Yeb.* 89b; *b. Naz.* 43b.

[21]*Spec. Leg.* 1.112–16, 247–56.

[22]*Ant.* 3.12.2 §277 (for the High Priest).

[23]E.g. *m. Naz.* 6.5; 7.1; *b. Naz.* 47b–48b; *y. Naz.* 7.1, 55d–56b; *Sifre Num.* §26 on 6.6; *Num. Rab.* 10.11; *Midrash ha-Gadol* on Num 6.6; *Tg. Neof.* Num 6.6; cf. *Semahot* 4.29–31, etc.

[24]Cf. Boertien 1971:166–79; on the principles of *Ohalot*, see recently Maccoby 1997.

[25]4QLev[c] 6.5; 11QpalaeoLev[a] frag. K 9; both attest the 'proto-Masoretic' text.

[26]4Q196 (Tobit[a]) 11.i.4; 4Q197 (Tobit[b]) 3.ii.11–12.

Temple at Jerusalem ruled out temporary Nazirite vows.[27] Instead, one finds various conventional assertions about the need for lawful burial, including statements about 'building the tombs of our fathers'.[28]

At the same time, there is other sectarian evidence to suggest the existence of a more rigorist position. The laws about corpse impurity in the *Temple Scroll* imply that the Qumran sect may have extended the Torah's priestly regulations on this matter to all members of the community.[29] More specifically, a relatively severe position would be entirely consistent with Josephus's account of the Essene requirement to break with one's family except under strict supervision.[30] Archaeological evidence confirms that Essenes or related groups avoided the protracted procedure of secondary burial, and consistently used individual rather than family tombs both at the Dead Sea sites of Qumran, Jericho, Ein el-Ghuweir and Ḥiam el-Sagha,[31] and in the apparently sectarian cemeteries recently unearthed at various locations around Jerusalem.[32] Although they do not constitute formal evidence, these practices would be entirely compatible with a reduced emphasis on family ties and the obligation to bury one's next of kin.[33]

What is more, there are reasonable grounds to doubt the broad acceptance in first-century halakhah of the particular Tannaitic exception for High Priests and Nazirites in the case of the 'abandoned corpse', even if the general principle of burying the unattended dead as an act of kindness is clearly attested at least since the book of Tobit.[34] Philo for one entirely omits the concession of

[27]So e.g. Boertien 1971:27.

[28]Cf. 1QM 11.1 (the enemies' corpses are left with no-one to bury them); 11QT 48.10–13 (the need for discrete burial places; cf. 49.5 – 51.5 on corpse impurity); 4QPrEsther[d] (=4Q550) 1.6 ('when you die I will bury you'); 4QVisions of Amram[b] (=4Q544) 1.1–3 (building the tombs of our fathers, burying the dead; cf. 4QVisions of Amram[c] 1.ii.11, 15, 17).

[29]See especially 11QT 48.11–14; 49.8–9; cf. Yadin 1983:1.324, 327; Swanson 1995:181, 188. Note, too, that E. Eshel 1997 interprets 4Q414 frag. 2 in relation to corpse contamination; others have seen here a baptismal liturgy.

[30]E.g. *War* 2.8.6 §134: τὰς δὲ εἰς τοὺς συγγενεῖς μεταδόσεις οὐκ ἔξεστι ποιεῖσθαι δίχα τῶν ἐπιτρόπων.

[31]Cf. Hachlili 1992:792–3; H. Eshel & Greenhut 1993:256–8 [NB in this article the site is variously spelled Ḥiam el-Sagha, Ḥiam el-Sa'gaha, Ḥiam El-Sa'laha and Ḥiam El-Sa'raha].

[32]One such tomb has turned up in the Mamilla area west of the Old City, two at East Talpiot, and most recently over 50 at Beit Safafa. See Kloner & Gat 1982:76; Zissu 1998, 1999.

[33]Cf. also Hachlili 1993:263.

[34]Tob 1.17–18: it is one of the expressions of Tobit's charity (ἐλεημοσύνη = נמילות הסדים) that he buries the bodies of Jews thrown outside the walls of Nineveh. Cf. 2.3–9; 12.12–13; see also 2 Macc 12.39.

the מת מצוה (i.e. the abandoned corpse) from his discussions of the Torah passages about the High Priest (Lev 21.11) and about the Nazirite (Num 6.6), while unambiguously reiterating in both cases the prohibition of burying parents.[35]

Additional doubt is cast on the state of first-century halakhah on this matter by the discussion in Mishnah *Nazir* 7.1. That passage records considerable disagreement between the late first-century R. Eliezer b. Hyrcanus and his colleagues about whether even an unattended corpse should exempt the Nazirite and the High Priest from maintaining their purity at all costs. It seems that the universal mandate of the abandoned corpse may not have been formalized until the early Tannaitic period, when it came to be grounded in the requirement of Lev 21.1 that a priest may not incur corpse impurity בעמיו, i.e. when he is 'among his people'. The unattended dead whom a priest might come across in the open countryside was by implication excluded.[36] Intriguingly, even the Parable of the Good Samaritan may imply that the principle of the unattended corpse was not in fact universally recognized in pre-70 halakhah: seeing a man who was 'half dead' (ἡμιθανῆ), the Priest and the Levite take the precaution of walking by 'on the other side' – presumably in order to avoid overshadowing a potential corpse and thereby contracting impurity that would ritually disqualify them from their temple duties (Luke 10.30–32).[37]

It is, incidentally, far from clear that the hypothetical case of the neglected corpse is the situation envisaged in Matthew 8.22 par., regardless of whether the father is assumed to be near death or just

---

[35]Philo, *Spec. Leg.* 1.113–15, 250. Quite how Professor Hengel can deduce from such texts Philo's 'manifest . . . tendency to relax this ritual stipulation' (1996:11n. 26) is not clear to me. Philo does indeed discover an allegorical, 'spiritualizing' perspective in these laws (*Agr.* 175–8; *Immut.* 87–90; *Leg. All.* 1.17; cf. also the application to the Logos in *Fuga* 109, 113), but it is of course fundamental to his exegetical approach that spiritual interpretation does not negate literal observance. Note his famous critique of the pure allegorists in *Migr.* 89–93.

[36]Cf. *Sifra* Emor 1 on Lev 21.1 (§211.1). See also Boertien 1971:163, citing M. Petuchowski.

[37]On this subject cf. now also Bauckham 1998. Although conceding that both the duty of burial (of the מת מצוה) and the principle of saving life (פיקוח נפש:, cf. p. 7 above) are early, Bauckham suggests that the determining principle of the parable is instead the overriding (and unparalleled) priority of the love command (ibid., pp. 481–5). But while the double commandment undoubtedly governs both the context of the parable (Luke 10.25–29, 36–37) and the substance of Jesus' teaching (see Chapter 1 above), there is perhaps no need to downplay the rhetorical effect in the parable's Palestinian setting of a (regular) priest and a Levite neglecting even a doubtful מת מצוה because of how it might affect their ritual status. That such scruples sometimes affected attitudes to mourning and burial seems clear, for example, from the Tannaitic story of an ordinary priest who was compelled by his colleagues to defile himself at Passover in order to bury his wife (see 29 n. 19 above).

deceased.[38] J. A. Bengel's passing surmise that there may have been other sons (*ad* Matt 8.22; cf. similarly Derrett 1985:77) is by no means the far-fetched rationalization that a number of commentators have accused it of being. The point in our context is simply the inquirer's request to honour the widely attested expectation (cf. e.g. Tob 6.13–15; *m. Ket.* 11.1) that children should provide for their ageing parents' burial. It is children who are in the first instance responsible for the burial of their parents, as indeed honouring one's parents was one of the 'acts of kindness' (גמילות חסדים) which have no prescribed limit (*m. Peah* 1.1). To tend the unburied could even be conceived in imitation of God, who clothes the naked, visits the sick, comforts the mourner and, in the case of Moses, buries the dead (*b. Sot.* 14a; cf. Deut 34.6).[39] Given this high regard, burial of one's parents could indeed be set aside only in the most exceptional circumstances. It is the apparent denial of this most basic act of charity that gives Jesus' statement its undeniably shocking directness. Nevertheless, the present scenario of burying a parent is likely to be a different matter from that of an abandoned corpse, as indeed these two situations are always distinguished in the relevant rabbinic discussions.

Interpreting the Interpreters

In the end, it seems that a thinly disguised theological agenda drives the prevailing exegesis of the passage. This of course is inevitable for most of us, and not inherently problematic. What matters is to try and perceive how it affects one's reading of the evidence.

While Professor Hengel assures his readers that Jesus was not in principle opposed to works of kindness, he is just as certain that 'any casuistic legal codification was repugnant to him' (1996:9 n. 21). Jesus, we are told, categorically rejected ritualism (1996:11 n. 27). His answer to this potential disciple 'in a unique way expresses his sovereign freedom in respect of the Law of Moses and of custom in general'; 'any cultic or ritual basis was ... far from his thoughts' (1996:11). Quite how we know all this about Jesus' thoughts is not

---

[38]Immediate burial was the norm, as corpses would not normally be left overnight; the point of the tradition, therefore, is that the demands of the Kingdom rule out even a brief delay. McCane's attempt (1990; cf. earlier, Meyers 1971:54 n. 31, 82 n. 37) to interpret our saying in relation to secondary burial, i.e. the gathering of bones into ossuaries after decomposition, remains unconvincing on both contextual and semantic grounds. The relevant terminology in these cases is always that of 'gathering (and burying) the *bones*' rather than of 'burying the person'.

[39]See further Davies & Allison 1991:53 n. 157.

clear. Tertullian, who pointed out the saying's point of contact with the Old Testament laws about High Priests and Nazirites, is summarily pigeonholed as 'the lawyer Tertullian'.[40]

Is it unreasonable to see here traces of that age-old platonizing Christian cliché, according to which the pure gospel of Jesus, untainted by the trappings of law and religion, triumphs over the casuistry and ritual of Judaism? Especially in their more recent works, Professors Hengel and Sanders have clearly shown themselves to be far less prone to such facile historical dichotomies than some of those who quote them. Nevertheless, their conclusions on this subject still seem to echo the contrast of gospel versus law, sovereign grace versus ritual observance, Jesus versus Judaism – a polarity that in its undiluted form could be traced from its invention by followers of Paul to its systematic endorsement by Marcion and his various ancient and modern sympathizers.

Could it be that, by hastily sweeping the legal context of Jesus' saying under the carpet, the dominant interpretation has in fact missed an important clue to its possible background of meaning? Post-World War II New Testament scholarship found in the 'criterion of dissimilarity' an opportune peg, whose ideological convenience far outstripped its rather flawed and limited use as an indicator of the authentic Jesus. It is disturbing to note how apologists for both liberalism and confessional conservatism have continued to find refuge in assuming the *a priori* likelihood of assertions about Jesus' radical distinctiveness vis-à-vis a Torah-centred Judaism. The implausibility of occasional Jewish and other programmes to assert a wholly observant and uncontroversial Jesus should not prevent us from adopting a pragmatic posture that will assess each case on its own merits.

We come, then, to the first of my two major conclusions for this paper. It is a largely negative one, and perhaps the only one that can be stated with some degree of confidence: Matthew 8.22 par. is unlikely to mean what the prevailing consensus takes it to mean. Its undeniably provocative flavour notwithstanding, the assumed radical contrast with any and all Jewish halakhah begins to evaporate on closer examination.

---

[40]1996:11; cf. Tertullian, *Adv. Marc.* 4.23. Others who have appealed to these passages include Plummer 1909:130; Klemm 1969:62; Glombitza 1971:19; Schweizer 1976:220–1; Klemm 1969:62 n. 3 also lists H. Grotius and J. J. Wettstein among earlier writers; cf. also Derrett 1985:76.

Possible Ways Forward

Where might this leave us with regard to the interpretation of our saying? Three options remain open.

A Renewed Case for the Consensus?

First, it must be admitted that logically the consensus view might still be correct. It is indeed possible that Jesus deliberately shocks his potential disciple with a saying designed to stress that his kingdom-centred ministry and identity entitle him to a sovereign autonomy from Torah and tradition. My contention here is simply that while theoretically conceivable, the case for this view remains to be made – and the evidence commonly adduced for it does not support the conclusion.

If this first explanation fails, however, the meaning of our text becomes more, rather than less, difficult.

Reinterpretation as Prophetic Drama?

A second option, not wholly incompatible with the first, would be that Jesus simply provokes the potential inquirer to a symbolic action of prophetic significance. Just as Jeremiah was instructed to boycott all mourning of the dead in order to symbolize the coming disaster for Judah and Jerusalem (Jer 16.5–9), so Ezekiel became a sign of the destruction of Jerusalem and the Temple by not mourning the death of his wife (Ezek 24.16–24). These prophetic parallels are widely acknowledged; even Professor Hengel rightly warms to them (1996:12). Usually, of course, they are construed in classic Well-hausenian fashion as standing outside or even in contrast to the legal tradition of the Pentateuch (so also Hengel). We need hardly point out, however, that they were certainly not understood in this fashion by Jesus or anyone else in Second Temple Judaism, whatever one might make of their literary origin.

Nevertheless, prophetic drama of this kind is certainly a conceivable explanation. Several incidents in the gospel tradition can be helpfully understood as symbolic actions, perhaps especially Jesus' cleansing of the Temple and the institution of the Last Supper.[41] At the same time, it is by no means clear that the present logion qualifies under the same heading. Unlike the events in Jerusalem, the present incident concerns not Jesus' own action but

---

[41]See Hooker 1997.

his command to a follower. Those other two episodes also differ from our logion in being accompanied by unambiguous words of explanation, like most of the prophetic actions of the Old Testament prophets.[42] More importantly, no action is in fact reported as having been carried out. Instead, our saying is kept deliberately terse and gnomic, either to maintain a sense of enigma or perhaps more likely because it is assumed to be self-interpreting. Finally, it is worth noting that even if the prophetic drama genre were appropriate, such a parallel would in any case provide no comfort to an interpretation of our passage as showing Jesus in deliberate breach or suspension of the Law. Neither the biblical prophets themselves nor the ancient Jewish versions and interpretations portray their parabolic actions as overriding or contradicting the Torah.

A Third Option?

We must obviously leave open the possibility that someone might come up with a better argument for the Hengel/Sanders consensus, whether on the grounds of established halakhah or on those of a prophet's provocative action. Meanwhile, however, we shall devote the final part of this paper to another interpretative context. If this uninterpreted saying does *not* intend a radical rejection of Jewish law and tradition, what *else* might it have been assumed to mean in the first-century setting? The following remarks on this subject are brief and somewhat experimental, deliberately intended as an *entrée* to further discussion rather than as a full-blown hypothesis.

My proposal here will be to focus on one of the two mandatory legal exemptions from the duty to bury one's parents. By taking a halakhic approach, I do not of course mean that Jesus' teaching should be read in keeping with the academic genre of halakhic discourse, nor indeed that this is the primary perspective even in this episode. Jesus was neither rabbi nor scribe, and there is little point in denying the obvious harshness of his saying when compared with the attitudes in texts like Tobit. Nevertheless, if one accepts that Jesus was in some meaningful sense conversant with the cultural and religious milieu of first-century Palestine, then the issue of his relationship to the traditions of Judaism cannot simply be subsumed under the later image of Jesus as the revealer of a radical *nova lex*. Chapter 1 above documents the extent to which the Jesus

---

[42]Compare additionally Isa 20; Ezek 4–5; 12; Hos 1–2. Cf. Stacey 1990:141–2, 205–7 and *passim*.

tradition continues to manifest a significant halakhic awareness, if only as a natural reflection of the general setting in which it originated and continued to function for some time.

Of the two Old Testament legal traditions discussed above, the High Priestly one may be safely set aside for present purposes. Although it is of course true that some circles in the early church came to view both Jesus and (in a different sense) James the Just in high priestly categories, there is no evidence that this aspect features either in the original episode or in its redactional treatment by Matthew and Luke.[43] Any sacerdotal overtones would here arise only by secondary analogy from a Nazirite link (see below), if that could be demonstrated.

Here, then, I would like to propose for further discussion the possibility that the most likely subtext in the earliest setting of our logion may be found in Nazirite motifs. Although occasionally mooted,[44] this has to my knowledge never been seriously considered in the secondary literature. If the 'Jesus *versus* the Law' scenario cannot be sustained, might this possibility offer a way forward?

Nazirite Halakhah

A Nazirite connection seems at first sight to be so far-fetched as to render any discussion unnecessary. There is no evidence in the Gospels that either Jesus or his disciples manifested the obvious signs of Nazirite devotion. Far from being a teetotaller, Jesus seems to have been a frequent guest at feasts and developed a reputation for being a 'glutton and a wine-bibber' (Matt 11.19 par.). The Gospels are not interested in the length of his hair or that of his disciples, and there is no apparent concern about corpse impurity either at the house of Jairus (Mark 5.22–43), at Nain (Luke 7.11–15) or at the tomb of Lazarus (John 11.1–44).[45] More clearly still, we find no reference to the appointed sacrifices marking the end of a Nazirite vow.

What point, then, might there be in seeking a Nazirite explanation of our logion? Probably very little, if the question is put as directly

---

[43]*Pace* Schniewind 1960:114; Glombitza 1971:19–20, who argue that Jesus operates as High Priest here.

[44]E.g. in Bernheim 1997:90; Derrett 1985:223–6 (though taking an allegorical line); Schweizer 1960.

[45]Nevertheless, one wonders if it might be significant that Jesus seems to attend no burials (not even that of Lazarus) and appears to approach no dead person other than those he restores to life.

as that: there is nothing to suggest that either Jesus or his inquirer are speaking as Nazirites.

There are, however, a number of additional contextual observations to be taken into account, beginning with the redactional triplet of sayings about radical discipleship in which our logion appears (Matt 8.19–22; Luke 9.57–62). It is certainly in keeping with what we know of Jesus' teaching about discipleship that he described membership in the kingdom of God by adopting various images of radical dedication. These include resolutely setting out to plough a field, leaving behind one's family, having no home to sleep in, planning to build a large building, going to war against a superior enemy, and even taking up one's cross daily to follow Jesus like a condemned criminal going to his execution. (This last has been thought a possible adaptation from a slogan of Jewish militant nationalists.[46]) In all these and similar cases, a concrete and familiar image is used to illustrate his challenge to 'bring one's life to a point' by investing all that one is and has in the service of God.

If such a reading is even approximately correct, however, it would in a first-century Jewish context make Nazirite connotations or comparisons eminently plausible. It is worth illustrating this briefly, both from a Jewish and from an early Christian perspective.

1. The Old Testament and Judaism

Not only Samson[47] (Judg 13.7) but Samuel, too, was regarded as a lifelong Nazirite, as is clear already in the 4QSam[a] and LXX texts of 1 Sam 1.11, 22.[48] Both in biblical and in subsequent Jewish thought, Nazirites were regarded as uniquely dedicated to God, and temporarily comparable in status to priests, as both alike are pure and 'holy to the Lord' (note Lev 21.6 with Num 6.8).[49] Philo, in fact,

---

[46]E.g. Luke 14.26–33 par. Cf. Hengel 1989:260, 271, following Schlatter 1925:264 and 1929:350; cf. Brandon 1967:57.

[47]Cf. recently Stipp 1995.

[48]LXX 1 Sam 1.11 inserts οἶνον καὶ μέθυσμα οὐ πίεται. Whether in order to avoid implying corpse contamination or for other reasons, Josephus tones down 1 Sam 15.33 to suggest that Samuel (evidently a Nazirite according to *Ant.* 5.10.3 §347) merely 'gave orders' for Agag to be put to death: *Ant.* 6.7.5 §155. Cf. also Sir 46.13 (Heb.); *m. Naz.* 9.5 on Samuel, and 1.2 on becoming a Nazirite 'like Samson'. See further Boertien 1971:201–7, and on the underlying textual questions cf. also Catastini 1987; Tsevat 1992; Ulrich 1978:39–40, 165–6. The possibility of a Nazirite link with Samuel in the Lucan infancy narrative is also entertained by Davies & Allison 1988:1.276.

Absalom later came to be seen as a lifelong Nazirite (*b. Naz.* 4b; *Num. Rab.* 9.24); Joseph was a temporary Nazirite (e.g. *Gen. Rab.* 98.20; cf. Vulgate Gen 49.26 par. Deut 33.16: *nazareus* = נזיר); cf. also Caleb in Num 32.12 (Symmachus & Theodotion).

[49]It has occasionally been suggested (e.g. by Berger 1996:330) that there could be a link with this phrase in the demon's exclamation in Mark 1.24 par.; cf. also John 6.69.

explicitly affirms that Nazirites were for the duration of their 'Great Vow' to consider themselves as priests in active service (τὸν χρόνον ἐκεῖνον ἱερᾶσθαι, *Spec. Leg.* 1.249). Philo speaks of the Nazirite vow in exalted theological terms: the supreme offering that transcends ordinary material offerings is the consecration of oneself, which demonstrates an inexpressible piety and an abundant love of God. As in Tannaitic midrash, the Nazirite vow manifests the dedication of oneself to God: 'This is why this practice is rightly called the Great Vow: for the greatest possession which anyone has is himself'.[50] The Nazirite's ritual purity, too, symbolizes his complete devotion to God, and Philo compares the case of inadvertent corpse defilement to that of being caught in unintentional sins (*Agr.* 176). A popular if somewhat enigmatic story told of the High Priest Simeon the Just's (third century BC) encounter with a handsome young Nazirite confirms that this vow was indeed understood as a symbol of sanctification and personal devotion to God.[51] In discussing why the passage about the Nazirite (Num 6.1–21) follows immediately on that about the unfaithful wife (Num 5.11–31), one Tannaitic passage advises that anyone who happens to see a woman engaging in adulterous ways should immediately abstain from wine.[52] This spiritual and even penitential dimension of the Nazirate was perhaps already implicit in the fact that the prescribed offerings in the Torah included in each case a sacrifice for sin (חטאת, Num 6.11, 14, 16).[53]

Despite the considerable personal and financial cost incurred by those who undertook them, Nazirite vows were clearly very popular in certain circles during the later Second Temple Period. Various sources speak of large numbers of Nazirites arriving at the Temple in fulfilment of their vows.[54]

This popularity of the practice is also indirectly confirmed by the highly developed halakhah assumed in the Mishnah and Tosefta:

---

[50]Philo, *Spec. Leg.* 1.248; cf. *Sifre Num.* 32 on 6.13.

[51]*T. Nez.* 4.7; *b. Naz.* 4b; *b. Ned.* 9b; etc.

[52]*B. Ber.* 63a (R. Yehudah ha-Nasi, *baraita*).

[53]Cf. Baumgarten 1996 on the original significance of this sacrifice. Note, however, the more negative interpretation of this connection in certain circles of later rabbinic Judaism. Thus, a widely attested tradition attributes to the anti-mystical and anti-ascetical Bar Qappara (early third cent.; his teacher R. Yehudah ha-Nasi apparently denied him ordination) the view that the 'sin' for which the Nazirite brings his sacrifice is that of having denied himself wine! See *b. Ta'an.* 11a (cf. R. Sheshet & R. Jeremiah, fourth cent.: ibid. 11b); *b. Naz.* 19a. See further Fraade 1986; for the diverse and often sceptical views of asceticism in late antiquity, cf. more generally Francis 1995; see also n. 56 below.

[54]In addition to 1 Macc 3.49, cited earlier, see e.g. Josephus *Ant.* 19.6.1 §294; *y. Ber.* 7.2 (11b40–5), etc.

the tractate *Nazir* (cf. *t. Nezirut*) offers numerous detailed regulations and conditions for the form and conduct of Nazirite vows. And despite the abrupt demise of temporary Nazirite vows after the events of AD 70[55] there still exists a significant Gemara on the subject in both Talmuds, perhaps because *Nazir* was a special topic within the larger and abiding subject of *Nedarim* ('vows'), which immediately precedes it in the Mishnaic sequence of tractates.[56]

What is more, the fact that both *Nazir* and *Nedarim* appear in the Mishnaic Order *Nashim* ('women') suggests the immense attraction that Nazirite and other vows evidently exerted over a great many women as well as men – perhaps because they offered to layfolk of both sexes and all walks of life a temporary share in quasi-priestly status, by means of a particularly engaging and respected expression of personal faith. Not only Queen Helena of Adiabene and Miriam of Palmyra, but even Agrippa II's otherwise not especially religious sister Berenice came to Jerusalem to bring her Nazirite offerings; indeed she stayed on past the outbreak of the Jewish revolt in AD 66.[57]

A good deal of corroborating evidence could be cited to document the popularity of Nazirite and related ascetic practices. Nazirites evidently had a high profile, as is clear from the fact that their sons could be named after them: so a splendid aristocratic family tomb at Mount Scopus has revealed the first-century ossuaries of one 'Hananiah son of Jonathan the Nazirite' and of 'Salome wife of Hananiah son of the Nazirite', and quite possibly also contains the sarcophagi of Jonathan himself along with his wife.[58] Here is a man from the time of Jesus who permanently bore the epithet הנזיר ('the Nazirite'), whether because of repeated short-term vows or a life-long vow, and who even bequeathed that name to his son and daughter-in-law. Pseudo-Philo's *Biblical Antiquities* show a sustained interest in Samson (e.g. 42.3), while various traditions about the mysterious teetotalling Rechabites of Jeremiah 35 appear to have been popular in the Tannaitic period.[59] Abstention from

---

[55]Note the question of what to do with Nazirite arriving in Jerusalem just after the Temple's destruction, *m. Naz.* 5.4. Temporary vows taken after the destruction are invalid (ibid.), although occasional instances of life-long Nazirite vows continued until modern times.

[56]The subject was apparently no longer studied by the Geonim, as indeed there is also some evidence attesting a certain resistance to ascetic practices of this sort (cf. n. 53 above). See also *EJ* 12.907, 910, and cf. e.g. *t. Nez.* 4.7; *b. Ned.* 9a–b etc.

[57]Josephus, *War* 2.15.1 §313–14. On Helena of Adiabene, see e.g. *m. Naz.* 3.6; Miriam of Palmyra (Tadmor) *m. Naz.* 6.11; *t. Nez.* 4.10.

[58]See Avigad 1971:196–8.

[59]See e.g. *Mek. Amalek* 4 (on Exod 18.27, ed. Lauterbach 2.187–8); *Hist. Rech.* 8–10 (on which see below).

wine and meat mark Reuben's repentance in *Test. Reub.* 1.10. Rules
about a variety of more general fasts and fast days abound, not least
in documents like *Megillat Taanit* and the Mishnah tractate
Taanit.[60] In case a date in the late first or early second century is
possible, we should also note the controversial wisdom text from the
Cairo Genizah edited first by Klaus Berger (1989) and then again in
somewhat polemical mode by Hans Peter Rüger (1991). That text
commends the Nazirite's fast over against the 'pleasure of the world'
(5.3),[61] and manifests a deliberate contrast between the joy of wine
and the pleasures of this world (6.2–3) on the one hand, and the joy
of the Torah on the other (6.4). Finally, Epiphanius speaks of a pre-
Christian Jewish group whom he variously calls Ναζαραῖοι (*Pan.*
19.5) and Νασαραῖοι (*Pan.* 29.7); the former at any rate are
presented as a distinct religious party alongside the Sadducees,
Essenes and others.

All in all, there can be no doubt about the popularity of Nazirite
vows and practices as a significant manifestation of Jewish piety in
the later second Temple period. This is particularly worth noting
inasmuch as prominent New Testament scholars have been known
to assert in print that at the time of Jesus there were no Nazirites at
all.[62]

2. *Jesus and the Gospels*

Evidence of early Christian interest in Nazirite motifs is inconsistent,
but remarkably intriguing. In Luke, John the Baptist's birth is
announced somewhat like that of Samson: we hear that he would
abstain from wine and strong drink for life (Luke 1.15; cf. 7.33 par.).
But no such statement is made about Jesus.

Matthew's infancy narrative has sometimes been thought to be
toying with a Nazirite connection in the fulfilment formula at
2.23 (Ναζωραῖος κληθήσεται).[63] His vague citation, however, suggests (i) that Matthew is deliberately evoking rather than quoting
from the Old Testament and (ii) that the precise textual link

---

[60]Cf. e.g. the discussion in Schürer 1979:2.483–4; Str-B 4.77–114. Note also the Jewish
Christian prescription of fasting in *Did.* 1.3; 7.4; 8.1 (and see Alon 1996 on the halakhah of
the *Didache*).

[61]'The fool mocks the Nazirite's fast, but praises the pleasure of the world':
אויל ילין צום נזיר וישבח האות עולם. I follow Rüger's reading of the damaged second half of the verse,
although I am not finally persuaded of his (and e.g. Veltri's 1992) arguments for a medieval
origin of this document.

[62]So e.g. Schweizer 1960:92, following M. Goguel.

[63]See e.g. Schaeder 1942:883, Schweizer 1960 and Berger 1996 as well as Davies & Allison
1988:1.26–7 and the sources they cite in n. 34.

may be somewhat tenuous in his own mind. In any case he wants of course to prove a prophetic link with Nazareth, not with Nazirites. Elsewhere, too, Jesus is typically identified as 'the Nazorean' (ὁ Ναζωραῖος; cf. Ναζαρηνός),[64] but Nazirite associations are notoriously difficult to substantiate.

Unlike John the Baptist, Jesus and his followers do not as a rule show ascetic tendencies (Luke 5.33; 7.34 parr.); this alone should urge a considerable reluctance in interpreting the identification of Jesus and the early Christians as 'Nazoreans' in even vaguely Nazirite terms.[65]

In the context of the Last Supper, however, Jesus utters a vow, attested in all three Synoptic gospels, which in its first-century context would have unmistakable Nazirite connotations: 'I shall not drink again of the fruit of the vine until that day when I drink it new in the kingdom of God' (Mark 14.25 par.). It is worth comparing this vow with the relevant criteria in Mishnah *Nazir*, which regards it as a sufficient declaration of Nazirite intent to say about a filled cup on the table, 'I will abstain from this' (*m. Naz.* 2.3). Similarly, an eschatological reference may be paralleled in vows such as, 'Let me be a Nazirite on the day when the son of David shall come' (*b. 'Erub.* 43a).

It is possible that the somewhat cumbersome phrase 'produce of the vine' (γένημα τοῦ ἀμπέλου) rather than merely 'wine' is of some significance. As it stands, it echoes the rabbinic term פְּרִי הַגֶּפֶן ('fruit of the vine', e.g. *m. Ber.* 6.1) but is not paralleled in the LXX or in biblical Hebrew. If it is not simply an early occurrence of the Mishnaic idiom, it may be in keeping with the regulations for Nazirites, who were to abstain from every product derived from grapes (Num 6.4 מִכֹּל אֲשֶׁר יֵעָשֶׂה מִגֶּפֶן, i.e. LXX ἀπὸ πάντων ὅσα γίνεται ἐξ ἀμπέλου), explicitly including vinegar, seeds and skins (Num 6.3–4).

Regardless of this matter of detail, however, there exists an interesting correlation with a well-known *crux* of the passion narrative, viz. the question of whether Jesus does or does not accept the drink offered to him on the Cross. All four Gospels mention such an episode, but each handles it differently. Mark and Matthew in fact have two incidents: the first is before the crucifixion, the Roman executioners' offer of wine (οἶνον) scented with myrrh (gall in

---

[64]Matt 2.23; 26.71; Luke 18.37; John 18.5, 7; 19.19; Acts 2.22; 3.6; 4.10; 6.14; 22.8; 26.9. Ναζαρηνός: Mark 1.24; 10.47; 14.67; 16.6; Luke 4.34; 24.19. Contrast also ὁ ἀπὸ Ναζαρεθ: Matt 21.11; John 1.45; Acts 10.38.

[65]So e.g. recently Berger 1996. For the meaning and identification of 'Nazoreans', see the fuller study of Mimouni 1998.

Matthew), probably to numb the pain (Mark 15.23/Matt 27.34). In the second incident, an anonymous bystander presents Jesus on the point of death with a sponge dipped in vinegar (ὄξος, Mark 15.36/Matt 27.48). In the former case, Mark's Jesus pointedly refuses the offer, while Matthew's tastes but then rejects it. In the latter, it is unclear whether in fact he drinks any of it before expiring with a loud cry. Luke has only the soldiers' initial offer of vinegar (23.36, προσφέροντες). John's Jesus openly announces that he is thirsty, 'in order that the Scripture might be fulfilled' (19.28, ἵνα τελειωθῇ). Someone brings him (προσήνεγκαν) a spongeful of vinegar; he takes it and then expires with the words, 'It has been fulfilled' (19.29–30).

For an assessment of these passages it is vital to note that the phrase ἐπότισάν με ὄξος ('they gave me vinegar to drink') occurs in LXX Ps 68.22 (=69.21), a Psalm of individual lament that influenced the composition of the passion narrative. Given this Old Testament formulation, the tradition's emphasis on the prophetic fulfilment theme accounts adequately for the tensions between the gospels. Without denying the possibility that the Marcan double tradition might be early, the redactional trend would be to enhance the links with Psalm 69 and thus to downplay Jesus' refusal of the offer of vinegar. Precisely that refusal, however, would make excellent sense in the light of his Nazirite vow at the Last Supper.

3. The Rest of the New Testament

Nazirite vows remain similarly marginal elsewhere in the New Testament, except for some interesting hints in Acts. Although Luke's reliability on this point has been doubted, there are good reasons for thinking that Paul was under a Nazirite vow while at Corinth (Acts 18.18; note Koet 1996; Horn 1997). He cuts his hair while still abroad at the port of Cenchreae, although we do not know whether this is because he had completed his vow[66] or because that vow had in fact lapsed as a result of corpse impurity (Num 6.9–12). Paul then drops off Aquila and Priscilla at Ephesus and proceeds straight to the Holy Land, making a special journey to

---

[66]It is difficult to be certain about the halakhah on whether Nazirite hair could be cut outside the land, and indeed about the extent to which less formal practices would have pertained in the diaspora. It seems reasonable to infer from the cumulative evidence of t. Nez. 1.5; 4.6; m. Naz. 3.6; 6.8b; 7.3 that vows were contracted and could be valid outside the Holy Land, even if the Hillelites required of diaspora Nazirites a brief symbolic period of another thirty days' Nazirate in Jerusalem. In any case m. Naz. 6.8 suggests that the shaving of the hair and the offering of sacrifices were not always carried out together. Cf. Boertien 1971:92–3; Koet 1996:138, 140 n. 46.

Jerusalem (and presumably the Temple) on his way back to Antioch (18.21–22). Later, his purpose in going up to Jerusalem is to 'bring gifts of charity to my people and offerings ... in the temple' (24.17–18). He undergoes the appropriate seven-day purification (21.26–27; cf. 24.18; *m. Naz.* 7.3; *b. Naz.* 54b; Philo *Spec. Leg.* 3.205) and prepares to pay for the appropriate sacrifices for four poor Christian Nazirites who are just coming to the conclusion of their vows (21.23–26; cf. 24.17–18). It is unclear whether he offers the Nazirite sacrifices for himself, too; certainly Mishnaic halakhah suggests that anyone coming from outside the Land would have had to spend at least another standard period of thirty days as a Nazirite before being able to complete a valid vow.[67]

Other Nazirite allusions in the New Testament are few and far between. It has occasionally been suggested that the 'weak' Christians of Romans 14–15 might be Nazirites, because of their abstention from wine and meat. Nazirites, however, do not abstain from wine for reasons of purity (Rom 14.14, 20; cf. Dan 1.8), and are unlikely to take offence because *others* drink wine (14.21). Abstention from meat is not expected in either written or oral Torah, although some might vow to abstain from it. John the Baptist, for instance, ate no meat except locusts, which like fish were not considered meat and were explicitly allowed to those who had vowed to abstain from meat (*m. Ḥul.* 8.1).[68] The abstention of Romans 14–15 is more likely related to concerns about the possible contamination of food purchased from Gentiles.[69]

4. *Other Early Christian Evidence*

A puzzling and widely debated interest in Nazirite matters continued in early Christianity, and came in due course to be associated with the early monastic movement.[70] Presumably following the precedent

[67]M. *Naz.* 3.6; cf. 6.3; *m. Ed.* 4.11. However, note also *m. Naz.* 7.3 for the view that contamination by 'land of the Gentiles' (in Palestine?) does not render the vow invalid. *T. Nez.* 1.5 also takes Nazirite vows in the diaspora for granted: 'Naziriteship applies in the Land and abroad.'
For the standard period of thirty days for Nazirite vows of unspecified length, see further e.g. Josephus, *War* 2.15.1 §313; R. Mattan later deduced the 30–day duration of Nazirite vows from Num 6.5: קדש יהיה, 'he shall be holy'; יהיה has the numerical value of 30 (*b. Naz.* 5a = *b. Ta'an.* 17a; *b. Sanh.* 22b; cf. *Num. Rab.* 10.10 etc.).
[68]Locusts were regarded as clean unless specifically contaminated (Lev 11.22; cf. e.g. *m. Ḥul.* 3.7; *m. Uktzin* 3.9), even when bought from a Gentile's store (*m. 'Abod. Zar.* 2.7). Note, too, that John is specifically said to have eaten *wild* honey (μέλι ἄγριον, Mark 1.6 par.), which unlike domestic bees' honey was regarded as exempt from purity concerns: *m. Makš.* 6.4.
[69]See already Dan 1.8, 16; cf. further E. P. Sanders 1990a:272–83; Tomson 1990:168–76.
[70]Cf. e.g. Basil, *Ep.* 44.1, and see Berger 1996:328 and n. 17, citing Gregory of Nazianzus, *Or.* 42.26 (*PG* 36.489C), et al. In later Hebrew, the word נזיר came to denote a monk.

of Jesus 'the Nazorean', Jews are quoted in Acts 24.5 as including Paul and other Christians in 'the sect of the Nazoreans'.[71] The precise meaning of this term has been widely debated and cannot be fully discussed here. Suffice it to say that on purely philological grounds the connection with Nazareth, favoured by a variety of writers since Epiphanius (*Pan.* 29.6),[72] seems less close than that with the Septuagint's term ναζιραῖος (Judg 13.5; 16.17; Lam 4.7; 1 Macc 3.49).[73] Certainly the vast majority of Jewish Christians were not, and were not perceived to be, from Nazareth; nor was first- or second-century Nazareth a prominent centre of Christianity. Another favoured explanation, derived from the word נצר (the messianic 'branch': Isa 4.2; 11.1; Zeph 3.8; 6.12), suffers from being still more remote philologically, and from a lack of relevant explanation or citations in the New Testament.[74] Yet another possibility is that the word simply renders the later rabbinic term for Christians, נוצרים, which could mean something like 'watchers' or 'observers' (e.g. of the Torah: see Prov 28.7).[75]

At the end of the day, it must be admitted that the resolution of this matter probably remains outside our grasp for the time being. But regardless of the intricacies of the terminological argument, patristic sources agree that the different groups known as Nazoreans or Nazarenes included above all Jewish Christians, whose beliefs are variously described and whose practices do not necessarily overlap with those of classic Jewish Nazirites. A similarly intriguing thread seems to run from the previously cited traditions about the

---

[71]See further Tertullian, *Adv. Marc.* 4.8: Jews call Christians *Nazaraei* because they are the 'Nazirites' of whom Lam 4.7 says that they are 'whiter than snow'. So LXX, Vulgate. Cf. also Epiphanius, *Haer.* 29.6.

[72]Cf. also H. Schaeder, *TWNT* 4.874–9.

[73]Berger 1996:324 n. 6 lists 32 cases of Hebrew *yod* becoming *omega* or *omicron* in LXX. Even within the Hebrew MS tradition, transference of this sort is not uncommon. Hebrew *zayin* (as in 'Nazir', נזיר) is most typically transliterated by *zeta*, whereas the letter *tzade* in 'Nazareth' (נצרת) should be expected to go to *sigma*, as also in LXX renditions of names such as Nebuchadnezzar, Zephaniah, etc. (but note the exceptions discussed in Schaeder 1942:884). See further Berger 1996:323–5; note also the Vulgate's terms *nazareus* (Gen 49.26; Num 6.18–21; Deut 33.26; Judg 13.5, 7; 16.17; Lam 4.7; 1 Macc 3.49), *nazarenus* (Amos 2.11–12).

[74]Another interesting possibility, not widely noted, is the contested phrase נצירי ישראל (*Qere'* נצורי) in Isa 49.6, where the Servant is appointed to bring light to the nations and salvation to the ends of the earth, and to restore 'the preserved (?) of Israel'. It is of interest that LXX has τοῦ κληθῆναί σε for MT מהיותך. Davies & Allison *ad loc.* appeal instead to Isa 4.3 קדוש יאמר לו.

[75]Cf. further Pritz 1988:11–18. Similarly note the consistent Syriac description of Christians as *naṣrayya*, subsequently adopted by Persians, Armenians and Arabs alike (Schaeder 1942:880).

Rechabites to the early Christian hermits and the *Story of Zosimus*.[76]

Perhaps the most directly relevant piece of the patristic puzzle for our purposes is Hegesippus's partly legendary description of James the Just, which strongly resembles the lifelong vegetarian Nazirite (cf. the 'Nazirite like Samson', *m. Naz.* 1.2): James was holy from his mother's womb, drank no wine and ate no meat, and did not cut his hair (Eusebius, *Eccl. Hist.* 2.23.5).[77]

5. Summary of the Evidence

The practice of Nazirite vows, whether formally or informally contracted,[78] was extremely popular in first-century Palestine, apparently common among both the lower classes and the well-to-do. Nazirites were a well-known phenomenon wherever observant Jews lived and congregated; and long-term or life-long Nazirites with their distinctive long hair would have been a familiar sight in public places. In this context, the Mishnah shows that the popularity of Nazirite practices had generated a whole range of popular idioms, allusions and modes of conduct that formed a basic cultural staple and thus would be widely recognizable. At any one time there were members of the community whose distinctive priest-like dedication to God was often apparent by their hair, who abstained from wine and whose obligation to purity before God was greater even than their duty to their parents.

Spiritually, Nazirite vows offered non-priestly Jews (whether male or female, Num 6.2) an opportunity to dedicate themselves voluntarily to God in a tangible way for either a short or a longer period. Philo's interpretation of the custom is highly suggestive in this respect, as we saw; but later rabbinic homiletical developments also favour such an understanding. Thus the story cited earlier about Simeon the Just (third century BC) illustrates the fact that the Nazirate is to be undertaken only 'for the Lord' (Num 6.2), as being of benefit in defeating human pride.[79] *Numbers Rabbah* similarly

---

[76]See e.g. the abstemious figure Zosimus in *Hist. Rech.* 1.1 and *passim*. Note further Knights 1993, 1997, who argues that this document probably does not belong among the OT Pseudepigrapha, *pace* J. H. Charlesworth.

[77]According to the *Gospel of the Hebrews*, after the passion of Jesus, James swore to eat no bread until he should see him risen from the dead: Jerome, *De Viris Inlustribus* 2 (cf. Schneemelcher 1991:1.178).

[78]Many abstained from wine and meat even without taking the formal vows: *b. B. Bat.* 60b; *b. Šab.* 139a.

[79]*Sifre Num.* 22 (on 6.2) and parallels (e.g. *t. Nez.* 4.7; *b. Ned.* 9b; *b. Naz.* 4b; *Num. Rab.* 10.7 [on 6.2]).

interprets the Nazirite's long hair in terms of moral grief and compunction, designed to defeat the evil impulse and to keep oneself free from sin;[80] in God's eyes this dedication makes the Nazirite the equal of the High Priest (10.11).

Socially, the Nazirite institution invited an unusual degree of solidarity across class boundaries. This is evident in the common practice of wealthier citizens defraying the expenses of poorer Nazirites. Just as Simeon b. Shetah with his brother-in-law Alexander Jannaeus had done this for 300 Nazirites (y. Ber. 7.2, 11b40–45) and Agrippa I for others (Josephus Ant. 19.6.1 §294), so Paul did this for four Jewish Christians who had come to Jerusalem to complete their vows (Acts 21.23–26).

Conclusion

Jesus had no family of his own, and no fixed abode; his message and ministry manifested and called for the sort of discipleship that put the kingdom of God before familial obligations: 'whoever loves father or mother more than me is not worthy of me' (Matt 10.37 par.; cf. 12.50 par.). Somewhat unusually but no doubt symbolically, Jesus himself abstained from marriage – as did other first-century Jews.[81] Perhaps because of his early position as a follower of the more visibly Nazirite John the Baptist, Jesus came to be popularly identified by the epithet 'the Nazorean'. The fact that he nevertheless did *not* on the whole abstain from wine and meat, as John had done, apparently caused a certain amount of puzzlement and required explanation. His message and lifestyle nonetheless remained a radical one, which shared with the Nazirite way of life a comprehensive vision of holiness (note Num 6.5, 8) and purity as constituted by God.[82] And although Jesus is frequently seen to be at

---

[80]*Num. Rab.* 10.10; cf. 10.2–4 (e.g. 10.4 end: 'if one wishes to sanctify himself so as not to be tripped up by whoredom he should separate himself from wine').

[81]One might compare the somewhat complex literary and archaeological evidence for celibacy among Essenes (Philo, *Hyp.* 11.14–17; Pliny, *Nat. Hist.* 5.73; Josephus, *War* 2.8.2 §120–1, 2.8.13 §160–1; *Ant.* 18.1.5 §21; also CD 12.1–2 par. 4QD^c 3.i.17 on mandatory sexual abstinence within Jerusalem) and *Therapeutae* (Philo, *Contempl.* 68). While rabbinic evidence is admittedly scant, it is at least worth noting the occasional estimation of sexual abstinence as an expression of purity and holiness: e.g. Moses and the Israelites at Sinai (Exod 19.15; *b. Šab.* 87a; *'Abot R. Nat.* A 2; *Tg. Ps.-J. Num* 12.8); cf. David and his men in 1 Sam 21.4. *M. Yeb.* 6.6 implies that sexual abstinence is permitted to men who already have children, and to women. As early as Jer 16.1–4, the prophet is instructed not to marry. On rabbinic elements of sexual asceticism cf. further Horbury 1979:117. And quite apart from his Nazirite vow Paul, too, was evidently celibate by choice (1 Cor 9.5; cf. 7.7).

[82]See e.g. Chilton 1992:121–6, 135–6; and cf. pp. 10–12 above.

odds with more 'lenient' Pharisaic interpretations of the Torah, even
his own divergent views in fact almost always remain well within the
range of attested halakhic positions.

In this context, Jesus' challenge to a prospective[83] disciple to 'let
the dead bury their own dead' would indeed raise eyebrows. But it is
by no means necessary or even plausible to see it as a significant
attack on the Torah, or even as deliberately requiring disobedience
to it (so Hengel, Sanders). Instead, the notion of a special religious
duty transcending even basic family obligations is one that would
have been culturally familiar to Jesus' audience, regardless of
whether they agreed with him or not. In the broader context
of widespread Nazirite practice, therefore, the saying easily fits into
a series of calls to discipleship illustrated from scenes of contemporary life, as we saw above (p. 37). It is at the same time consistent
with Jesus' radical but complex re-assessment of family ties *vis-à-vis*
a variety of contemporary Jewish assumptions, as attested by
passages like Mark 3.31–35 par.; 10.28–31 par. on the one hand
and Mark 1.29–31 par.; 7.8–13 par. on the other.

Our conclusion, therefore, is twofold: first, there is no evidence to
substantiate the assumption of a major clash between Jesus' saying
and a contemporary halakhah that had supposedly relaxed even the
biblical prohibitions for High Priests and Nazirites. As a result,
the supposedly paradigmatic function of this logion as indicative of
a radical critique of the Torah is without substance.

Our second conclusion is more tentative. Despite the ambiguity
surrounding terms such as 'the Nazorean(s)', it is clear that various
early Jewish Christians did manifest distinct Nazirite interests, and
indeed that Jesus himself appears to have uttered a Nazirite vow on
the eve of his execution. This evidence is too weak to support a direct
Nazirite setting for Matt 8.22 par., but it does provide a plausible
Jewish context in which the instruction to 'let the dead bury their
own dead' can be understood by way of analogy.

There is no doubt that within the broad bounds of late Second
Temple Judaism Jesus' charismatic and unconventional ministry
would have appeared daring and provocative to some observers.
Nor is there any doubt of the essential 'shock value' of Jesus' saying,
even in its clearly *ad hoc* and *ad hominem* setting comparable in tone
and substance to the charge given to the 'rich young ruler' (Mark
10.21 par.).

Professors Hengel, Sanders and others have laid valuable
groundwork for any future study of the text. Their interpretative

---

[83]In Matt. 8.21 he is already one of the disciples.

conclusions for Jesus' attitude to the Law, however, do not stand up to closer scrutiny. This paper has presented a moderate case for supposing that a broadly Nazirite symbolism may turn out to make acceptable sense of the saying's first-century Jewish setting. That setting may make it mean little more than, 'Come and follow me: those who are truly consecrated to God have even more important things to do.'[84] Regardless of the merits of that particular hypothesis, however, discussion of this text is bound to continue: *causa non finita est.*

---

[84]Cf. e.g. Beare 1981:214, though perhaps rather too flippantly and with insufficient awareness of the halakhic issues involved: 'Let that matter take care of itself.'

4

JAMES, ISRAEL AND ANTIOCH

It was in Antioch, Luke tells us (Acts 11.26), that the disciples were first called 'Christians' (Χριστιανοί), quite plausibly an official Roman designation for the adherents of a man called Χριστός.[1] But this is only the beginning of many puzzling questions. Were the followers of Jesus not previously identified with him as Messiah? Is it perhaps true after all that 'Christianity', as a movement publicly recognizable by its messianic belief in Jesus, was the invention of certain Hellenized Jews in Antioch?

And what was the role played by the Jerusalem leadership in all this? Protestant Pauline scholarship has long found in Galatians 2 proof positive of a deep and irreconcilable division between a law-free Gentile mission based at Antioch and the Jerusalem reactionaries under James the Just, who were very much the villains of the piece. They were irritated by Paul's cavalier approach to the Torah; and it was they who therefore invented the so-called Apostolic Decree *ex post facto,* as an attempt to extract from the Gentile mission at least a measure of Jewish respectability and decorum: 'we cannot ask for the whole Law but we must have some of it'.[2] All of Paul's troubles with Judaizing opponents from Galatia via Corinth to Rome can be understood as caused by Jerusalem's attempt to impose on his Gentile churches the Apostolic Decree (or something rather like it), and by his own stalwart resistance, for the sake of the 'law-free' gospel, to both the letter and spirit of that document.[3]

Was it *really* quite like that? We may or may not endorse this assessment, which with minor variations remains common to a majority of German and a good deal of British and American scholarship. But whatever our view of this matter, there can be no doubt that the real human and doctrinal dynamics of the apostolic church will remain a closed book to us until we can understand the beliefs

---

[1]See recently J. Taylor 1994; Hengel & Schwemer 1997:230 and *passim.* Cf. further Hengel & Schwemer 1998:350–1 on an inscription identifying the supporters of Cn. Calpurnius Piso, Roman governor of Syria in Antioch from AD 17 to 19 (*sic; pace* Hengel), as *Pisoniani* and those of his adversary Germanicus as *Caesariani.* Note also the NT's Ἡρῳδιανοί.

[2]So e.g. Barrett 1997:335; note the quotation from F. C. Baur and the reference to M. D. Goulder. At the same time, Barrett considers the Decree to be the invention of Hellenistic Christians, which Paul then did not accept: e.g. 1998:712.

[3]Cf. e.g. Käsemann 1942; Barrett 1963; Thrall 1980:51–5.

and motivations of Simon Peter and James the Just. Their role and influence in the fledgling church is arguably every bit as significant as that of Paul.

The so-called Antioch incident has been a central question for New Testament scholars for most of the past two centuries, and one that has given rise to an unmanageable deluge of secondary literature.[4] Recent times, moreover, have also seen a lively renewal of interest in the person of James himself.[5] This continuing flood of new scholarship has been largely published in the absence of new textual or archaeological data to add to our very limited basis of factual knowledge. As a result, the study of James the Just and his relationship with Antioch, Paul and the Gentile mission has lent itself to an unchecked proliferation of hypotheses. In New Testament scholarship, Antioch still seems to be a matter of *quot homines, tot sententiae*.

The issue at present is still mired on the one hand in method-ological problems pertaining to the two rather tricky sources we have in Acts and Galatians. On the other hand, one glance at recent treatments such as those of C. K. Barrett, M. D. Goulder or M. Hengel shows the extent to which the problem also continues to be bound up in a peculiarly intractable history of scholarly and confes-sional dispute. The developmentalist Hegelian view of early Christian history, as determined by conflicts over opposing funda-mentals and deeply intractable antagonisms, is still alive and well among the present-day heirs of F. C. Baur. (What is less well under-stood is the extent to which this point of view also perpetuates an ancient tradition of Christian supersessionism, such as that expressed by Jerome in his grumpy old man's rebuke of Augustine on the subject of the Antioch incident, *Ep.* 112.4–18.)

Given such a state of scholarship, one chapter cannot hope to 'solve' any of the major problems, nor to achieve anything by propounding yet another comprehensive hypothesis. My aim here is merely to shed a little light on the view that James the Just is likely to have taken of the city and the fledgling church at Antioch. Our first step will be to examine how the city and the Jewish community of Antioch might have been viewed by an inhabitant of Jerusalem in the mid first century. The second part of this chapter will then go on

[4]A recent full history of (mainly German) research is offered in Wechsler 1991:30–295; see earlier Kieffer 1982.

[5]Recent studies and surveys of the literature include Pratscher 1987; Adamson 1989; Wechsler 1991; Goulder 1994; Bauckham 1995, 1996; Painter 1997; Eisenman 1997; Bern-heim 1997; Wehnert 1997. For a survey of recent research on the Epistle of James, see also Hahn & P. Müller 1998.

to propose for discussion a number of relatively lightly argued theses on the likely rationale for James's view of Antioch. Whether the latter suggestions are eventually judged right or wrong, it is my hope that they may focus our consideration on certain key points of controversial significance, points that will in my view need to be resolved if future attempts at a fuller treatment are to become less arbitrary and subjective.

First-Century Antioch

As Frank Kolb recently reminded us in the *Festschrift* for Martin Hengel, the nature of our sources makes it virtually impossible to gain any sort of lifelike impression of the city of Antioch in the first century.[6] Our primary epigraphic sources extend to barely two hundred inscriptions over the entire period of the city's ancient history, an extraordinarily poor basis on which to assess a metropolis of Antioch's size. (One might compare the small city of Philippi, with only 10,000 inhabitants, which has thus far produced nearly 1,400 inscriptions.) With one mysterious exception,[7] none of the inscriptions relates directly to the Jewish community in the early imperial period. There are indeed a large number of coins, but these offer limited information on anything other than the political setting and the city's pagan cults; Jewish coins from Palestine are attested only in small numbers.[8] Other written sources for the first century include scattered comments of Josephus and the sometimes fanciful sixth-century chronicle of Malalas.

The excavations carried out in the 1930s admittedly had to contend with a vast ancient city, repeatedly destroyed by earthquakes

---

[6]Kolb 1996. In his moving travel account of this once great city, whose few remaining Christians look set to emigrate or die out within a generation, Dalrymple 1997:53 writes, 'It seems that barely one stone remains from what was once the third greatest metropolis in the Byzantine Empire and briefly, under Julian Apostate, its capital. ... Like Alexandria, its traditional rival, Byzantine Antioch is now just a city of memory, forgotten but for the conjectures of scholars.'

[7]The word ΓΟΛΒ is inscribed on a stele with menorah. See Downey 1952:15–51 and No. 24. Might this have marked a Jewish spelt store (Aram. גולבא, e.g. *b. Pes.* 35a; *b. Menaḥ.* 70b; cf. כסמין in Mishnaic Hebrew)? The significance of spelt, both as a basic staple and for halakhic reasons, is well documented in rabbinic sources: e.g. *m. Pe'a* 8.5; *m. Kil.* 1.1, 9; *m. Ḥal.* 1.1; 4.2; *m. Pes.* 2.5; *m. B. Meṣ.* 3.7; *m. Šebu.* 3.2; 4.5; 5.3; *m. Menaḥ.* 10.7; *m. Ṭ. Yom* 1.5.

[8]On the Jewish coins, see Waage 1952:87. Both Hasmonean and later Herodian (only Archelaus and Agrippa I) periods are represented, as well as the Roman procurators of the period from Augustus to Nero; perhaps the most interesting and suggestive find is a 'Year 2' (i.e. AD 67–68) coin of the war against Rome.

and now buried 6–10 metres under a flood plain.[9] Nevertheless, it now seems very disappointing that the work was executed on such a relatively small scale, consisting only of a few long sections and individual probes along the city's main north–south axis.[10] Nothing of substance emerged, for example, in relation to the entire Jewish quarter. The modern city of Antakya was recreated on a deserted site around 1800; a hundred years later, it still occupied only a very small footprint on the vast area of ancient Antioch.[11] By the end of the twentieth century, however, it had grown to a population of 130,000 complete with high-rise tenements, office blocks and increasing suburban sprawl; and the remaining scope for excavation of ancient Antioch is shrinking week by week.

It is a telling indication of the *status quaestionis* in Antioch scholarship that very little has moved since Downey's masterful work of forty years ago.[12] Kolb concludes, not unreasonably, that on the basis of the archaeological material we can say almost nothing about those cultural, ethnic and other aspects of Antioch's first- and second-century setting that would be of particular interest for an understanding of early Christianity in that city.[13] Despite the confidence displayed in a number of scholarly treatments, there seems little point in talking about the Jewish and Christian communities of Antioch without a clear acknowledgement that we still know very little.

The Jewish Community

In the Christian story, Antioch first features in the person of Nicolas of Antioch, a Gentile proselyte to Judaism who had emigrated to Jerusalem and there joined the Christian community, eventually becoming one of the seven first Deacons (Acts 6.5). By this time, the Jewish community of Antioch already had a long and sometimes tortuous history.

Antioch itself was, like Alexandria, a relatively brash upstart in the ancient Mediterranean world when compared to cities like Jerusalem,

[9]Cf. Kolb 1996:97; Lassus 1984:361; on the problem of flooding, with the concomitant need for canalisation, see also Feissel 1985; Grainger 1990:74–5; Wallace & Williams 1998:168; Millar 1993:86–9.

[10]Kolb 1996:105; cf. Lassus 1977:56–60, and see the excavation reports.

[11]See Grainger 1990:73–4 and cf. Lassus 1977:59, who reproduces H. Paris's mid-century map of modern Antioch superimposed on the ancient site.

[12]Downey 1961; cf. Hengel & Schwemer 1997:430 n. 949: 'The standard work is still Downey'; similarly Brown & Meier 1983:22 n. 51.

[13]Kolb 1996:99.

Damascus, Athens or Ephesus. It was only founded by Seleucus I Nicanor in 300 BC on the crossroads of important trade routes to Persia and the Far East, to Asia Minor in the north and to Egypt in the south. Although the city itself was landlocked, the nearby harbour city of Seleucia Pieria connected Antioch with destinations around the Mediterranean Sea. Despite its susceptibility to earthquakes and its desirability as the prize of successive warlords, Antioch continued to grow into a major metropolis of the ancient world, being ranked before long with Alexandria and Rome.[14] Antioch had grown in stature throughout the first centuries BC and AD, becoming the natural capital of the Roman province of Syria. Seleucia Pieria had been turned into a major naval base, and Julius Caesar had built new temples, baths, an aqueduct, a theatre and an amphitheatre. Not to be too far outdone, Herod the Great likewise furnished the city with a magnificently paved main street – even if Josephus's report of a marble colonnade over a length of 3.5 km may be somewhat exaggerated.[15]

Josephus claims that Jews had been granted citizenship rights at Antioch by the founder himself (*Ant.* 12.3.1 §119). Aside from this statement, the earliest evidence of Jewish settlement in Antioch is in the 170s BC, when the famous High Priest Onias III took refuge from his Palestinian rival Menelaos in Antioch's 'Beverly Hills', the pleasurable suburb of Daphne (2 Macc 4.33–34):[16] we hear, for example, of successful Jewish protests following Onias's subsequent assassination at the hands of Menelaos's 'hired gun'. Not only did the revered conservative Onias evidently consider Antioch a suitable haven of refuge, but it is also quite clear that substantial numbers at least of the more cosmopolitan inhabitants of Jerusalem regarded the citizenship of Antioch as a highly desirable prize since the second century BC. Indeed, Jason's administration in Palestine apparently made strenuous efforts to have even the population of Jerusalem enrolled as citizens of Antioch (2 Macc 4.9–10, 19).[17] And while the

[14]Josephus (*War* 3.2.4 §29) ranks it as 'indisputably third' (τρίτον ἀδηρίτως. . . ἔχουσα τόπον) after Rome and Alexandria.

[15]Josephus, *Ant.* 16.5.3 §148; *War* 1.21.11 §425. Kolb 1996:111 notes that the archaeological record points more plausibly to a colonnade dating from the time of Tiberius (as is claimed by Malalas).

[16]Note, however, the observation of Kolb 1996:101 that Daphne itself shows few signs of urbanisation prior to the third cent. AD. See further his pp. 102–3 on the attractions of Daphne.

[17]Similarly Downey 1961:109–10; Kraeling 1932:141; cf. more cautiously Barclay 1996:245. The situation is somewhat complicated by the Seleucid foundation or refoundation of several other 'Antiochs', including e.g. at Hippos, Dan and Gadara; the renamed Dan also had another 'Daphne' at the nearby springs. Josephus does not help matters by locating a place called 'Ulatha' near both the Syrian and the Danite Antioch (e.g. *Ant.* 15.10.3 §360; 17.2.1 §24). See further Avi-Yonah 1966:51; 1976:29, 107; Marcus & Wikgren in the LCL *Josephus*, 8:383 n. (f); cf. earlier Schlatter 1893:314–20.

author of 2 Maccabees clearly does not share Jason's enthusiasm for this course of action, prominent Jews of different persuasions continued to consider Antioch an attractive place in which to live and work. A large number of Jews took up residence in the city and in many cases became citizens there (cf. also Josephus, *War* 7.3.3 §44; *Ag. Ap.* 2.4 §39). Indeed, Antioch continued for several centuries to serve as a place of residence for important religious leaders; even in the Amoraic period famous Rabbis like Simlai and Isaac Nappaḥa are sometimes cited as teaching in the city.[18] In the first century, the highly visible signs of Herod the Great's recent munificence towards Antioch may well have boosted the Jewish community's prestige.[19]

The Jewish settlement (or settlements[20]) at Antioch was evidently younger than the ones in Alexandria and in a number of other Diaspora cities. In the first century it was probably numerically smaller than that of Alexandria, too, although it was nevertheless very large. Precise figures are very hard to come by: Kraeling's figure of 45,000 Antiochene Jews in the early empire was admittedly speculative and has come in for criticism.[21] Nevertheless, with Hengel & Schwemer 1997 we can in my view still agree that, on the justifiable assumption of at least 300,000 inhabitants (rather than merely citizens),[22] a total of 30,000–50,000 Jews seems entirely reasonable.[23] We must therefore assume a substantial and highly influential Jewish community.

There are many signs that the Jewish community in Antioch had by the first century become highly successful and well to do, and that it continued to be so for a considerable period of time. Although the rule of Caligula occasioned considerable suffering in Antioch and Alexandria alike, the larger economic context of Jewish life in the Syrian capital remained very pleasant and prosperous. Thus in the Second Temple period the Antiochene Jews evidently sent large contributions to Jerusalem; their importance to the welfare of

---

[18]E.g. R. Simlai, *y. Qid.* 3.15, 64d; R. Isaac Nappaḥa, *b. Ketub.* 88a, *b. 'Arak.* 22b; in the fourth century note also R. Jonah and R. Yose before the Roman governor Ursicinus in Antioch, in *y. Ber.* 5.1, 9a.

[19]So also Kraeling 1932:147.

[20]Kraeling 1932:143 thinks by the first century there were no less than three Jewish communities around Antioch: in the city, at Daphne, and in the agricultural plain where rice was grown (*t. Dem.* 2.1; *y. Dem.* 2.1, 22d11–12).

[21]Kraeling 1932:136; see Kolb 1996:110.

[22]These estimates admittedly vary immensely, from 100,000 to 500,000 people, although the latter figure is perhaps more appropriate to the fourth century than the first. As an example of a more conservative estimate, Feissel 1985:44 n. 51 follows Liebeschuetz in supposing that the figure may have been nearer 150,000 than 300,000; similarly Kolb 1996:101.

[23]Hengel & Schwemer 1997:189; cf. Riesner 1994:98.

Jerusalem is spelled out in a famous passage in Josephus (*War* 7.3.3 §43–45):

The Jewish race, densely interspersed among the native populations of every portion of the world, is particularly numerous in Syria, where intermingling is due to the proximity of the two countries. But it was at Antioch that they specially congregated. ... The Jewish colony grew in numbers, and their richly designed and costly offerings formed a splendid ornament to the Temple.

Josephus further reports of one exceedingly wealthy Babylonian Jew named Zamaris, who in the last decade of the first century BC seized upon the plain of Antioch as the best place to settle with his family of one hundred and his private army of five hundred mounted archers.[24] Even after the fall of the Temple, the wealth of Antioch remained legendary in rabbinic circles – the spices of Antioch were later said to be as good as cash (*b. Ketub.* 67a). Just as the Jerusalem church considered Antioch a good place to ask for famine relief, so we are told in the Talmud that second-century rabbis were still travelling there to request support for the poor scholars of Palestine.[25]

One of the most significant archaeological finds from Antioch is the large number of outstanding floor mosaics, which were clearly an important status symbol and fashion statement among the better off. 'The excavations have shown that in the whole area there was not a single better-class house without mosaic pavements decorating its entrance, halls, dining rooms, corridors and sometimes the bottoms of its pools.'[26] We have no reason to think that wealthy Jews would not have owned such houses. The early Christian community in Antioch, too, evidently included a number of relatively well-to-do people, as can be seen not only from its ability to send famine relief to Jerusalem (Acts 11.29–30) but also from members like Menahem of the court of Herod Antipas (Acts 13.1).[27] These mosaics tell an eloquent story of Antioch's opulence, enjoyment of life and

---

[24]Josephus, *Ant.* 17.2.1 §24. Herod later prevailed on him to move to Batanea.

[25]See the mission to Antioch of Rabbis Eliezer, Joshua and Aqiba: *y. Hor.* 3.7, 48a; par. *Lev. Rab.* 5.4; *Deut. Rab.* 4.8; cf. Acts 11.27–30.

[26]Cimok 1995:8.

[27]Cf. Meeks & Wilken 1978:15; Downey 1961:283–4. Note also that Barnabas, a Levite from Cyprus who was previously part of the church in Jerusalem, had sold a field in support of the church there (Acts 4.36–37). There is also a tradition that Theophilus made his large house available for the use of the church in Antioch (*Ps.-Clem. Rec.* 10.71). Eusebius (*Eccl. Hist.* 3.4.2) records a tradition according to which Luke, too, was a native of Antioch.

interest in moral philosophy as a popular topic for dinnertime conversation.[28]

Antioch, then, was of very considerable socio-economic importance for Jews in the Land of Israel; indeed it had come to be thought of as the 'great city' *par excellence*, as can be nicely demonstrated not only from Josephus (*War* 7.3.3 §43, cited above) but also from a number of Palestinian *baraitot*.[29]

It can be argued that, from the Tobiad all the way to the Amoraic period, Antioch and other parts of Syria consistently enjoyed a considerably higher profile in Palestinian Jewish texts than did Alexandria[30] or indeed any other part of the ancient world (except perhaps Babylonia, in the later period). In keeping with Josephus's assertions about Syria as being most densely populated with Jews, the extant Second Temple and rabbinic writings refer rather more frequently to Jews in Antioch and Syria than to the larger metropolis of Alexandria and the million or so Jews who lived in Egypt. This may no doubt be influenced by the easier overland routes and Roman administrative links between Palestine and Syria. Nevertheless, such considerations alone do not account for the status of Syria from the Palestinian Jewish point of view.

Jews and Gentiles in Antioch

In any discussion of first-century Antioch, therefore, it is useful to bear in mind that the Jews of that city were both more numerous and more prosperous than the Jews of Jerusalem. Their relations with the Gentile majority, moreover, appear to have been comparatively unencumbered by political scruples. At least in peaceful times, the predominant religious climate of the city among both Jews and pagans appears to have been one of relative tolerance.[31] Indeed,

---

[28]See Downey 1961:209–10. The mosaics manifest great popular interest in moral and philosophical themes: we may note the personifications and abstractions of figures suggesting time, power, renewal, the acquisition and use of wealth, pleasure, life, salvation, enjoyment, *megalopsychia*, *amerimnia*, memory and friendship (thus one finds naturally unfriendly animals depicted together, as in Isaiah 11). Downey writes, 'This collection of abstractions, found in one place, is almost unique in the Graeco-Roman world, and it brings before us, in a way literature could not, the interests of the people of Antioch and their curiosities and their speculations.' See also Levi 1944:312–14.

[29]Antioch was the largest city most Palestinian Jews could imagine; a stock phrase is 'even if it is a great city like Antioch': *t. 'Erub.* 3.13; *b. 'Erub.* 61b; *y. 'Erub.* 5.5, 22d; *y. Ta'an.* 3.5, 66d; also *Num. Rab.* 2.9.

[30]For Palestinian Jewish views of Alexandria and Leontopolis, see now Schäfer 1998.

[31]See Norris 1990:2372–3. Note, too, Josephus's comment (*War* 2.18.5 §479) that Antioch, Apamea and Sidon were spared the inter-ethnic violence that engulfed so many cities at the beginning of the first Jewish revolt in AD 66.

there is good evidence that Jewish relations with many Gentiles, including Gentile Christians, must often have been tolerably good: that, any rate, is clearly the flip-side of episcopal efforts from Ignatius to Chrysostom to dissuade the Christian faithful of Antioch from their continuing involvement with the local synagogue.[32]

Josephus claims, moreover, that very substantial numbers (πολὺ πλῆθος) of Greeks had become sympathizers of the splendidly furnished central synagogue, and that they enjoyed a measure of social integration with the Jewish population (κἀκείνους τρόπῳ τινὶ μοῖραν αὐτῶν πεποίηντο).[33] Once again this may explain why all the evidence suggests that the impetus for Jewish Christians to dissociate from meal fellowship with Gentiles originated in Jerusalem, and not in the Jewish community of Antioch.[34]

This in itself must raise questions for the continuing proliferation in New Testament studies of the 'all or nothing' assumption that observant Jews never ate with Gentiles and that those who surrendered this strict separation 'ceased to be Jews'.[35] To seek proof of a formal Jewish prohibition of commensality in anti-Semitic pagan

[32]Even Ignatius, although deeply opposed to Gentile Judaizing, was far less hostile to Jewish Christians: *Phld.* 6.1, 'it is better to hear Christianity from the circumcised than Judaism from the uncircumcised'. Cf. also Meeks & Wilken 1978:18, 'Moreover, if such a separation did take place around 70, it certainly did not mean the once-for-all isolation of the Judaeo-Christians from gentile Christians nor of Jews from Christians. The active influence of Judaism upon Christianity in Antioch was perennial until Christian leaders succeeded at last in driving the Jews from the city in the seventh century.' It is highly likely that this state of affairs was not restricted to Antioch. Note Jerome's comment in writing to Augustine (*Ep.* 112.13): 'until this day there is among the Jews throughout all the synagogues of the Orient (*per totas Orientis synagogas*) the so-called heresy of the Minim, which is condemned by the Pharisees even until now; popularly they are known as the Nazarenes, who believe in Christ, the Son of God,' etc.

[33]*War* 7.3.3 §45. Note similarly *War* 2.18.2 §463: Judaizing Gentiles were ubiquitous in Syria and were regarded as 'mixed up' or 'assimilated' (μεμιγμένον) with the Jews. (Smith 1987:66, 182 n. 33, rightly criticizes Thackeray (in the Loeb Classical Library) for rendering this term as 'neutrals'; Smith's own preference for 'persons of mixed stock', however, seems to me more speculative, as the context makes no reference to intermarriage.) Elsewhere, Josephus claims that all but a few of the women of Damascus had submitted to the Jewish religion (*War* 2.20.2 §§559–61).

[34]It is of course possible, as Prof. Horbury suggests to me, that 'those from James' may have come in response to conservative Jewish alarms raised in Antioch; but neither Luke nor Paul alludes to such a course of events.

[35]So e.g. Esler 1987:73–86, reiterated in idem 1998:94–7; cf. also earlier Str-B 4.374 ('so gut wie unmöglich'). Dunn 1993:119 rightly warns against monolithic views, and Barclay 1996 provides a more apposite paradigm for understanding the spectrum of Jewish belief and practice in the Diaspora. (Note, however, that Barclay's chosen brief of necessity affords little insight on the *Palestinian* view of the matter: in over 500 pages his book does not contain a single reference to the Mishnah, and only three to the Dead Sea Scrolls.) Jewish differences of opinion over accommodation and resistance to Gentile culture are perceptively explored in R. Goldenberg 1998:100–5 and *passim*.

authors' claims about Judaism, as many scholars do, is clearly to take the bulldozer approach.[36] The twentieth century should have taught us that anecdotal gossip and popular prejudice rarely furnish reliable evidence of a given ethnic community's real beliefs and intentions. Outright rejection of the Torah is only one of a wide range of possible scenarios for Jews eating with Gentiles – as is the case to this day. As even the earliest evidence from Daniel (1.3–17), Judith and the *Letter of Aristeas* (181–4) shows, a good many Jews clearly *did* eat in the company of Gentiles or even accept food supplied by them, without thereby surrendering their Jewishness or their respect for the Torah.[37]

Attitudes to this question evidently varied a good deal, depending on one's halakhic stance and perhaps one's geographic location. Observant Jews might adopt one of the following four positions: they could either

1. refuse all table fellowship with Gentiles and refuse to enter a Gentile house,
2. invite Gentiles to their house and prepare a Jewish meal,
3. take their own food to a Gentile's house, or indeed
4. dine with Gentiles on the explicit or implicit understanding that food they would eat was neither prohibited in the Torah nor tainted with idolatry.

This latter policy could, for example, be refined in the request to be given only vegetarian or other specified kinds of food – an option that even Paul explicitly legitimates in Romans 14.1 – 15.6.[38]

---

[36]Cf., a little more cautiously, Barclay 1996:436–7: 'It is impossible to understand how such complaints could be raised in different locations and across the centuries (from the first century BCE to the late second century CE) unless Jewish separatism at meals was commonly practised.'

[37]Cf. also Tob 1.11. See further E. P. Sanders 1990a:272–83; Tomson 1990:230–6; Rajak 1992 *passim*. Sanders (1990a:282) points out quite rightly that there is no reason to think cooking vessels used to prepare food for Jews were thought unclean if they had previously contained Gentile food. There is no established first-century halakhah for indirect impurity derived at two removes in this fashion (*contra* Esler 1987:85–6, 1998:98), just as the special arrangements for the shared meal in *Letter of Aristeas* say nothing about vessels. In relation to this document, Esler's argument is sustainable only by special pleading: he suggests that both the banquet manager Dorotheus and every one of his servants must have been Jews (1998:113–14). Sanders seems nearer the mark in stating that meal fellowship in this case is feasible because, in effect, Ptolemy eats food acceptable to Jews (1990c:178).

In this area, dogmatism is bound to lead to unrealistic conclusions. Especially away from the Judaean heartland, the situation is far more plausibly as Bergmann 1908:24 noted long ago: 'Es unterliegt auch keinem Zweifel, daß alle die eingehenden Kautelen, die von den Lehrern des Judentums für die Berührung mit dem Heidentum aufgestellt wurden, nicht immer und überall, besonders nicht in der Diaspora, rigoros innegehalten wurden; die Praxis war darin sicherlich milder als die Theorie.' Cf. again R. Goldenberg 1998 *passim*.

[38]Esler's (1998) complete silence on Rom 14.1 – 15.6 speaks eloquently.

Options (2), (3) and (4), moreover, would all be compatible with a shared Eucharist involving bread and wine.[39]

Within early rabbinic tradition, R. Eliezer ben Hyrcanus may be the best known Tannaitic exponent credited with the 'hard-line' assumption that Gentile intent is always idolatrous (*m. Hul.* 2.7).[40] It is probably the case that Gentiles were not normally thought subject to acquired ritual impurity.[41] Nevertheless, given the widespread Jewish conviction about the impurity of idolatry, it is clearly hard-line views about Gentile intentions that would most obviously incline conservative Palestinian Jews to consider it wholly 'unlawful' (ἀθέμιτον, Acts 10.28) for Jews to enter a Gentile's house and to eat with them (συνεσθίειν, Acts 10.28; 11.2).[42] The same position is reflected in the book of *Jubilees* (22.16), which was very popular among the Qumran sectarians; and Josephus confirms that the Essenes invariably bathed after contact with foreigners (and even with novices: *War* 2.8.10 §150).[43]

At first sight a similar trend appears to dominate many of the stipulations in Mishnah *'Abodah Zarah*.[44] Even here, however, *m. 'Abod. Zar.* 5.5 explicitly takes for granted the scenario of 'an Israelite eating with a Gentile at a table' (cf. *m. Ber.* 7.1); and Rabbi Meir is here also credited with a more open approach to the question of how an observant Jew might nevertheless eat with Gentiles.[45] Rabban Gamaliel of course is famously said to have frequented the baths of Aphrodite (*m. 'Abod. Zar.* 3.4); other regulations in the same tractate permit Gentile women to serve as wet-nurses for Jewish children (*m. 'Abod. Zar.* 2.1). At the same time, it is worth remembering that the stricter Mishnaic rules are attributed predominantly to the late first and second-century Judaean and Galilean rabbis; to the extent that such attributions are reliable, these views may well be coloured to some extent by the nationalistic fervour of their time, and are not necessarily representative of first-century Greek-speaking Jews at Antioch.

New Testament scholars still widely assume that the halakhah on

[39]Esler 1998:100, 107–8 assumes eucharistic fellowship with Gentiles to have been categorically ruled out for Jews.
[40]On Eliezer ben Hyrcanus, see Neusner 1973; Gilat 1984; and others cited in Stemberger 1996:70.
[41]See the documentation in Klawans 1995.
[42]See also *t. 'Abod. Zar.* 4.6: R. Shimon b. Eleazar prohibits dining in a Gentile's house even when taking one's own food and servants.
[43]Note also Schwartz 1998, who contrasts the highly polarized view of Gentiles taken in 1 Macc with that in 2 Macc.
[44]So e.g. Esler 1998:104–5.
[45]For further documentation see Tomson 1990:232–3.

Jew–Gentile table fellowship can be straightforwardly identified as 'all or nothing'. In fact, however, there was clearly a fairly broad spectrum both of halakhic opinion and of practice, both in Palestine and in the Diaspora.[46] It should in any case be self-evident that the large numbers of Gentile sympathizers in the Diaspora would be impossible to conceive without some measure of association and commensality.[47] Although some level of concern for the purity of foods is very widespread, outright refusal of all meal fellowship with all Gentiles is a rare and unusual counsel in Diaspora circles, as E. P. Sanders has shown: even *Joseph and Asenath*, which at one point affirms such a position (7.1), seems to remain inconsistent on this matter (cf. 20.8).[48] In the light of all this, Philip Esler's forceful and somewhat contrived denial of widespread commensality seems unreasonable, as has also been suggested by E. P. Sanders, B. Holmberg and others.[49]

This is not of course to deny that Antiochene Jews continued to have significant halakhic reservations about unrestricted intercourse with Gentiles. Thus their worries about the oil freely supplied in the city's baths are entirely in keeping with first-century Palestinian perspectives (and we are told the city's officials accommodated this concern by offering them financial compensation instead).[50] Similarly, the possible association of 4 Maccabees and the Hasmonean martyr tradition with Antioch[51] suggests a clear sense of loyalty to the Torah and the ancestral traditions. This alone, of course, does not dictate separation from Gentiles in practice.

One of the Antioch mosaics offers a particularly charming illustration of how a Jewish 'à la carte' approach might be imagined to work in practice.[52] A second-century house contained a mosaic depicting a small cold supper buffet. The courses are depicted in sequence; the table is decorated with a garland of flowers, and the food is served on silver dishes. Round flat loaves of bread are scattered about. The hors-d'œuvre consists of boiled eggs in egg-cups with spoons, cold salted pigs' feet, and artichokes. Apparently there

[46]Barclay 1996 and R. Goldenberg 1998 are among the more balanced accounts.

[47]Cf. Feldman 1993:45–83 *passim*.

[48]E. P. Sanders 1990a:275.

[49]E. P. Sanders 1990a:279–83; 1990b; Dunn 1993:119–21; Holmberg 1998; also Hill 1992:118–25, on Esler 1987:73–86 (cf. 1998). Cf. further S. J. D. Cohen 1989.

[50]Josephus, *Ant.* 12.3.1 §120; cf. John of Gischala's policy at Caesarea, *Life* 13 §74–5 par. *War* 2.21.2 §591–2. See further E. P. Sanders 1990a:272–83; Tomson 1990:168–76; Goodman 1990.

[51]See on this subject Hengel & Schwemer 1997:195–6.

[52]I am indebted to Downey 1961:212–13 for the following analysis; see also Norris 1991, Lassus 1984:366 and Cimok 1995, *inter alia*.

were cucumbers and other vegetables as well. This was followed by a fish served on a rectangular plate, a ham with a wine cup, then wild fowl. Finally there would have been a course of fruit (not preserved on the mosaic) followed by a round layer cake. There were no obvious reasons why Jews should not eat such a meal with a Gentile host who could respect his guests' preference not to eat pork or to participate in the customary libations.

Just as some, and probably many, Jews at Antioch worked and traded alongside Gentiles and frequented the theatre, gymnasia and circus games with Gentiles,[53] so many of the same people must have eaten with Gentiles, without ceasing to be Jews. As we noted earlier, it is telling that objections to the Jewish Christian practice of meal fellowship with Gentiles arose in Jerusalem and not in the Jewish community of Antioch. Among the large number of Jews in Antioch there were a good many who showed a relative latitude in their halakhic observance and, for all their sympathies with Jerusalem, were probably *not* naturally inclined to nationalism of the purist sort. Some Antiochene Jews apparently belonged to the Blues, one of the two major circus fan clubs.[54] It was a squabble between the Blues and the Greens that degenerated into a pogrom against Jews under Caligula in the year 39–40; this may well have been related to the simultaneous anti-Jewish riots in Alexandria and the unrest in Jerusalem over Caligula's policies towards the Temple. Crises in Judaea could rally Jewish sympathies in Antioch in support of Jerusalem, and precipitate significant tensions with Gentiles – though it is also important to note Josephus's explicit statement that this was *not* the case at the beginning of the Jewish Revolt of 66–70 (*War* 2.18.5 §479).

Antioch from the Perspective of the Land of Israel

In light of this rather limited but suggestive evidence, we can now turn to ask what sort of image of Jewish Antioch may have prevailed in first-century Jerusalem. It is fairly clear from a variety of sources that Syria had a somewhat doubtful status in relation to the Holy Land, being neither altogether part of it nor clearly abroad.[55] Aharoni rightly points out that while the Mediterranean, the Jordan,

[53]For a summary of the diaspora evidence, see e.g. Feldman 1993:59–63 and *passim*.

[54]Schenk 1931:188 documents Caligula's preference for the Greens; it is also worth noting that the violence against Jews appears to arise as a consequence of the Blues publicly insulting the Greens in the theatre (Malalas 10.244.20–25). Cf. further Hengel & Schwemer 1997:184–5.

[55]See Neubauer 1868:292ff.; Neaman 1971:88–103; Stemberger 1983; Hengel 2000.

the Desert and the Wadi el-Arish provide natural boundaries to the west, east and south, the Holy Land's only natural boundaries in the north are the Taurus and Amanus mountain ranges.[56] As promised to Abraham and Moses and said to have been conquered by David, the Holy Land extended to the north and east of Lebanon all the way to the Taurus Mountains and the River Euphrates.[57] This same vision of the Land had been more explicitly re-affirmed at the time of Ezekiel (Ezek 47.15–17; 48.1).

The northernmost point in many of these cases is said to be Lebo-Hamath, a place of uncertain identification which in the biblical text usually marks the boundary of the Land.[58] At the dedication of the Temple Solomon had celebrated in the company of 'all Israel, the great congregation (קָהָל גָּדוֹל, LXX ἐκκλησία μεγάλη), from Lebo-Hamath to the Wadi of Egypt'.[59] The same definition of the Land occurs as early as Amos 6.14. What is more, the Deuteronomic history preserves evidence that after the political loss of these boundaries the restoration of the original Holy Land was still understood to remain a divine command: thus the otherwise objectionable king Jeroboam II is praised for restoring the boundaries 'according to the word of the LORD ... by his servant Jonah son of Amittai, the prophet' (2 Kgs 14.25–28).[60] Another text worth mentioning is Obadiah's assignment to returning exiles of the coastline up to Zarephath near Sidon (Obad 20), which of course is the scene for an important story about Elijah (1 Kgs 17.8–23) that is later taken up

---

[56]Aharoni 1979:65.

[57]Gen 15.18 (cf. 49.13); Exod 23.31; Num 13.21; 34.7–9; Deut 1.7–8; 11.24; (34.1–3); Josh 1.4; 1 Kgs 4.21, 24; 2 Chr 9.26. Note also that the Davidic census explicitly included Kadesh and Sidon (2 Sam 24.6–7). On Ituraea see also Freyne 1988:169, 193, who rightly dismisses earlier suggestions (e.g. Schürer 1890:1.293; Schürer & Vermes 1979:2.7–10) that the Judaized 'Ituraeans' of Josephus Ant. 13.11.3 §318 must be Galileans (cf. Josephus's careful delineation in War 3.3.1 §35–40 of Galilee as bordering on Tyre and its dependent territories). Pace Freyne (1988:169), however, their conqueror was not in fact Alexander Jannaeus but Aristobulus. See p. 64 below.

[58]Num 13.21; 34.8; Josh 13.5; Judg 3.3; 1 Kgs 8.65; 2 Kgs 14.25; 1 Chr 13.5; 2 Chr 7.8; Ezek 47.15, 20; 48.1; Amos 6.14.

[59]See the parallel in 2 Chr 7.8. Cf. also 1 Chr 13.5: David assembled (NB LXX ἐξεκκλησί-ασεν) 'all Israel' from the Shihor of Egypt to Lebo-Hamath in order to bring back the ark of the covenant. For the influence on early Christianity of Septuagintal conceptions of the 'congregation' (ἐκκλησία) as Israel, see Horbury 1997.

[60]'He restored the border of Israel from Lebo-hamath as far as the Sea of the Arabah, according to the word of the LORD, the God of Israel, which he spoke by his servant Jonah son of Amittai, the prophet, who was from Gath-hepher. ... He recovered for Israel Damascus and Hamath, which had belonged to Judah ...'. Solomon had earlier conquered 'Hamath-zobah' and built storage towers there, according to 2 Chr 8.3–4; but this could be Hamath, a town further south on the river Orontes. Cf. also Hengel 2000:66.

in the Jesus tradition.[61] In the Second Temple period, this sort of utopian perspective continues, for example, in the Qumran *Genesis Apocryphon*, in which the land promised to Abraham predictably extends to the Euphrates. This latter document explicitly names several cities well to the north of Galilee[62] and locates the northern border at 'the mountain of the Bull' (תורא טור), probably the 'Taurus' or 'Taurus Amanus' range that later features similarly in Targumic and rabbinic texts (see below).[63]

Politically, various Jewish conquests may reflect this ideological tendency to describe the Holy Land in the maximal dimensions envisaged in the biblical record. So, for example, it is worth noting the Hasmonean proclivity to project a Jewish presence in Syrian lands wherever a power vacuum lent itself to such adventures. Jonathan Maccabeus, we are told, despatched 3,000 Jewish auxiliary troops to put down a mutiny in Antioch against the Seleucid king Demetrius II – even if doubtless such aid may in part have been a bargaining chip designed to curry political favours in return.[64] Similarly, following the destruction of the Samaritan Temple and the conquest of Idumaea in the South by John Hyrcanus in 129 BC, in

---

[61]Luke 4.25–27. This text seems at first sight to assume that both Zarephath and (implicitly) Damascus lie outside the land of Israel. Most translations and commentaries take it in this sense: Elijah went not to any of the widows in Israel but *instead* to a Gentile one outside it. The point of the challenge to Jesus in 4.23, however, is not that he works miracles outside the Land but that he works them in the (culturally mixed) Capernaum rather than in his (more conservative Jewish) hometown. This view of the Sea of Galilee evidently underlies Matt 4.13–16, too; and of course Jesus, like Elijah, travels to the land of Tyre and Sidon (Matt 15.21 par), and esteems its spiritual potential rather more highly than that of Chorazin and Bethsaida (Matt 11.21 par).

BDR 448.9 rightly points out that the phrase εἰ μή can occasionally be equivalent to exclusive ἀλλά (Matt 12.4; Rev 21.27), although several of the cited examples are by no means self-evident. Overall, the sense of the 'single exception' clearly predominates in the LXX (e.g. Judg 7.14; 4 Kgs (= 2 Kgs) 6.22; 2 Esdr 12.2 (= Neh 2.2); Eccl 3.22; 8.15; Isa 40.28; Dan θ' 6.6; Jdt 9.14; Sir 16.2; Wisd 7.28; 17.11; Bel 1.5; cf. *Pss. Sol.* 18.12) and governs the vast majority of the over 60 occurrences of οὐ…εἰ μή in the NT. A certain ambiguity may well derive from an underlying Aramaic אלא (= לא אם), which can encompass both meanings (cf. BDR 448.9, citing J. Wellhausen and G. Harder).

Only a most tentative case is possible for the relevance of this passage to our question. Still, in the text as it stands the point is *not* that Jesus ministers *outside* Israel, but rather that he does so away from his traditional πατρίς, among the most dubious and marginal people ἐν τῷ Ἰσραήλ.

[62]1QapGen 21.11–12: note Gebal (Byblos) and Qadesh (near Emesa).

[63]For this interpretation, cf. e.g. Alexander 1974:206, 249, who follows Honigman in assuming that 'Taurus'/'Tauros' in Latin and Greek may itself simply be a transliteration of an underlying Aramaic תורא. See further Weinfeld 1993:208.

[64]1 Macc 11.43–51; cf. Josephus, *Ant.* 13.5.3 §135–42. Bikerman [= Bickerman(n)] 1938:71–2 sees this Jewish action as 'concession politique de leur part, récompensée par des privilèges royaux'.

104 his successor Aristobulus invaded Ituraea to the north of Galilee. In both cases we are told that the inhabitants were permitted to remain 'in the land' (ἐν τῇ χώρᾳ) only if they were circumcised and lived by the laws of the Jews – a practice that, for all its Machiavellian political benefits, seems certain to be related at least in part to an idea of the restoration of Jewish land.⁶⁵ The coherence of politics and ideology is nicely illustrated by the Jewish historian Eupolemus, writing in the Hasmonean period, who describes the conquests of David as explicitly including Idumaea, Ituraea, Tyre as well as Commagene by the Euphrates.⁶⁶

Herod the Great is another interesting case in point, if undoubtedly less driven by Jewish religious devotion. A hint of Roman readiness to recognize Jewish claims on 'Greater Palestine' may be present in the fact that the provincial administration evidently allowed the Jewish king Herod considerable political leeway in Syria. Josephus in fact claims that when for a brief period Herod threw his support behind Julius Caesar's assassin Cassius, the latter recognized Herod's strategic importance by giving him a force of cavalry and infantry – and assigning him responsibility for all of Syria (Συρίας ἁπάσης ἐπιμελητὴν καθιστᾶσιν).⁶⁷ Augustus, we are told, took a comparable view, instructing the procurators of Syria to obtain Herod's approval for all their policies (Ant. 15.10.3 §360). After Herod's death, the Romans allotted to various of his Jewish relatives the care of parts of Syria that lay well to the north of what might plausibly be claimed as

---

⁶⁵Josephus, Ant. 13.9.1 §257–8, 13.11.3 §318; cf. 13.15.4 §397: Pella in Transjordan was demolished by Alexander Jannaeus because its inhabitants would not embrace the Jewish way of life (τὰ πάτρια τῶν ᾽Ιουδαίων ἔθη).

We should perhaps note in passing a baraita attested in b. Sot. 33a (cf. Cant. Rab. 8.13) to the effect that 'Yoḥanan the High Priest' once heard a bat qôl come out of the Holy of Holies and say (NB in Aramaic), 'The young men who went out to war have gained a victory at Antioch' (נצחו טליא דאזלו לאגחא קרבא לאנטוכיא). This looks like a garbled reference to John Hyrcanus, whom Josephus reports as having heard a voice in the Temple assuring him that his sons had just defeated Antiochus Cyzicenus in battle at Samaria (Ant. 13.10.2–3 §275–81, 282).

⁶⁶Eupolemus quoted in Eusebius, Praep. Ev. 9.30.3–4; cf. Fallon 1985, Holladay 1992.

⁶⁷War 1.11.4 §225 (note that in Ant. 14.11.4 §280 the assignment is only of Coele-Syria). It may even be worth noting that Herod the Great, though hardly impelled by conservative Jewish regard for the holiness of the Land, seems in his numerous campaigns to have pursued territorial gains throughout the biblical land of Israel, but not outside it. It would be interesting in this regard to debate the status of his campaign in 38 BC to relieve Mark Antony at Samosata in Commagene, in the extreme north-eastern corner of Syria between the Euphrates and the Taurus mountains (Josephus, Ant. 14.15.8–9 §439–47; War 1.16.7 §321–2). Note, on the other hand, Herod's many munificent gifts to cities well outside the Land (War 1.21.11–12 §422–8); and his expedition to aid Marcus Agrippa's campaign on the Black Sea in 14 BC (Ant. 16.2.2 §16–23). Cf. also Hengel 2000:61.

political Palestine.[68] Finally, we should perhaps at least mention the chronicler Malalas' astonishing tale (10.245) of 30,000 men being despatched from Tiberias under the Jewish Priest Phineas to pillage Antioch in revenge for the anti-Jewish pogrom there in AD 39–40. This account is frequently, and probably rightly, dismissed as straining historical credulity a good deal too far.[69] At the same time, it could be worth just one more thought at least from the geographic perspective: leaving aside the historical improbabilities, an action of this kind might make a certain amount of *ideological* sense if Antioch is regarded as part of the biblical Holy Land.[70]

More interesting still are the Palestinian Targums on the Pentateuch, which, despite their uncertain final date, are widely agreed to reflect a good many popular homiletical traditions of the first and second-century synagogue.[71] Several of these Targumim explicitly envisage the border at Antioch, which they identify with the biblical Lebo-Hamath.[72] Similarly, 'Riblah' at Numbers 34.11 becomes 'Daphne', thereby further highlighting the significant standing of Antioch's posh suburb in Palestinian Jewish consciousness. Another piece of evidence in support of this perspective may possibly be present in much later rabbinic references to Pappus and Lulianus, apparently two martyrs of the revolt under Trajan, who were said to have set up banks 'from Acco to Antioch' to supply the needs of those immigrating from 'the Exile' (לעולי גולה, *Gen. Rab.* 64.10), a term typically applied to

---

[68]E.g. *Ant.* 19.8.1 §338: Chalcis was ruled by Herod's grandson Agrippa II, who was later given extensive lands to the north and east of Galilee (Batanea, Trachonitis, Gaulanitis and north as far as Abilene: *Ant.* 20.7.1 §138; *War* 2.12.8 §247; cf. *Life* 11 §52). His daughter was given in marriage to king Azizus of Emesa (on the Orontes river), after the latter agreed to be circumcised (*Ant.* 20.7.1 §139); other descendants of Herod were assigned Cetis in Cilicia and even Armenia (*Ant.* 18.5.4 §140).

[69]So e.g., quite cautiously, Schenk 1931:188–92; followed by Hengel & Schwemer 1997:184–6 and others.

[70]Hengel & Schwemer 1997:432 n. 954 suggest somewhat implausibly that the High Priest in question is Phanni (Phanasus), who was appointed by the Zealots at the beginning of the Jewish War (*War* 4.3.8 §155; *Ant.* 20.10.1 §227). It is certainly true that reprisals to relieve Jews in Palestinian and Syrian towns were launched in the early weeks of the war (Josephus, *War* 2.18.1 §458–60). The main problem with Hengel's identification would seem to be that Josephus specifically refers to Antioch as being (with Apamea and Sidon) one of the only *undisturbed* towns at the beginning of the Revolt (*War* 2.18.5 §479).

[71]See e.g. Kaufman 1994, 1997; Hayward 1989; Gleßmer 1995.

[72]*Frg. Tg.* and *Tg. Neof.* on Num 34.8; *Tg. Ps.-J.* on Num 13.21 ('up to the roads into Antioch', possibly implying that Antioch itself is outside, as Alexander 1974:183 thinks; or perhaps it is merely an attempt to interpret the phrase לבוא in 'Lebo-Hamath'). *Num. Rab.* 10.3 similarly identifies the Hamath of Amos 6.2 (cf. 6.14) as 'Hamath of Antioch'; cf. *Lev. Rab.* 5.3; *Yalqut* to Amos (p. 545). Indeed, as Alexander rightly points out, 'The identification of *Hamath* with *Antioch* is standard in early Jewish texts' (1974:207; cf. ibid. pp. 181, 187).

Babylonia.[73] Since Acco itself was even in the first century arguably part of the Holy Land[74] and Antioch wealthy enough not to need other people's loans, these are presumably banks set up in aid of those newly arrived in the biblical Promised Land. One might compare the wealthy Jewish aristocrat mentioned earlier, who arrived in the Land from Babylonia with his large clan and private army and decided to settle in the plain of Syrian Antioch before being induced by Herod to help colonize Transjordan instead.[75] A later midrash envisaged that in the messianic age the exiles returning from the Diaspora would burst into song when they reached the top of Mt Taurus Amanus (*Cant. Rab.* 4.8.2).

The Rabbis still frequently assume a border at Amanah, a mountain whose sole biblical mention occurs in a list of northern mountains in the Song of Songs (4.8).[76] The precise location of this site is difficult to determine, and has generated a certain amount of debate.[77] Both Targumic and rabbinic sources typically locate it at Mount Amanus just northwest of Antioch. This is a range that marks the border between Syria and Cilicia and forms a southern extension of the Taurus mountains,[78]

[73]On Pappus and Lulianus, see Horbury (forthcoming), to whom I am indebted. Lulianus is described in *Sifra* Beḥuqqotay 5 on Lev 26.19 (§266.1.4) as 'the Alexandrian' (לוליינוס אלכסנדרי), quite possibly a reference to the Syrian Alexandria (modern Iskenderun, Turkey: cf. Strabo, *Geogr.* 14.5.19; Ptolemy 5.14.2) on the coast 40km north of Antioch, across the Syrian Gates (Pass of Beilan) and not far from the entrance to the Cilician plain.

[74]See, however, the doubts expressed in the Amoraic period, e.g. in *y. Šeb.* 6.1, 36c (R. Aḥa b. Jacob); cf. already *m. Giṭ.* 1.2 (R. Yehudah bar Ilai regards Acco as outside the land for the halakhah of divorce bills, R. Meir as inside the Land).

[75]Note also that Pappus and Lulianus' interest in fostering Jewish return and settlement in the Land may go hand in hand with their being martyred at Laodicea-on-Sea (modern Al-Ladhiqiya in Syria, a little way south of Antioch).

[76]See Neubauer 1868:5–10. See above on *m. Šeb.* 6.1 (cf. 9.2) and *m. Ḥal.* 4.8; also *t. Ḥal.* 2.11; *y. Šeb.* 6.2, 36c; *b. Giṭ.* 8a.

It is an interesting bit of *Wirkungsgeschichte* to note that an early eighteenth-century splinter group of the Württemberg pietist movement emigrated to Iowa in 1842 and founded a community called Amana. Among their various ventures was the Amana Society, whose commercial initiatives later led to the popular Amana brand of domestic appliances (see www.amana.com).

[77]This is due not least to the fact that while Mt Hor marks the *northern* boundary according to Num 34.7, another mountain of that name is in Num 20.22–28 said to be the site on which Aaron dies, 'on the border of the land of *Edom*' (v. 23; cf. Num 33.37–39; Deut 32.50). The fourteenth-century Jewish traveller Estori ha-Parḥi (c. 1282–c. 1357) identified it as *Jebel-el-Akra* just north of today's Syrian-Turkish border, and barely 20 miles south of Antioch. See Ha-Parchi 1897: ch. 11, ed. Luncz p. 250; cf. Neubauer 1868:8, although he (mistakenly?) cites ch. 2 of the Berlin edition.

[78]For the position of Mt Amanus, see e.g. Strabo, *Geography* 14.5.18. The same location seems already to be presupposed in the book of *Jubilees* (8.21; 9.4); cf. Alexander 1982:208. See further Alexander 1974:204, who also plausibly suggests on the basis of *Exod. Rab.* 23.5 and *Cant. Rab.* 4.8.2 that the identification with the biblical Mt Amanah was based on assonance. Other texts that locate the northern border at Mt Amanus include *m. Ḥal.* 4.8; *m. Šeb.* 6.1; *t. Ter.* 2.12; *t. Ḥal.* 2.11; *y. Ḥal.* 4.7, 60a.

although it has occasionally been suggested that the 'Taurus' of the rabbinic phrase 'Taurus Amanus' could itself be a part of the Amanus range (perhaps near the pass known as Beilan or the 'Syrian Gates').[79] Even Avlas of Cilicia (אוולס דקלקי) is explicitly said to mark the border in several potentially early passages;[80] if this is to be identified with the so-called 'Cilician Gates' (Πύλαι Κιλίκιαι) rather than somewhere nearer the pass of Beilan,[81] the ideal Land of Israel might on that reckoning be thought to include even the Cilician plain and with it, for example, the city of Tarsus. It is worth noting that during Paul's lifetime this area did in fact form an integral part of the integrated Roman province of Syria, and became incorporated into the new province of Cilicia only under Vespasian in AD 72; a province of 'Syria and Cilicia' is probably presupposed in Gal 1.21 and Acts 15.23, 41.[82]

On the whole, however, rabbinic literature tends to greater ambiguity and caution in its definition of the Land.[83] Judaism may well have tended to a more pragmatic view after the catastrophic wars against Rome, being chastened by the need to recognize that the true dimensions of the land of the Jews were in reality and for the foreseeable future always going to remain very much smaller. A similar tendency towards greater realism may be in evidence in Josephus: his apparently more modest contemporary estimation of the Land not only suits his apologetic purpose but coincides with what may have been a late first-century rabbinic shift of perspective,

[79]So e.g. Alexander 1974:205, following Honigman. See also n. 81 below.

[80]Tg. Ps.-J., Neof. and Frg. Tg. on Num 34.8; contrast t. Šeb. 4.11 (where Avlas appears to be nearer Galilee). Josephus suggests that the area from 'Amanus and Taurus' outward is inhabited by the sons of Japheth (Ant. 1.6.1 §122) and Ham (1.6.2 §130), thus suggesting that Mt Amanus is regarded as a significant boundary for Shem as well. Jdt 2.25, too, seems to envisage Cilicia as the southern border of Japheth.

[81]See e.g. Jastrow s. v. אבלס (p. 7); Treidler 1975:287–8. McNamara 1995:10–11 leaves the matter wide open: the Avlas de-Qilqi is either the pass of Beilan at the Syrian Gates (as Alexander 1974:208 supposes), or the plain of Cilicia beyond that pass, or even the narrow stretch of sea between Cyprus and Cilicia known as the 'Cilician trench' (αὐλών) in Pliny, Nat. Hist. 5.130 (cf. similarly Neubauer 1868:431 n. 4). See also Josephus, Ant. 13.15.4 §397: if Κιλίκων αὐλών in that passage is not a mistake, there may have been a similarly named locality in Transjordan (but Alexander 1974:208 plausibly follows Schalit in emending to Ἁλυκὸς αὐλών, i.e. 'Valley of Salt').

[82]See Bing 1992:1024; Hemer 1989:172, 179; Riesner 1994:236. Note especially the evidence of Codex Sinaiticus in all three passages, which presupposes a province called Συρία καὶ Κιλικία (in Acts 15.41 this is also supported, inter alia, by Alexandrinus and the Majority Text).

[83]Neubauer 1868:6 writes, 'Quelques rabbins veulent que les frontières de la Palestine indiquées dans la Bible, soient considérées comme frontières réelles, quand il s'agit de l'exercice des devoirs religieux; d'autres restreignent beaucoup plus la signification de "Terre d'Israël".' What he fails to identify is the apparent change in the prevailing opinion during the early Tannaitic period.

as we shall see in a moment.[84] Such a note of political pragmatism, at any rate, would make sense of the fact that later texts (and e.g. the Babylonian *Targum Onkelos*) usually restrict the size of the Land to more realistic dimensions.[85] Later *halakhot* more commonly assume that Antioch and Syria are outside the Land.[86]

Without undue reliance on precise rabbinic attributions, it is worth thinking seriously about the Mishnah's explicit suggestion that around the end of the first century the official halakhic treatment of Syria and Antioch changed from an original 'Greater Israel' position to a more realistic estimation of the Holy Land. Mishnah *Hallah* 4.7–8 records a discussion between two famous rabbis of the second Tannaitic generation, Rabban Gamaliel II and Rabbi Eliezer. The latter affirms that Syrian land bought from Gentiles must be treated like *Eretz Israel* for the purposes of both tithes and the Sabbath year law, while Rabban Gamaliel disagrees and proposes instead a three-zone rule that identifies the northern limits of the Land at Kezib (= Akhzib), just south of today's border with Lebanon at Rosh ha-Nikra, a line that is explicitly justified in the light of post-exilic realities.[87] Syria on this view is an ambiguous halakhic zone between the Diaspora and the land of

---

[84]Josephus forgoes a detailed description of the Land, and appears to skip Num 33–36 from his running account of the wilderness events in *Ant.* 4.7.3 §171–2. Although he relates that the Hebrew spies explored the land of Canaan all the way north to Hamath, in keeping with Num 13.21, he assigns no contemporary name to this place (but see *Ant.* 1.6.2 §138: Hamath = Epiphaneia, in N. Syria). Weinfeld 1993:214 –16 notes a shift in Josephus towards cities and the Temple on the one hand, and a spiritualization of Land theology on the other.

[85]Even *Targum Pseudo-Jonathan* to Num 34 shows signs of such redaction, as Neubauer 1868:430 already noted; cf. further Alexander 1974:207 and McNamara & Clarke 1995 *ad loc.* Several of the more outlying areas are moved nearer to the land: Tiberias, for example, takes the place of Antioch in v. 8 and a line nearer Damascus is envisaged in v. 10.

[86]So explicitly *b. Git.* 44b (cf. Neubauer 1868:8–9); and note e.g. the differing halakhah for the sale of slaves (*y. Git.* 4.6, 46a), divorce certificates (*m. Git.* 1.2, Rabbi Yehudah bar Ilai [mid- second cent.]: even Acco and Ashkelon count as outside the Land), and the fruit of young trees (*m.'Orl.* 3.9: doubtful *'Orlah*-fruit is forbidden in *Eretz Israel* but permitted in Syria). Note also the tradition (e.g. in *y. Šeqal.* 6.2, 50a; *y. Sanh.* 10.7, 29c) of an exile at Daphne = Riblah, associated with the story of 2 Kgs 25.6 and Jer 39.5; 52.10–30.

[87]*Sifre* Deut 51; cf. e.g. *t. Šeb.* 4.6, 11; *t. Hal.* 2.6; *y. Dem.* 2.1, 22d; *y. Šeb.* 6.2, 36c; so also the Rehov Inscription, line 13. See Sussmann 1981:152 and cf. Safrai 1983:209; Neusner 1973:2.176–7 rates the attribution to Eliezer as merely 'fair' tradition. The date of this halakhic shift may conceivably owe something to the end of Agrippa II's Herodian rule in Syria, as Prof. W. Horbury suggests to me. Note further the comparable dispute between the third-generation Tannaite R. Yose (b. Halafta) and Eleazar b. Yose on whether the biblical boundaries are reckoned to belong to the Land: the former denies and the latter affirms this (*t. Ma'as. Š.* 2.15). Elsewhere, R. Eleazar b. Yose is similarly credited with the view that the territories on the boundaries of the Land are equivalent to *Eretz Israel* (*t. B. Qam.* 8.19). In the Amoraic period it may be worth comparing the somewhat different dispute in *y. Dem.* 2.1, 22c between R. Eleazar (b. Pedat) and R. Yohanan (b. Nappaha), as to whether the majority even of the more modestly defined *Eretz Israel* is in the hand of Israelites or in the hand of Gentiles.

Israel proper.[88] The Mishnah laconically notes that after a period of compromise Rabban Gamaliel's view eventually prevailed. It is certainly confirmed in a famous *baraita* also found in the inscription from the synagogue at Reḥov in Galilee.[89] Even in these more pragmatic texts, of course, the halakhah for the Sabbath year and dough offerings still recognizes at least an ambiguous zone from Akhzib to the Euphrates and Amanah, which is not actually treated as Diaspora. The more modest perspective is evidently a counsel of practical expediency rather than a clear change of principle.[90] In the same context of tractate *Ḥallah*, we find the statement that at the time of the Temple the offering of first fruits brought by one Ariston from Apamea was accepted on the principle that 'he who owns land in Syria is like one who owns land in the outskirts of Jerusalem'.[91] Even under the developed three-zone model, for example, the mid-second-century rabbis of the Mishnah agree that one may not sell land to Gentiles either in Palestine or in Syria (*m. 'Abod. Zar.* 1.8).[92]

Thus, although no systematic view emerges, we may say that one important perspective in the earlier rabbinic sources is reflected in the Tosefta's bald assertion that 'everything from the Taurus

[88]Cf. similarly *m. Šeb.* 6.1; *m. Dem.* 1.3; see also *m. Šeqal.* 3.4 on the halakhah for *terumah* and *m. 'Abod. Zar.* 1.8 for the lease or sale of land to Gentiles.

[89]See Sussmann 1981; Stemberger 1996:37 and the references cited in n. 87 above. Note, however, that the inscription (like its rabbinic parallels) lists 'doubtful cities' in the regions of Tyre, Naveh and Transjordan – suggesting that there were cities in these regions that for purposes of the Sabbath year halakhah counted as part of the Land.

[90]Similarly, it is worth noting R. Yoḥanan's rejection in *y. Sanh.* 3.2, 21a of the idea that the law court in Tiberias has a higher authority than that in Antioch. Cf. further the definition offered by Safrai 1983:209, 'The Land of Israel was defined as the land upon which Israel lived in the context of its being the Promised Land, free of idolatry, not worked on the Sabbath or the Sabbatical Year.'

[91]M. Ḥal. 4.11; cf. *b. Giṭ.* 8a; contrast *m. Ḥal.* 4.10 on Alexandria. An ossuary discovered in the Kidron valley in 1990 mentions one Ariston of Apamea (ארסטון אפמי), apparently a proselyte also called Judah (יהודה הגיור), who had moved to Jerusalem: see Ilan 1992:150–55. Ilan remains cautious on the identification of this man with the one in the Mishnah passage; but the possibility is certainly not remote. 'Apamea' also features in *Tg. Ps.-J.* to Num 34.10. I remain unpersuaded of Alexander's argument (1974:212–13; cf. p. 215) that Paneas/Caesarea Philippi is meant here: 'Paneas' is separately mentioned in v. 11 as being further south. Commenting on Ezekiel 47, Jerome separately attests this tradition (Alexander 1974:217 calls it a 'mis-reading') of the border at *Syrian* Apamea; see n. 94 below.

[92]R. Aqiba is similarly reported as saying that in Syria Jews may not sow, plow or weed during the Sabbath year (*t. Šeb.* 4.12); and even R. Gamaliel II required only one batch of dough offering in Syria as in Palestine (*t. Ḥal.* 2.5). Cf. further Safrai 1983:210–11; and note the Reḥov synagogue inscription cited above. Cf. also *m. Yad.* 4.3 on Egypt, Babylon, Ammon and Moab as clearly *outside* the Land and subject to quite different halakhic rules. On the general issue, note further Safrai 1983:207–9 and *passim*; also Weinfeld 1983 on Transjordan.

Amanus downwards is the land of Israel'.[93] And for all the halakhic moderation of Rabban Gamaliel and the 'official' Talmudic line, Jerome informs us that (some) Palestinian Jews still held this view around the year 400.[94]

This notion of Antioch as part of the Holy Land of course sounds quite preposterously remote from what one would normally regard as Jewish Palestine – which is perhaps why New Testament scholars seem not to have seriously considered such a possibility.[95] Mental maps, however, usually speak more eloquently about people's true perceptions than political ones. (On moving to Britain I was disturbed to find that Vancouver, once at the centre of my world maps and worldview, is at the very end of the world on British maps.) At a time of heightened messianic expectations for the restoration of the Holy City and the Land, it is not unreasonable to suspect that the utopian dimensions of the biblical promises would once again come alive in the hopes of observant Jews, just as they had previously done at the time of Ezekiel.[96]

Quite plausibly, therefore, many first-century Palestinian Jews regarded Antioch as the gateway from the Exile to the Holy Land, and thus fraught with a considerable symbolic significance. For religious Jews concerned about the redemption of the Twelve Tribes, Antioch's status as a large metropolis inside the biblical Promised Land might well carry special halakhic sensitivities.

Four Theses on James the Just and Antioch

With the foregoing observations in mind, I wish to propose four brief but controversial theses for discussion, in the hope that debate on these may help to narrow down the interpretative options regarding James's intervention. My starting point will be an attempt to take both Acts and Galatians more or less at face value in light of what has been said so far, acknowledging tensions and contradictions wherever necessary, but without resorting either to grand harmonies or to grand polarities and conflict theories. It will also be useful to

---

[93]See e.g. t. Ḥal. 2.11; y. Šeb. 6.2, 36c; b. Giṭ. 8a.

[94]Jerome, Comm. on Ezek 47.15–17 (CCL 75.721); Quaest. in Gen. 10.18 (CCL 72.14). A well-attested variant of Num 34.11 in the Vulgate places Riblah contra fontem daphnim, 'opposite the spring of Daphnis'. Cf. Alexander 1974:216; McNamara 1995:9–10.

[95]Thus, among recent authors, even the opposing positions of Esler 1998:106, E. P. Sanders 1990c:172; Tomson 1990:228–9; Hill 1992:134; Bauckham 1995:423 etc. all assume that Antioch is outside the Land.

[96]On the ideological function of such utopian texts within the OT, cf. also Kallai 1983:76–9; Smend 1983:96–9 and passim; Weinfeld 1993:52–75, 99–120.

bear in mind that our main interest here is confined to James rather than Paul or Peter; the latter would require separate studies.

1. The Mission from James is solely addressed to Jews and not to Gentiles; it must be carefully distinguished from Jewish and Judaizing opposition to Paul.

The phenomenon of Jewish embassies and letters of instruction from Palestine is well established and may on the Christian side be represented in the Epistles of James and Jude, as well as in several stories in Acts.[97] In keeping with this tradition, the Jacobean mission probably came in the form of a reasoned request for solidarity rather than an authoritative demand for compliance.[98] Paul's report, along with the evidence of comparable Jewish embassies from Jerusalem, makes it likely that James's intervention will have been in the form of an earnest appeal.

All the evidence, therefore, suggests that the 'men from James' (τινας ἀπὸ Ἰακώβου, Gal 2.12) genuinely represented him and were not pretenders or impostors. More importantly, they and their mission must be carefully distinguished from Paul's opponents in Galatians and elsewhere, including in Galatians the false brethren (ψευδαδελφοί 2.4; cf. 2 Cor 11.26), the agitator (ὁ ταράσσων, 5.10), the troublemakers (οἱ ἀναστατοῦντες, 5.12) and those who fear Jewish persecution and therefore undergo and promote circumcision (6.12–13, note οἱ περιτεμνόμενοι). The same is true *a fortiori* for the 'super-apostles' of 2 Corinthians (ὑπερλίαν ἀπόστολοι 11.5–13; cf. 12.11). In all these cases, the Pauline opponents are people who make a direct approach to *Gentiles* in order to persuade them to be circumcised. In none of them is there any mention of table fellowship or of the name of James.[99] The

---

[97]Just as Rabban Gamaliel wrote to the Jewish communities in the south, in upper and lower Galilee and in Babylonia, so James arguably writes to the 'Twelve Tribes in the Diaspora' in the NT Epistle that bears his name. (Similarly, the address of 1 Peter may conceivably denote Christians in those areas of 'the Diaspora' that lie just beyond the ideal boundaries of the Promised Land.) See *t. Sanh.* 2.6; *b. Sanh.* 11a, etc. and cf. recently Niebuhr 1998; Taatz 1991; Bauckham 1995:423–5. In the third and fourth centuries there seems to be considerable evidence of authoritative instructions to the Diaspora being sent by the Patriarch of Palestine in Tiberias: see Feldman 1993:71–2 and note Libanius' letter to Priscianus (LCL No. 131) in AD 364.

[98]*Pace* N. Taylor 1992:129–30.

[99]So also Pratscher 1987:71–2. In this regard it is perhaps worth noting once again the old chestnut of F. C. Baur (followed by W. Lütgert, W. Schmithals and others), who supposed that the 'Christ party' at Corinth (1 Cor 1.12) were those who stressed close links with the original followers of Jesus at Jerusalem. There is no evidence for this position in the context; if it were true, we would certainly expect ἐγὼ δὲ Ἰησοῦ. The case against this view is well summarized in Schrage 1991:146–8, who more plausibly suspects a case of Pauline irony.

opponents and agitators are far more likely related to the unauthorized Jerusalem Christians mentioned even in the Apostolic Decree of Acts 15.24 (cf. 15.1–2): they are people 'whom we did not send', but who have gone out among the Gentile Christians and 'said things to disturb you and unsettle your minds'.[100]

By contrast, the men from James address themselves solely to Jewish Christians; and this would of course be the only appropriate stance in keeping with the Jerusalem agreement as reported in Gal 2.7–9. James appeals to the constituency for which he feels responsible, and on a topic of particular relevance to Jewish life in the Holy Land. (See also below.) His emissaries therefore cannot be Judaizers, as is still often presupposed.[101]

Correspondingly, James's embassy did not oppose the Gentile mission. Nothing indicates that James made any effort to renege on the Jerusalem agreement (Gal 2.9) to recognize a separate mission to the Gentiles. Nor was his intervention in any sense designed to promote the circumcision of Gentiles. There is no evidence from Galatians, Acts or any New Testament texts that James advocated this. Indeed it is worth noting that even the Apostolic Decree actually presupposes the *rejection* of any idea that Gentiles must be circumcised; it is logically impossible to affirm both the Decree and Gentile circumcision at the same time. Even in Galatians, this bitterest and most polemical of his letters, it is not James whom Paul accuses of 'forcing Gentiles to Judaize', but Peter: Paul's main complaint is not that James advocates separate Jewish and Gentile Christian communities, but that Peter first accepts and then rejects table fellowship.

Another important corollary, therefore, is that despite frequent assertions to the contrary, the mission from James was *not* in any straightforward sense about food, nor about Gentile carelessness in matters of purity or idolatry. Had the problem been merely the purity of the food consumed at common meals, this could have been easily rectified. We should in that case have expected a conditional or partial withdrawal from commensality, such as making it dependent on Gentile compliance with principles of the kind enunciated in the Apostolic Decree. What we find instead is a *complete* withdrawal by the entire Jewish membership of the church

---

[100]Barrett 1998:741 hangs on to the view that these people were men genuinely commissioned, who nevertheless 'may have gone beyond their brief'. More likely, given what both Luke and Paul actually do say about James in Acts 15, Gal 2 and elsewhere, is that they were people who were precisely *not* charged by James but nevertheless claimed to address the Gentiles as official spokesmen of the Jerusalem church. The difference is subtle but important.

[101]So rightly Pratscher 1987:81 and n. 132, with documentation.

at Antioch, with the exception of Paul. The decision appears to be to reject not certain kinds of food but any and all commensality *per se*. The problem, in other words, was not the food but the company.[102] This we saw above to be a fairly hard-line stance, which would not perhaps have been widely held outside the Jewish heartland.

This in turn means that the request from James did *not* concern anything like an imposition of the Apostolic Decree.[103] Indeed it is best interpreted without reference to that document. The 'Decree' enunciates widely agreed Jewish principles for Gentile behaviour, which almost certainly represent common ground between Paul and Peter.[104] Regardless of that particular point, however, these principles are clearly irrelevant to the problem as it presents itself in Antioch. Neither the Jacobean mission nor the Apostolic Decree is fundamentally about food; but the former is concerned about *Jewish* behaviour and the latter about *Gentile* behaviour.[105] (Galatians 2 in fact does not even claim that James's intervention explicitly opposed table fellowship, but rather that this was what the Antiochene church concluded.) In any case, Paul in Galatians 2 does not object to anything remotely relevant to the principles enunciated in the Decree. What is more, he himself goes on just a few years later to agree that the mission to the Jews must be observant (1 Cor 9.20; cf. p. 171 below), and even to endorse the idea that Jewish–Gentile meal fellowship must allow for Jewish believers to abstain from meat or wine (Rom 14.1 – 15.6).[106]

2. James's motivation was in part political.

It remains unclear whether James's concerns about the church at Antioch were primarily political or primarily religious. Most likely both elements were present, and closely interrelated. There is in any case enough evidence of *political* pressure on the Jerusalem church to suggest that the politically motivated plea for solidarity must have been at least part of the reason for James's embassy to Antioch.[107] This was a measure not so much of cowardice but of *Realpolitik* in the Jerusalem of the 40s. Just as the wording of Mark 13 may well

---

[102]Cf. Bernheim 1997:177.

[103]*Contra* Catchpole 1977:442 and many others.

[104]Cf. e.g. Dunn 1993:124; Borgen 1988; see also Chapter 7 below.

[105]Cf. Bauckham 1995:438, 462.

[106]See also n. 38 above, and for the importance of 1 Cor 9.19–23 see Richardson 1980. Cf. Wehnert 1997:139–41, 271, who offers the suggestive, but in my view ultimately unpersuasive, argument that Paul later changed his mind on the Apostolic Decree.

[107]So e.g. Jewett 1971; Pratscher 1987:85; Dunn 1983:183–6; Hengel & Schwemer 1997:245–55 and *passim*.

reflect something of the Jerusalemite alarm at Caligula's intended 'abomination of desolation' in the Temple,[108] so we may assume that in the aftermath of that assault, and in the subsequent pro-establishment persecution under Agrippa I, the Jerusalem church survived only because of its visible support for the Jewish national institutions.

Luke deliberately parallels the 'trials' of Jesus and of Stephen, and implies that Stephen's execution and the subsequent persecution of his followers were due to his radical critique of the Temple, in explicit appeal to Jesus. These events could have occurred in the mid-30s, while Caiaphas was still in office, as the *Pseudo-Clementine Recognitions* suppose (e.g. 1.71).[109] Although the Twelve survived that persecution, it may well be that in the aftermath of Caligula the nationalist hand had been strengthened by a sympathetic Agrippa to the point where the position of the original disciples had become untenable. As the closest followers of a man associated with threats against the Temple, they were obvious targets for persecution: James the son of Zebedee was killed in this context, and the popularity of that measure encouraged Agrippa to turn his attention next to Peter (Acts 12.2–4). Peter escaped, but had to leave the city and arrived before long in Antioch.

Writing to Thessalonica in AD 50 (1 Thess 2.14–16), Paul shows himself aware of recent persecutions of the Palestinian Jewish church, which he explicitly sets in parallel to the opposition suffered by Jesus. In addition to the events of AD 43–44, it is worth noting the remarkably precise suggestion in Malalas (10.247) to the effect that a further significant Jewish persecution of the apostles and their followers took place in AD 48 ('in the eighth year of Claudius'), i.e. during the time of Ventidius Cumanus's bloody tenure as procurator (AD 48–52).[110] While the nature of the evidence makes confirmation of this suggestion impossible, very recent persecution of this kind is certainly plausible and would lend a vivid colour to the proceedings at Antioch.[111] Galatians 6.12 may be another case in point, with its

---

[108]See Theissen 1992:151–65. Cf. Dan 12.11; Mark 13.14 par.

[109]Some have supposed the possibility of High Priestly action during the interregnum after Pilate's deposition in AD 36, comparable to the execution of James the Just under Annas the son of Annas (Josephus, *Ant.* 20.9.1 §200–3). See also the discussion in Riesner 1994:52–6.

[110]Josephus, *Ant.* 20.5.2 – 6.3 §103–36; *War* 2.12.1–7 §223–45. Hengel & Schwemer 1997:241 point out that AD 48–49 was probably a Sabbath year, which would have accentuated the famine and added to public tensions.

[111]For a positive estimation of Malalas' note, see Riesner 1994:175; cf. Schenk 1931:200–1. I offer a fuller discussion of these events, also in relation to 1 Thess 2.14–16, in Bockmuehl forthcoming.

apparent background of Jewish persecution 'for the cross of Christ'. This would be all the more significant if, as on balance I think likely, Galatians must be dated considerably earlier than the usual assumption of AD 54 or 57, quite possibly in the near aftermath of the Antioch incident itself.[112]

It is also important to bear in mind that the Jerusalem church may have been concerned about the mobility of their enemies: just as the accusations of Paul's adversaries followed him from the Diaspora all the way to Jerusalem (e.g. Acts 21.21, 27–28), so also scandalous reports about practices in the Antiochene church could easily travel to Jerusalem and be used against a church under persecution there.

All this makes highly plausible an appeal to Christians in Antioch for an exercise of consideration and solidarity in their possibly fairly recent[113] practice of freely associating with uncircumcised Gentiles. It also lends dramatic definition to Paul's statements about those, including Peter, who manifest 'fear of the circumcision' (Gal 2.12; cf. 6.12). Far from being a fear of the authority of James,[114] this may well be motivated by the concrete circumstances in Judaea and Jerusalem of the 40s and 50s, where only a thoroughly Jewish mission could hope to be tolerated. In these circumstances, any politically defensible integration of Gentiles, especially within the biblical Land, might only be possible by 'requiring them to live as Jews' (cf. Gal 2.14 τὰ ἔθνη ἀναγκάζεις Ἰουδαΐζειν) – a point of view to which James appeals, and to which Peter gives way.

3. James's religious motivation can be construed in light of the teaching of Jesus.

In trying to fathom James's possible reservations about an integrated church of Jews and Gentiles, it is relevant to bear in mind Jesus' own

---

[112]Paul's angry account suggests that his memory of these events is still quite vivid; his reproachful description of Peter here contrasts notably with the far more respectful picture in 1 Cor. Paul also seems to look back on the foundation of the (South) Galatian churches in AD 47–48 as relatively recent: he declares himself astonished that the Galatians have 'so quickly' deserted the gospel (1.6) at a time when they should still have in mind the visual image of the apostle's demonstration of Christ (3.1). The reference to the beginning of his mission to Galatia at 4.13 (τὸ πρότερον) cannot be taken as evidence that Paul had already visited more than once. The apparent de-emphasis of Gal on Israel's salvation history and covenantal theology, much noted in recent scholarship (see e.g. Longenecker 1998:5–23, 174–9), may well have suited the polemical context in which Paul found himself having to justify his Gentile mission apart from Jerusalem and Antioch. Even if this were true for Gal, however, Rom and 1 Cor show that, upon calmer reflection, Paul's reaction did not last.

[113]Dunn 1993:117, citing Burton, suggests that the freer meal fellowship may itself be the result of the Jerusalem Council.

[114]So again recently Painter 1997:69.

apparent avoidance of Gentiles and Gentile cities in Galilee, as well as his pre-Easter command to the disciples to go nowhere 'among the Gentiles' (Matt 10.5). This prohibition is evidently ethnic rather than geographic in intent. Jesus himself is depicted as happily travelling to the region of Tyre and Sidon (where he stayed in a (presumably Jewish) house, Mark 7.24), to Gaulanitis, the Decapolis and Samaria, all of which represent part of the idealized dimensions of the biblical Holy Land as assigned to the nine-and-a-half lost tribes. In describing the disciples who came to follow Jesus, the gospel tradition characterizes the new people as representing all parts of the biblical land of Israel: 'a great multitude from Galilee followed; also from Judaea and Jerusalem and Idumaea and from beyond the Jordan and from about Tyre and Sidon a great multitude, hearing all that he did, came to him' (Mark 3.7–8). The drastic and surprising nature of Jesus' stance is particularly well illustrated in Matthew by his response to the Syro-Phoenician woman who comes to him well inside the Roman province of Syria, only to be told, 'I was sent only to the lost sheep of the house of Israel' (Matt 15.24).[115]

This geographic dimension of his mission to the lost sheep of the house of Israel may well form an important corollary to Jesus' obvious programmatic interest in the Twelve Phylarchs and the Twelve Tribes.[116] As Sanders and others have shown,[117] Jesus' ministry can be properly understood as a Jewish restoration movement. The restoration of the twelve tribes was widely expected to be part of the eschatological work of Elijah or the Messiah; according to the *Psalms of Solomon*, for example, God would in the messianic period gather his people 'and divide them according to the tribes on the land'.[118] Jesus' appointment of the twelve disciples deliberately reflects this notion of a restoration of all Israel: they are the ones who 'will sit on twelve thrones, judging the twelve tribes of Israel' (Matt 19.28 par. Luke 22.30). Their mission appears in part to be territorially defined: they will not have gone through all the towns of Israel before the Son of Man

---

[115]All this would seem to suggest the need for a more differentiated reading of the evidence than that offered by W. D. Davies 1974:336–65. It could be worth speculating whether the theme of baptism in the Jordan might for John have had connotations of the second Exodus (as perhaps it later did for Theudas: Jos., *Ant.* 20.5.1 §97–9), whereas Jesus' ministry focused on the arrival of the Kingdom in the Land itself.

[116]See Horbury 1986 cf. Allison 1998:141–5.

[117]See e.g. E. P. Sanders 1985, 1993; McKnight 1999.

[118]*Pss. Sol.* 17.28–31, 50; cf. e.g. Sir 36.11; 48.10 (Elijah); 4 Ezra 13.39–40 (Messiah); 1QM 2.1–3; and of course passages like Ezek 47.13; Isa 49.6. See further documentation in Horbury 1986; E. P. Sanders 1985:95–8.

comes (Matt 10.23).[119] Both Matthew and Luke offer tantalizingly brief but explicit glimpses of an interest in the land of the northern tribes, where Jesus lives and travels;[120] and in a potentially anti-zealot logion of Matthean redaction we find that it is the humble who will 'inherit the Land' (Matt 5.5).

James's rising influence coincided with the disappearance of the Apostles from Jerusalem. Although listed in the early tradition of 1 Cor 15 as an original witness of the resurrection, James's prominence was greatly enhanced when the apostolic base in Jerusalem was eroded by persecution. In particular, it seems clear that the three years from the death of Caligula in 41 to the death of Agrippa in 44 brought about a sustained persecution of the original Apostles, including the execution of James the son of Zebedee and the removal of Peter from Jerusalem (Acts 12.1–17). This in turn apparently precipitated a shift in the leadership of the Jerusalem church, as a result of which the 'Twelve' gave way to the 'Pillars' and to James and the Elders as the central authority.[121] Peter and John clearly still belonged to the 'Pillars' at the time of the Antioch incident, though not, it seems, for very much longer:[122] significantly, James appears together with Peter and John in Gal 2.7–9, but by himself in 2.12. Peter arrived in Antioch several years after the end of his leadership in Jerusalem in AD 42–44.[123] James and those who remained were faithful to the vision of national redemption in Jerusalem; Hegesippus describes James as a Nazirite who prayed continually in the Temple to ask forgiveness for the people (Eusebius, *Eccl. Hist.* 2.23.5–7).

James's request, or at least the Antioch church's reception of his request, may be usefully understood in the light of this national emphasis in the ministry of Jesus, and against a geographic background in which Antioch was seen as part of the Promised

[119]In this respect one may also wish to reconsider Jesus' recruitment of Simon the Zealot (and possibly Judas Iscariot along similar lines?), as one who might well be sympathetic to a Land-based restoration theology. Another influence on Jesus may be the potential Land symbolism implied in his baptism in the Jordan.

[120]Jesus' home is in the 'land of Israel' (γῆ Ἰσραήλ, Matt 2.20–21), and his ministry is in the land of Zebulon and Naphtali (γῆ Ζαβουλὼν καὶ γῆ Νεφθαλίμ: Matt 4.13–15), which reaches far to the north. The Lucan infancy narrative appears to assign importance to Anna's belonging to the tribe of Asher (see recently Bauckham 1997, although he suspects a connection more specifically with the Median Diaspora).

[121]So also Pratscher 1987:68; Bauckham 1995:427 and *passim*; Hengel & Schwemer 1998:244–5. Contrast Painter 1997:42–44 and *passim*.

[122]Hengel & Schwemer 1998:244–5, 253 and nn. 1266, 1327 point out that the Apostles are mentioned for the last time in relation to the Decree: Acts 15.2, 4, 6, 22–23; 16.4.

[123]Cf. Bauckham 1995:440–1, '... the persecution of Agrippa I (AD 43 or 44) was the point at which the Twelve ceased to be the leadership of the Jerusalem church.'

Land. The Messiah's ministry was understood to be carried out for the Twelve Tribes of Israel by the twelve Phylarchs.[124] And the new mission to the Gentiles should not be conducted in such a way as to compromise Jesus' mission to Israel – a point that could carry particular weight within the scriptural borders of the Twelve Tribes. The mission to the house of Israel in the Land of Israel is a matter that the Jerusalem agreement had left firmly within the jurisdiction of the Pillars (Gal 2.9). This might also explain why James intervenes in Antioch but not, for example, in Alexandria, Corinth or Rome.

Two additional corollaries are worth noting. First, despite our earlier remarks it is interesting to observe the geographic dimension even of the Apostolic Decree, which fits squarely with this view of affairs in Jerusalem. As reported in Acts 15, this document is addressed in the first instance to *Gentile* believers 'in Antioch, Syria and Cilicia' – areas that on the argument here presented are either part of the ideal Holy Land or at any rate immediately contiguous with it.[125] This certainly confirms that the Decree cannot have been the subject of the mission from James. At the same time, however, it is highly significant that the stipulations of the decree are taken precisely from those passages of the Pentateuch that legislate for Gentiles living in the land of Israel. Richard Bauckham has effectively demonstrated that the prohibitions of the decree are precisely those that in Leviticus 17–18 apply to *Gentiles* living 'in the midst of' (בתוך) the house of Israel.[126]

And secondly, it could be that Paul understood his task in no less geographic terms than did James. Even the pre-Christian Paul's intervention in Damascus may be subject, *ceteris imparibus*, to comparable reasoning about the Land. Both cities were just inside the Scriptural *Eretz Israel*, as is reasonably clear also from the status of Damascus in the Dead Sea Scrolls.[127] For a self-declared nationalist ('zealot', indeed) like Saul of Tarsus,[128] the integrity of polity and practice was essential if observant Jewish life in the Land was not to be compromised. Outside the Land, practices like the Sabbath year, tithes or purity were possible at best in a very partial

---

[124]Cf. Horbury 1986; Bauckham 1995:423. Note also *Ep. Apos.* 30.

[125]Note, however, that Paul and Barnabas are depicted in Acts 16.1–4 as taking the Decree beyond Cilia into Galatia: to Derbe, Lystra and Iconium. In 21.25, James evidently assumes that the Decree applies to *all* Gentile believers.

[126]Bauckham 1995:459–61; see also the Targumic background, as highlighted by Wehnert 1997:219–38; and cf. p. 167 and n. 95 below.

[127]'The land of Damascus' is outside 'the land of Judah' but is not obviously in 'exile' or outside Israel. See e.g. CD 6.5 par. 4QD^a 3.ii.20–21; 4QD^d 2.12; cf. *Tg.* Zech 9.1.

[128]See Phil 3.5–6; Gal 1.13–14; cf. Rom 10.2; also Acts 9.1–2. The 'zealot' dimension of the pre-Christian Paul is explored e.g. in J. Taylor 1998; cf. Hengel 1991:69–71 and *passim*.

manner: Jews arriving in the Land from abroad, for example, were by definition unclean, just as Gentile land was unclean.[129] Within the Land, however, a life by the biblical purity laws was feasible and appropriate caution could be exercised. James and Saul of Tarsus had very different methods and reasons for their respective interventions in the Jewish Christian communities in Antioch and Damascus; but both were arguably motivated by their concern for national redemption.

Despite brief mentions in Acts 15.41 and Gal 1.21 we have no reason to think that Paul ever regarded areas of Palestine, Syria or Cilicia to be specifically his mission field for taking the gospel to the Gentiles. He seems to found no churches there, even in his native Tarsus.[130] And despite his claim in Rom 15.19 to have begun his ministry 'from Jerusalem', there is little evidence of any extended activity in these regions. Apart from Antioch, Paul shows remarkably little interest in the churches in any of the other Gentile cities in the Land of Israel.[131] At the same time, as Rainer Riesner has argued, it may be that Paul operated with a geographical understanding of the Gentile world that derived from the prophecy of Isaiah 66.19, interpreted to denote a Gentile mission field beginning with Tarsus and arching from there via Asia Minor through the Greek islands to Spain (הָאִיִּים הָרְחֹקִים, 'the distant islands').[132]

4. At Antioch, the differences between James and Paul were more halakhic than theological, and had been exacerbated by the Jerusalem Council.

Nothing in Luke or Paul explicitly suggests that James had fundamental *soteriological* disagreements with Paul, or that his mission was anti-Pauline in intent. Of course, it would be unwise to assume that theology and halakhah could ever be entirely uncoupled. To

[129]Cf. e.g. Safrai 1983:206–7; Klawans 1995; Tomson 1990:228–9, following G. Alon.

[130]Note, however, Acts 15.41, which assumes his 'strengthening' of existing churches. Riesner 1998:266 sees Tarsus mainly as 'an ideal point of departure' for missionary activity to the north and west.

[131]Note Acts 16.1 (Syria and Cilicia); 18.22 (Caesarea), 21.3–9 (Tyre, Acco, Caesarea), though these all seem to be passing visits to churches Paul did not found. It could be worth speculating if this is why Paul's letters to Asia Minor, Greece and Rome remain silent about the Decree, without contradicting its substance.

[132]Riesner 1994:213–25. See also Scott 1995:151–9 and *passim* on the influence of Genesis 10 in defining Paul's view of his mission field; he is one of the few scholars to recognize that a potential dispute over the boundaries of the Land might be involved, although he does not explore this further (note pp. 158–9). Others have in the past proposed a straightforwardly territorial interpretation of the Jerusalem agreement, but this is rightly dismissed in Murphy-O'Connor 1996:142–3. On Spain as the end of the world, see Neubauer 1868:417.

some degree, the one inevitably informs the other; and all the evidence plausibly implies significant differences of emphasis, approach and interpretation of the theology that Paul shared with Peter and James. Indeed, despite their joint affirmation of the Gentile mission, we shall see that their underlying *ecclesiological* assumptions may well have differed considerably (pp. 81–2 below).

Nevertheless, it is important that Paul's rebuke of Peter in Gal 2.14–21(?) clearly stresses common ground far more than differences—his ἡμεῖς (vv.15–17) must include not only Peter, but by implication James as well.[133] In other words, theological differences between them can undoubtedly be identified, but the explicit sticking point of the confrontation at Antioch is halakhic: 'You are a Jew, yet you have been living like a Gentile, not like a Jew. How can you compel Gentiles to live like Jews?' (Gal 2.14).

In the area of halakhah, then, there are obvious disagreements between James and Paul. While the influence of Jesus may be primary, I would venture the suggestion that James is closer to a number of positions attributed to R. Eliezer ben Hyrcanus, both about the halakhah of *Eretz Israel* and about the extent to which one could trust Gentiles not to commit idolatry.[134] If James did regard Antioch as part of the Land, issues of purity would matter more literally there than in the Diaspora, where purity concerns were difficult to enforce consistently.[135] Although Gentiles might not attract impurity in relation to the biblical laws about food or corpse impurity,[136] they and their land were regarded as effectively impure by virtue of being tainted with idolatry and the associated immorality.[137]

By contrast, the churches of Antioch and the Pauline mission presumed the intention of Gentiles to be free from idolatry unless expressly stated otherwise. Even Paul, of course, instructs his churches not to eat with Christian idolaters (1 Cor 5.11 συνεσθίειν) or to consume meat in cases where the supplier's idolatrous intention is explicit (1 Cor 10.28–29[138]). It seems plausible that Paul would

---

[133]It would admittedly be worth re-examining James 2 in this connection, but that chapter's polemics can best be understood as addressing the way in which an Antiochene or Pauline type of soteriology had been abused in certain circles.

[134]In this connection it is interesting to note the rabbinic tradition of R. Eliezer's conversation with Jacob of Kefar Sikhnin about a logion of Jesus, in *t. Ḥul.* 2.24.

[135]Cf. Safrai 1983:207, 'Full Jewish life can only be practiced in Israel, not only because of the precepts which could only be fulfilled there, but because those who dwell in foreign lands live in perpetual defilement, with no possibility of acheiving [*sic*] purification.'

[136]Cf. Klawans 1995.

[137]See Tomson 1990:222–36; Klawans 1997, 1998; Safrai 1983:206–7, following G. Alon.

[138]On the halakhic function of the term συνείδησις in 1 Cor 10 see Tomson 1990:208–16; cf. also pp. 158, 168 below.

also have differed from James on the applicability of *Eretz Israel* halakhah in Antioch. Was it part of the mission to Israel or part of the mission to 'those not under the Law' (1 Cor 9.21; cf. Gal 2.7–8)?

There is no evidence to support the frequent assumption, especially in German scholarship, that the Jewish Christians at Antioch church had simply abandoned Jewish observance in the interest of a 'law-free' Gentile mission.[139] As Dunn rightly points out, the phrase 'to live like a Gentile' in Gal 2.11 is an intra-Jewish taunt, relative to what it means to 'live like a Jew', and it does *not* imply a complete abandonment of all Jewish observance.[140]

The Jerusalem Council may well have created or at least aggravated this problem in the first place. Whether or not the Council produced the Apostolic Decree (and unlike many scholars I think this remains entirely plausible), the proceedings of Acts 15 and Galatians 2.1–10 fully validated a Gentile Christian mission. What they did not do was to address the resultant problems of polity and fellowship.

Paul's vision of Jews and Gentiles united by faith in Christ derived from Deutero-Isaiah and followed a halakhah in keeping with that ecclesiology, according to which 'all the nations' would be gathered in the last days (Isa 66.18–21).[141] Based perhaps on their interpretation of Jesus' own pattern of table fellowship (Rom 14.14; cf. Mark 7.19c), Paul and the Antiochene church had evidently come to adopt a relatively liberal purity halakhah that could accommodate the Gentiles. James's vision of the Gentiles, by contrast, derived from Amos 9, if Acts 15 can be believed.[142] For him, the messianic

---

[139]So again recently Hengel & Schwemer 1997:197, according to whom the church at Antioch had no significant contact with synagogues, circumcision and ritual commandments having lost their significance. (The authors do not tell us how they know any of this.) Even Jewish Christians 'will at first have circumcised their own children, simply to avoid the charge of apostasy.... However, in common with Gentile Christians they will have dispensed with the observance of ritual regulations, while following them in dealing with Jews who observed the law strictly.' The only justification offered is the dubious assurance that 'this basic attitude again goes back to the preaching of Jesus, for whom the commandment to love pushed the ritual law into the background' (p. 198, although they acknowledge that 'critical of the law' might more appropriately characterize Paul's position than 'law-free'). On the latter claim about Jesus, see Chapters 1–3 above; cf. also Bauckham 1998a.

[140]Dunn 1993:128, in criticism of H. D. Betz.

[141]The formulation of N. Taylor 1992:135 seems insufficiently precise: 'Paul took his stand on principle in a matter on which James, Peter, and Barnabas exercised pragmatism rather than dogma.'

[142]Acts 15.16–17: note the extensive discussion of this passage in Bauckham 1996. See also Chilton 1998:40–2, who suggests that James' interpretation of Acts 9.11 may share with that of Qumran (4Q174 3.10–13; CD 7.15–17) a dual concern in a messianic renewal that is at the same time a restoration of the Torah (note Acts 15.21; Jas 2.8).

redemption would indeed find its eschatological corollary in the Gentiles seeking the Lord (Acts 15.17; LXX Amos 9.12), but this carried no necessary implications for any sort of integrated polity.[143]

At the end of the day, there is perhaps nonetheless reason to think that the halakhic differences with James at Antioch were held at bay for the sake of the one gospel: what Paul rejects as reprehensible is not the conduct of James but that of Peter.

Conclusion

We have found evidence that religious and political considerations may have forced James's hand in his intervention at Antioch. It seems worth exploring the possibility that both the Jerusalem agreement and the subsequent dispute at Antioch may have had a territorial dimension. James is seen to interfere only here, but nowhere else in the areas of the Pauline mission, and neither in Galatians nor in Acts do we hear that James resisted Jewish–Gentile meal fellowship in any part of the Diaspora proper. James's action is consistent with the *political* desire if possible to secure a *modus vivendi* for the church in Jerusalem, and with a widely attested *religious* perspective in which Antioch would be understood in terms of the biblical dimensions of the Land promised to the Twelve Tribes, who had been the focus of Jesus' mission to Israel. This remains of course no more than a hypothesis, but it is one that may well account for the situation better than many of the more commonly proposed explanations.

James's intervention, Peter's accommodation and Paul's rigid refusal despite being in a minority of one, may each in its own way have contributed to the emergence of a separate group publicly known as *Christianoi* – Gentile believers in Christ whose public image could no longer be most obviously identified in association either with pagan cults or as sympathizers of the Jewish community.[144]

---

[143]Cf. similarly Chilton 1998:37–40.

[144]Hengel & Schwemer 1997:183 suggest that the emergence of a separate Gentile identity at Antioch may have been facilitated by the population's hardening anti-Jewish attitudes in the years 39–40, coinciding with Paul's arrival from Tarsus in the company of Barnabas. The same would presumably again be the case in 48, if Malalas 10.245 is correct. Whether or not Hengel is right on this point, any politically-motivated Gentile desire to distance themselves from the Jewish community after AD 40 might well have been reinforced for existing or prospective Gentile Christians by the events of Gal 2.12–13. (It remains the case, of course, that the evidence for strained Gentile Christian relations with the Jewish community at Antioch in the first and second centuries is very slender indeed.) Knox 1925:196 thinks that the decision to evangelize the Gentile world from Antioch was itself a direct result of the controversy in that city; but this seems unlikely in view of Gal 1.16–21.

Christianity may well owe its subsequent survival to the fact that it followed neither the Petrine and Jacobean nor indeed the Pauline stance at Antioch, but embraced both the former and the latter together as the apostolic foundation of the Church.[145]

---

[145]Cf. Holtz 1986:357. Despite Antioch, it was only Marcionite or Jewish Christian extremists who denied the 'catholic' belief that Peter and Paul later jointly laid the foundation of the church at Rome (so e.g. Irenaeus, *Haer.* 3.1.1, 3.3.1; cf. already *1 Clem.* 5.1–6).

PART TWO

Jewish and Christian Ethics
for Gentiles

5

NATURAL LAW IN SECOND TEMPLE JUDAISM

We move in Part Two of this book from the halakhah of Jesus and the Palestinian Jewish Christians to the formulation of Christian ethics for the new Gentile churches. What resources did first-century Judaism offer for a translation of Jewish morality to the wider Graeco-Roman world? And what was the role played by these traditions in the ethical teaching of the early Christian mission to Gentiles?

Broadly speaking, universal ethics in ancient Jewish thought can be discussed under two headings: positive law and 'natural' law. This distinction is somewhat arbitrary, and in any case there is a certain amount of overlap between the categories, as we shall see. Nevertheless, it is a useful distinction at least for descriptive purposes. Some texts argue for universal laws that God has simply revealed as such in the Torah. Others, however, emphasize the existence of laws whose universal validity is in keeping with perceived and agreed facts about the created order and the nature of human flourishing.

The former category is generally captured by the moral commands of Genesis 1–11, and more particularly by the laws for aliens in Leviticus 17–18 and other chapters in the Torah and the Prophets. It is these these laws that eventually came to be expounded in the so-called Noachide Commandments of rabbinic literature, which will be the subject of Chapter 7.

The second category, by contrast, can be seen especially in certain Old Testament prophetic and wisdom passages that support moral propositions from a natural state of affairs. More specifically, we find it in certain later authors who developed such Jewish arguments in dialogue with the emerging Stoic doctrine of a divine law according to nature (νόμος φύσεως or the like). It is this latter category which will form the subject of the present chapter.

We shall need further clarification in due course (see also pp. 113–16 below). In the meantime, however, it will be appropriate to indicate some areas that on this definition are *not* here under discussion. I will postpone the subject of positive universal law and thus of the Noachide Commandments, except in passing.[1] Similarly, lines will need to be drawn in relation to wisdom literature: aside

---

[1] Note on this subject Chapter 7 below.

from the general observation that moral exhortations are here often drawn from observations of a natural state of affairs, I shall concentrate more specifically on cases where universal moral injunctions are derived from perceptions of the created order by functional analogy rather than merely poetic simile. Thus, 'Go to the ant, thou sluggard' (Prov 6.6 AV) is in: it offers an inductive analogy drawn from the behaviour of ants to human behaviour. On the other hand, 'Dead flies make perfume stink' (cf. Eccl 10.1) is out, since Qohelet applies this observation obliquely, by poetic simile, to the fact that folly can sometimes outweigh wisdom and honour.[2] Moreover, I shall here omit the more general comparisons or observations about the created order; our interest is in natural law and not in 'natural theology' or 'natural revelation'.[3] 'The heavens declare the glory of God' is arguably a true statement about the created order; nevertheless, it does not directly address the issue here at hand. The concern here is not epistemology but ethics derived from nature (though of course the two are sometimes closely linked in the area of apologetics).

The Old Testament

We begin with some basic observations about the Old Testament. Three reasons may be offered to account for the relative importance assigned to this section in a study of the Second Temple period. First, and at the risk of some controversy, one might well argue that the majority, though by no means all, of the texts here cited, do indeed date from the post-exilic period in their canonical form, and are therefore perfectly relevant to a study of Second Temple Judaism. Secondly, even the pre-exilic elements of the Bible were part of what was arguably one of the most important Jewish documents in the Second Temple period. And thirdly, it will become clear in the course of this chapter that post-biblical Jewish views on natural law are *in nuce* already anticipated in the Torah.

---

[2]Von Rad's discussion (1957:422–3) of correspondence in wisdom literature cites examples of both kinds, but without drawing the distinction. Prov 25.23; 26.20; 27.17, 20 are not really functional analogies; Eccl 13.1 may come close. Going beyond the realm of ethics, a good illustration of 'poetic simile' from the Psalms is Ps 42.1 ('As a deer longs for flowing streams, so my soul longs for you, O God'). A particularly interesting form of the teleological argument for the existence of God in Ps 94.9 is based on 'functional analogy': 'He who planted the ear, does he not hear? He who formed the eye, does he not see?'

[3]On natural theology in the Bible, see e.g. Barr 1993.

Introductory Observations

Without being side-tracked on peripheral questions, it is worth recalling some general characteristics of the ancient Near Eastern thought world, before going on to the more specific considerations governing Old Testament moral thinking about creation.

Henri Frankfort comments on the much greater immediacy with nature that was the universal experience of ancient civilizations: society and human moral agency were for them always imbedded in community, and intimately dependent upon nature and cosmic forces.[4] For the ancients, nature is by no means inanimate or dumb, as much of Western civilization has supposed ever since the Renaissance. Instead, it speaks with a voice that makes powerful claims of allegiance not only in regard to human self-understanding, but also in the area of practical conduct.

In Old Testament and Jewish thought, more specifically, God and his creation never ultimately speak with two distinct voices. Although of course it is true that ancient Israel had no abstract concept of 'nature' or of the 'cosmos',[5] God's voice is clearly heard both in creation and in the Torah, and the two are fundamentally related. And while there is thus, significantly, no 'law of nature' terminology as describing a reality distinct from the law of God, the Hebrew world view does operate on the assumption that all creation expresses God's law and moral purpose, and all of God's law is law according to nature.

This is clear as early as the account of Gen 1–11, where (after the initial state of *tohu wabohu*, 1.2) there is really never any ἀνομία, any 'lawless moment': everything proceeds according to God's command. As soon as he is created, Adam receives a divine command about his relation with the created order (Gen 2.16–17). At the same time, however, the serpent's invitation to 'become like God' constitutes a powerful warning both about the presence of evil in creation, and perhaps about its innate potential for idolatry in particular. The serpent's lie is a lie about nature: idolatry denies the

---

[4]'The world appears to primitive man neither inanimate nor empty but redundant with life; and life has individuality, in man and beast and plant, and in every phenomenon which confronts man – the thunderclap, the sudden shadow, the eerie and unknown clearing in the wood, the stone which suddenly hurts him when he stumbles while on a hunting trip. Any phenomenon may at any time face him, not as "It", but as "Thou". In this confrontation, "Thou" reveals its individuality, its qualities, its will. "Thou" is not contemplated with intellectual detachment; it is experienced as life confronting life, involving every faculty of man in a reciprocal relationship. Thoughts, no less than acts and feelings, are subordinated to this experience' (Frankfort 1949:14).
[5]Von Rad 1957:424.

natural ordinance that God is God and man is man. As early as the covenant with Noah, the patterns of creation are said to reflect the faithfulness of God and demand a clear and corresponding moral respect from humanity in terms of the protection of life (Gen 9.1–17). God's creation of human beings makes them inherently sacrosanct, so that to take their life is to contradict their God-given nature.[6] Both Cain and Lamech are guilty of such contradiction: Abel's blood, we hear, 'cries out from the earth' (Gen 4.10). The idolatrous intention (Gen 11.4) of the Tower of Babel, finally, closes the narrative of Gen 1–11 with another warning against man trying to become God.

The inclusion in the Psalter of 'nature psalms' like 19, 29, 33 and 147 indicates that God's word in nature was considered a corollary and extension of his word in the Torah.[7] Thus, what might be called 'laws of nature' in the Psalms are not considered in either impersonal or Deistic fashion as in Stoicism, but they are the dependent and personal word of the Creator, indeed specifically of the God of Israel. The laws of the universe are not the independent edicts of autonomous nature but the direct corollary of God's sending forth his word to the earth.

For the Old Testament it is always the Lord who remains the lawgiver, and not some cosmic competitor.[8] In view of the problem of evil, apocalyptic literature later adopted a potentially more dualistic perspective on creation, but for the majority of the Second Temple period the idea of God's sovereignty over the created order prevailed unchallenged.

Following on from this more general perspective on the matter, we now turn to a number of passages from each of the three parts of the Hebrew canon.

The Torah

As we have seen, at several points even prior to the giving of the Law at Sinai, the biblical text seems to make allowance for moral principles that correspond to 'the way things are', rather than being derived from a specific positive command of God. Corruption, violence and wickedness are repeatedly cited as intrinsic justification for the Flood (Gen 6.5, 11–13). Dinah's brothers are outraged at her

---

[6]Thus e.g. J. Barton 1979:3; cf. Gehman 1960:111–12.

[7]See Greidanus 1985:42; cf. Kraus 1978:958 (the דבר that controls nature has become known to Israel in the revelation of the דברים).

[8]Horst 1961:249 speaks of the Old Testament's 'Yahwizing of natural law'. Cf. further Greidanus 1985:51.

rape on the simple grounds that 'such a thing ought not to be done' (Gen 34.7). Similar appeals to self-evident standards of morality are found elsewhere in the Old Testament (e.g. Abimelech in Gen 20.3–4 [cf. Deut 22.22–27], 20.9; Tamar in 2 Sam 13.12) and may well imply the acceptance of an unwritten, quasi-natural law.[9] One could even point to the remarkable role played by Jethro as a jurisprudential advisor to Moses in Exodus 18.[10]

The Pentateuchal laws themselves give every impression of being positive law in the straightforward sense. The vast majority of them are prefaced by a formula like, 'The LORD spoke to Moses, saying ...'. There is no attempt, and no intention, to represent this legislation as anything other than divine in origin. Nevertheless, as James Barr points out, in terms not of form but of substance many of them show a certain organic indebtedness either to the laws of surrounding nations (e.g. in the Covenant Code, Exod 21–23) or to the dictates of common sense (Barr would include much of the Decalogue) – thereby demonstrating their relevance to the natural law tradition.[11] Beyond the examples cited by Barr, even the Deuteronomic blessings and curses attached to the renewal of the covenant in Deut 27–28 might be interpreted in these terms. Nevertheless, this reading of the laws 'against the grain' tends of course to play down Scripture's *internal* emphasis on the Sinaitic covenant as positive legislation, which is significant for our purposes of determining the Jewish idea of natural law.

The Prophets

It is, however, in the prophets that we perhaps come closest to a biblical notion of law according to nature. Here is not the place to resolve the old scholarly puzzle about the chronological and socio-logical relationship between the composition of the Law and that of the Prophets.[12] Suffice it to say that the connection is a complex one even in the post-exilic texts; and prophetic moral instruction, more often than not, tends to appeal to authorities other than the Law of Moses.

Of particular significance to our subject here is the work of John

[9]Cf. Gehman 1960:113.

[10]See further Barr 1990:12.

[11]Cf. Barr 1990:17, 'There are ... cases which on the surface appear as revealed law and are so expressed, but where the actual content makes very good sense if we think of it as derived from the social experience of the community.'

[12]On this subject see e.g. Zimmerli 1963; Clements 1965; and the classic work of Wellhausen 1905.

Barton, who has demonstrated the prevalence, especially in the prophets, of a pertinent notion of 'poetic justice'. Taking up a suggestion of C. S. Rodd about Genesis 18.25 ('Shall not the Judge of all the earth judge justly?'), Barton concludes,

The very possibility of asking the question does seem to indicate that men may obtain their moral norms not just from what God chooses to reveal, but from the perception of some ethical principle inherent in the way things are: from a socio-logical perspective, we might say by the projection on to the universe of moral principles drawn from the consensus view of the society of which the storytellers form a part.[13]

Barton would assign to this category a good deal of the moral teaching in Isaiah, beginning with the opening indictment against Israel's unnatural rebellion (1.2–3): 'Hear, O heavens, and listen, O earth; for the Lord has spoken: I reared children and brought them up, but they have rebelled against me. The ox knows its owner, and the donkey its master's crib, but Israel does not know, my people do not understand.' A similar case is the woes in chapter 5 and elsewhere (e.g. 29.16) against those who 'call evil good and good evil, who put darkness for light and light for darkness, who put bitter for sweet for bitter' (5.20). There is a sustained polemic even in later parts of Isaiah against the unnaturalness of sin, and the folly of idolatry in particular (J. Barton 1979:5–6): this sin is lampooned as a kind of 'cosmic nonsense', which twists the sane perspective on the cosmos that would persuade humanity to acknowedge and revere the one true God (J. Barton 1979:7). This same kind of 'cosmic nonsense' argument prevails in a good many other prophetic passages, whether about Israel's sin or Gentile idolatry (see also Deut 4.28). Amos 6.12 asks, 'Do horses run on rocks? Does one plow the sea with oxen? But you have turned justice into poison and the fruit of righteousness into wormwood.'

This argument from the 'unnaturalness' of sin is not strictly phrased in terms of natural law. Thus in the last mentioned example, the running of horses on the rock provides only a limited analogy to the turning of justice into poison. Nevertheless, the argument condemns the corruption of what is perceived and acknowledged to be a healthy state of nature. There is assumed to be a shared perception of God-given physical and moral order in the cosmos, to which humanity owes allegiance.[14]

[13]J. Barton 1979:4–5; cf. Rodd 1972:137–9.

[14]Sometimes this same argument about natural justice can also be applied more specifically to the positive revelation given to Israel: Jer 8.7 uses this familiar argument in lamenting, 'Even the stork in the heavens knows its times; and the turtledove, swallow and crane observe the time of their coming; but my people do not know the ordinances of the LORD.'

Similar arguments are found throughout the prophets, some explicit and others rather more subtle. Perhaps the most widely discussed passage in this regard is Amos 1–2. The prophet here denounces Israel's neighbour countries, not for their failure to keep the Torah (only Israel is so judged, 3.2), but for their transgressions against an assumed international consensus on just warfare and the treatment of innocent civilians.[15] While the argument is again not strictly based on nature, the passage begins by showing the wrath of God on human sin manifested in the withering of shepherds' pasture on Mount Carmel (1.2). Amos 1.9 explicitly charges Tyre with neglect of the 'covenant of brotherhood' – i.e. clearly a principle rooted in the nature of human kinship and relationship. Despite their basis in convention rather than positive law, these principles evidently carry a divine sanction.[16] They relate arguably to the nations overstepping the boundaries of what is recognizably just and fitting in the conduct of human affairs. Where human beings dispense with the constraints of equity in the greedy pursuit of power, they are by implication guilty of unnatural hubris and must face the fire of their Creator's wrath.

I cannot here deal with all the related passages,[17] but before moving on it is perhaps worth drawing special attention to a pre-exilic passage which, in a kind of reverse natural law argument, explicitly links the sins of Israel with the ecological disasters that have befallen the land:

There is no faithfulness or loyalty, and no knowledge of God in the land. Swearing, lying, and murder, and stealing and adultery break out; bloodshed follows bloodshed. Therefore the land mourns, and all who live in it languish; together

[15]See J. Barton 1980:55; also Horst 1961:241–2. It is of course true that the Deuteronomic school in particular did endorse the wholesale destruction of Canaanite towns, e.g. Num 21.1–3; Deut 3.6; 7.1–6; 25.17–19; Josh 8.1–29. Nevertheless, it appears that prophetic perspectives on the ḥrm tradition were rather more nuanced and critical, at times even turning it against their own people: note e.g. Hos 1.4 (on which see e.g. G. I. Davies 1992:54–5 and cf. 2 Kgs 10); Isa 43.28; Jer 25.8–9. Note Saul's 'bloodguilt' in relation to the Gibeonites, 2 Sam. 21.1. See further Soggin 1990; Horbury 1985 helpfully discusses post-biblical interpretations of this tradition.

[16]Pace J. Barton, e.g. 1980:43; cf. also Houston 1982.

[17]Certain other texts similarly indict the Gentiles for their iniquity, blasphemous insolence and gratuitous violence, sometimes linking such judgement with ominous signs of upheaval in the cosmos (e.g. Isa 13.11–13, Ezek 28–29, etc.; see further pp. 95–6 below on Dan 4.28–32).

In a different vein, it could be argued that the indictment against the sacrifice of blemished animals in Mal 1, while undoubtedly influenced by the laws of the Torah, seems to appeal more directly to some inherent standard of right and wrong: 'Try presenting that to your governor; will he be pleased with you or show you favour? says the Lord of hosts' (1.9). Even the Gentiles, by implication, do not do such a thing: for among them God's name is great and 'in every place incense is offered to my name, and a pure offering' (1.11).

with the wild animals and the birds of the air, even the fish of the sea are perishing. (Hos 4.1–3)

Scholars have repeatedly pointed out the close connection between the Decalogue and the offences here listed by Hosea; in this case at least, then, one may well wish to posit an early natural law connection in the Hebrew understanding of the Ten Commandments.[18]

The Writings

The third part of the canon opens up a number of additional literary forms in which the natural law argument finds expression. These include above all the wisdom literature and related material in the Psalms.

The book of Job is often adduced in this regard, as being particularly clear in its use of moral arguments from the created order. Two contrary but nevertheless characteristic examples may suffice for now. Job's friend Zophar represents a typical wisdom sentiment when he concludes from observation that the pursuit of wickedness is unprofitable: 'Do you not know this from of old, ever since mortals were placed on earth, that the exulting of the wicked is short, and the joy of the godless is but for a moment?' (20.4–5). Of course, a degree of moral ambivalence arises for Job and for the Psalmists from the corresponding lament that the wicked do in fact seem to prosper while the righteous suffer. This emerging recognition of the problem of theodicy turned out to be an important contributing factor in paving the way for a transcendent eschatology of judgement and resurrection, a development that gathered pace from about the third century BC. For present purposes, however, the ambivalence of Zophar's simple consequentialist argument from nature means that it increasingly gives way to a more ethnocentric, nationalized view of wisdom in which creation attests the Torah.[19]

Job 31.13–15, on the other hand, is a powerful moral argument based on the analogy of relationships. Job asks,

If I have rejected the cause of my male or female slaves, when they brought a

---

[18]Nevertheless, it may be significant to point out that this sort of easy connection occurs here in what most would regard as an eighth-century document, and thus in the only one of the passages under discussion which can be clearly dated before the exile. This may be relevant to the difficult redaction critical position of the Decalogue within its literary context in Exodus. But it also may relate to J. Barton's apparent belief (1979:8) that the OT texts of 'poetic justice' are chiefly pre-exilic.

[19]Occasional exceptions include e.g. Sir 13.1 ('Whoever touches pitch gets dirty').

complaint against me; what then shall I do when God rises up? When he makes injury, what shall I answer him? Did not he who made me in the womb make them? And did not one fashion us in the womb?

Two points are being made: one, the master should do to the slave as he would like to be treated by God who is his own master. The second point, however, is based on the nature of creation: our self-evident human equality of standing before God requires us to treat all other human beings equitably and with fairness.

In another setting it would be desirable to discuss especially the relevance of the book of Proverbs for the natural law question. Nevertheless, my earlier point bears repeating: despite its unselfconscious matter-of-factness about the world, much of Israelite wisdom literature offers only the complex counsel of experience rather than moral principles derived from the created order by inductive analogy.[20] It is the character of the vast majority of Israelite proverbs that the stable door is, as it were, locked only after the horse has bolted.[21] The playfully descriptive element predominates and is rarely developed into the prescriptive, so that there is no embarrassment even about completely contradictory insights.[22] The overtly theoretical and harmonizing intention of later wisdom literature develops only gradually with the post-exilic rise of the scribal schools.

Our section on the Writings concludes with two little vignettes: one from Daniel and one from the Psalms, each illustrating an important aspect of the post-exilic development of the natural law argument. The book of Daniel contains a powerful symbolic argument against the unnaturalness of pagan idolatry, a theme repeatedly encountered in the prophets and carried over into post-canonical Jewish literature. The second dream of King Nebuchadnezzar in chapter 4 follows the episode of the three young men thrown into the furnace for refusing to worship the king's golden image. As predicted in this dream, interpreted by Daniel, and finally announced by a heavenly voice, a decree of the heavenly Watchers changes the king's mind and manner for seven years (Dan 4.16, 25, 32; cf. LXX 4.33ᵃ; 4QPrNab) from that of a human being to that of an animal, in order that he (4.25, 32) and all human beings

---

[20]See von Rad 1957:415–39. Cf. p. 419: 'Die Weisheit tastet die Erscheinungswelt auf Ordnungen hin ab, läßt dann aber die jeweilige Erfahrung durchaus in ihrer Besonderheit stehen.' See also von Rad 1970, chapters 7 and 9. J. Barton 1999:17 characterizes wisdom ethics as 'advice on how to get on, rather than training in the pursuit of the virtuous life'. For him, it is in the end to the OT *narratives* that one must turn for what he calls an 'implicit' virtue ethic (ibid., pp. 18–20).

[21]Cf. von Rad 1957:418 and n. 10, citing A. Jolles.

[22]Von Rad 1957:420.

(4.17) may learn 'that the Most High is sovereign over the kingdom of mortals, and gives it to whom he will'. Nebuchadnezzar's offence, clearly, is his idolatrous megalomania, as manifested both in his setting up of the golden statue, and in the more immediate context by his wanton arrogance: 'Is this not magnificent Babylon, which I have built as a royal capital by my mighty power and for my glorious majesty?' (Dan 4.30).[23] Deluded disregard for his merely human nature leads to a punishment in kind: viz., the manifest perversion of that very humanity into the mind of a man who is alienated from human society and in all his behaviour like an animal (Dan 4.33).[24]

My last Old Testament illustration involves just a couple of observations about Psalm 19. The dating and origin of this Psalm are widely disputed, but for present purposes I suggest that like Psalms 1 and 119 it expresses the emerging Torah piety of the post-exilic period. In its canonical form at least, the Psalmist's celebration of the perfection of the glory of God revealed in creation is matched and surpassed by the even greater perfection of the Torah. The two main sections of the poem are linked by the phrase, 'and nothing is hid from its heat' (v. 7 Heb.),[25] as well as by the repeated imagery of the Torah's shining light (v. 9 Heb.).[26] And it is precisely this easy

---

[23]It is worth comparing this sentiment with that reported of Herod's son Agrippa I in Acts 12.22.

[24]The LXX elaborates on Nebuchadnezzar's chastisement in several interesting ways. Thus the voice announces that the angels are to persecute the King during his madness, and his arrogance is punished by being bound while his opulent house is given to another (4.32). Of particular relevance to our topic is the idea that his flesh and heart are changed; he walks around naked with the wild animals and is subject to visions and hallucinations (4.33[b]). His restoration to sanity, as in Qumran's Prayer of Nabonidus (4QPrNab), is here explicitly linked to the forgiveness of his sins, which he receives when he prays to the great God of gods and King of kings (4.34; cf. 36). He is admonished that the glory (δόξα: cf. 4.29–30 with v. 34) belongs to God, and is only then restored to his rightful station (and his δόξα, v. 36), in which he now faithfully serves God and all his holy ones (v. 37[a]). This is contrasted explicitly with the impotent gods of the nations, who can neither kill nor make alive nor do anything significant (ibid.).

The theme is closely related to the idea that contempt of creation results in the corruption of humanity's own nature in the image of the very thing they craved. Anticipated in Hosea (9.10), this theme comes to fruition in later Jewish writings and seems to underlie the important natural law passages about idolatry and immorality for example in Wisd 13–14 (with 15.6: 'Lovers of evil things and fit for such objects of hope are those who either make or desire or worship them') and Romans 1.19–32. See also Wisd 11.16: 'One is punished by the very things by which one sins'; 12.23, 27; 2 Kgs 17.15 ('they went after false idols and became false, etc.'); and cf. Ps. 115.8.

[25]Cf. Craigie 1983:183.

[26]V. 9:מאירת עינים; for בר used of the sun as 'bright' rather than merely 'pure' (NRSV, etc.) cf. LXX τηλαυγής; also Cant 6.10. On the widespread Jewish idea of the Torah as a light, see also Bockmuehl 1990:28 n. 29. See Cooper 1994, who also discusses David Qimḥi (c. 1160–1235) et al.

It has repeatedly been pointed out that the twin emphases of the Psalm could be seen as a meditation on the themes of Gen 1–3. Clines 1974 argues that each of the attributes of the Law of the Lord contributes an allusion to the Tree of Knowledge. See also Craigie 1983:182–3.

juxtaposition of Torah and creation[27] which prepares the way for the overwhelming assumption in Hellenistic Jewish writers that the Torah is self-evidently a law in full accordance with nature, indeed the most perfect expression of such a law. It is in this Psalm, then, that we get a glimpse of what became the mainstream view of natural law in Second Temple Judaism. This view is neither that there is a law of nature given in addition to the law of the Torah, nor that there is nothing but the Torah. Instead, creation itself demands life in accordance with the will of the Creator, and the Torah, or at least the principles it embodies, are the most perfect expression of a law that is in accordance with creation rightly understood.

Apocrypha and Pseudepigrapha

We come, then, to the vast body of post-biblical Jewish literature. Here, even more than for the Old Testament, my selection of texts and issues must be restricted and indeed to some extent arbitrary. Three further sections make up the remainder of this chapter. The first, 'Apocrypha and Pseudepigrapha', is admittedly something of an ill-defined grab-bag of writings. It has come to be used in the scholarly community for those Jewish religious writings of the post-biblical period that were transmitted over the centuries primarily in Christian circles. Next, I shall offer a brief and in some ways equally heterogeneous section on the Dead Sea Scrolls and early rabbinic literature. Finally, Philo and Josephus come into view not only as the two most prolific Jewish writers of the period, but also as the ones who make the most substantial contribution to our subject.

The Apocrypha

We come first to the Apocrypha, i.e. the additional books included in the LXX but not in the Hebrew canon. It is here for the first time in the LXX that we find use of the Greek word φύσις to express the idea of 'nature', though most of these texts do not bear directly on

---

[27]Similarly anticipated in Deut 4.6–8; and cf. e.g. Ps. 119.89–91, 96. LXX Ps. 118 (= 119).89–91 offers an explicit verbal parallel: just as the word (and truth, v. 90) of God *abides* for ever, so the earth *abides* and 'the day' *abides* at his command (3x διαμένει). The parallel between Torah and nature is as in Psalm 19.

Barr 1990:16–17 points out that the 'Torah' of Ps. 19, or indeed of Ps. 119.89–91, is never identified as a *book* of the Law. This is indeed so, although there can be little doubt as to how Second Temple Judaism came to understand these Psalms. Note also that the 'Torah' of Ps. 119 can be declared orally (v. 13) *and* contains wonderful things to be observed with the *eyes* (v. 18). See further Levenson 1987.

our subject. I shall restrict myself to highlighting just a few of the most relevant passages.

Like several other Apocrypha, the book of Tobit contains instructions of a generally sapiential character, such as Tobit's instructions to his son in chapter 4. Among these, the closest we come to a natural law argument is the negative formulation of the Golden Rule encountered in 4.15: 'What you hate, do not do to anyone.' From a basic state of affairs (everyone hates ill-treatment), a plausible inference is here adduced (everyone should refrain from mistreating others). This is not the only possible conclusion (affirmation of a pecking order would be another), but it is a legitimate analogical argument from the nature of human relations (as perceived by social consensus).

The book of Ben Sira is perhaps the apocryphal work most closely related to the genre of Old Testament wisdom. Thus, much of its advice is generally related to a reflection on nature, but without involving conscious inductive analogy or extrapolation for the realm of ethics. It is clear from Sir 42.15 – 43.33 and elsewhere that Ben Sira does have a kind of natural theology; like the book of Wisdom, indeed, he follows contemporary Hellenistic thought in stressing the cosmic universality of wisdom in nature.[28] Nevertheless, aside from a general doxological exhortation (40.30) there is no attempt to deduce a universal morality from the created order. What is more, for Ben Sira the picture is further complicated by the fact that much of his teaching can in fact be seen as indebted to the Torah, even as a form of Torah interpretation. This at any rate is clear from his own views about the Torah and its exposition (e.g. Sir 24 and 39), and it is further stressed by the translator's insistence in the Prologue that his grandfather wrote on the basis of his expertise in 'the Law, the Prophets and the other ancestral books'. There is, moreover, a well-known emphasis on priestly concerns (e.g. 7.29–31; 50.1–21). Like Baruch (4.1) or Mishnah *'Abot* (6.7); but unlike the earlier wisdom literature (incl. e.g. Ahiqar[29]), Ben Sira stresses that the pursuit of wisdom must in the first instance be concerned with Torah (9.15 etc.). Wisdom does rule over creation (and in this sense the Torah is clearly 'according to nature', but her rule is explicitly focused in her home in Zion (Sir 24.3–12). Ben Sira is a Torah scholar first and foremost, and thus resembles the rabbis after him more than the prophets before him. We find little interest here in apologetics or international ethics.

---

[28]See Sir 24 and note the discussion in Hengel 1973:288–90.
[29]See Lindenberger 1985:485–6 and *passim*.

Matters are different for the Wisdom of Solomon, composed perhaps in Alexandria, which appears from the very beginning to make a more public and international appeal. 'Love righteousness, you rulers of the earth, think of the Lord in goodness and seek him with sincerity of heart' (Wisd 1.1; cf. 6.1–11). Ethics is emphatically international: 'Because the spirit of the Lord has filled the world, ... therefore those who utter unrighteous things will not escape notice, and justice ... will not pass them by' (1.7–8). The Epicurean perse-cutors of the suffering righteous in chapter 2 are condemned on the grounds of a universal morality, and the Torah is mentioned at most in passing (2.12?). Pseudo-Solomon is happy to describe right-eousness and morality in terms of virtue (ἀρετή : 4.1; 5.13; 8.7); indeed for the first time in Jewish literature this is defined in terms of the four classical Platonic virtues: wisdom 'teaches self-control and prudence, justice and courage' (8.7). Wisdom's teaching is, at the same time, explicitly linked with her intimate involvement in creation (7.15–22), so that virtue and nature are linked. Nevertheless, it is patently obvious from chapters 10–18 that Wisdom is first and foremost involved with the nation of Israel; as far as salvation history is concerned, her stance is distinctly partisan for the people of God. Indeed, where necessary she will overcome or alter the course of nature in the interest of redemption: it is not creation that saves but the Creator himself (16.7–8, 12, 26; 19.6–12, 18–22).

At the same time, it is highly significant that despite this partisan stance of wisdom, the moral content of her teaching remains firmly universal in both scope and rationale. Thus, idolatry is an irrational act contrary to nature, whether in Israel's worship of serpents and animals in the desert (11.15–16) or the pagan's adoration of the work of his own hands (13.10 – 14.31). The sins of the Canaanites are described so as to make them seem self-evidently evil and irrational by contemporary Hellenistic standards (12.4–5: 'merciless slaughter of children, ... sacrificial feasting on human flesh and blood'). Unrighteousness is folly; and as in the prophets, the worship of irrational animals (12.23–24; 15.18) and inanimate objects (13.10–19; 15.15–17) is seen to be a manifest nonsense by the very nature of creation: 'people are mortal, and therefore what they make is dead' (15.17; cf. *Letter of Aristeas* 134–6). In a poignant analogy from the Letter of Jeremiah, idols are 'like a scarecrow in a cucumber bed, which guards nothing' (70); and the twin stories of Bel and the Dragon similarly have Daniel poking fun at the worship of both animals and inanimate objects.

Going beyond this issue in a way that closely anticipates the argument of Romans 1, Wisdom 14 argues for an intrinsic and inevitable connection between idolatry and the resulting immorality of religion and life (14.22–29). False religion produces false and destructive lifestyles, and once again the author resorts to describing this immorality in terms that any contemporary Stoic or middle Platonist would have recognized as behaviour contrary to reason: pagan religious cults, murder, deceit, perjury, sexual debauchery, etc.

Finally, I may mention in passing 4 Maccabees, which is included as an appendix in the Slavonic Apocrypha. This work of the first century AD presents its message to fellow Diaspora Jews (18.1) in the language of Stoic philosophy: reason rules supreme over the emotions, and the classical virtues are exalted (1.1–6, 18 and *passim*). More specifically, the Jewish Torah is held up as the consummate expression of the commands of virtue and reason (1.34; 2.4–5, 23; etc.). The author of 4 Maccabees explicitly resists any attempt to define nature in such a way as to bypass the Law: when Antiochus taunts Eliezer for refusing to eat pork as a gift of nature (φύσις, 5.8), the saintly priest replies by affirming the primacy of the divine law with its teaching of the virtues (self-control, courage, justice and piety[30]). He turns Antiochus's argument on its head: if indeed the law is given by God, 'we know that in giving it the Creator sympathizes with us according to our nature'.[31] It is not nature that is the final arbiter over the Torah; instead, nature and Torah can be seen to correspond to each other, as both proceed from the same God.

The Pseudepigrapha

Post-canonical Jewish literature includes a remarkable number of works that could be described as apologetic in whole or in part. Given the biblical background we have established, as well as the emerging Greek philosophical trends to which we shall refer below, it is not surprising that 'natural law' arguments flourished in the period here in view.

Within the limitations of this chapter, it is impossible to do justice

---

[30]In Xenophon and sometimes in Philo, piety or religion replaces prudence as the fourth virtue. Note e.g. Philo, *Mos.* 2.216. The same notion that the Law teaches the classical virtues is widely found; in addition to Philo, see e.g. already Aristobulus in Eusebius, *Praep. Ev.* 13.13.8; cf. Tit 2.12.

[31]4 Macc 5.25: οἴδαμεν ὅτι κατὰ φύσιν ἡμῖν συμπαθεῖ νομοθετῶν ὁ τοῦ κόσμου κτίστης. NB the NRSV translation seems defective. Contrast H. Anderson 1985:550, 'We know that the creator of the world, in giving us the Law, conforms it to our nature'; similarly Urbach 1987:292.

to the wealth of available material. For our purposes I shall single out three documents of particular importance: the *Letter of Aristeas*, the *Testament of Naphtali*, and the sayings of Pseudo-Phocylides. Dating from around the same time as several of the Apocrypha we discussed, these documents provide important corroboration and development of the emerging natural-law arguments.

First, we turn to the *Letter of Aristeas*, probably written in the second century BC. In his description of the Jewish law, the author affirms the thesis that God has 'set down everything similarly in regard to natural reasoning [πρὸς τὸν φυσικὸν λόγον καθέστηκεν]' (143). Although fully defending the literal observance of the ritual laws, the *Letter of Aristeas* also insists that these laws have profoundly rational explanations and often a symbolic moral purpose (161–6 and *passim*). The work then proceeds on this assumption, in that the universal morality propounded at the banquet is offered by the wisdom of the Jewish scribes. Natural law, once again, is another way of stating that the Torah is in keeping with the facts of creation and, more importantly, vice versa.

The *Testaments of the Twelve Patriarchs* contain a host of moral teaching cast in universal language. Nevertheless, it would be a mistake to ignore this collection's repeated and usually exclusive address to Jews,[32] or indeed its explicit concern for Torah piety, including matters of ritual law.[33] Although in many ways typical of Jewish Hellenistic ethics, much of the instruction is not of direct relevance to our subject here. One passage in the *Testament of Naphtali*, however, stands out as providing a particularly clear moral analogy from creation:

Sun, moon and stars do not alter their order; thus you should not alter the Law of God by the disorder of your actions. The gentiles, because they wandered astray and forsook the Lord, have changed the order, and have devoted themselves to stones and sticks, patterning themselves after wandering spirits. But you, my children, shall not be like that: in the firmament, in the earth, and in the sea, in all the products of his workmanship discern the Lord who made all things, so that you do not become like Sodom, which departed from the order of nature. Likewise the Watchers departed from nature's order; the Lord pronounced a curse on them at the Flood. On their account he ordered that the earth be without dweller or produce.[34]

The argument here could hardly be clearer: the natural order,

[32]E.g. *Test. Dan* 5.5, 8; *Test. Naph.* 4.1; but see *Test. Sim.* 7.2, a Christian interpolation. The ethics in the *Testaments* may well be a kind of Jewish or Jewish Christian edification for proselytes.

[33]See e.g. Slingerland 1986:45–8, in criticism of an earlier article by Howard C. Kee.

[34]*Test. Naph.* 3.2–5 (trans. Kee 1983:812); for the sin of the Watchers, cf. their unnatural intercourse with women in *Test. Reub.* 5.6; 2 Pet 2.4; Jude 6.

perceived in creation, calls for certain orderly patterns of human behaviour, which are also in keeping with the Law of God. The preceding context in chapter 2 further explains that the divine order in the creation of humanity requires that one should 'do nothing in a disorderly manner, arrogantly, or at an inappropriate time'. While 3.1 warns against avarice and empty speech, 4.1 further condemns 'the wickedness of the Gentiles and the lawlessness of Sodom'. The Law of the Lord is in accordance with creation, and the perceptible pattern of creation is a pattern of moral meaning and significance.

A similar argument occurs in Pseudo-Phocylides, our third and final witness from the Pseudepigrapha.[35] Here, the orderly movements of heavenly bodies are taken as an argument against strife and envy:

> Do not envy (your) friends their goods, do not fix reproach (upon them). The heavenly ones also are without envy toward each other. The moon does not envy the much stronger beams of the sun, nor the earth the heavenly heights though it is below, nor the rivers the seas. They are always in concord. For if there were strife among the blessed ones, heaven would not stand firm.[36]

Creation itself suggests the Creator's desire for harmony rather than discord as most conducive to life on earth. The argument may seem banal, but its rationale is eminently relevant to our subject.

Two other examples from Pseudo-Phocylides may be adduced. Both are concerned with sex, the first with the licit and the second with the illicit sort. In good Jewish fashion (cf. e.g. *b. Yeb.* 61a–64a, etc.), the author enjoins marriage as part of the good order of creation: 'Do not remain unmarried, lest you die nameless. Give nature her due, you also, beget in your turn as you were begotten' (175–6). Creation is designed to survive by sexual reproduction, in which human beings therefore ought to play their part. As might already have been supposed on the basis of this argument, male and female homosexual behaviour is ruled out a few lines further on by the example of animal behaviour: 'Do not transgress with unlawful sex the limits set by nature. For even animals are not pleased by intercourse of male with male. And let women not imitate the sexual role of men' (190–2). The biological accuracy of this assertion is not here under discussion; suffice it to say that the argument from the *normal* pattern of animal sexuality was widespread in ancient Judaism and early Christianity,[37]

---

[35]Several of the other Pseudo-Greek poets are similarly relevant in this regard; see e.g. Attridge 1985:825–30.

[36]Ps.-Phoc., 75–9 (van der Horst 1985). On the subject of envy in similar universal contexts, cf. e.g. Tob 4.7, 16; Sir 14.10; also Rom 1.29.

[37]Cf. Philo *Abr.* 135; *Spec. Leg.* 2.50; Rom 1.27 on homosexuality; and *b. Šab.* 65a; *b. Yeb.* 76a on lesbianism.

even though occasional exceptions were known.[38] The normal teleology of nature confirms the Torah.

To close this section, it is appropriate to say a few words about the role of natural law in the Jewish apocalypses. For obvious reasons, one will not find in these documents very much of interest for our purpose: it is the visionaries' profound experience of alienation from the observable world of nature and history which leads them to turn to heavenly revelation in the first place. For the apocalyptists, the observable world itself has become profoundly hostile to faith, and its testimony to a just and provident Creator is no longer unambiguous. They manifest a deep sense of alienation between the present, visible experience and the ultimate reality of God. On the other hand, just as in the book of Job one finds an awareness of natural justice despite a frequent sense of moral gloom and alienation, so also many of the Apocalypses finally refuse to surrender to a completely dualistic cosmology. Their conception of the natural order, however, is divided between the evils and corruptions of this world and the vision of a tranquil and transformed creation in the heavenly realms. Led astray by fallen angelic powers who reveal unlawful secrets (e.g. *1 Enoch* 8–10), human evil here on earth causes untold devastation and oppression of the created world. In heaven, however, the tranquil motion of the stars joins the hosts of angels worshipping God in a setting of transcendent beauty, which foreshadows the redemption appointed to descend to earth. The apocalyptic visionaries are shown the sovereignty of God in the cosmological mysteries of heaven precisely because they are not available on earth. And yet, the very linkage of astronomical and meteorological observation with heavenly truth suggests the writers' unwillingness to surrender the idea that creation at least ought to, and in some cases does, embody the moral will of the Creator.[39]

The Dead Sea Scrolls and Early Rabbinic Literature

We come now to the shortest section of this chapter. Its very brevity is revealing, as neither the Dead Sea Scrolls nor rabbinic Judaism show a marked interest in questions of natural law. Centred as they are on conducting Torah study in the land of Palestine and in the Semitic languages of Palestine, their concern for philosophical and apologetic questions in the Hellenistic vein is virtually non-existent.

[38]Cf. Pendergraft 1992.
[39]Cf. further Bockmuehl 1990:33–5.

The Dead Sea Scrolls fix their interest narrowly and nationalisti-
cally on the positive revelation fully present in the Torah.

One finds no more than a handful of moral appeals to creation.
The most familiar and perhaps the clearest of these is the
Damascus Document's argument against divorce by appeal to the
Creation account, which shall serve as our sole example. CD 4.21
describes those who are 'twice caught in fornication by taking two
wives while they are both alive, whereas the principle of creation
is, 'Male and female he created them' [Gen 1.27]' (my translation).
While this does involve a moral reference to creation, it is nevertheless important to note that, just as in Jesus's use of the same
argument (Mark 10.5–9 par.), the decisive appeal is arguably to a
passage of Scripture rather than to a natural phenomenon –
though of course in this case the distinction may be negligible.[40]

The so-called 'Book of Mysteries' (1Q27) is also of interest. It
shows both a passionate affirmation of the universal validity of
justice and yet an equally firm scepticism about the practicality
of natural law: the Gentiles universally do not abide by it, and will
therefore fall under judgement.

Do not all nations (עמים) loathe sin? And yet, they all walk about under its influence.
Does not praise of truth come from the mouth of all nations (לאומים)? And yet, is
there perhaps one lip or one tongue which persists with it? What people would wish
to be oppressed by another more powerful than itself? Who would wish to be
sinfully looted of its wealth? And yet, which is the people not to oppress its
neighbour? Where is the people which has not looted [another] of its we[alth?]
(1Q27 1.i.9–11, *DSSSE*)

---

[40]Note also the absence of the usual tag (e.g. 'as it is written') identifying a Scripture
quotation.

Two recently published passages of a sapiential character may also be mentioned. The first
comes from a collection of proverbs that shows no signs of sectarian origin and therefore may
have circulated more widely: 'Just as lead melts, an unstable person cannot stand in fire'
(4Q424 1.5). Although this employs an appeal to creation, the argument is arguably strained
and in any case probably lies closer to a poetic simile than to a functional moral analogy.
Secondly, a curious esoteric wisdom text about the 'mystery of existence' has come to light,
which includes among other things an exhortation about honouring one's father and mother.
Here the reader is advised to serve his parents because they have guided him and God has
appointed them over him (4Q418 10.ii.18). The first reason given might be regarded as an
appeal to natural equity in the nature of human relationships. Dr T. H. Lim of Edinburgh
University suggests to me that a kind of reasoning from nature may also underlie the
regulations in 1QSa 1.7–19 about the activities appropriate to different stages of life, including
marriage at the age of 20 (1.10).

Horoscope-like texts such as 4Q186, 4Q318 or 4Q561 appeal to natural phenomena to
derive not moral but eschatological discernment. Berger 1972:526 cites the use of the phrase
משפט בריאתו in CD 12.15 as an expression of natural law; but its application to the appropri-
ateness of roasting or boiling locusts makes this rather implausible.

The striking resonance of this argument with such passages as Wisd 13–14 and Rom 1.18–32 certainly indicates the broad currency of such arguments in late Second-Temple Judaism. Nevertheless, it is clear that few if any specific conclusions can be drawn from this text for any constructive assessment of 'natural law' at Qumran.

Beyond that, a more general point of contact might be found in the Dead Sea sectarians' intense concern for calendrical matters. As early as the book of *Jubilees* (second cent. BC), the plea for a solar rather than lunar designation of months makes reference to the fact that the latter corrupts the regular course of the year, causing the festivals to fall on different days.[41] Even so, however, this insight into the calendar appeals explicitly to a positive divine commandment rather than to an observation of nature; indeed *Jubilees* laments the fact that the rest of Israel have been led astray by their diligent observation of the moon (*Jub.* 6.36). Other texts meriting further study might include 4Q185 and 4Q416–424. But even then, the Dead Sea texts seem on balance to manifest the sort of distaste for universal moral discourse that is the usual hallmark of reclusive sects.

Among the rabbis, explicit examples are also few and far between.[42] The Torah is God's exclusive gift to Israel, and it contains the only truths worth knowing (*m. 'Abot* 5.22). Rabbi Jacob said, 'If a man was walking by the way and studying and he ceased his study and said, 'How fine is this tree!' or 'How fine is this ploughed field!' the Scripture reckons it to him as though he was guilty against his own soul.'[43] This mindset is by and large blissfully unperturbed by questions like the philosophical justification of morality. Thus in one famous story the first-century Rabban Yohanan ben Zakkai, challenged by a pagan about the apparently magical practices prescribed in relation to the Red Heifer (Num 19), dismisses the man with a quasi-scientific explanation. However, when the pagan has left, the Rabban's disciples question their master about the inadequate answer he had given. His reply speaks volumes: 'The dead body does not really defile; the water does not really purify; but God has said, I have ordained an

---

[41]*Jub.* 6.32–38; cf. 1QS 1.14–15, 10.5; 1QH 20(= 12).5–9; see now also 4Q320, 4Q321, and 4Q325 (calculation of the solar priestly courses) and 4Q252 (on which see also Lim 1992).

[42]Urbach 1987:323 cites Felix Perles and Hermann Cohen in support of the (implausible?) idea that while rabbinic ethics is normally theonomous in formulation, the few apparent exceptions may be due to Hellenistic influence. More likely is perhaps the possibility mooted above: viz., that natural law reasoning cannot thrive in communities that retreat, by choice or force of circumstance, into a cultural ghetto.

[43]*M. 'Abot* 3.8, trans. H. Danby 1933; cf. 3.19.

ordinance, I have decreed a decree; it is not permitted to you to transgress it' (*Num. Rab.* 19.8; cf. *Tanḥ.* Ḥuqqat 26; *Pesiq. Rab Kah.* 4.7). Whether nature bears out the truth of the Law is neither here nor there: what matters is the divine commandment.

Ephraim Urbach writes that, in contrast to Hellenistic Judaism, for the Rabbis 'the Torah is not according to Nature';[44] they usually took the viewpoint of a revelational positivism that allowed them to be playfully nonchalant about instances where the Torah appeared to be contrary to nature.[45]

However, a small number of texts might be said to be *compatible* with a natural law argumentation, at least in the form that the Torah expresses a fundamental law that is also implied in creation. One or two passages are early, but few if any can be confidently dated to the Second Temple period. Anonymously, a well-known passage at the end of Mishnah *Sotah* mourns the passing both of the great sages of Israel and of the natural health and prosperity of the land and people.[46] A Tannaitic tradition in *b. Yoma* 67b claims that the prohibitions of idolatry, immorality, bloodshed, robbery and blasphemy should have been written as law even if they had not been in the Torah.[47] The third-century R. Yoḥanan said, 'Had the Torah not been given, we would have learnt about modesty from the cat, robbery from the ant, and fornication from the dove.'[48] Later midrashim assert that when God created the world, he first consulted the Torah (e.g. *Gen. Rab.* 1.1). There is thus merely a tenuous link with the natural law tradition; it was in the end Maimonides who tied the natural law argument to the rabbinic tradition by explicitly equating it with the Noachide commandments.[49]

On the other hand, if one were to cast one's net more widely, it would become apparent that at least the Mishnah's less overtly Scripture-based formulation of halakhah does in practice appeal to many creational patterns and phenomena. This could be said to be true for a good number of the technical rules about materials that

---

[44]Urbach 1987:292; cf. also his citation of J. Heinemann, p. 324 and n. 26.

[45]Urbach 1987:292.

[46]*M. Sot.* 9.12–15; note, conversely, that ominous natural phenomena are in the same passage seen to foreshadow the coming of the Messiah (9.15). Possibly related is the curious statement in *m. Roš Haš.* 1.2 that the world is judged four times a year: 'at Passover, through grain; at Pentecost, through the fruits of the tree; on New Year's Day all that come into the world pass before him like legions of soldiers ...; and at the Feast of Tabernacles they are judged through water [i.e., presumably, rain: see n. 50 below].'

[47]Cf. similarly *Sifra*, Aḥarei Mot 13 on 18.4 (§194.2.11); etc.

[48]*B. 'Erub.* 100b bottom (אילמלא לא ניתנה תורה היינו למידין צניעות מחתול וגזל מנמלה ועריות מיונה).

[49]See the discussion in Novak 1983:294–300; cf. K. Müller 1998:210–14.

pass on impurity, the properties of ritual baths, or even what to do if it rains on the Feast of Tabernacles.[50]

Philo and Josephus

We come then, lastly, to the two great Jewish Hellenistic authors of the first century, Philo of Alexandria and Flavius Josephus.

Philo of Alexandria

There is abundant evidence especially in Philo; and his treatment of the subject has given rise to a considerable scholarly debate, to which we cannot do justice now.[51] In particular, two key concerns have been the origin of his natural law terminology and his use of the Greek tradition of an 'unwritten law', ἄγραφος νόμος. In an article in 1968, Helmut Koester concluded his study of the phrase νόμος φύσεως with the unguarded claim that because he could find no clear prior attestations of this term, Philo himself was 'most probably' the *creator* of the theory of natural law.[52] Responding to Koester's assertion in 1978, Richard Horsley showed that while it was undoubtedly on the intellectual cutting edge, Philo's natural law argumentation nevertheless follows that of Cicero two generations earlier. Horsley came to somewhat more sober conclusions:

> The parallel passages on the law of nature in Philo and Cicero derive ultimately from a Stoic tradition on universal law and right reason. ... But this Stoic tradition had been reinterpreted by a revived and eclectic Platonism upon which both Cicero and Philo drew. ... The key figure in the Platonic revival and the thinker upon whom Cicero and (probably) Philo depend was Antiochus of Ascalon, the head of the Academy in the early first century, who devoted much of his energy to a reinterpretation of Stoic ethics. ...[53]

Here is not the place to evaluate or to rekindle this debate. Instead, I shall confine myself to a brief presentation of the outline of Philo's natural law reasoning, taking into account the discussion in Koester, Horsley and elsewhere.

Philo follows contemporary Stoic perspectives in depicting the universe as a vast *polis* constituted ultimately by right reason (ὄρθος

[50]Rain at Tabernacles is a sign of a curse (*m. Ta'an.* 1.1), which can be compared to 'a slave who came to fill the cup for his master and he poured the pitcher over his face' (*m. Suk.* 2.9). One may only vacate the *Sukkah* if it rains so heavily that the porridge spoils (ibid.).

[51]See e.g. Koester 1968, Horsley 1978, N. G. Cohen 1992, 1993; Martens 1992; Flückiger 1949; Heinemann 1927; Hirzel 1900.

[52]Koester 1968:540.

[53]Horsley 1978:36.

λόγος) or the law of nature (νόμος φύσεως).[54] Mediated by the Logos, the divinely given universal law of nature stands over against the positive laws of the various human states.[55] However, rather than distinguishing between 'nature' and 'God', Philo links these two terms closely. Nature often means the nature of God; indeed sometimes the two become virtually interchangeable.[56] The law of nature therefore is never an immanent legal entity, but always remains the divine law of creation:

The Father and Maker of the world was in the truest sense also its Lawgiver. ... He who would observe the laws will accept gladly the duty of following nature and live in accordance with the ordering of the universe, so that his deeds are attuned to harmony with his words and his words with his deeds.[57]

What can we say about the content of this law of nature? In principle, it does not appear to differ from the content of the Torah itself. The order of the whole world is in harmony with the Law and vice versa;[58] indeed the Torah's written laws are but copies of the law of nature.[59] But even prior to and apart from the Mosaic Law, nature's law is present as an unwritten law (ἄγραφος νόμος) which the virtuous observe intuitively.[60] In his idealizing description of the Patriarchs, Philo always assumes that they embody this unwritten law of nature, as indeed they are themselves personified laws, ἔμψυχοι καὶ λογικοὶ νόμοι (*Abr.* 5; cf. 276), the originals of which the laws themselves are copies (*Abr.* 3).[61] More than that, the Patriarchs 'gladly accepted conformity with nature, holding that nature itself was, as indeed it is, the most venerable of statutes, and

[54]This natural law is intelligible by human reason, which faithfully reflects the divine image: *Opif.* 69, 146; *Mut.* 223. Cf. Horsley 1978:55.

[55]*Jos.* 28–31; *Mos.* 2.48; *Opif.* 3, 143–4. The law of nature is given by God: e.g. *Mos.* 2.48.

[56]E.g. *Contempl.* 70: 'nature' created all people free; cf. *Opif.* 143. See further Koester 1968:531–3; Goodenough 1935:51–2 and 1962:65.

[57]*Mos.* 2.48 (LCL). Cf. *Q. Gen.* 4.90: 'law is an invention of nature, not of men.' It is worth bearing in mind the possible influence of a widely attested association of passages like Prov 8.22 and Gen 1.1, implicitly linking wisdom/Torah with the beginning (NB ראשית/ἀρχή) of creation. For the identification of wisdom and Torah, see e.g. Prov 29.18; cf. Bockmuehl 1990:63–4.

[58]So e.g. *Opif.* 3.

[59]The Mosaic laws are 'stamped ... with the seal of nature herself' (*Mos.* 2.14), 'the most faithful picture of the world-polity' (*Mos.* 2.51).

[60]On the unwritten law in Philo, see also Martens 1992.

[61]See Koester 1968:535; Goodenough 1962:33–4; Martens 1992:43 n. 31, 1994b. The notion of an 'implanted' or 'innate' law in the *Apostolic Constitutions* is possibly relevant: see *Apos. Con.* 1.4–5; 2.8–11; 11.1–4; 12.39–43; and cf. recently Synek 1998. Rom 2.14–15 may also be related.

thus their whole life was one of happy obedience to law' (*Abr.* 6; *Mos.* 2.14; *Prob.* 62).

More specifically, the laws of nature include first of all the subordination of creation under the Creator (*Plant.* 132), but beyond that apparently also several of the commandments of the Decalogue.[62] Infanticide 'overturns the statutes of nature' by demolishing what she builds (*Virt.* 132–3; cf. Josephus *Ag. Ap.* 2.24 §202 on abortion). Even some of the more specialized laws of the Pentateuch may be cited in this context, including those against cross-breeding (*Spec. Leg.* 3.46–7) and yoking together unequal animals (*Spec. Leg.* 4.204). Philo condemns slavery, too, as

annulling the statute of Nature, who mother-like has born and reared all men alike, and created them genuine brothers, not in mere name, but in very reality, though this kinship has been put to confusion by the triumph of malignant covetousness, which has wrought estrangement instead of affinity and enmity instead of friendship. (*Prob.* 79 LCL)

Equality before nature implies equality before God, with resulting moral obligations.

In addition to these and other specific laws (e.g. about sexual behaviour: *Abr.* 135–7; *Spec. Leg.* 3.37–42), there are a few rather more general rules that are also called 'laws of nature'. These tend to fall into the category of proverbial sayings or truisms, and do not in fact amount to any moral requirement at all: examples include the regularity of the seasons (*Spec. Leg.* 4.208, 215) or the idea that the wise man holds all fools in subjection (*Prob.* 30).[63]

Flavius Josephus

A few remarks, finally, on this Jewish historian whose lifetime spans the transition from the Second Temple Period to early rabbinic Judaism. Josephus picks up on many of the arguments as well as the terminology already discussed above, in Philo and elsewhere.

Josephus is convinced that Moses calls his readers to a rational study of the nature of God from his works, and then to imitate that model practically (*Ant.* 1.Proem 4 §19).[64] Just as for Philo, the law of nature can come to be synonymous with the will of God (e.g. *Ant.* 4.8.48 §322; 17.5.3 §95; *War* 3.8.5 §374 on the reality of natural death). In any case Josephus clearly shares the contemporary Jewish

[62]*Decal.* 132 murder; *Spec. Leg.* 4.212 greed; cf. *Decal.* 98 on sabbath rest, also 142.
[63]Koester 1968:537 n. 4.
[64]Abraham is for him the model of a virtuous man who did this: *Ant.* 1.7.1 §155–6. Cf. a similar claim in *Gen. Rab.* 39.1.

conviction that all the regulations of the Torah conform to nature: even for the obscure details attending the construction of the Tabernacle, he insists that the whole assembly is intended specifically as an imitation of the nature of the cosmos, μίμησις τῆς τῶν ὅλων φύσεως.[65] While no particular moral implications attach to this belief, it is in keeping with the common Jewish understanding that all the Torah is according to the law of nature.[66] This finds particular moral application in the argument against suicide as 'repugnant to that nature which all creatures share' and as an act of godlessness against the Creator. More specifically, even animals do not deliberately kill themselves – 'so firmly rooted in all things is the law of nature, the will to live' (War 3.8.5 §370; cf. 374, 378). Another requirement of the law of nature is to bury the dead (War 3.8.5 §377; 4.6.3 §382; cf. on this subject Chapter 3 above).

Perhaps the most wide-ranging argument for the Torah as being according to the law of nature is mounted in the well-known summary of the Law in Ag. Ap. 2.22–30 §190–219 (cf. also 2.21 §184–9). While the specific connection with the νόμος φύσεως terminology is lacking, this section includes statements about sexual relations being 'natural' only between man and wife (2.25 §199), and it extols the gentleness and humanity (φιλανθρωπία) of the Law (2.29 §213). It is worth mentioning, too, that Josephus in this passage shares the notion of Aristobulus and others[67] that the Greek philosophers in fact studied Moses and thus arrived at their moral understanding of the world (e.g. Ag. Ap. 2.16 §168, 36 §257, 39 §281). 'Just as God permeates the universe, so also the Law has found its way among all mankind' (2.39 §284). Torah and nature are in harmony.

Conclusions

I offer my conclusions in the form of five summary theses, three general and two more specific ones.

1. Strictly speaking, there is no 'natural' law in Second Temple Judaism. That is to say, we have seen that neither the Hebrew Bible nor post-biblical Jewish literature allows for a moral authority in nature that is somehow distinct from that of God himself. Law,

---

[65]Ant. 3.6.4 §123; cf. 3.7.7 §180–7; War 5.5.4 §212–13; also Philo, Mos. 2.88, 117–21 and passim. I am indebted for this observation to Dr. Paul Spilsbury.

[66]For Aristobulus (Eusebius, Praep. Ev. 13.12.9), even the sabbath is according to the law of nature.

[67]Aristobulus, in Eusebius, Praep. Ev. 13.12.1–2; cf. Artapanus, in Praep. Ev. 9.27.4; Philo, Spec. Leg. 4.61; cf. Aet. 19; Her. 214; Mos. 2.12.

inasmuch as it carries any real authority, is never 'natural' in the sense of being anything other than divine in origin.

2. The law of nature is in keeping with the Law of God. This is merely the corollary of the previous point. Creation, rightly perceived (i.e. according to revelation and common convention), manifests the purposes of the Creator. And to the extent that a moral law is suggested by the order of creation, this law therefore agrees with the Law of God. This means not that any given phenomenon by itself is thought to constitute a law (see e.g. on 4 Maccabees, above), but that by rightly observing the regular *patterns* of creation one can discern both order and purpose as intended by the Creator.

3. The Law of God is in keeping with the law of nature. The unity of the Creator demands that his voice in positive, special law does not contradict his voice in the order of creation. Although we found exceptions to this in certain rabbinic texts, by and large there is a consistent concern to see the Torah as the supreme expression of the law according to nature, and to interpret nature in conformity with it. That is to say, not only is the Torah in accord with nature, but nature, rightly understood, endorses the Torah.

4. More specifically, the idea of a law according to nature is well-established except, apparently, in Palestinian scribal circles. This simply reflects our discovery that in texts like Sirach, the Dead Sea Scrolls, and early rabbinic literature the natural law motif is not highly developed. These writings concentrate on their traditional practice of Torah interpretation and seem relatively uninterested in the more theoretical and apologetic derivation of ethics from creation. It may also be worth considering that certain scribal circles increasingly came to distinguish carefully between halakhah and haggadah, and to concentrate on the former.

5. The idea of a law according to nature is well established prior to Philo. This final conclusion lends support to R. A. Horsley's critique of H. Koester's thesis; and it suggests furthermore that Philo's development of natural law theory is in fact indebted not only to Stoic ideas of the preceding two generations, but to a well-documented and long-standing tradition within Second Temple Judaism itself.

NATURAL LAW IN THE NEW TESTAMENT?

In its own attempt to articulate a universal morality, early Christianity turned in the first instance to norms and principles inherited from ancient Judaism, which provided a ready point of departure in dealing with pagan contemporaries. As we suggested at the beginning of the last chapter, 'public' moral discourse in ancient Judaism and early Christianity usually appealed to the moral authority either of positive universal law or of 'natural' law. We traced this latter question in the Old Testament and in Second Temple Judaism, concluding that despite a lively tradition of 'natural' theology and ethics, Judaism almost invariably subordinated moral arguments from nature to the teaching of the Torah.

We now turn in this chapter to ask about the New Testament authors' appropriation of this same tradition. To what extent, if at all, did they employ moral appeals to a commonly perceived state of affairs in creation? Here, too, we will find the evidence to be slender but highly significant.

'Nature' and other Conundrums

As in the previous chapter, it will be evident from the problem definition that the 'fishing net' to be used in our trawl through the New Testament must be determined phenomenologically rather than by a given concept of 'natural law', be it ancient or modern. That is to say, we are interested in whether and how the writers themselves appeal in their moral argumentation to a perceived state of affairs in the created order, as distinct from a direct appeal to written revelation. Nevertheless, given the controversy that has long surrounded 'natural law' arguments especially in relation to the New Testament, it may be worth devoting a brief excursus to a couple of pertinent methodological problems before launching into our discussion of the texts themselves.

'Natural Law' or Convention?

Our investigation is unfortunately burdened by a long history of Christian philosophical discussion of 'natural law' arguments. That discussion has frequently appealed to Romans and other New Testament texts in the context of Graeco-Roman and later thought, a fact that significantly complicates our definition of terms.

Since the Enlightenment, a gathering chorus of philosophers, theologians and jurists has pointed out (i) that 'nature' is impossible to define; (ii) that, regardless of the definition, its phenomena are ambiguous, contradictory, and a function of culture; and (iii) that in any case no moral obligation can ever be said to follow from a state of affairs: 'is' cannot entail 'ought'. Twentieth-century advances in the sociology of knowledge have produced widespread agreement about the importance, and the difficulty, of differentiating between (a) a moral appeal ostensibly to 'nature', and (b) an argument from what is merely *perceived* to be 'natural' within given cultural contexts.[1] This is quite apart from the precise meaning of contested passages from Aristotle to Augustine and Aquinas.

In biblical scholarship, these arguments have taken hold somewhat indirectly, such as in the interpretation given to passages like Acts 17 and Romans 1–2 under the currently waning influence of Karl Barth; and, perhaps more generally, as part of the widespread retreat from moral theology proper to post-modern deconstructions of ancient or modern religion.

A certain reticence about the philosophical viability of many traditional natural law arguments is doubtless healthy. Nevertheless, the evidence of Chapter 5 leaves little doubt that the ancient writers, whether Jewish or Christian, Greek or Roman, *did* in fact frequently appeal to 'nature' or to the created order in formulating moral arguments. For all its complications, therefore, our question certainly retains its contextual validity for a study of early Christian ethics.

Given Christianity's more deliberate outreach to Gentiles, however, it becomes all the more important to understand the Christian 'natural law' argument in its wider Graeco-Roman setting.

Hellenistic thought since Aristotle saw a close overlap, in both concepts and terminology, between natural law, unwritten law, and custom. Thus, the extended discussion in Aristotle's *Rhetoric* makes it clear that there was thought to be a universally accepted unwritten law[2] which served at the same time as the foundation of a morality 'according to nature'.[3] Similar sentiments recur in Xenophon, Demosthenes and many other Hellenistic writers.[4]

---

[1]See e.g. Bubmann 1993:267–80, on writers like W. Korff and Klaus Demmer; also e.g. Novak 1998:188–90.

[2]νόμος κοινός ... ὅσα ἄγραφα παρὰ πᾶσιν ὁμολογεῖσθαι δοκεῖ: *Rhet.* 1.10, 1368b7.

[3]κοινὸν δὲ κατὰ φύσιν: 1.13, 1373b4.

[4]Xenophon, *Mem.* 4.4.5ff. cites Socrates regarding unwritten universal laws (τούς γ᾽ ἐν πάσῃ, ἔφη, χώρᾳ κατὰ ταὐτὰ νομιζομένους, 4.4.19). Cf. further Hirzel 1900:3–11; and more generally Flückiger 1954; Maschi 1937; Lombardi 1946, 1947.

A comparable overlap prevailed in early Imperial Roman thought, in which natural law and the unwritten international law (*ius gentium*) on the one hand were contrasted with the positive law of the state (*ius civile*) on the other. We find this notion especially in Cicero, who regards the *ius gentium* to be part of the unwritten law that applies to all people everywhere and derives from universal practice; institutions that are common to all peoples enter into the 'law of nature'.[5] It was of course usually recognized that unwritten law could be peculiar to certain communities. Nevertheless, both Cicero and the second-century jurist Gaius clearly identified *ius gentium* with natural law,[6] although later Roman legal authors by and large did not.[7] Cicero's view on this matter was bolstered by his close link between natural law and his notion of the common good.[8]

To be sure, actual ancient usage of the φύσις terminology merely corroborates the difficulty of distinguishing effectively between nature, truth regarded as self-evident, and universal custom or convention: the term φύσις could encompass them all. At times, the most obvious modern equivalent of 'nature' is simply that of 'common sense'.

There is, as a number of authors have rightly noted, room for considerable confusion in this correlation. For Aristotle and others, it is precisely a moral principle's universal acknowledgement that shows it to be 'natural' and therefore universally valid; and yet it is not always clear whether the force of such law derives from its self-evident truth or its universal usage.[9] Nicholas 1996 points out the related confusion between the principles of natural law and the actual positive law of the *ius gentium*, a distinction not recognized by Cicero and Gaius.[10]

[5]Cf. Levy 1949; Horsley 1978; van Zyl 1986; Nicholas 1996; Voigt 1966.

[6]See e.g. *Tusculanae disputationes* 1.30.30: 'omni autem in re consensio omnium gentium lex naturae putanda est'; Gaius, *Inst.* 1.1; 1.2.2; 2.1.11. Cf. further van Zyl 1986:66; Ricken 1994:138–9; Arkes 1992:251–60, 266–7, 274–5; also Jolowicz 1952:102–5, with reference to Cicero's *De Off.* 3.5.23; *De Har. Resp.* 14.32; also Weiss 1917; Nicholas 1996. On Gaius, see more generally H. Wagner 1978.

[7]See e.g. Waldstein 1988, 1993, 1994, although the evidence may be more ambivalent for Gaius (references cited above; cf. e.g. Stein 1974:314–15; Ricken 1994:139–40; Winkel 1993; Wagner 1978 *passim*). Even Ulpian, in D.1.1.1.3–4, seems to indicate that *ius gentium* can at least be *derived* from *ius naturale*. On the vague and varying significance of the terms 'nature' and 'natural', even in classical Roman legal thought, see further van Zyl 1986:56–7; Nicholas 1962:56–7 and 1996; Stein 1974:314–15 and *passim*; also Waldstein 1983.

[8]E.g. *De Officiis* 1.7.22; 3.6.30; see especially Mayer-Maly 1971; van Zyl 1986:68.

[9]Cf. Ricken 1994:136–8, who points out that even Plato's notion of φύσις remained sufficiently vague to permit him to accommodate quite different uses of the term within the same context (e.g. in *Laws* 875a–d).

[10]Nicholas 1996:835: 'natural law is law which ought to be universally applied and *ius gentium* is law which is in fact so applied'.

As we saw in Chapter 5, the Jewish philosopher Philo of Alexandria, too, drew on related Stoic traditions and identified the unwritten law explicitly and specifically with the law of nature.[11] Under his influence, patristic authors of the second and third centuries went on to develop the natural law tradition in a Christian vein.[12]

The New Testament authors arguably make no explicit use of the Graeco-Roman natural law tradition, as we shall discover; and this must be seen as an important caveat in relation to earlier studies of the subject. What is more, even for the broader issue of the New Testament's moral appeals to the created order, it is instructive to note that the philosophical distinctions between 'nature' and culture were evidently not as neatly drawn in the ancient world as they came to be in some medieval and subsequent Christian thought.[13] At the same time, and in spite of justified modern philosophical and theological qualms, Graeco-Roman and NT authors in their different ways confirm the antiquity of both the substance and the terminology of natural law discourse. Most ancient writers shared the unquestioned assumption that humanity's place in the social and natural order implied fundamental principles of morality; and that these were continuous with all good systems of positive law, and recognized by cultured peoples everywhere. Not only Greeks and Romans but Jews and Christians, too, argued in such terms,[14] if only to make their moral discourse possible in an intercultural world. Their theologically based presupposition of a universal ontology, moreover, served as the indispensable framework for their covenantal worldview.[15]

Criteria of New Testament Ethics?

Somewhat tangentially, a second methodological concern relates to the underlying *criteria* of New Testament ethics. Why are some actions right and others wrong? Given the overwhelmingly

[11]Thus most clearly Horsley 1978. Cf. further Martens 1992:43 n. 31 and *passim*; Goodenough 1962:65–6; see also above, p. 107. In demonstrating the dependence of Philo on an established tradition, Horsley argues specifically against Koester 1968.

[12]For documentation, see e.g. Ricken 1994:140–2, with reference to Justin (e.g. *2 Apol.* 2.4), Tertullian and others. See also Lactantius (*Inst.* 6.8–9), who follows Cicero.

[13]See above, p. 115 nn. 7, 9.

[14]Important previous studies include Barr 1990, 1993; Dodd 1953; Horsley 1986; Koester 1968. See further Chapters 5 above and 7 below.

[15]Cf. Novak 1998:61, who notes, 'In Scripture itself the covenant has a universal precondition as well as a universal consequence, ... an ontology as well as an eschatology.' See further Novak 1998:178 and *passim*, together with the comments of Oakes 1999:49.

theological way in which the New Testament thinks about law, including 'natural' law, it is not surprising that legal (or 'halakhic') aspects of its ethics continue to be downplayed or even resisted in scholarly discussion. And yet, why is it that the apostolic writers appear to regard the Old Testament's Sabbath and feast day legislation as optional, whereas its principles of sexual morality evidently remain in force? The New Testament's apparent de-emphasis of 'ritual' laws in favour of more general, 'moral' ones has of course been noted throughout Christian history; but the *reasons* for this distinction are rarely understood.

The question of moral and legal criteria of Christian ethics also arises from the early church's evident adoption of many Graeco-Roman conventions. These include lists of virtues and vices, household codes (*Haustafeln*) – and indeed moral arguments from the created order. At the same time, and just as in the Old Testament, the relationship with contemporary popular ethics is clearly complex and by no means uncritical. Pagan assumptions about morality, even 'natural' morality, could never *as such* be binding. True, both Jews and Christians frequently found common ground with Stoic morality and made much of certain Graeco-Roman concepts of virtue, convention, and natural law. But it is important to note that pragmatic considerations cannot satisfactorily explain which practices were commendable and which were not. Pagan morality inevitably entailed religious connotations, many of which clashed with fundamental tenets of Christianity.[16] Even from the perspective of the Graeco-Roman background, therefore, the question of criteria is once again inevitable.

A more specific attempt to address this question will be offered in Chapter 7. In the meantime, it will suffice to bear the issue in mind as we proceed to ask about the New Testament's appeal to universal moral laws of 'nature' and convention.

Jesus and the Gospels

Direct moral appeals to the created order are relatively rare in the Gospels. It is historically likely that Jesus confined his ministry largely to Jewish audiences, and the tacit assumption underlying virtually all of Jesus' teaching is a context of Torah-observant

---

[16]This is a case ably made by H. D. Betz 1988:200–1. Even as regards Stoicism, however, it is important to remember that the second-century apologists distinguished carefully between Stoic morality (which they affirmed) and Stoic pantheism and fatalism (which they rejected). Cf. Justin's criticisms in *1 Apol.* 43; *2 Apol.* 7; and see Chadwick 1966:21.

Judaism, as we saw in Chapter 1. While Jesus may at times radically differ from certain forms of Pharisaic interpretation and launch virulent attacks on the Temple establishment, many of his presuppositions are held in common with his opponents. The differences are over the *interpretation* of a shared ethnic and religious Judaism, in which the issue of cross-cultural dialogue about universal law would perhaps rarely arise.[17]

The same is true, by and large, for the original *Sitz im Leben* of the Jesus traditions as transmitted in Palestinian Jewish Christianity. To be sure, at least the Marcan and Lucan redactions do of course betray a Gentile setting and orientation. Even in the special material of the evangelists, however, we are hard pressed to find moral arguments pertinent to the question here at hand. In some ways these matters seem to arise rather more typically in the apologetic passages of Acts and the Pauline corpus.

The available material conveniently divides into positive and negative appeals to nature and universal convention. To acknowledge this is to give away from the start one important conclusion of this chapter: the New Testament's attitude to the concept of natural law is profoundly ambivalent. Appeals to nature are employed only where they fit ethical priorities that have already been established on other grounds.

Positive Use of Natural Law

To establish the existence of a moral appeal to nature in the Jesus tradition, we may begin with what I take to be two fairly straightforward examples. The first is the positive form of the Golden Rule in the Sermon on the Mount: 'Do to others as you would have them do to you.' Although the philosophical weakness and inadequacy of this logion as a straightforward ethical principle has often been pointed out,[18] it is clearly attested in Q (Matt 7.12 par. Luke 6.31) and seems to be an authentic part of the teaching of Jesus.[19] Somewhat like Jesus' re-affirmation of the commandment of

---

[17]Note, however, Loewe 1966 on the universal applicability even of some inner-Jewish halakhic categories; and cf. further A. F. Segal 1995 and Chapter 7 below.

[18]See again recently Alexander 1997:382 and *passim*.

[19]Other early allusions (partly in the 'negative' formulation also encountered e.g. in Tobit 4.15: cf. p. 98 above) include *Did.* 1.2 and *1 Clem.* 13.2; cf. *Gos. Thom.* 6; *P. Oxy.* 654.5. Lyonnet 1967:151 n. 2 points out that the Fathers do not normally distinguish between the 'positive' and the 'negative' form of the Golden Rule. Alexander 1997 shows the evidence for the rabbinic attribution of the 'negative' Golden Rule to Hillel (*b. Šab.* 31a) to be inconclusive.

neighbourly love (Mark 12.31 par.), the Golden Rule argues from an assumed universality of basic human needs and desires. That is the moral function both of the Golden Rule's ὅσα ἐὰν θέλητε ('whatever you would wish') and of the love commandment's ὡς σεαυτόν ('as yourself'). Their humanity is what moral agents share; and the tradition manifests a deep trust that human beings intrinsically understand fundamental human needs. In its Palestinian setting, the Rule's specific practical validity as a summary of the *Torah* obviously also relies significantly on its symbiosis with a shared Jewish cultural and covenantal context. Nevertheless, the uncomplicated assumption of a kind of natural reciprocity and commonality of human needs suggests the acceptance of a moral category that is general and self-evident, rather than positively revealed in the Torah.[20]

Another relatively obvious case is Jesus' argument with the Pharisees about hand-washing. Although the debate is in the first instance clearly about interpretative approaches to the Torah, Jesus' clinching statement is what might be called an argument from 'the way things are', namely that unclean foods enter not the heart but the stomach before being expelled again, into the sewer (Mark 7.19).[21] The created order itself shows that contaminated foods merely pass through the body and do not affect the heart, but evil has its very seat in the heart and comes from within. The argument in effect is based on 'common sense': it takes for granted a pragmatic wisdom rooted in the universality of human experience.

We may point to a few other moral arguments formulated generally with reference to the natural world. Significantly, most of these are found in the parables and in the wisdom traditions of the synoptic sayings material ('Q'); and Chapter 5 above reminded us that it is of course in wisdom that we would expect to find Judaism's easiest point of contact with a tradition of natural theology.[22] Examples from 'Q' include the call to lay up lasting heavenly treasure away from moths and rust (e.g. Matt 6.19–20 par.), to trust in God's provision like the birds and the lilies of the field (Matt

---

[20]Compare also J. P. Brown 1993 for a study of Luke 6.27–38 against a general Graeco-Roman background of natural law (focusing on the themes of recompense as well as friendship and enmity).

[21]The authenticity of this saying is disputed, but does not in any case affect our argument here.

A similar 'common sense' resolution of moral argument about the Torah is the question that follows the parable of the good Samaritan: 'Which of these do you think was a neighbour to the man who fell among robbers?' (Luke 10.36). The Pharisee is required to have recourse to a criterion outside revelation. Cf. Johnson 1982.

[22]See above, p. 94 and *passim*; cf., however, Collins 1998 on the abiding tensions between revelation and natural theology even in Alexandrian texts like the book of Wisdom.

6.26–28 par.), and the assurance that like a human father God will
give his children good things when they ask him (Matt 7.7–11 par.).
Similarly, we find sayings about building one's house on the rock
(7.24–27 par.), putting new wine into new wineskins (9.16–17
par.), reading the signs of the times like the signs of the weather
(16.2–3 par.), and knowing a tree by its fruit (7.16–20, 12.33 par.;
we shall return to this theme below).

Despite such initially promising clues, however, it is important to
acknowledge that much of this material is at best of indirect
relevance for our problem. Even where the Jesus tradition does
engage questions of universal morality, the relevant precepts or
principles are not so much *derived* from nature or convention but
rather *illustrated* from that source – a point that is particularly clear
in the parables. The resulting logic is that of simile rather than of a
direct functional analogy, and its authority is based on common
sense rather than on any sort of deductive reasoning from the created
order. More typically, Jesus' teaching clearly takes for granted the
Jewish context of revealed Torah, which undergirds virtually everything else he says. A good illustration of this is his teaching on
divorce: Mark 10.6–8 (par.) grounds the prohibition of divorce in
the created order, and yet it does so on the strength of a direct
scriptural quotation (Gen 2.24). This is 'natural law' only in a highly
contingent sense, if at all; and the Jesus tradition offers little evidence
of any systematic moral appeal to nature.

Nevertheless, several 'borderline' examples can be highly
revealing. Jesus' well-attested reply to the question about payment of
Roman taxes is one such case: 'Give to Caesar what is Caesar's, and
to God what is God's' (Mark 12.17 par.). Jesus here affirms a separation of political loyalties by accepting both the legitimate
universality and the limited jurisdiction of government. On one level
this is of course an evasive answer, one that refuses to offer either a
theological endorsement of Roman rule or, on the other hand, an
incitement to rise up and depose it. In that sense it might serve as a
radical disavowal of Machiavellian *Realpolitik*, and thus a denial of
the quest for power as an end. Of course the statement also means
what it does *not* say: refuse to give to Caesar what is God's alone;
and do not withhold in the name of God what is Caesar's rightful
claim. Either way, however, this statement flies in the face of the
Palestinian politics of violence, both of the revolutionary and of
the establishment kind. For present purposes, we must note that
Jesus' saying amounts to a tacit recognition of universal social
realities pertaining to human society. It affirms not the goodness but
the *legitimacy* of government – and its contingent right to the loyalty

of citizens. The moral point of reference here is not exactly 'nature'; but Jesus nevertheless appeals to a universally established social order almost as part of 'the way things are'. Theologically, the effect is profoundly anti-idolatrous, affirming both the sovereignty of the Creator and the sociality of his creatures.

Four other marginal passages merit brief discussion in this section, one from 'Q', two from Luke and one from Matthew.

The passage from 'Q' takes up the recurrent motif of a tree and its fruit, and identifies morality as a function of character.

Either make the tree good, and its fruit good; or make the tree bad, and its fruit bad; for the tree is known by its fruit. You brood of vipers! How can you speak good things, when you are evil? For out of the abundance of the heart the mouth speaks. The good person brings good things out of a good treasure, and evil person brings evil things out of an evil treasure. (Matt 12.33–35 par. Luke 6.43–45; cf. Matt 7.16–20)

While no specific ethical precept is here attached, this piece of characteristic teaching nevertheless relies for its moral point on a functional analogy with creation. It is 'in the nature of things' that being and doing cannot be separated, which means that there is an intrinsic link between human behaviour or speech and human character.

In my second example, the Lucan Jesus appears to offer an adaptation of Proverbs 25.6–7. He advises guests at a banquet to choose a lower seat than they deserve, because this will more likely lead to promotion and honour rather than shame (Luke 14.7–11). While for Luke an eschatological application of this passage is quite likely (14.11), its basic moral point is once again derived *analogically*, from universal social convention and 'the way things are' (a host determines seating based on honour), rather than deontologically, from revealed truth. Another, equally robust case in Luke is the parable of the dishonest steward, which leads Jesus to commend the use of money to make friends (Luke 16.1–9). Here, too, wisdom's discernment of reality should guide the use of money by the children of the Kingdom.[23] In other words, they are to learn from 'nature' to be 'wise (φρόνιμοι) as serpents and innocent as doves' (Matt 10.16).

Returning to the Matthew's Sermon on the Mount, finally, we hear that God sends his sun and rain equally on the just and the unjust (5.45). This statement is used to counter what might be called an *insufficiently* creational kind of morality: to love and to greet only

---

[23]In the same context, 'you cannot serve God and mammon' (v. 13) may endorse a similarly pragmatic critique, not of money but of idolatry.

one's friends is just what tax collectors and Gentiles do (vv. 46–47). Jesus, however, uses the Creator's indiscriminate bounty and blessing to call for behaviour that altogether transcends ordinary generosity.[24] The 'greater righteousness' of the kingdom must imitate God's gifts in creation: Jesus calls for a counter-commonwealth of love and forgiveness that covers those who loathe us as well as those who like us. By appealing to God's lavish work in creation, Jesus corrects and challenges human behaviour that is petty, partisan and merely conventional: for him, the Creator himself shows that such actions are in fact not sufficiently 'natural'. The divine voice in creation here is *not* reducible to the voice of human habit or convention.[25]

Negative Use of Natural Law

The Jesus tradition, then, does contain a number of measured moral appeals to the created order. Against this, however, must be set several important passages in which Jesus takes up a seemingly 'natural' state of affairs only to subject it to subversion and critique. On the one hand, of course, we find a respect for common customs and institutions, and an ethic that is indeed deeply compatible with universal social needs and human aspirations. On the other hand, the disciples are repeatedly challenged not to give unquestioning assent to the seemingly natural assumptions of the status quo: despite a hearty affirmation of creation, mere allegiance to existing conventions is not good enough.

One of the key subversive texts in this regard appears in the context of the second great statement about the Graeco-Roman political system, a kind of foil to the earlier passage about paying taxes to Caesar:

So Jesus called them and said to them, 'You know that among the Gentiles those whom they recognize as their rulers lord it over them, and their great ones are tyrants over them. But it is not so among you; but whoever wishes to become great among you must be your servant, and whoever wishes to be first among you must be slave of all. For the Son of Man came not to be served but to serve, and to give his life a ransom for many.'[26]

---

[24]In a traditional wisdom context like Qohelet, one might have expected a statement like this to be followed by a warning to enjoy the day of prosperity and avoid excessive righteousness or wickedness (Eccl 7.14–17).

[25]It is worth noting in this regard the clash between natural law and the convention of slavery, which was recognized by first-century Stoics like Seneca and by classic Roman legal writers. See further Marcic 1964.

[26]Mark 10.42–45; cf. Matt 20.25–28; Luke 22.25–27.

On an initial reading, this text might appear merely xenophobic, expressing a characteristically conservative Jewish antipathy for the political practices of other nations. However, the case is perhaps a little more complex than that. First, Jesus observes the seemingly universal (and arguably 'common sense') fact that those with power tend to make the most of it: rulers exercise dominion. What is more, verse 43 even seems to take for granted the pursuit of 'greatness' as a normal part of the human quest for acceptance and recognition. At the same time, however, Jesus profoundly subverts the 'natural' Graeco-Roman political conventions pertaining to the whole system of power and personal advancement: his counter-kingdom is built on the exercise of ambition not through conquest and empire, but through self-giving service. Nature's kingdom might seem to those in power to teach the survival and success of the fittest, even 'the divine right of kings' (as later writers put it). The counter-kingdom of Jesus, however, expresses authority through humility and exalts the servant, the children, the little ones. Thereby the universal human conventions of power are deeply undermined.

From a canonical perspective, it is particularly significant to note the telling Lucan addition, 'And those in authority over them are called "benefactors"' (22.25). While affirming the virtues of benefaction elsewhere,[27] Luke here calls into question the selfish exploitation and status-seeking connected with the ubiquitous Graeco-Roman system of patronage and benefaction.[28]

The paradox seems to be that loyalty to an existing institution (e.g. giving Caesar his due) can nevertheless go hand in hand with a deep structural distaste for its whole way of operating. The criterion for this disapproval lies expressly *not* in nature, public convention or common sense. Instead, it is rooted in a mentality that owes a lot to the Isaianic Servant Songs, and which is particularly embodied in the life and work of Jesus himself. In this case, Jesus deconstructs and reinvents convention.

Once we are alerted to this possibility of a deep ambivalence in the

---

[27]Cf. 7.5; 8.1–3; 19.8; NB Acts 10.38: Jesus διῆλθεν εὐεργετῶν. See also Lull 1986.

[28]In his important study, Winter 1994 unfortunately dispatches this verse in one footnote (p. 40, n. 50). He asserts, but makes no effort to prove, that 'the prohibition (ὑμεῖς δὲ οὐχ οὕτως) is not against Christians operating as benefactors.' Luke's obvious approval of the use of wealth for the common good is of course incontestable (cf. Zacchaeus, the Centurion who built the synagogue at Capernaum; Barnabas, Cornelius, Lydia, and others). But whether this really amounts to a call for full-scale participation in the contemporary benefaction system is surely another question. Winter's emphatic denial of any ambivalence in this regard (pp. 200–2 and *passim*) might be thought to sit uneasily with Jesus' views on the privacy and secrecy of almsgiving in general and on the social recognition of benefactors in particular (Matt 6.2–4, a passage which Winter never mentions).

Gospels' use of 'natural' conventions, a similar pattern begins to emerge in several other cases.

Here, I would like merely to single out the Synoptic teaching on *marriage and the family*. Jesus appeals to the Creation account in order to honour marriage as indissoluble except by adultery (Matt 19.3–9 par.).[29] He loves little children and repeatedly takes them in his arms and lays hands on them (Mark 9.36; 10.16 par.); children are said to be closest to the Kingdom of God. On the other hand, he himself apparently remained unmarried and may have endorsed the ideal of celibacy for the sake of the kingdom of heaven in terms that to Jewish ears would sound highly provocative (Matt 19.10–12). Luke is particularly strong about the implications: Jesus' hyperbole about the loyalties of the true disciple here includes even hating one's wife and children (14.26); elsewhere Luke preserves the statement that those who are worthy of the age to come do not marry at all (20.34–35 par.)[30].

We are confronted with a deep ambiguity here. Marriage is strongly affirmed as integral to the original design of creation, and yet even marriage clearly takes second place to the requirements of the Kingdom of God and the new creation – where, according to an almost certainly authentic tradition, Jesus thought it would have no place.

Closely related is Jesus' teaching on family life. Not only are children important to him, but parents figure prominently in his teaching; as we saw earlier, he assumes that they naturally give good things to their children (Luke 11.11–12 par.). He is concerned for the families of his disciples and heals Peter's mother-in-law (Mark 1.30–31 par.). He reaffirms the commandment to honour father and mother (Mark 7.10; 10.19) and is profoundly incensed at the Pharisaic *Corban* legislation, which compromises that commandment (Mark 7.9–13 par.). He raises a widow's only son at Nain (Luke 7.11–16) and the daughter of a distraught synagogue official and his wife (Mark 5.22–24, 35–42).

On the other hand, he clearly refuses to recognize his own family when they come to see him, declaring instead that his disciples are his true family (Mark 3.31–35). He has come to bring strife between children and their parents and, less surprisingly perhaps, between daughter-in-law and mother-in-law (Matt 10.34–35 par.). Most notoriously in recent scholarship, he forbids one potential disciple to bury his father (Matt 8.21–22 par.).[31]

---

[29]See Chapter 2 above.

[30]Note that Mark 12.25 confines this state more clearly to the age to come.

[31]Cf. Chapter 3 above on this text.

In all these cases, a harsher clash between obligations to the order of creation and to the Kingdom of God seems difficult to imagine. We might of course quibble about the authenticity of one or another of these sayings, particularly those preserved only in a single tradition. Nevertheless, it seems difficult to avoid the conclusion that there is a deep ambivalence at the very heart of the Jesus tradition: he expressed both positive and starkly provocative ideas on the subject of marriage and the family. Endorsements of the perceived order of creation stand side by side with cases of profound subversion or subordination of that same order.[32]

A similarly contradictory picture emerges in relation to several other relevant topics, including those of money,[33] manual labour,[34] and provision for future needs.[35] In each case there is a general affirmation of behaviour in accordance with creational realities, which is then profoundly relativized by the demands of the kingdom of God. (It seems, however, to be a delightfully revealing exception that one of the few areas of natural activity to emerge virtually unscathed is that of hospitality, food and drink.[36])

Finally, it is especially in some of the more apocalyptic passages that the Son of Man's coming judgement harshly disrupts not only human sin and injustice but also any merely customary recourse to nature or convention. 'On that night there will be two in one bed: one will be taken and the other left; two women will be grinding meal together: one will be taken and the other left' (Matt 24.40–41 par.). Apparent 'normality' may not be taken for granted in the Kingdom, as we have already seen in relation to the subject of marriage. The man with only one talent may not just hide it and bide his time (Matt 25.18, 24–29 par.). The parousia will be like the days

[32]See also S. C. Barton 1994 on the ambivalence of this tradition.

[33]Luke 8.1–3; 16.1–9. It is of course important to contrast this with more critical statements about Mammon, the selling of possessions, etc.

[34]A critical attitude to labour is arguably present in the story of Mary and Martha (Luke 10.41), as in Matt 6.28. Contrast the parables about labour; e.g. Matt 24.46 par. It is significant that the Gospels use the idea of work can refer both to manual labour and to ministry for the kingdom: Matt 9.37–38; 10.10; Luke 10.2, 7; cf. similarly 1 Thess 2.9; 5.12–13; Rom 16.12; 1 Cor 15.58; 2 Cor 10.15. Cf. further Schelkle 1978; M. Davies 1985; for the Graeco-Roman world more generally, see e.g. Millett 1996; Garnsey 1980.

[35]Luke 14.28–32 par. Other examples might be said to include the parable of the Ten Virgins; preparations for the Last Supper; Judas's reported tenure of the money box, the provision for Jesus' ministry on the part of wealthy women supporters (Luke 8.1–3) etc. For notes 33–5, see further Hengel 1974:60–4 and *passim*.

[36]The authenticity of this perspective may be made more plausible by controversies like Matt 11.18–19 par. Luke 7.33–35.

of Noah: 'They were eating and drinking, and marrying and being given in marriage, until the day Noah entered the ark, and the flood came and destroyed all of them' (Matt 24.37–39 par.). In Luke 13, the 'natural' cry for retributive justice in the face of Pilate's massacre of pilgrims meets only with Jesus' stark rebuff: 'unless you repent, you will all perish likewise' (Luke 13.1–3).

Quite what this subversion of natural conventions *positively* means for Christian ethics is not really spelled out. Nevertheless, Jesus' ministry makes it clear that *extraordinary* acts of mercy are required: this emerges, for instance, from the Sermon on the Mount and from the judgement scene of Matt 25. For the Jesus tradition, the moral order of creation is part of the will of God; and yet the *right reading* of creation is not self-authenticating, but remains contingent on the perspective of the Kingdom.

The Acts of the Apostles

The two-volume work of Luke-Acts is widely acknowledged to show a heightened concern for social and political issues.[37] From the opening chapters of his Gospel, we find Luke offering *public* theology, repeatedly concerned to embed sacred story in secular history, and showing how the gospel addresses and transforms the world. This is a dimension to which we shall return more explicitly in the penultimate chapter of this book.

A generally positive approach to public social and political conventions certainly suits Luke's overall perspective. The Empire in Acts is not the Whore of Babylon, but rather the governing authority that secures the general setting for the spread of the gospel. Along with the Pastoral Epistles, Luke-Acts is for this reason one of the least apocalyptic of all New Testament documents. The gospel and the conventions of Roman culture and public morality are for Luke not finally incompatible: when shrewdly used, these natural conventions serve as an instrument and almost a kind of 'preparation of the gospel', in which the church can grow and flourish.[38]

Nevertheless, while much of this may be indirectly relevant to our subject here, *explicitly* moral arguments from nature are less common.

Most pertinently, perhaps, both in Lystra (Acts 14) and Athens

---

[37]See e.g. Cassidy & Scharper 1983; Esler 1987; Seccombe 1982; Neyrey 1991, and a host of other works on wealth and poverty in Luke.

[38]See also Esler 1987:201–19.

(17) Paul's evangelism of Gentiles is seen to take as its point of contact an appeal to creation and the Creator. The primary point of these two speeches is epistemological rather than moral, i.e. concerned with the knowledge of God rather than the derivation of ethics. Somewhat surprisingly, perhaps, the word φύσις does not occur in either passage.[39] Nevertheless, using a common Jewish Hellenistic appeal to the Creator who is greater than his creation,[40] the Lucan Paul argues from the supremacy of this Creator against the idolatrous folly of worshipping other creatures, before going on to introduce the message of Jesus Christ.[41]

A small number of other examples could be found,[42] but the lack of explicit appeal to the created order means that much of Acts falls outside the narrow scope of this study.

Paul

While the study of Paul's use of 'natural law' reasoning languished in the closing decades of the twentieth century,[43] social aspects of Pauline Christianity have been the subject of a burgeoning scholarly industry.

Of particular relevance to our purposes here is the question of Paul's knowledge and use of the public social conventions of the Hellenistic world. These have been studied from a variety of angles by scholars like W. C. van Unnik (1954, 1975), F. W. Danker (1982), P. Marshall (1987), E. Judge (1984a, b), J. P. Sampley (1980), B. W. Winter (1988, 1994) and many others. Particular attention has been paid to Paul's positive employment and critical revision of Hellenistic *rhetorical* conventions; writers who come to mind in this regard include H. D. Betz (1972, 1979), G. A. Kennedy (1984), R. Jewett (1986) and many others.[44] Key texts under examination have been and continue to be the Corinthian, Galatian and Thessalonian Correspondence. All these studies have produced a wealth of information about the Hellenistic social and rhetorical

---

[39]See also Koester 1974:271 n. 202.

[40]For documentation, see Chapter 5 above.

[41]Cf. Gärtner 1955.

[42]Note e.g. Paul's deft appeal to his Roman citizenship in Philippi, Jerusalem, and Caesarea, employing it to advance the gospel to Rome (16.37–39; 21.39; 22.25–29; 23.27; 25.11).

[43]Explicit studies of natural law in Paul are few and far between; after Dodd 1953 and Austgen 1969 (and perhaps Lyonnet 1967), even ostensibly pertinent writers like Aune 1995 (cf. 1996), Wischmeyer 1996 and Seifrid 1998 have not engaged the subject directly.

[44]See e.g. Forbes 1986; Litfin 1994; Classen 1991, 1993; D. F. Watson 1995; R. D. Anderson 1996.

conventions that were widely taken for granted in the environment in which Paul worked.

It would obviously be the task of a major monograph to draw all these strands together in a treatment of Paul's approach to Christian ethics. Even within the more limited purview of this chapter, however, the ancient mind's close linkage between 'nature' and universal social convention invites a brief indication of some of the most relevant areas for our purposes. On the domestic front, the most important theme is that of the *Haustafel,* the household codes of Colossians, Ephesians, the Pastorals and 1 Peter, with their specification of the different roles within the given social reality of the Hellenistic household.[45] Within the larger arena of the *polis,* we encounter most obviously the formalized catalogues of *vices and virtues,*[46] which despite their distinctively Christian content continue to have much in common with Stoic lists as reformulated in Hellenistic Jewish contexts.

These qualities overlap with a second complex of topics relating to *public decorum,* including considerations of dress and public decency, courtesy or *urbanitas,*[47] loyalty to the state, good citizenship, public unobtrusiveness and peaceableness (ἡσυχία). Related to this notion of decorum is the semantic field composed of numerous stereotypical terms for social propriety,[48] several of which appear, for example, in Phil 4.8.

A further group of public conventions can be related to *social welfare.* Included among these must be the system of patronage[49] and public benefaction,[50] attitudes to work and manual labour,[51] economic self-sufficiency,[52] philanthropy (φιλανθρωπία),[53] various issues concerning hospitality to strangers, etc.

Last but not least, there is the use and critique of Hellenistic *rhetorical conventions* in Paul's correspondence. Among the most relevant of these for the field of ethics may be the patterns of commendation and

---

[45]Cf. Crouch 1972; Schrage 1988:244–57 and *passim.*

[46]See e.g. Vögtle 1936; Wibbing 1959; Herr 1976:87–115; cf. also Balch 1981:21–80 and Charles 1997:99–127, with special reference to 1 and 2 Peter, respectively.

[47]See Procopé 1991.

[48]E.g. ἄξιον, πρέπον or πρέπει, ὄφειλον, δεῖ, τὰ μὴ καθήκοντα, εὐάρεστον, εὐσχημονῶς, τέλειον, ἀγαθόν, etc.

[49]E.g. Saller 1982; Konstan 1995.

[50]See e.g. van Unnik 1954, 1975; Danker 1982; Winter 1988, 1994, ch. 3.

[51]Grant 1978:66–95.

[52]Note αὐτάρκεια in Phil 4.11; 1Thess 4.12; Eph 4.28; cf. the works of Winter and Judge, cited above.

[53]See Hiltbrunner 1994; Pearson 1997; cf. also Chadwick 1992 on *humanitas.* On philanthropy and other ancient provisions for social welfare, see Bolkestein 1939:67–286 (Greece), 287–379 (Rome) and the useful synthesis on pp. 418–37; and see e.g. Hands 1968, Fuks 1979–80, and the essay collection by Kloft 1988.

blame, honour and shame, wisdom and folly,[54] and the conventions and assumptions surrounding Paul's views and practice of 'boasting'.[55]

In the broadest possible sense, many of these different perspectives bear at least indirectly on the moral dimensions of 'nature' and 'convention'.

Precisely what might be meant by 'nature', however, is an issue of some uncertainty even in Paul's writings. The term φύσις, which is absent from the gospels and Acts, is in the New Testament found primarily in the Pauline corpus.[56] Paul uses it of the original state of creation; as we shall see, in some cases this seems to be buttressed by an implicit appeal to universal custom and consent. As in the case of Jesus, however, many existing social conventions continue for Paul to be deeply ambivalent, and must be handled with considerable discretion: some are cautiously affirmed, while others are profoundly subverted in light of Paul's theology of the cross.

In the interest of conciseness, we shall here confine ourselves to a brief discussion of three explicit or at least clearly implicit moral appeals to nature: Romans 1.26–27; Romans 2.14; and 1 Corinthians 11.14.[57]

Romans 1.26–27

Recent commentaries tend to agree that in Romans 1.19–32 Paul adapts a Jewish Hellenistic argument about knowing the Creator from creation. This in turn is taken to show that pagan idolatry, in its immoral denial of creation, constitutes a manifest nonsense, an evil contrary to nature. The same argument recurs in various forms as early as Isa 40.18–31; 44.9-21; Psa 115.4–8; Jer 2.27–28, etc.; the closest parallel is widely recognized in Wisdom 13–14.[58] The logic of this argument goes something like this:

1. God's existence and power, although invisible, are revealed in creation and can be known by observing the created order.
2. The pagans thus knew about God and should have given him the glory. They are without excuse.

---

[54]Cf. e.g. Malina 1981; Pilch & Malina 1993.

[55]Cf. Davis 1999:130–88 and *passim*.

[56]It occurs 11x in Paul (Rom 1.26; 2.14, 27; 11.21, 24 (3x); 1 Cor 11.14; Gal 2.15; 4.8; Eph 2.3), twice in Jas 3.7 and once in 2 Pet 1.4. All of its 12 uses in the LXX occur in 3–4 Maccabees and Wisdom, i.e. books first composed in Greek.

[57]It is perhaps also worth mentioning Aune 1995, who proposes several interesting (if ultimately unconvincing) parallels between Paul's linkage of death/resurrection and ethics on the one hand and the *commentatio mortis* theme in contemporary pagan texts on the other.

[58]Gal 4.8 also confirms Paul's view that idolatry is contrary to nature.

3. Instead, they pervert the natural order to make idols out of created things, and treat them as gods.

4. Idolatry leads to shameless and abominable immorality, which is itself an instance of worshipping the creature instead of the creator.

Here we are concerned not so much with the controversial epistemological question of a natural *knowledge* of the Creator, about which twentieth-century scholarship engaged in much spirited debate. For Paul as for Hellenistic Judaism, however, some such perception of God from creation clearly seemed possible – not indeed by human ingenuity, but by divine revelation (ὁ θεὸς γὰρ αὐτοῖς ἐφανέρωσεν, Rom 1.19).

What is of primary interest here is the *moral* argument. Misdirected worship of the creature in place of the Creator (1.25) leads logically to God's surrender of pagans to the resultant sexual perversions of 1.26. Where he is spurned in favour of idols, God gives idolaters up to the objects and consequences of their misplaced desires. The same argument about a sexual perversion of 'nature' is found, for instance, in Philo, Wisdom and Jewish testamentary literature.[59]

The context makes it plain that the appeal to 'nature' here (παρὰ φύσιν, v. 26) is in fact an appeal to the same created order which calls for the distinction between creature and creator. Homosexual intercourse is chosen as the paradigmatic sin only in the sense that it was for Judaism *the* pagan sin *par excellence*, and virtually unknown in Judaism itself.[60] Indeed in 1 Corinthians 6 Paul is the first attested writer to use the rare Greek word ἀρσενοκοίτης, which appears to be a literal translation of the common halakhic term משכב זכור, 'one who lies with a male'.[61] To the Jewish mind, this demonstrated a prime example of pagans using the human body contrary to the purpose for which it was intended in the order of creation. Joseph Fitzmyer explains the train of thought as follows:

The human being who fails to acknowledge God and turns from him, who is the source of life and immortality, seeks rather a vicarious expression of it through the misuse of the natural procreative faculty. ... Homosexual behavior is the sign of human rebellion against God, an outward manifestation of the inward and spiritual rebellion.[62]

---

[59]Philo, *Abr.* 135; *Spec. Leg.* 2.50; 3.37; Wisd 14.12–27; *Test. Naph.* 3.2–4; *Test. Jos.* 7.8.

[60]On the 'paganness' of sexual perversion, note especially *Ep. Arist.* 152; Josephus, *Ag. Ap.* 2.24 §199; *Sib. Or.* 3.594–600. See also Ziesler 1989:78; Fitzmyer 1993:286.

[61]The phrase derives from the positive (rather than 'natural') law of Lev 18.22, which in 18.26 is declared to apply to both Jews and aliens.

[62]Fitzmyer 1993:276. Cf. Hays 1996:385–9; Furnish 1979:58–78; E. P. Sanders 1991:110–13; more generally Sacchi 1973.

Even in this paradigmatic context, however, sexual perversion is of course only one among many pagan sins, as Rom 1.28–32 goes on to show. Denial of God's sovereignty over his creation distorts the mind and leads 'naturally' to *all kinds* of wickedness. As elsewhere, Paul's ensuing catalogue of vices is less clearly Christian and innovative than his catalogues of virtues: instead, he lists sins that are more easily identified as such by existing (albeit primarily Jewish) categories.[63]

We should note that Paul takes his 'natural' point of reference in relation not primarily to immorality but to idolatry. The fundamental argument concerns misdirected worship of the creature. Immorality in that sense may also be παρὰ φύσιν, but this simply follows upon the prior 'unnaturalness' of idolatry.

Romans 2.14–15

In the past, scholars frequently considered Romans 2.14–15 to be the key New Testament passage on natural law.[64] Paul seems here at first sight to allow for the possibility of a 'natural' law observance by Gentiles. Upon closer examination, however, the passage turns out to have remarkably little to say about our subject. At best, it allows for the possibility that some Gentiles might 'naturally' (φύσει) keep the requirements *of the Torah*.[65] What is in view is the possibility that some of the Torah's stipulations (τὰ τοῦ νόμου) might be kept instinctively by Gentiles who do not actually know them.[66] Paul's concern, in other words, is not some sort of separate 'natural law', but rather a 'natural' or common-sense *knowledge* of the one Law of God, subjectively mediated by the individual's moral consciousness. Paul's allowance for the universality of this organ of moral epistemology is indeed significant, in that it establishes the sphere of creation as a valid arena of Christian moral discourse.[67] With respect to the positive *substance* of Pauline ethics, however, there is not in fact a great deal to learn here.

[63]Cf. also p. 14 and n. 30 above.

[64]For references see e.g. the brief discussion in Fitzmyer 1993:306–7.

[65]Martens 1994a points out that, according to Stoic thought, only a rare sage would in fact follow the demands of nature.

[66]Cf. Fitzmyer 1993:309; also Seifrid 1998:122–3.

[67]Cf. e.g. Lohse 1989. Prof. Francis Watson rightly draws my attention to Bonhoeffer's views on the incarnation as vindicating life and ethics in the natural world – which Bonhoeffer calls the 'penultimate' realm. See Bonhoeffer 1955:143–5; cf. Feil 1985:144–6. Cf. also more recently the rather different conceptions of a Christian theology of 'nature' in O'Donovan 1994:58–67; Pannenberg 1993:72–113 and *passim*.

1 Corinthians 11.14

Despite its superficially trivial appearance, Paul's most explicit appeal to nature as a moral authority is at the same time his most perplexing. 'Does not nature itself (ἡ φύσις αὐτή) teach you that if a man wears long hair, it is degrading to him, but if a woman has long hair, it is her glory?' (1 Cor 11.14–15). Innumerable interpretations of this passage have been advanced, although they have frequently made insufficient philosophical and exegetical distinctions. C. H. Dodd in his famous essay on 'Natural Law in the New Testament', for instance, fails to use the term 'nature' with adequate precision, or to distinguish between 'nature' and 'common sense'.[68]

This text is admittedly a hermeneutical jungle. Several relevant points may, however, be made. First, Helmut Koester rightly notes that hair and beards constituted a popular topic in contemporary Stoic diatribe about what might be in keeping with 'nature'.[69] For Paul's younger contemporary Epictetus of Hierapolis (c. 55–135), for example, hair is nature's bequest; like the voice, it is God's evident outward sign to distinguish male from female, a sign that should be preserved and not confused (*Diss.* 1.16.9–14). A man who removes his facial hair in effect objects against nature's decision that he should have been born male (*Diss.* 3.1.27–30).[70]

---

[68]Dodd 1953:133. Moral principles according to nature must be distinguished from the epistemological question of a *natural knowledge* of morality.

[69]Cf. Koester 1974:257.

[70]It is worth quoting at length from 3.1 (LCL), a passage whose Corinthian associations provide important background information for Paul's statement: 'Young man, whom do you wish to make beautiful? In the first place, know who you are and then adorn yourself appropriately. You are a human being; and this is a mortal animal which has the power of using appearances rationally. But what is meant by "rationally"? Conformably to nature and completely. What, then, do you possess which is peculiar? Is it the animal part? No. Is it the condition of mortality? No. Is it the power of using appearances? No. You possess the rational faculty as a peculiar thing: adorn and beautify this; but leave your hair to him who made it as he chose. Come, what other appellations have you? Are you man or woman? "Man." Adorn yourself then as man, not as woman. Woman is naturally smooth and delicate; and if she has much hair (on her body), she is a monster and is exhibited at Rome among monsters. And in a man it is monstrous not to have hair; and if he has no hair, he is a monster; but if he cuts off his hairs and plucks them out, what shall we do with him? Where shall we exhibit him? And under what name shall we show him? "I will exhibit to you a man who chooses to be a woman rather than a man." What a terrible sight! There is no man who will not wonder at such a notice. Indeed I think that the men who pluck out their hairs do what they do without knowing what they do. Man, what fault have you to find with your nature? That it made you a man? What then? Was it fit that nature should make all human creatures women? And what advantage in that case would you have had in being adorned? For whom would you have adorned yourself, if all human creatures were women? But you are not pleased with the matter: set to work then upon the whole business. Take away – what is its name? – that which is the cause of the hairs: make yourself a woman in all respects, that we may not be mistaken: do

Countless visual representations of ancient hairstyles suggest that men's hair tended indeed to be kept relatively short, presumably to facilitate mobility in labour, war and sport. If Acts 18.18 is anything to go by, Paul himself had short hair, which was only temporarily allowed to grow for the purpose of fulfilling his vow. Sculptures and frescoes show that women's hair in the first century was generally longer but wrapped around the head in braids,[71] thus enhancing the natural beauty of the head.[72]

Paul's appeal to 'nature' in this context does of course have a great deal to do with ancient custom and convention. Contrary to a widely held misconception among commentators, however, Paul himself actually appeals to a contemporary argument about *intrinsic* distinctions between men and women. Indeed φύσις here *does* mean 'the natural order', 'the way the world is', as perceived by a widely held first-century Graeco-Roman consensus about civilized life. On this view, it was precisely the mark of savage barbarians or of the sexually dissolute to deviate from this order of nature.[73] Sculpture and literary sources agree that women in first-century Corinth wore

---

not make one half man, and the other half woman. Whom do you wish to please? The women? Please them as a man. "Well; but they like smooth men." Will you not hang yourself? And if women took delight in catamites, would you become one? Is this your business? Were you born for this purpose, that dissolute women should delight in you? Shall we make such a one as you a citizen of Corinth and perchance a prefect of the city, or chief of the youth, or general or superintendent of the games? Well, and when you have taken a wife, do you intend to have your hairs plucked out? To please whom and for what purpose? And when you have begotten children, will you introduce them also into the state with the habit of plucking their hairs? A beautiful citizen, and senator and rhetorician. We ought to pray that such young men be born among us and brought up.'

[71]E. Pottier et al. as cited in Murphy-O'Connor 1990:809; also Thompson 1988.

[72]Cf. Achilles Tatius 8.5.4: σεσύληται τῆς κεφαλῆς τὸ κάλλος (of a female slave whose head had been shaved).

[73]Julius Caesar, *De Bello Gallico* 5.14 writes, 'All the Britons, indeed, dye themselves with woad, which occasions a bluish color, and thereby have a more terrible appearance in fight. They wear their hair long, and have every part of their body shaved except their head and upper lip. Ten and even twelve have wives common to them, and particularly brothers among brothers, and parents among their children ...' In the first century AD, Lucan, *Bellum Civile* 1.497–9, writes of *formerly* savage 'Ligurian tribes, now shorn, in ancient days | First of the long-haired nations, on whose necks | Once flowed the auburn locks in pride supreme'. Plutarch, however, was well aware that even the Spartans used to have a different view: Lysander (d. 395 BC) wore his hair 'very long, after the ancient custom, and growing a generous beard. For it is not true, as some state, that because the Argives, after their great defeat, shaved their heads for sorrow, the Spartans, in contrary fashion, let their hair grow long in exultation over their victory; nor was it because the Bacchiadae, when they fled from Corinth to Lacedaemon, looked mean and unsightly from having shaved their heads, that the Spartans, on their part, became eager to wear their hair long; but this custom also goes back to Lycurgus. And he is reported to have said that a fine head of hair makes the handsome more comely to look upon, and the ugly more terrible.' (*Lysander* 1.1–3; cf. Herodotus 7.208–9).

their hair long, but neatly braided and coiled or tied on top of their heads.[74] It is particularly interesting to note that, contrary to their custom elsewhere, female devotees of the Isis cult in first-century Roman Corinth apparently anointed their hair *and covered it* with a linen cloth; Corrington suggests that this was to show themselves behaving in a seemly Roman fashion.[75]

The particular argument of this passage, however, derives from the fact that in this context the perversion of hairstyles denoted a perversion of sexual identity. For a man to wear female hairstyle was a way of communicating effeminacy and thus homosexuality. It is likely, therefore, that for Paul men's long hair is 'unnatural' not just by common convention or sentiment, but especially because of what it is perceived to denote in the moral realm. As we saw in Romans 1, both Paul and Hellenistic Judaism decried homosexual acts as *intrinsically* contrary to the created order.[76]

At the same time, the reference to 'nature' (1 Cor 11.14) is not for Paul the highest authority, the knock-down argument that settles the matter. Instead, it is a parting shot that appeals to a kind of lowest common denominator[77]: οὐδέ, used similarly in 5.1, suggests a translation along the lines of 'doesn't even nature teach you otherwise?' Unlike Cicero, Paul would certainly *not* agree that 'we shall never err if we follow nature'.[78] He himself does not hesitate to depart from nature in the name of the gospel, as is obvious from his remarks both about the funding of his ministry in 9.7 and about celibacy in chapter 7. Paul seems instead to be quite aware of the ambivalence of 'nature'; and this awareness may well lurk behind his concession in 11.16 that the appeal to a consensus about 'nature' will not persuade everyone.

Other Possible Uses of Natural Law

From time to time one encounters the opposite argument, namely that the idea of compliance with a public moral consensus is essentially alien to Paul. On this reckoning, the Christian commendation of public conventions only surfaces in the supposedly more bourgeois ethic of the deutero-Pauline epistles, especially the

---

[74]See Thompson 1988.

[75]See Corrington 1991:229, also cited by Schrage 493 n. 27, in relation to 1 Cor 11.5. The female initiates depicted in the frescoes of the Villa dei Misteri at Pompeii wear their hair tied up, and the only one who does not is being beaten: cf. Thompson 1988:112.

[76]Note especially Ps.-Phoc. 212; see also Murphy-O'Connor 1990:809, and p. 130 above.

[77]Cf. Schrage 1995:521, to whom I am indebted in the following comments.

[78]*De Officiis* 1.28.100; cf. related sources cited in Schrage 1995:521 n. 208.

Pastorals in their pre-occupation with ordered households and respectable Christian leadership.

It is of course true that Paul's ethics can be markedly counter-cultural, as we shall see below (pp. 137–40). At the same time, however, the concern for a credible Christian presence in the normal and natural fibres of human society pervades the Pauline corpus from the very earliest to the very latest letters. This is a point of sufficient importance to merit the brief discussion of several additional passages.

Within a few months of founding the church at Thessalonica in the year 49/50, the Apostle urges Christians there 'to aspire to live quietly, to mind your own affairs, and to work with your hands ... so that you may behave properly towards outsiders and be dependent on no one' (1 Thess 4.11–12; cf. 2 Thess 3.10–11). Without formulating a considered view of 'nature' or public polity, this stance clearly takes for granted the existence and moral significance of the public realm – and thereby implies the need and legitimacy of a public moral discourse.

Christian ethics, then, remains for Paul intelligently attuned to public social conventions, so as to cause no impediment for the gospel. At the same time, as Edwin Judge and others have suggested, the demand to work for one's living is a reaction against the parasitic abuse of the patronage system in the Thessalonian church, and may moreover endorse a widespread public distaste for the practices of certain Cynic preachers.[79] This viewpoint is closely analogous to that which recurs in Ephesians 4.28 and of course in 1 Timothy 2.2. To cause no offence and live irreproachable public lives is commended to all, and especially to Christian leaders (cf. further 1 Cor 10.31–33; Col 4.5–6; 1 Tim 3.7).

Implicit appeals to 'nature' or universal convention are also present in a number of other passages in 1 Corinthians, notably in the incest case of 5.1 ('immorality ... of a kind that is not even found among pagans')[80] and in the public disorder problem of 14.23 (church order is required not least because outsiders will 'say that you are out of your mind'; cf. v. 40). The almost incidental nature of these appeals to public decorum, however, cautions against the construction of any systematic Pauline appeal to nature.

[79] Judge 1984b:23; Winter 1984:42–60; cf. Barclay 1993:523, who suggests an intentional contrast with the behaviour of Cynic preachers.

[80] A man's sexual union with a stepmother was condemned both by Jews (e.g. Lev 18.8; 20.11; *m. Sanh.* 7.4) and by Gentiles – at least by Romans, whose sexual *mores* were often stricter than those in Egypt or Greece. Cf. Schrot 1979; Tomson 1990:97–103; Murphy-O'Connor 1990:803.

Finally, Romans 13.1–7 merits a further comment under this heading. This much-debated passage deals with the political authority of Roman magistrates. It does so at a time of relative peace in the early years of Nero's rule: Jewish Christians had recently returned to Rome after the expulsion under Claudius in AD 49, and were perhaps still in a somewhat nervous political state. The discussion of taxes in this passage also fits in general with the increasing public unrest over calls for tax reform during this period.[81] A third background factor for Paul's writing may have been the popularity of the emperor cult in his own context of the eastern empire: could Christians justifiably pay taxes to one who elicited competing worship as a divine Saviour?[82]

The actual argument in these verses is in fact straightforward and remarkably similar to what appears in contemporary Jewish and Christian literature on the subject.[83] For our purposes, it is worth noting that Paul grounds his instructions in what he clearly regards as a universal creational given: political authority is the exclusive gift and prerogative of God (v. 1), who alone can delegate it to civil government. This delegation gives a divinely sanctioned authority even to the Roman administration as God's servant for the common good (εἰς τὸ ἀγαθόν, note verses 4, 6). But it also *limits* the legitimate exercise of that authority (verse 7; cf. also the εἷς κύριος of 1 Cor 8.6). The universality of this argument for the rightful authority of government is clear both from the general tone of verse 1 and from the much-noted absence of christological reasoning.

As already in 1.19 and 2.15, therefore, Paul's moral canvas is here unrestricted. He appeals to moral intention ('conscience', συνείδησις, v. 5) and takes for granted not only substantial agreement with diaspora Jewish political thought but also, it seems, a conscious Roman Christian engagement with society's public institutions.[84]

Two additional dimensions of Paul's stance here are worth bearing in mind. First, Christian respect for civil government also had strategic and *practical* connotations for the church in these early

---

[81]See Tacitus, *Annales* 13.50–1; Suetonius, *Nero* 10.1.

[82]On these background considerations, see further e.g. Fitzmyer 1993:35–6, 662–3; Friedrich et al. 1976; E. Bammel 1984.

[83]See Jer 29.7; Ezra 6.10; cf. further Prov 8.15–16; Sir 4.27; Wisd 6.3–4; Bar 1.11; 1 Macc 7.33; *Ep. Arist.* 45; Josephus, *War* 2.10.4 §197; *Ag. Ap.* 2.6 §76–7; *m. 'Abot* 3.2; and cf. the famous third-century dictum of Mar Samuel: דִּינָא דְּמַלְכוּתָא דִּינָא, '[even] the [secular] government's legal decision is a [valid] legal decision' (*b. B. Qam.* 113a; see n. 86 below). In the NT, see 1 Pet 2.13–17; Tit 3.1; John 19.11.

[84]Cf. e.g. Fitzmyer 1993:663.

years of Nero's rule. Paul does not formulate a full-fledged political theory. In particular, he does not address the question of what might be the appropriate response when government does *not* punish the wicked and reward the good (though 2 Thess 2.7, if authentic, suggests that he is aware of the problem). For now, the gospel can be advanced by affirming the legitimate authority of Rome – even when the gospel's advantage may be the Christian's personal disadvantage, as the Apostle himself acknowledges in Phil 1.12–14. Paul's position in this respect is remarkably consistent with the one we encountered in Acts.

And secondly, this passage (along with 1 Peter 2.13) contains an implicit affirmation not just of the government's penal authority, but apparently also of the public honouring of good citizens and benefactors in the Roman institution of patronage (as, for example, van Unnik and Winter have suggested).[85] Even if this reference to benefaction may be somewhat tenuous, other Pauline passages clearly commend doing good to one's fellow human beings even beyond the confines of the church: Gal 6.10; Rom 15.2; 1 Cor 10.32; cf. 1 Pet 2.17.

We do not of course have here a derivation of political ethics from 'natural law'. Nevertheless, Romans 13 shows itself to be indebted to the long-standing diaspora Jewish tradition of respecting secular political institutions as universally God-given and entitled to human allegiance. It is also a point of view that is remarkably compatible with later rabbinic ideas of the legitimacy of Gentile government[86] – along with the Noachide obligation to establish and honour civil authorities and lawcourts, which we will encounter in the next chapter.

Paul's Critique of Public Convention

In addition to such Pauline arguments from common sense and universal 'natural' usage, however, we also find a significant countercurrent to the easy symbiosis with 'natural law' and Graeco-Roman convention that the preceding comments might seem to imply. Paul is consistently clear about the Christian *discontinuity* with 'the world' and its way of reasoning. The contrast between the old and the new way of life is a constant theme. Christians no longer think and live as

---

[85]See p. 128 and n. 50 above.

[86]דינא דמלכותא דינא: the judgement of the (Gentile) government is a valid judgement (so e.g. *b. Git.* 10b; *b. Ned.* 28a; *b. B. Qam.* 113a–b; *b. B. Bat.* 54b). See further K. Müller 1998:90, 196–7.

the pagans do (e.g. 1 Thess 4.5; 2 Cor 5.15–17; Eph 4.17–19); the old desires of the flesh must be put away (Gal 5; Rom 6, 8, 12), and Christians progress from being ψυχικός, unspiritual (1 Cor 2.14; 15.44, 46) to being the people of the Spirit. They have left behind the elementary principles (στοιχεῖα) of the world (Gal 4.3, 9; Col 2.8, 20). Having been transferred from darkness to light (Col 1.12), they are to shine as beacons of light in a perverse generation (Phil 2.15).

This kind of reasoning comes into its own above all in Paul's 'theology of the cross', classically spelled out in the passage about wisdom and folly in 1 Corinthians 1.18–2.10. Here Paul undermines many of the seemingly 'natural' Graeco-Roman conventions that his Corinthian readership apparently takes for granted. The whole cultural edifice of status, wealth, and wisdom is attacked from the perspective of the cross of Christ. Here the politics of ambition and advancement is shown up as folly, and all human pedigree and achievement turned on its head.

That text does not of course *directly* address the issue of natural morality or public convention. What we can say, however, is that Paul's theology of the cross leads to a significant transformation of many of the ethical patterns one might expect to find in a Graeco-Roman 'natural law' argument.

Another obvious example of such metamorphosis appears in Paul's lists of virtues. Although he adapts existing structures of paraenesis from Stoic and Hellenistic Jewish thought, subtle alterations suggest a profound christological re-orientation. The themes of humility, meekness, love, joy or peace would not be expected in a Stoic catalogue of virtues: indeed it has often been pointed out that the Christ-like virtues of meekness and humility were in fact terms of derision in Graeco-Roman thought.[87] Status, commendation and freedom are all found in a Christian's relationship with Christ.

Regardless of one's views on authorship, another parenetical form that shows evidence of this Pauline transformation is the *Haustafel* of Colossians and Ephesians (cf. 1 Peter). Here, loyalty to existing creational institutions is retained on the basis of a complete christological re-orientation. Despite all their language of propriety and decency in affirming natural orders, the moral argument of these household codes for the most part is formally based neither on convention nor on nature, but on an appeal to revelation in Christ.[88]

---

[87]In secular Greek, the term ταπεινοφροσύνη rarely appears, and then in a derogatory sense to denote servile weakness, obsequious grovelling or on the other hand mean-spiritedness (e.g. Epictetus, *Discourses* 3.24.56; see W. Grundmann in *TDNT* 8:1-27).

[88]So e.g. Col 3.17 (ἐν ὀνόματι κυρίου Ἰησοῦ), 18, 20 (ἐν κυρίῳ), 22 (ἐν ἁπλότητι καρδίας φοβούμενοι τὸν κύριον), 23 (ὡς τῷ κυρίῳ καὶ οὐκ ἀνθρώποις), 24 (τῷ κυρίῳ Χριστῷ δουλεύετε), 4.1 (καὶ ὑμεῖς ἔχετε κύριον ἐν οὐρανῷ). Similarly Eph 5.20 – 6.9, although 6.2 appeals to the Decalogue.

Paul himself, a middle-class Roman citizen, artisan and trained scholar, does not shy away from identifying himself regularly as a slave (δοῦλος). He advises masters to do the same, treating their slaves as brothers, and slaves to regard themselves as the freedmen of the Lord (1 Cor 7.22; Col 4.1; Phlm). In regard to earthly institutions, Christians render respectful service not as a 'natural obligation' but for the sake of Christ. At the same time, the old racial and sexual hierarchies of power that were rooted in the conventions of 'nature' are reconceived in Christ (cf. Gal 3.28; Col 3.11).

This same paradox of simultaneous affirmation and subversion, previously encountered in the teaching of Jesus, continues to the very latest of Paul's writings. Thus, Philippians 4.8 would seem to confirm that the demands of the gospel encompass what is good for humanity in general: 'Finally, beloved, whatever is true, whatever is honourable, whatever is just, whatever is pure, whatever is pleasing, whatever is commendable, if there is any excellence and if there is anything worthy of praise, think about these things.' The general Hellenistic nature of this list of virtues has often been pointed out: aside from the address to Christian believers (ἀδελφοί), it contains little or nothing that could not have been written as part of contemporary Stoic moral exhortation.[89] The paradox is that after his repeated development of a stark *antithesis* between Christ and the world (note especially Phil 1.27–30; 2.15, 21; 3.2–14, 18–21), Paul now offers a properly inculturated Christian exhortation in the philosophical vernacular of Roman Philippi.[90] Arguments like these were later used by Clement of Alexandria and other patristic writers to show the compatibility of Christian and classical virtues.[91]

In spite of the emphases of Romans 13 and related passages in the Pastorals, the theme of *citizenship*, too, is subject to serious reorientation in Paul's thought. Writing to the church in the Roman colony of Philippi, which took pride in its privileged status of citizenship, Paul insists that first and foremost a Christian citizen's conduct must be worthy, not of the public institutions of the Empire, but of the gospel of Christ (Phil 1.27). Indeed a Christian's primary citizenship is not in Rome but in heaven, from where the real Redeemer will come (Phil 3.20); Galatians 4.26 expresses this in terms of allegiance to the

[89]Cf. e.g. Engberg-Pedersen 1995, and more generally Pohlenz 1949; Sevenster 1961.

[90]Contrast this idea with passages like Phil 2.1, 5–11, where the Christian mind comes to expression in Christ-like virtues of compassion and humility – qualities, in other words, that would strike an alien and contrary note within the cultural world of the moral pagan. Cf. Bockmuehl 1997:250.

[91]Cf. Pelikan 1993:129, 141; also Chadwick 1966:15–17, 39, 103–5.

Jerusalem above.[92] It hardly needs mentioning, of course, that Christian apocalyptic literature like the Johannine Apocalypse makes rather heavy weather of the contrast between Christ and a political power that is perceived in largely demonic terms. On the other hand, as we shall see in Chapter 8, second-century apologetics managed, rather like Paul, to combine the themes of exemplary citizenship with that of Christians as citizens of every country and of none.[93]

In this connection, finally, we should recall that despite the New Testament's generally positive attitude to Christian contributions to society, the Graeco-Roman system of benefaction and patronage comes in for repeated criticism. We encountered several such occasions in Jesus and Paul (e.g. Luke 22.25; 1 Thess 4.12), and must here merely note the sustained parody of the Hellenistic conventions of praise and commendation in 2 Corinthians.[94] Chapter 3 plays on the custom of letters of commendation, while the whole tenor of chapters 1–7 stresses the theme of strength through weakness and suffering. The self-seeking achievements of Paul's opponents in 2 Corinthians 10–13 are similarly deconstructed from the perspective of Christ's power in weakness. As Edwin Judge has shown, in the Corinthian correspondence Paul enters into a head-on confrontation with the mechanisms of power in the Roman patronage system, and puts in its place the unusual concept of οἰκοδομή or building up.[95] In place of the self-seeking and calculating relationships of clients and patrons, we find Christ who gives the indiscriminate gifts of grace and of the Spirit (1 Cor 12.4–11; cf. Eph 4.7–12 etc.).

Conclusion

This chapter clearly remains incomplete in its coverage of both topics and texts. It would be interesting, for example, to discuss the virtual absence from New Testament ethics of *aesthetic* considerations.[96]

---

[92]One might compare Ephesians, which stresses the Gentile Christians' incorporation into the commonwealth of Israel as fellow citizens with the saints (2.12, 19). Hebrews later also offers the imagery of the Christian's citizenship of the heavenly Jerusalem (12.22) along with his or her existence on earth as a foreigner (11.13 and *passim*), and as one whose place is outside the city (13.12–14).

[93]Note *Diogn.* 5.4, 9, and see Roldanus 1987. Contrast Winter 1994:12, 200–2 and *passim*, whose argument perhaps does not allow sufficiently for the prominence of this theme of exile.

[94]Cf. e.g. Davis 1999; Heckel 1993; Savage 1996.

[95]Judge 1984b:22–4.

[96]As a possible exception note, perhaps, the passages on women's hair in 1 Cor 11; 1 Peter 3.4; Phil 4.8; contrast Luke 21.5; Matt 23.27.

Further consideration of the complex cultural role of honour and shame as 'natural' or conventional motivating factors would also be useful. More careful documentation of the *social setting* of the natural law argument would be difficult, but nonetheless highly desirable: although it is broadly attested in literature under Stoic influence, to what sort of audience could it presume to appeal?[97]

We have concentrated on the traditions associated with Jesus and Paul, as containing arguably the most fruitful material. Nevertheless, a more complete study would also need to consider the scattered evidence in the remainder of the New Testament writings, including especially the epistles of James and 1 Peter. James is of interest because of its largely sapiential approach to ethics.[98] In some cases, this Christian wisdom makes specific reference to natural phenomena (e.g. 1.9–11; 1.22–25; 3.3–5, 7–12). Bearing in mind the distinctions drawn above at the beginning of Chapter 5, however, these arguments are largely concerned with *illustration and analogy*, not with a moral appeal to a 'natural' state of affairs.[99] The First Letter of Peter, too, has a strongly developed interest in Christian witness in the midst of adversity. The writer repeatedly appeals to the notion that Christian moral behaviour is *inherently* persuasive of an unbelieving or hostile public: God has ordained that doing right should serve to 'silence the ignorance of the foolish' (2.15; cf. 2.12; 3.1–2). Similarly, the author takes for granted that the message implied in right conduct is both universally intelligible and persuasive to the human mind – a conviction that furnishes a rudimentary platform for his instructions about Christian public ethics. At the same time, of course, it is also true that 1 Peter never develops this thought into a formal moral appeal to creation.

Three final points may serve as a conclusion. We have seen in the

---

[97]For the New Testament, unlike perhaps for Philo, the answer to these questions would in any case rest on rather slender and diffuse evidence, and an obvious literary or rhetorical *Sitz im Leben* has not emerged from our study. It is also worth noting how the fledgling Christian communities throughout the Empire would almost constantly have had to face the problem of justifying the Christian way of life in terms intelligible to a hostile or indifferent majority. Apologetic concerns, including those relating to morality, were at times not just of academic interest but a matter of life and death; but at at no time in the first three centuries of our era did Christianity enjoy the protection of civil and religious rights. The public face of Christian morality was a constant concern, as the pages of the New Testament make very clear. See further Chapters 8–9 below.

[98]Cf. e.g. Baker 1995 and the important new study of Bauckham 1999:29–111, 152–5, 203–5.

[99]Note e.g. the fading of riches compared to Middle Eastern grass that withers at the onset of summer, 1.9-11. The only exception may be 3.11–12, where the compatibility of a tree and its fruit reinforces the call for personal integrity in speech.

Gospels and in Paul a remarkable confluence of attitudes to moral arguments from 'nature'.

1. On the one hand, the Gospels, Acts and Paul freely affirm and use a variety of observations from the created order in contexts of moral instruction. In this regard, early Christianity agrees substantially with Jewish wisdom[100] and to some extent with Stoic moral teaching. Without affirming a simplistic physical deontology, there is nevertheless a shared awareness of an underlying 'hierarchy of goods'[101] that transcends the complex specificities of time, place and custom. Human beings are created by God in a certain way and for a certain purpose: and the way things are with all of us has implications both for the common-sense possibility of moral knowledge and for the practical responsibilities arising from that knowledge. The health of the world demands that the Creator's sovereignty should be respected, and what he has made must not be perverted. God affirms his creation, but is distinct from it: and certain human responses are intrinsically incompatible with that fact. Such moral references to 'nature' are never straightforwardly deductive in form, but tend instead to constitute an informal appeal to universal common sense ('does not nature itself teach you . . .?'), a rhetorical consensus-building device drawing on shared assumptions about God and the created order.

2. At the same time, the created world is also fundamentally in need of redemption. The perception of 'nature' and public convention is for the New Testament remarkably ambivalent as a source of moral authority, and needs in significant respects to be transcended.[102] Both Paul and the Gospel tradition show a deeply subversive attitude to 'natural' morality, shaped largely by considerations of soteriology, eschatology and resultant moral implications. We find that conventional obligations and expectations are profoundly relativized and sidelined in the face of the coming kingdom of God, which is the kingdom not of the fittest and strongest but of Christ crucified. The inauguration of the new age in Christ means that early Christianity is critically selective in its acceptance of earlier moral assumptions.[103] Natural law is never simply identical with revelation, and can certainly never substitute for it.

---

[100]Compare Irenaeus, *Haer.* 4.13.4: all precepts of natural law are shared with the Jews (*naturalia omnia praecepta communia sunt nobis et illis*).

[101]A phrase used by Arkes 1992:274–5.

[102]It is interesting to compare the illuminating, if somewhat atypical perspective of 2 Peter 1.4, with its call to escape the corruption of this world (κόσμος) in order to participate instead in the *divine* φύσις.

[103]Cf. Schrage 1988:201, citing V. P. Furnish.

3. And finally, this fact throws us back to the question of criteria: which 'natural laws' and which public conventions are for Christians authoritatively valid, and which are not? For an answer to this, however, New Testament ethics invariably turns to *positive* law: that is to say, to the articulation of an ethic for Gentiles and above all to the authority of the person, word and work of Jesus. In other words, the New Testament authors' description of the created order is invariably underwritten by the incarnation and resurrection of Christ; it can never be considered other than *ex post facto*. Christ is both its source and its destiny, ὅτι ἐξ αὐτοῦ καὶ δι᾽ αὐτοῦ καί εἰς αὐτὸν τὰ πάντα (Rom 11.36; cf. Col 1.16). And yet, from this vantage point, it is all the more remarkable that the early Christian focus of attention still always remains the created *universe* and all its citizens. The moral theatre of redemption is nothing less than *the world* that God has loved. Creational givens are at once relativized, embraced and redeemed in the light of Christ's resurrection, and of the renewal of creation that he promises and we await. ὃ γέγονεν ἐν αὐτῷ ζωὴ ἦν, καὶ ἡ ζωὴ ἦν τὸ φῶς τῶν ἀνθρώπων (John 1.4).

7

THE NOACHIDE COMMANDMENTS AND
NEW TESTAMENT ETHICS

Late twentieth-century Europe and especially North America have witnessed the gradual corrosion of their public moral consensus; as a result, meaningful ethical discourse in society has become increasingly difficult. Alasdair MacIntyre, one of the shrewder commentators on this process, writes,

> The most striking feature of contemporary moral utterance is that so much of it is used to express disagreements; and the most striking feature of the debates in which these disagreements are expressed is their interminable character. . . . There seems to be no rational way of securing moral agreement in our culture.[1]

Where a shared foundation of morality cannot be assumed, how can one speak about right and wrong? After decades in the cultural wilderness, the issue of public ethics is more pressing than ever.

To appreciate this peculiarly post-Constantinian and 'post-modern' problem can in turn raise our awareness of related concerns in the experience of the ancient church, forced as it was to discover what the God of Israel might require of Gentiles who believed in Christ. At the Apostolic Council in Jerusalem it was resolved that Gentiles can be saved *as Gentiles*, without needing to convert to Judaism. To be sure, this in itself was quite a revolutionary step. But it is one thing to say that Jews and Gentiles together constitute the people of God; quite another, to define the common life of that new covenant people. Unlike the Torah, the New Testament never uses 'Thou shalt' or 'Thou shalt not', except in quotations;[2] and it never grounds a moral precept purely and simply on 'thus it is written'. On what positive grounds, then, did the early Church talk to Gentile believers about ethics, if the Mosaic laws as such could not now be the basis of appeal?

Closely related to this internal Christian discussion is the second, much wider problem of how Jews and Christians in general spoke about ethics to a largely indifferent or adversarial public in the Roman imperial setting of a pluralistic paganism with its very different moral systems – be it for purposes of apologetics, evangelism, or catechesis.

---

[1]MacIntyre 1981:6. Cf. more generally Bloom 1987; Bellah et al. 1985.
[2]Thus also Daube 1981:89–90.

As one contribution to the study of that larger issue, this chapter will consider the relevance to the New Testament of the Noachide Commandments, as a key formulation of Jewish ethics for Gentiles. The argument here will be that when they are assessed on a continuum of biblical and post-biblical halakhah for aliens, the Noachide Commandments and their pre-rabbinic predecessors are an important pointer to the criteria and rationale that fuelled concrete ethical instructions of the Apostolic mission to the Gentiles.

Methodological Concerns

Before going on to discuss the *topos* of the Noachide Commandments as such, I wish to introduce a few additional considerations of method, pertaining both to this particular subject and to the more general question of early Christianity's formulation of a universal ethic. Preliminary reading suggests at least three methodological obstacles to such a study, as we turn from 'natural' to positive law.

Law as a Topic of Early Christian Ethics

For Gentile Christianity, the Torah could not *as such* be assumed to function as law. This fact, however, in turn gives rise to a host of related historical problems. Did the concrete substance of its ethics have a specifically Christian character? Which concepts or principles, if any, *did* have the force of moral law? Obvious illustrations of this dilemma include the problem of purity in mixed Jewish-Gentile congregations, as well as Paul's decisions about sex and idolatry in 1 Corinthians 5–10.

However, any discussion of this fundamentally legal problem soon runs into a curious dearth of relevant secondary literature. True, there is a real glut of *meta-legal* treatises on the New Testament, and to a lesser extent on the early Patristic period. That is to say, we do have numerous studies of Jesus' or Paul's *view* of the Law, as well as miscellaneous New Testament *theologies* of Law.[3] Few scholars, however, have considered the properly legal, halakhic aspects of the subject. That is to say, few have bothered specifically to ask the question, 'What is the New Testament's applied ethics or *halakhah* – and how does it work?'

It is not tautologous, then, to affirm that there is a need to think about law *legally* and morally, rather than primarily in terms of a

[3]So again Heikki Räisänen's survey (1992:252–77).

(Christian) *theology* of law. A few scholars like D. Daube and
J. D. M. Derrett have published work along these lines; more recently,
P. J. Tomson and A. F. Segal have contributed valuable studies.[4]

'Law' vs. 'Gospel'

Following scholars like C. G. Montefiore and K. Stendahl, E. P.
Sanders has received the lion's share of the credit for debunking the
traditional Protestant assumption that first-century Judaism was a
fundamentally 'legalistic' religion, unacquainted with the grace of
God as taught by Jesus and by Paul. A great deal has been written
on this subject in the last twenty-five years.

However, the logical corollary of this thesis on the *Christian* side
was not specifically addressed by Sanders, and has remained virtually
untreated in scholarly literature. I refer to the parallel assumption of
an antithesis of 'Gospel' vs. 'Law' in the teachings of Jesus, Paul, and
the early church. This crypto-Marcionite perspective tacitly underlies
much of the past century's Protestant theological literature, and
appears to have deep roots in the sixteenth- and seventeenth-century
Lutheran orthodox debates about the so-called 'third use of the law'
(*tertius usus legis*), favoured by Calvin and Melanchthon but
opposed by the hyper-Lutherans. Many Lutheran authors to this day
discount that law (any law, whether Mosaic or otherwise) might
have a role to play in Christian ethics. Other modern manifestations
of this include the continuing assertions that Jesus or Paul 'annulled'
or 'abrogated' the law (a claim apparently first made by Origen)[5],
and probably the recurring intimations that New Testament passages
of concrete ethical instruction or practical community discipline are
somehow theologically retrograde and sub-Christian.[6]

The Problem of Universal Law

The third significant issue was already raised in a related form in
Chapter 6 (see above, pp. 113–16): the widespread academic
suspicion besetting any study of universal or 'natural' law. As we
concluded there, the actual ancient usage of the concept of a divinely
sanctioned universal law is sufficiently well established to make its

---

[4]E.g. Derrett 1970, 1982; Daube 1956:55–105; A. F. Segal 1990, 1995; Tomson 1990. For
the underlying problems, it is still worth consulting Dodd 1951:64–83.

[5]Even that attribution, of course, might be contested. But see e.g. *C. Cels.* 5.48; 7.26; and
cf. p. 14 and n. 28 above.

[6]Cf. J. Barton's apt summary (1999:16) of E. P. Sanders' work: 'Paul himself is not always
Pauline in the sense defined by Luther.'

study a legitimate exercise. For the more limited purposes of the present chapter, it suffices to reiterate that ancient Jewish and Christian writers shared the unquestioned assumption that humanity's common place in the world implies certain universal principles of right and wrong – principles that were divinely stipulated, continuous with all just systems of *positive* law, and recognizable by cultured peoples everywhere. Modern philosophical distaste for such lines of argument should not cause us to ignore their considerable importance in the sources.[7]

Form and Substance in New Testament Ethics

Textbooks of New Testament ethics are for the most part united in stressing a radical innovation in the theological *form* of early Christian ethics. The moral demand of Christianity, writes W. D. Davies, 'is concentrated in the Person of Christ'.[8] Certainly for the New Testament as a whole there can be little doubt about the defining significance of the person and work of Christ. The resulting unique orientation of early Christian ethics gives rise to several interesting developments. In particular, one notes a shift in most New Testament authors from the Torah to Christ as the formal motivation, authority and example in Christian moral discourse.

In its *substance*, however, New Testament ethics is much less radically changed. In addition to the teaching and example of Jesus, most scholars perceive a generally Jewish Hellenistic background, which the Christians derived from their contact with the diaspora synagogue. In particular, several authors have noted the influence of synagogal exhortation and catechesis-like instruction drawn from certain passages in the Torah.[9] Increasingly, scholars are also beginning to acknowledge the formative influence of Jewish Torah interpretation on New Testament ethics, especially in Paul.[10] This use of Torah is obviously selective (it concentrates on 'nuggets' from passages like Exod 20 or Lev 18–20); but it may represent a kind of ethical *testimonia* tradition.[11]

---

[7]Cf. recently Barr 1990, 1993; J. Barton 1998; earlier scholarly treatments include Dodd 1953, Koester, 1968 and R. A. Horsley 1978. See Chapters 5–6 above, *passim*. Novak 1998:22–44 offers a sustained argument that natural law traditions are necessarily assumed as part of the conceptual structure of covenant and of halakhah.

[8]W. D. Davies 1972:315. Cf. Schnackenburg 1986:25; Schrage 1988:8.

[9]See e.g. Thyen 1955; Niebuhr 1987; Hodgson 1976; Carrington 1940; Gottlieb Klein 1909; Seeberg 1903; Selwyn 1947:365–466.

[10]So e.g. Holtz 1981, Reinmuth 1985, Rosner 1994; Finsterbusch 1996.

[11]See Harris 1916–20; cf. also Hodgson 1976, Carrington 1940 and others.

At the same time, recognizing the Torah's general influence on New Testament ethics raises numerous further questions when it comes to the more concrete methodological and moral issues. What were the *criteria* for the selection of Pentateuchal material for Christian ethics? Why, for example, is Pauline ethics never based *purely and simply* on the Torah?[12] Why is the Old Testament's Sabbath legislation optional, whereas its sexual morality evidently is not? On what grounds did early Christianity de-emphasize many of the so-called 'ritual' laws of the Hebrew Bible but stress the more general, 'moral' ones? Having previously alluded to questions like these,[13] it will be the aim of the present chapter to outline one historically viable approach.[14]

Even from a purely Gentile point of view, the problems of early Christian ethics are no less significant. Nowadays it is often argued that in terms of social ethics, the New Testament, Paul and the deutero-Paulines above all, simply swallowed much of the contemporary value system as a quick way to gain societal recognition – and to suppress the influence of unruly women, slaves, charismatics and millenarians.

This argument, however, is flawed in at least two ways. First, it assumes that religion and ethics are as unrelated for Paul as they seem to be for some of his modern interpreters. The early Christians were perhaps not quite so crudely pragmatic. And secondly, as H. D. Betz has shown, it fails to recognize that not only Christian teaching but popular Hellenistic morality, too, was in fact inalienably *religious*. Precisely for this reason, a Christian (or for that matter a Jew) could not simply regard popular Graeco-Roman morality as neutral; as a whole, it was positively other and *pagan*.[15] This applies to a host of issues relating to food, commerce, magic, sex, prostitution, etc. It is clearly true, as we saw in Chapter 6, that the New Testament at times appeals to 'public' conventions of morality (e.g. 1 Cor 5.1; 1 Tim 2.2; cf. also 1 Cor 11.14; 14.23; and the household codes). Nevertheless, the relationship with contemporary popular ethics is complex and by no means uncritical. Although both Jews

---

[12]Cf. Schrage 1988:206 (excepting Rom 12.19); Westerholm 1986–87:232.

[13]See above, p. 117.

[14]The classic answer, disqualifying 'civil' and 'ceremonial' laws based on a kind of systematization of Hebrews, is hardly satisfactory. Indeed the very distinction between moral, civil and ceremonial laws, aside from being unknown to the Old and New Testaments and to Judaism, is legally unworkable and practically awkward. Who would confidently classify the laws about gleaning or the taking of a bird's nest, not to mention the Sabbath and the command about images?

[15]Cf. H. D. Betz 1988:200–1.

and Christians often found allied ideas in Stoicism and were able to endorse certain Graeco-Roman concepts of virtue, convention, and natural law, philosophical convenience alone does not satisfactorily explain which practices were acceptable and which were not. The criteria of selection clearly must be sought elsewhere.

It is in this question of the *rationale* of New Testament ethics that the Noachide Commandments will prove to be relevant. They provide an external perspective on what second-century rabbinic Judaism considered the halakhah to require of righteous Gentiles – precisely the question which, *mutatis mutandis*, Christian Jews had asked themselves a century earlier. The remainder of this chapter will introduce some of the relevant texts and issues, concluding with reflections on a few of the most notable points of contact with the New Testament.

The Noachide Commandments

Briefly put, the *topos* of Noachide Law in rabbinic thought governs relations between Jews and non-Jews, and is thus a kind of functional equivalent to the Roman *ius gentium*.[16] Its basis lies in the conviction that God gave certain pre-Sinaitic laws equally to all humankind, laws that may therefore form the ethical foundation of Jewish dealings with Gentiles.

Antecedents

The rabbinic argument about Noachide Commandments takes its cue explicitly from the Bible. We must therefore begin by taking a brief look at key Old Testament passages that bear on the issue of ethics for Gentiles.

Genesis 1–11

The point of departure here must be Genesis 1–11. Genesis 2.16–17 is God's first explicit command to humanity, a fact which made it a key text for rabbinic Judaism:

וַיְצַו יְהוָה אֱלֹהִים עַל־הָאָדָם לֵאמֹר ....

A literal translation might read,

---

[16]B. Cohen 1966:1.26–7; Novak 1983:xiii. Note that it is therefore *positive* law, as distinct from 'natural' law (cf. the Roman *ius naturale*). Nevertheless, Novak 1998:191–2 (cf. 149–73, 182) offers the plausible but controversial argument that Noachide law is at the same time 'the Jewish way of thinking natural law' (p. 191). Cf. p. 115 above.

'And the LORD God commanded regarding (the) man, saying. ...'

Not implausibly, the Rabbis took Genesis 2.16 to mean that there were commandments relevant to all human beings. With a bit of clever midrash, the idea of six commandments given to Adam was commonly rooted in Genesis 2.16–17: the prohibition of idolatry, blasphemy, adjudication, homicide, illicit sex, theft.[17] Regardless of this particular bit of fanciful eisegesis, it is surely correct to take note of the fact that God gives Adam a *command* (ויצו). This command is significant, and was apparently seen to be so not just by the Rabbis, but also by earlier writers including Sirach[18] and Philo.[19]

It is instructive to observe some of the human sins described in Genesis 1–11. Adam and Eve are expelled for disobeying God's command of 2.16 and for wanting to be like God (3.5), which could be seen as an act of blasphemy. The Promethean serpent is cursed for deception (3.14). Cain and Lamech murder a man and raise the question of just retribution (4). God's reason for sending the flood is the violence (חמס, 6.11, 13) of humanity. Ham is guilty of exposing his father's uncovered nakedness (9.20–27; cf. Lev 18; גילוי עריות in the Noachide Commandments); unlawful sex of a different kind is perpetrated by the 'sons of God' in chapter 6. God also establishes a covenant with Noah and his descendants, with positive commands against bloodshed and the consumption of blood from an animal (Gen 9.4–6, what came to be known as the law of the torn limb, cf. *Gen. Rab.* 34.13: אבר מן החי).[20] Genesis 11, finally, almost by way of an *inclusio*, describes the urban, cultural equivalent of wanting to be God: 'Come, let us build ourselves a city, and a tower with its top in the heavens, and let us make a name for ourselves' (11.4).

One might argue, then, that Genesis 1–11 already endorses a number of very general moral precepts which could be taken to apply to humanity as a whole. In particular, divine commandments to both Adam and Noah are mentioned. Other pre-Sinaitic principles might be drawn from the rest of Genesis (e.g. Dinah's rape and its aftermath, Gen 34; Onan's refusal of Levirate marriage, Gen 38); but arguably most of these are neither in legal form nor clearly

[17]*Gen. Rab.* 16.6; cf. 24.5; *Deut. Rab.* 2.25; *Cant. Rab.* 1.16; *b. Sanh.* 56b; *Pesiq. Rab Kah.* 12.1.

[18]In a context of creation and God's covenant with all mankind, Sir 17.14 affirms, 'He said to them, "Beware of all evil." And he gave *commandment* to each of them *concerning the neighbour* [περὶ τοῦ πλησίον].'

[19]Philo, e.g. *Leg. All.* 1.90–108. On the tradition of commandments given to Adam, see further K. Müller 1998:62–4.

[20]For the link between bloodshed and blood consumption, see e.g. Milgrom 1997; cf. Flusser & Safrai 1986.

universal in application. Two clearly legal regulations, circumcision (Gen 17) and the rule about not eating the thigh muscle on the hip socket (Gen 32.32), are given respectively to the descendants of Abraham and of Jacob.[21]

The Mosaic Laws

As for the Pentateuchal legislation proper, this is revealed explicitly to Israel in the context of the Sinaitic covenant (so at least thought the final redactor, and Jewish interpreters after him). Nevertheless, within this corpus there are many laws of universal moral appeal and influence, not the least of which are the Ten Commandments, the only piece of Sinaitic legislation understood to have been revealed by God directly to the people (note Exod 20.1, 19, etc. in Jewish interpretation). Although they, too, are explicitly addressed to Israel (Exod 20.2) and include commandments whose moral appeal arguably was not universal (Sabbath, images), a good deal could indeed be said about their 'public' significance both for Second Temple Judaism (Philo, *Decal.*; Josephus, *Ant.* 3.5.4–5 §90–92; *m. Tamid* 5.1; the Nash papyrus, etc.) and for early Christianity.[22] Their early interpretation shows that the Ten Commandments, addressed by God directly to all the people gathered at Sinai, were frequently regarded as standing out in importance from the rest of the Torah. However, in view of the fact that the New Testament itself cites them only rarely (Matt 19.18–19 par.; Rom 13.9), and never in their entirety, it seems justifiable here to leave consideration of the Decalogue for a separate treatment. Still, it is important to note that its distinctive origin and status evidently contributed to its being viewed by Philo[23] and early Christian writers[24] as a summary of natural law.[25]

Specific legal requirements for Gentiles are present only in the context of legislation about *gerim*,[26] i.e. resident aliens (and, in a few negative laws in Deuteronomy, *nokhrim*, i.e. unfriendly foreigners).[27]

---

[21]Rabbi Yose ben Ḥanina et al. concluded that pre-Sinaitic laws repeated at Sinai applied to all, but the others only to Israel: *b. Sanh.* 59a–b. Antecedents to the Noachide laws in the pre-Sinaitic stories are also explored in Novak 1998:27–61; cf. Millard 1995:85–8 and *passim* on Gen 9.

[22]For the different early Christian and Jewish views of the Decalogue, see recently Freund 1998; for the Jewish perspective cf. more generally B.-Z. Segal & G. Levi 1990.

[23]See e.g. Philo, *Decal.* 24 and *passim*; cf. also p. 109 above.

[24]So e.g. Irenaeus, *Haer.* 4.15.1; *Apos. Con.* 20.

[25]For the distinction in both Judaism and Christianity between the Decalogue, given by God, and other laws given through Moses, see e.g. Horbury 1988:759–60.

[26]*Toshab* is always accompanied by another term, especially *ger*.

[27]*Zar* appears to be a more general term for 'outsider'. For an up-to-date treatment of these probably mainly post-exilic laws, see van Houten 1991; cf. also more generally C. Bultmann 1992.

These laws fall into two categories. The first extends Israel's social welfare rights to the *gerim* (incl. fair trial, Deut 1.16; Sabbath and festival rest, Exod 20.10; 23.12; Deut 5.14; 16.11, 14; and support mechanisms for the disadvantaged, Exod 23.9; Lev 19.10; 23.22; 25.6–7; Deut 26.11–13; 27.19).[28] The alien has full rights of citizenship; in a strikingly parallel expression, Leviticus 19 commands both 'you shall love your fellow citizen as yourself' (ואהבת לרעך כמוך, 19.18) *and* 'you shall love the alien as yourself' (ואהבת לו כמוך, 19.34).

The second category of laws consists of positive *commands* applying to *gerim* along with the rest of Israel. These are for the most part concentrated in the Holiness Code of Leviticus 17–26, and here chiefly in 18–20. Without going into detail at this point, all the explicit examples pertain to three basic categories: (a) laws relating to God – improper sacrifice, including sacrifices to idols (17.8–9, 20.2–5), as well as blasphemy (24.10–16); (b) laws relating to homicide and injury (24.17–22), the killing of animals (24.18) as well as the eating of animals' blood (17.10–16)[29]; (c) illicit sexual relations (Lev 18, 20[?]). A fourth and special case seems to be the treatment and redemption of Israelite slaves (25.47–55).[30]

The Prophets and Writings

A great deal more could easily be said in this regard, including evidence from the historical books;[31] but here I should like to make just one or two remarks about the prophetic oracles against the nations, before moving on to the Noachide Commandments proper. Perhaps the most important prophetic passage is once again Amos 1–2, which we encountered earlier.[32] Amos here pronounces God's judgement on Israel's neighbour countries, not for their failure to keep the Torah (only Israel has this privilege, 3.2), but for their transgressions against an assumed international consensus on just warfare and the treatment of innocent civilians. John Barton's study

---

[28]Nevertheless, *gerim* could participate in the Passover only if they were circumcised (12.43–49): the *ben-nekher* must not eat of it (Exod 12.43), but a circumcised *ger* may.

[29]There seems to be a conflict over whether resident aliens may eat an animal that dies of itself or has been torn by wild animals: Lev 17.15 appears to forbid this, while Deut 14.21 allows it to be eaten by the resident *ger* or sold to the *nokhri*.

[30]Contrast Israelite treatment of alien slaves, Lev 25.25–26.

[31]Cf. e.g. the Ammonite abuse of David's friendly ambassadors in 2 Sam 10; Elijah's rule about the treatment of prisoners of war, 2 Kgs 6.22 (and cf. LXX); Ruth; Haman in Esther; and note the decrees of Cyrus and Darius in Ezra, and of Nebuchadnezzar and Darius in Dan 3–4; 6.

[32]For this section cf. also p. 93 above.

of these passages has shown that they take for granted an informal Ancient Near Eastern protocol of international law, which pertains to such acts as the plundering of innocent towns, wholesale massacre, infringement of boundary rights, disturbing the dead, cannibalism, etc.[33] Despite their basis in convention rather than positive law, these principles are understood to carry divine sanction.[34]

There are numerous prophetic passages addressed to the foreign nations, mostly in a context of divine judgement. Some of these are merely the promised removal of those who now oppose the people of God, and are less relevant for our purposes. But others explicitly indict the foreigners for their iniquity, blasphemous arrogance, and gratuitous violence (Isa 13.11, Ezek 28.2–10, etc.).

Other texts are more inclusive, and relate to both Israel and the nations. Even leaving aside the eschatological visions of Gentiles coming to receive Torah from Mount Zion in the eschaton (Isaiah 2; Micah 4), one finds a number of universalizing ethical precepts. Thus it is not insignificant that the well-known summary of Micah 6.8 is addressed not to Israel but to humanity at large: 'He has told you, O 'adam, what is good; and what does the LORD require of you but to do justice and to love mercy and to walk humbly with your God?' Perhaps the most striking passage, however, is Ezek 33.23–26, where the moral standard of those who are left behind during the exile has even dropped below that required of resident aliens:

The word of the LORD came to me: Mortal, the inhabitants of these waste places in the land of Israel keep saying, 'Abraham was only one man, yet he got possession of the land; but we are many; the land is surely given us to possess.' Therefore say to them, Thus says the Lord GOD: You eat flesh with the blood, and lift up your eyes to your idols, and shed blood; shall you then possess the land? You depend on your swords, you commit abominations, and each of you defiles his neighbour's wife; shall you then possess the land?

This constellation of sins including violence and blood offences, idolatry, and adultery is hardly accidental.[35] These are the minimum requirements expected of those who live in the land of Israel. Ezekiel indicts the conceit of Israelites whose moral standards have fallen

---

[33]J. Barton 1980:55.

[34]*Pace* J. Barton; cf. Houston 1982:216–17.

[35]Dependence on swords is presumably another term for relying on violent and bloody means to achieve one's purposes; the term *tô'ēbah* ('abomination') is a general term for that which is repugnant to God (see e.g. Waltke 1979).

below those required of resident aliens (cf. Lev 18–20), and who nevertheless think they will inherit the Land.[36]

Wisdom literature constitutes an additional body of potentially relevant Old Testament material. Its universal ethical character applies not just in much of Proverbs but also in contexts like the code of honourable conduct which is assumed in Job 31.[37] Nevertheless, very little of the biblical wisdom material is explicitly addressed to non-Israelites. Further work is clearly necessary in this area, but for present purposes it will suffice to note that the rabbinic doctrine of Noachide laws does not appeal for its scriptural justification to the wisdom literature of the Old Testament.

Post-Canonical Texts

As soon as we move beyond the bounds of the canon, there are numerous texts of considerable relevance to the subject of universal ethics. Detailed consideration of these passages must be left for another occasion, but the most important links in the apocryphal and pseudepigraphal writings include the Book of Wisdom (notable for its connection of Gentile idolatry with sexual immorality and other corruptions, 14.12–31[38]), various texts from the *Sibylline Oracles* 3–5,[39] and especially *Jubilees* 7 and Pseudo-Phocylides.[40]

Some readers may wonder about the omission from this short list of the *Testaments of the Twelve Patriarchs*, among other documents. This is because, although clearly there is considerable overlap in

---

[36]He may also be implicitly refuting the appeal to Abraham, since that patriarch was a man who explicitly *kept* God's commandments (Gen 26.5 etc.; cf. Philo, Rabbis, etc.). A similar point was made earlier by Hosea, who links Israel's immorality with environmental disaster in the land itself (Hos 4.1–3): 'There is no faithfulness or loyalty, and no knowledge of God in the land. Swearing, lying, and murder, and stealing and adultery break out; bloodshed follows bloodshed. Therefore the land mourns, and all who live in it languish; together with the wild animals and the birds of the air, even the fish of the sea are perishing.' Clearly the implication seems to be that where the inhabitants of Israel flagrantly disregard even the basic moral requirements for residence, the land itself rebels.

A similar doctrine may be implied in the curses of Deuteronomy 28, although they apply to the whole of the Torah. Note also that Paul seems to employ an equivalent argument in Rom 2.17–32.

[37]The relevance of this passage is noted e.g. in Gordis 1986:63. Cf. pp. 94–5 above.

[38]For this link see also Exod 34.15–16; Rom 1.23–27; Gal 5.19; 1 Thess 4.3; Rev 2.14, 20; and cf. Simon 1981:423, 429–30.

[39]Cf. e.g. *Sib. Or.* 3.36–45, 185–91, 235–45, 373–80, 593–6, 732–40, 758 ('The Immortal in the starry heaven will put in effect a common law for people throughout the whole earth'), 762–66; 4.30–4; 5.165–74, 386–93, 430–1. See also 12.110–12.

[40]Cf. further *Ep. Arist.* 131–6, 168–9, 171 and *passim*.

ethical content,[41] these texts do not profess to be speaking either to or about Gentiles. Most of the ethical material in the *Testaments* is explicitly addressed to Jews, and Gentiles are almost always written off.[42]

Jubilees 7.20, however, is worth quoting for its particular proximity to the Noachide Commandments. In his testament of Noah, the writer includes a number of ethical requirements:

> [Noah] bore witness to his sons so that they might do justice, and cover the shame of their flesh, and bless the one who created them, and honour father and mother, and each one love his neighbour, and preserve themselves from fornication and pollution and from all injustice.

Later verses mention bloodshed (7.23–24), consumption of blood (7.28–33), and the offering of firstfruits. This list contains some unusual precepts, and the context acknowledges that Noah's descendants will in fact *not* keep these laws. Nevertheless, this is the earliest extant Jewish text that explicitly links Gen 9 with a universal ethic for the children of Noah (cf. also 1QapGen 6.6–9).

Pseudo-Phocylides is a particularly difficult case.[43] This first-century author's[44] teachings are indeed universal in flavour, and no addressees are specified. Moral instruction concentrates on principles relating to murder, injury, property, sex, adjudication, and protection of the weak.[45] There are clear conceptual links with the Old Testament passages about resident aliens, and a number of scholars have assumed a direct familiarity with the Noachide Commandments.[46] However, the work includes a number of biblical laws which in their original setting have nothing to do with Gentiles (e.g. protecting the stranger, 39–40; sparing the mother when taking a bird's nest, 84–5 [Deut 22.6–7]). What is more, in Ps.-Phocylides, as indeed in the *Testaments of the Twelve Patriarchs,* the failure to address blasphemy and idolatry might

[41]*Test. Reub.* 3.3–6; [*Test. Levi* 14.5–6]; *Test. Jud.* 18.2–6; *Test. Iss.* 3.3–8; 4.2–5; 7.2–6; *Test. Dan* 5.5–6; *Test. Gad passim*; *Test. Asher* 2.1–10; 4.2–5; *Test. Benj.* 4.1–5; 6.2–7; 8.1–3.

[42]E.g. *Test. Dan* 5.5, 8; *Test. Naph.* 4.1; but see *Test. Sim.* 7.2, a Christian interpolation. The ethics in the *Testaments* may well be a kind of Jewish (or Jewish Christian) instruction for lay people.

[43]Secondary literature on Jewish Hellenistic moral teaching includes the works of K. Niebuhr and H. Thyen, cited earlier; see also Crouch 1972; Küchler 1979.

[44]An emerging scholarly consensus favours a date in the first century BC or AD. See Thomas 1992:22; van der Horst, e.g. 1985:567–8.

[45]Thus also Niebuhr 1987:14–15.

[46]E.g. Guttmann 1927:112 and F. Siegert, as cited by van der Horst 1985:569 n. 34; cf. Schürer/Vermes 1986:3.690. Relevant passages of Ps.-Phoc. include especially 3–6, 8–12, 18, 32, 58, 135–6, 147–8, 154.

seem peculiar if we were dealing with a typical Jewish admonition to Gentiles. For these reasons it seems best to allow that this Jewish author will have written with at least a partly Jewish audience in mind.[47]

Nevertheless, it cannot be denied that, in terms of both its content and its fictional setting as Greek lyrical poetry, the work of Ps.-Phocylides is composed *as if* addressed to a much wider audience. In his definitive study on Ps.-Phocylides, J. Thomas concludes that while this text does not reflect the Noachide Commandments as such, it clearly *does* manifest a concern with what he calls 'the Noachide question' (*die Noachidenfrage*), i.e. the problem of moral obligations for non-Jews.[48] Thus, the date and character of Ps.-Phocylides make this document an important link between the biblical laws and the fully developed rabbinic doctrine of Noachide Commandments.

Two other writers of direct relevance are Philo and Josephus,[49] both of whom were briefly discussed for their views of natural law in Chapter 5 above. Here, too, the limited purpose of this chapter requires a postponement of fuller discussion. While their works are highly pertinent to questions of universal ethics, they do not with equal frequency address the question of the halakhah *for Gentiles*, which lies at the heart of the Noachide Commandments. (H. A. Wolfson in particular is probably mistaken in affirming too close a link between Philo's ethical theory and the Noachide Commandments.[50])

Various other texts could be cited, including the Slavonic 2 *Enoch*, in which one recent study also finds much of the same reasoning that later becomes explicit in the Noachide Commandments.[51] Evidence from the Dead Sea Scrolls might of course have been highly valuable;

[47]Thus also Schürer/Vermes 1986:3.690; Alon 1996 (also cited as Alon 1967 by van der Horst 1985:566; and see Krauss 1903:32–3.

[48]Thomas 1992:228–35, 355–9.

[49]Especially Philo's *Hypothetica* and *Leg. Gai.* as well as Josephus's *Ag. Ap.* 2.16–30 §§157–219 are of interest here; note also Herod's speech about the mistreatment of his ambassadors, in *Ant.* 15.5.3 §127–46.

[50]See Wolfson 1947:2.182–7, who points *inter alia* to Noah having acquired 'all the virtues' (*Abr.* 34).

[51]See Böttrich 1992:184, 'Die Themenkreise der materialen Ethik im slHen stimmen ohne Rest mit jenen Themenkreisen überein, die in der späteren rabbinischen Theologie unter dem Stichwort der noachidischen Gebote zusammengefaßt wurden.' Note his discussion on pp. 185–9, documenting every one of the seven laws from 2 *Enoch*. The question remains, of course, whether the mere presence of related ethical material suffices to establish a link with the Noachide Commandments. See further Guttmann 1927:98–114, and cf. other texts like Ps.-Menander; *Test. Abr.* A 10.5, 9, 11; B 12.6, 9, *Apoc. Abr.* 24.5–9.

but the sectarians appear to keep their own counsel of intolerance and remain virtually silent on the subject of ethics for Gentiles.[52]

The Rabbinic Doctrine

Early rabbinic literature harbours conflicting attitudes to the ethical behaviour of Gentiles. The stricter view, perhaps especially prevalent in the first half of the second century around the revolts under Trajan and Hadrian, assumes that dealings with Gentiles should be kept to a minimum, since the unspecified intention of a Gentile must always be assumed to incline towards idolatry.[53]

The more lenient view, representing a Hillelite strand and related Amoraim, tends to allow that there are righteous people among the Gentiles who conform to a minimum level of morality, and that meaningful trade and communication with them is indeed possible.[54] Related to this is the famous early second-century debate between Rabbi Eliezer ben Hyrcanus and Rabbi Joshua b. Ḥananyah about whether any Gentiles will be saved (*t. Sanh.* 13.2). Basing himself on Psalm 9.17, Rabbi Eliezer said: 'None of the Gentiles (*goyim*) has a portion in the world to come, as it is said, "The wicked shall return to Sheol, all the Gentiles who forget God." ' Pointing out that this Psalm condemns only those Gentiles who *forget* God, Rabbi Joshua countered: 'Therefore there are righteous people among the nations (*'ummot*) who have a portion in the world to come.'[55] Certain leniently inclined later Rabbis in fact concluded that Gentiles outside

---

[52]But see perhaps the difficult passage CD 9.1 (par. 4QD[b] 17.ii.8–9): 'Every man who shall extirpate any human being shall be put to death according to the laws of the nations (בחוקי הגוים).' Derrett 1983 sees here a Jewish authority's forced application of Noachide laws in order to protect Jews against resident aliens. In the absence of more specific contextual information, however, Derrett's interpretation seems speculative. Somewhat more significant for our purposes is CD 12.6–11 on contact with Gentiles, in which there are some halakhic similarities with the mishnaic *'Abodah Zarah* (see below): one must not kill Gentiles for gain, or sell them any slaves, clean animals, grain or oil – 'lest they sacrifice them'. On the wider problem of the halakhah at Qumran, see *inter alia* Sussmann 1994 and Qimron 1994.

[53]סתם מחשבת נכרי לעבודה זרה: R. Eliezer b. Hyrcanus, *M. Ḥul.* 2.7. Cf. *b. Sanh.* 60b on Gentile wine; and see Novak 1983:116. Compare the similar opinion at Qumran, just noted: clean animals may not be sold to Gentiles lest they sacrifice them to idols, בעבור אשר לא יזבחום (CD 12.8).

[54]Cf. the more detailed argument in Tomson 1990:208–16.

[55]Rab Yehudah bar Yehezqel (third cent.) later spoke of the 'thirty righteous people among the nations of the world [צדיקי אומות העולם] by whose virtue the nations of the world continue to exist' (*b. Ḥul.* 92a). The sectarian documents in the Dead Sea Scrolls, by contrast, appear to assume the universal destruction of the Gentiles in the judgement: 1QH 12(=4).26, 1QpHab 13.1–4, etc.

Palestine are not idolaters, since they simply follow their ancestral customs.[56]

The doctrine of the Noachide Commandments resides somewhere along this divide, being used both by those (like Joshua b. Ḥananyah?) who see them as useful criteria to assess Gentile morality, and those who think that since Gentiles have disregarded even these basic laws, they are a lost cause.[57] We may also note what might be called the 'soteriological' dimension of this discussion in the recurring motif of 'a share in the world to come'.[58] (As we shall see below, this motif correlates well with the guiding question of 'what Gentiles must do to be saved', which Acts 15.1 sees as the motivation behind the Apostolic Council.)

Aside from the passage in *Jubilees* 7, the first explicit mention of the Noachide Commandments in the formal sense occurs in the Tannaitic period. The *locus classicus* is an anonymous tradition in Tosefta *'Abodah Zarah* 8.4: 'Seven commandments were given to the children of Noah: regarding the establishments of courts of justice, idolatry, blasphemy, fornication, bloodshed, theft [and the torn limb].'

על שבע מצוות נצטוו בני נח

על הדינים ועל עבודה זרה ועל קיללת השם ועל גילוי עריות

ועל שפיכות דמים ועל הגזל [ועל אבר מן החי][59]

The precise date of this tradition is impossible to establish. However, its inclusion in the Tosefta means that this explicit formulation of the Noachide doctrine certainly dates from before the end of the third century;[60] and the fact that Rabbi Meir (fl. c. 130–60) comments on it in the immediate context makes a date in the first half of the second century highly probable.[61] (Tannaitic passages like *m. Ned.* 3.11 also clearly assume a well-established halakhic category of the 'Noachide'.)

---

[56]*B. Ḥul.* 13b: R Ḥiyya b. Abba, quoting R. Yoḥanan bar Nappaḥa (both Amoraim).

[57]The Gentiles were unable to keep the Noachide laws: *Sifre Deut.* 343 (Deut 33.2; ed. Finkelstein, p. 396); *Mek.* Baḥodesh Yitro 5 (ed. Horovitz/Rabin, p. 221); R. Abbahu in *b. B. Qam.* 38a: the Gentiles have forfeited their right to legal protection by failing to keep the Noachide Commandments.

[58]This point is rightly noted by K. Müller 1998:80–6; cf. 72–80. See also p. 164 below.

[59]The seventh is missing from Zuckermandel's text (based on MS Erfurt), but is present in MS Vienna and the Alfasi edition. It is, moreover, contextually required by the word 'seven'.

[60]There is now a strong scholarly consensus on a final redaction of the Tosefta no later than the late third or early fourth century. See Stemberger 1996:157, also with reference to J. Neusner; Goldberg 1987:283–4.

[61]Cf. e.g. K. Müller 1998:47; Millard 1995:80–1, 84, both of whom date the Noachide commandments to the time of Hadrian.

Throughout the Talmudic era this doctrine never seems to assume a fixed and final definition. Various opinions add or substitute a number of interpretative extrapolations transmitted in the names of Tannaitic Rabbis; these pertain to the prohibition of sorcery and related activities, castration, and forbidden mixtures.[62] Others restrict the Noachide Commandments to idolatry alone or to idolatry, blasphemy and adjudication.[63] The most widely encountered version, however, has seven commandments given to the sons of Noah.[64] The substance of these commandments, roughly speaking, corresponds to those Pentateuchal laws for which the death penalty is given to an Israelite.[65]

Later midrashim from the third century on speak of six commandments given to Adam (based on Gen 2.16, discussed earlier), the seventh (prohibition of the torn limb) to Noah after the flood, an eighth to Abraham (circumcision); a ninth to Jacob (regarding the thigh muscle on the hip socket); and then Israel at Sinai received all the commandments.[66] One fourth-century Rabbi cites thirty commandments;[67] elsewhere we are told that these thirty are the commandments which the Noachides *will* accept one day, i.e. in the Messianic age.[68]

In spite of the variations, certain basic principles emerge. Gentile obligation remains basically unaltered by the Sinaitic covenant.[69] The Noachide laws form the basic ethical foundation for both Jews and Gentiles: the extensive discussion in Tractate *Sanhedrin* concludes that 'there is nothing permitted to Jews which is forbidden to Gentiles'.[70] Observance of the Noachide

---

[62]*B. Sanh.* 56b (Ḥidqa, Simeon [b. Yoḥai], Yose [b. Ḥalafta], Eleazar [?], an anonymous Tanna of the school of Manasseh), 59b; cf. *t. 'Abod. Zar.* 8.6–8. See also K. Müller 1998:28–30.

[63]*B. Sanh.* 56b bottom: Yehudah (b. Ilai), Yehudah b. Batira, both second cent.

[64]Other Tannaitic texts include *b. Sanh.* 56a bottom [*baraita*]; *Mek.* Baḥodesh, Yitro 5 (R. Simeon b. Eleazar; ed. Horovitz/Rabin, p. 221); *Sifre Deut* 343 (Deut 33.2; ed. Finkelstein, p. 396) cf. further *b. 'Abod. Zar.* 2b bottom; *Gen. Rab.* 34.8, etc.

[65]*B. Sanh.* 56b (*baraita*); cf. art. 'בן נח', *Encyclopaedia Talmudit* 3.350 and n. 65.

[66]Thus explicitly *Exod. Rab.* 30.9; *Cant. Rab.* 1.2.5; cf. *Tanḥ.* Yitro 2.7 (ed. Buber 2.35); *Gen. Rab.* 16.6; *Deut. Rab.* 2.25, etc.

[67]E.g. *b. Ḥul.* 92a bottom (Ulla [bar Ishmael]).

[68]Y. *'Abod. Zar.* 2.1, 40c16 אילו שלשים מצות שעתידים בני נח לקבל (attributed to Rab, mid-third cent.); cf. *Gen. Rab.* 98.9. Cf. Krauss 1903:34; he thinks the thirty laws are based on Lev 19 and served not for Noachides but as catechetical instruction for proselytes (ibid., 40). The thirty are sometimes thought to be included in the seven: cf. art. 'בן נח', *Encyclopaedia Talmudit* 3.350 (שם).

[69]Novak 1983:53.

[70]*B. Sanh.* 59a: ליכא מדעם דלישראל שרי ולעובד כוכבים אסור; the only exceptions mentioned are the laws of seizing a beautiful woman in war (Deut 21.10–14) and theft of things worth less than a *prutah* (cf. *b. Sanh.* 57a).

Commandments also served to define the status of a resident alien.[71]

A more detailed discussion of the individual laws must be left for another occasion,[72] but two important final observations are in order before proceeding to examine the relevance of this subject to the New Testament. The first is that the core of the Noachide Commandments is explicitly made up of three capital offences, viz. fornication, bloodshed, and blasphemy or idolatry. Only for these three is a Noachide said to be liable to the death penalty[73] – and it is interesting that for the Christian consensus of the first three centuries these remain the 'mortal' sins that necessarily entail excommunication.[74] Given the importance of laws for aliens in the Old Testament, it is highly significant that these three offences are precisely those which the Rabbis at Lydda in the second century agreed to make the minimum test of allegiance *even for Jews*. A Jew must rather die than commit these offences:[75]

R. Yoḥanan said in the name of R. Simeon ben Yehoṣadaq: By a majority vote, it was resolved in the upper room of the house of Nitzah at Lydda that on pain of death a person may commit any transgression in the Torah – except idolatry, fornication, and bloodshed.

א"ר יוחנן משום ר"ש בן יהוצדק
נימו וגמרו בעליית בית נתזה בלוד
כל עבירות שבתורה אם אומרין לאדם עבור ואל תהרג
עבור ואל יהרג
חוץ מעבודת כוכבים וגילוי עריות ושפיכות דמים:

In other words, the minimum requirements for living in the Land may not be circumvented by either Jews or Noachides.[76]

Finally, the Rabbis not only presupposed ancient traditions of universal law, but at least in some cases they also appear to have endorsed the idea that the Torah expresses a fundamental law in keeping with nature (see Chapter 5 above). Several relevant passages are particularly close to the Noachide Commandments. A Tannaitic tradition in *b. Yoma* 67b claims that the prohibitions of idolatry,

---

[71]B. 'Abod. Zar. 64b: כל שמקבל עליו שבע מצות שקבלו עליהם בני נח. Cf. further Hoffmann 1885:121–2; also Novak 1983:14–19.

[72]See further art. 'בן נח', *Encyclopaedia Talmudit*, 3.348–62 (שסב–שמח), especially 349–57; also Novak 1983:53–254 and 1998:149–73; K. Müller 1998.

[73]R. Joseph (bar Hiyya, d. 333), citing Rab (d. 247): 'For three crimes is a Noachide put to death: ... for fornication, bloodshed, and blasphemy' (על גילוי עריות ועל שפיכות דמים ועל ברכת השם). R. Shesheth adds ועל עבודת זרה, 'and for idolatry' (*b. Sanh.* 57a).

[74]See e.g. Tertullian, *Pud.* 5.15; Origen, *Or.* 28.10; Canons 1–2 of the Council of Elvira (c. 306); and cf. K. Müller 1998:200–8; Sahlin 1970; Flusser & Safrai 1986:179–81.

[75]B. Sanh. 74a. For a similar point, cf. Novak 1983:32.

[76]See already Ezek 33.23–26, cited in *t. Soṭ.* 6.9; cf. *Jub.* 23.14; 30.15; CD 4.15–18.

immorality, bloodshed, robbery and blasphemy should have been written as law even if they had not been in the Torah.[77] And R. Yoḥanan (third cent.) said, 'Had the Torah not been given, we would have learnt about modesty from the cat, robbery from the ant, and fornication from the dove.'[78] There is thus an overlap in content between the Noachide and natural law traditions, as we suggested above. Maimonides later made that link explicit.[79]

As David Novak has shown, the Noachide Commandments were a functional part of rabbinic law, without at the same time having to be formally enforced. On the one hand, they served as an internal point of reference within Jewish self-understanding, helping Judaism to situate itself *vis-à-vis* a multicultural Gentile world.[80] On the other hand, this doctrine upheld the biblical notion of an international morality that makes ethical communication possible. It did so against the background of the widespread Graeco-Roman ideas like the *ius gentium*, natural law and unwritten law, which applied to all humanity equally. The validity and usefulness of these commandments does not depend on anyone keeping them perfectly, as some of the Rabbis realized: they are a point of reference.[81]

Noachide Law and the New Testament

The requisite brevity of our discussion here makes it advisable to concentrate on the Synoptics, Acts, and Paul, with a necessary emphasis on Acts 15 and 1 Corinthians 5–10.

Both historically and conceptually, the key problem of New Testament ethics is this: while the exalted Jesus is both its motivation and highest authority, the historical Jesus in fact had little or nothing to say about the *content* of an ethic for Gentiles. The New Testament writers themselves take a variety of approaches to this problem.

Mark

Mark concentrates on the teaching of Jesus, whom he sees as fulfilling the prophetic tradition (e.g. 1.2–3; 4.12; 9.1–8); Jesus' divinely sanctioned teaching is superior to the traditions of his

[77]Cf. *Sifra* Aḥarei Mot 13 on 18.4 (§194.2.11), discussed earlier (p. 106 above). The comparison between Noachide and natural law is also made by A. F. Segal 1990:195 (cf. 1995 *passim*).

[78]*B. Erub.* 100b bottom; cf. p. 106 n. 48 above.

[79]See the discussion in Novak 1983:294–300; cf. A. F. Segal 1990:195; K. Müller 1998:210–14.

[80]Thus Novak 1983:xviii and cf. 1998:174–93.

[81]Novak, 1983:xvii–xviii: these laws serve as a 'formal model'.

Jewish contemporaries. Although the Markan Jesus does occasionally dabble in contemporary halakhic debate,[82] his ethic is focused on an authoritative call to faith, discipleship and watch-fulness for the Kingdom of God. His audience is probably Gentile (7.3–4; 15.39) and has apparently already resolved the problem of the Jewish law by dispensing with the dietary and purity regulations (7.19).[83] Ethical content is based on love of God and one's neighbour, and on a selection of the Ten Commandments (12.29–30; 10.19). In addition to the authority of Jesus, we have no indication of which, if any, Old Testament commandments apply.

Matthew

Matthew, writing for a mixed community, takes greater pains over the definition of ethics; the Torah is here more explicitly affirmed (5.17–20 and *passim*). His Jesus consistently opposes the Pharisees, but does not sidestep the issue of the Torah's validity. Instead, he offers an alternative halakhah, which is the prophetic fulfilment of the Torah in his person and teaching (5.17–18; 11.13; cf. also 19.3–9). Although in practice endorsing the Jewish interpretative principle of 'making a fence' around the commandments to prevent their erosion (5.21–48; cf. *m. 'Abot* 1.1; 3.13), Jesus is explicitly opposed to oral traditions that constrain or limit the truly important commandments of the Law (τὰ βαρύτερα τοῦ νόμου, 23.23): love of God and of neighbour, and the second Table of the Decalogue (19.16–19; 22.36–40). In the end, Jesus' teaching and interpretation of the Law is the highest authority; and this alone is what the Apostles are to teach the new, Gentile community of his disciples (28.20). But although Matthew clearly tries to formulate a 'Jesus halakhah' (e.g. in 5.21–48; 19.3–9), many questions remain wrapped in diplomatic silence. Thus, issues like circumcision, purity and food laws are not dealt with, although leprosy (8.2–3; 10.8; 11.5), evil spirits (10.1; 12.43) and, by implication, pigs (7.6; 8.30–32) are evidently still unclean. Purity, tithing and phylacteries are significant but depend on inward purity (15.19–20; 23.5, 23, 25–26). Other than the teaching of Jesus, once again no clear criteria for Gentiles emerge.

---

[82]Mark 3.4 (a debate later reflected, and comparably resolved, in *m. Yoma* 8.6), 7.11 (*m. Ned.* 9.1; 11.4), 12.14, etc.

[83]Against this current consensus in scholarship see, however, the important caveat of Sariola 1990 and Dautzenberg 1998: a careful, dispassionate reading of Mark provides little evidence that the evangelist has come to anything like a systematic position on the Law. Cf. also Chapter 1 above.

Luke-Acts

Luke's perspective, although unsystematic and untechnical,[84] is one of harmony between Jews and Gentiles. In addition to characteristics in common with the other gospels, Luke particularly endorses the Old Testament's concern for the poor and oppressed. He affirms the priority of healing over the Sabbath (13.10–17), and develops a well-known penchant for exemplary character narratives. The Torah is fulfilled in Christ, and is thus not something that separates Jews from Gentiles in the new era he has inaugurated.

It is in Acts, however, that Luke poses the key questions for the new Gentile mission. Beginning with Peter's experience in his mission to Cornelius (Acts 10.9–16, 34–35, 47–48) and continuing with Paul's turning to the Gentiles in Pisidian Antioch (13.46–52), the question of an ethic for Gentile believers becomes unavoidable.

This issue comes to a head in the so-called Apostolic Council of Acts 15. Regardless of one's perspective on the historicity of the account, Luke's report pinpoints the central halakhic problem with great accuracy: should Gentiles who believe in Christ be treated as proselytes or as Noachides? It should be noted carefully that the primary point in this Lucan account is *not* that of table fellowship in mixed congregations (unlike Gal 2.12 and *pace* most commentators[85]), but more generally the halakhic status of Gentile believers: verse 1 clearly defines the question as being about what Gentiles must *do* to be saved.[86]

The maximalist case was being advanced by Christian Pharisees who argued, not without plausible justification, that covenant membership requires full conversion. Peter's opening argument at the Council is that people like the household of Cornelius have in

---

[84]Cf. Blomberg 1984.

[85]English scholarship, following F. C. Burkitt and T. W. Manson (both as cited in W. D. Davies 1980:117–18), has usually tended to argue that the Apostolic Decree was a working compromise for the sake of table fellowship, which Paul accepted and later (Gal 2) dispensed with. German scholarship, followed by English scholars like C. K. Barrett and M. D. Goulder, has on the whole taken the supposed tension with Gal 2 to mean that the Decree was a later Antiochene invention which Luke inserts at this point (see the commentaries, e.g. Haenchen and Barrett, *ad loc.*).

Acts 15 and Galatians 2.7–10 would seem to concur that the Apostolic Council confirmed the integrity of the Gentile mission. The sticking point arose later (2.12) over the issue of table fellowship, for reasons we discussed earlier (see Chapter 4 above).

[86]See also p. 159 above on the 'soteriological' dimension of the Noachide laws. Like some other commentators cited in the previous note, Fitzmyer (1998:556–7) would appear to beg precisely this question – not only in view of 15.1 and the framing of the Decree (15.19, 28), but also in the incongruous claim that the Decree concerns 'only a *modus vivendi* of Gentile among Jewish questions', and 'no salvific purpose'. These two issues are not so easily separated.

fact *already* been saved, *as Gentiles* (note also v. 9: 'in cleansing their hearts by faith he has made no distinction between them and us'), and there is therefore no need to make them converts. Paul and Barnabas offer supporting evidence.

James's speech, far from being a compromise, in fact accepts Peter's argument and simply spells out the halakhic consequences. If indeed it is the case that in Christ these Gentiles have a portion in the world to come (to adapt Rabbi Joshua's language), i.e. that they are saved *as Gentiles*, then it suffices to apply to them the same ethical principles that would in any case apply to righteous Gentiles living with the people of Israel, i.e. resident aliens.[87]

The form in which these principles are given shows signs both of Lucan redaction and of considerable subsequent textual variation.[88] For our purposes, however, what matters most is that in their original text form the principles themselves are strongly reminiscent of the second-century lists of Noachide Commandments: 'to abstain from what has been sacrificed to idols and from blood and from what is strangled and from fornication' (ἀπέχεσθαι εἰδωλοθύτων καὶ αἵματος καὶ πνικτῶν καὶ πορνείας, 15.29; cf. 15.21; 21.25).

Two of these commandments are a reasonably straightforward anticipation of the Noachide Commandments regarding idolatry and sexual sin – in their most common halakhic applications as idol meat consumption and extramarital sex.[89] To complete the core triplet of Jewish capital crimes, it would be convenient if one could take αἵματος as 'bloodshed', and πνικτῶν as the practical equivalent to the law of the torn limb. Unfortunately, in the context it is more likely

---

[87]See the texts discussed on pp. 152–3 above. Note further passages like Exod 12.49; Lev 19.34; 24.22; Num 9.14; 15.15–16, 29, which suggest that *in principle* the same law governs both Jews and Gentiles in the Land. (In practice certain distinctions do seem to apply, as was seen above.) This same overall point has found significant development in recent treatments by T. Callan 1993, R. Bauckham 1995, 1996, and J. Wehnert 1997.

[88]Useful recent treatments of the Lucan redaction of this passage include Wedderburn 1993; Wehnert 1997:33–82. The complex text critical questions are helpfully summarized in Metzger 1975:429–34; cf. Wehnert 1997:21–32.

[89]There is no need to restrict εἰδωλόθυτον specifically to the context of a pagan temple, as Witherington has variously argued (e.g. 1993, 1998:460–3). His position requires one (a) to ignore the entire Jewish tradition we have examined here, (b) to assume Christian interpolation in passages like 4 Macc 5.2 (1998: 459) and (c) to take for granted that the Torah's laws about Gentiles constitute 'the wrong social context' (p. 465). Witherington denies that 'ritual' (i.e. halakhic) concerns could be at stake, since the Decree seems inadequate to regulate table fellowship; but of course it explicitly concerns halakhah for Gentiles, and not commensality. He also, curiously, cites Bauckham 1996 to the effect that there are no exact Jewish parallels to precisely the four stipulations of the Decree (465 n. 429), only to pass over in silence Bauckham's own perfectly reasonable and constructive interpretation from Lev 17–18.

On πορνεία see e.g. F. Hauck & Schulz 1967; and cf. further Barrett 1987:52, 54; Simon 1981:422–3.

that *both* these terms pertain to the consumption of unacceptable meat. 'Western' MSS, indeed, have famously adjusted the text to produce a less ritual, more moralizing emendation of the Decree, in which its stipulations are paired with the Golden Rule. A possible argument *against* the dietary reading of αἵματος might seem to be the unlikelihood of repetition in an otherwise tightly abbreviated list. Halakhically, however, we are dealing with three carefully defined forbidden foods: food sacrificed to idols, meat with blood still in it (*nᵉbēlah*, i.e. probably including that which died by itself[90]), and meat from an animal that was not properly slaughtered (i.e. 'strangled' or possibly also 'torn', *tᵉrēfah*).[91]

At the same time, while the *shedding* of blood may not be explicitly mentioned, it is in fact both taken for granted and implicit in the wording of the Decree itself. Unlike idolatry and fornication, the prohibition of homicide could (like incest; cf. 1 Cor 5.1) have been presupposed as self-evident even among cultured Hellenistic Gentiles. More specifically, however, Genesis 9, Leviticus 24 and later Jewish interpretation shows that laws about animal and human blood are closely related in context: for both man and animal, their blood is their life and is therefore taboo.[92] It is therefore safe to take αἵματος as a dietary injunction with broader implications. Although it applies to the consumption of animal blood here, in the context of Jewish halakhah that prohibition extends *a fortiori* to the shedding of human blood, just as the avoidance of idol food obviously extends to the prohibition of idolatry. As it stands, the Decree addresses *both* 'moral' and 'ritual' offences (note τῶν ἀλισγημάτων 'defilements', v. 20).[93] Moral and dietary arguments belong inseparably together, and it is highly instructive to consult Tertullian, Eusebius and others on the continued prohibition of blood consumption in the church

---

[90]The connection of blood consumption with eating what dies of itself is clear in Lev 17.10–15, where both are forbidden to the alien (contrast Deut 14.21); cf. also Ezek 4.14; 44.31.

[91]Nahum 2.12 appears to identify 'torn' (*tᵉrēfah*) with 'strangled' meat. For the latter, cf. *Jos. Asen.* 8.5; 21.14; and see also E. P. Sanders 1990a:275 and more fully Wehnert 1997:221–32. K. Müller 1998:164–5, 199 also rightly argues that, despite the distinction between the strangled animal and the 'torn limb', the two remain closely related in the prohibition of blood consumption.

[92]Gen 9.4–5; Lev 24.17–22; cf. also *Jub.* 6.7–12; 7.23–33; Philo *Spec. Leg.* 4.122 (condemning the sacrificial practices of pagan priests). See similarly Milgrom 1997 on the link between blood consumption and bloodshed.

[93]Thus also Hurd 1965:250–3, and Barrett 1987:54; *pace* Simon 1981:415–16, 426–7; Wehnert 1997:212 (cf. Bockmuehl 1999), and many commentators Cf. Flusser & Safrai 1986.

of the second and later centuries, in the West as much as in the East.[94]

This kind of analysis shows the concise Jewish development of laws about resident aliens to be of considerable relevance in explaining the choice of ethical requirements in Acts 15.[95] Even if Gentiles are saved as Gentiles, they must be exhorted to abide by those commandments that already apply to them in Scripture and its interpretative tradition.

Paul

Finally, a few comments on Paul. It was W. D. Davies who proposed the first sustained argument for the relevance of the Noachide Commandments to the substance of Paul's ethics.[96] In that assertion he is almost certainly right. He is almost certainly wrong, however, on a number of subsidiary points. First, the nature of the evidence does not support claims such as 'that Paul was familiar with the Noachian commandments cannot be doubted' (p. 115); as we saw, the Noachide Commandments as such were probably not explicitly formulated before the second century. The *principles* of a Jewish universal ethic can be clearly established for the Second Temple period, as we saw earlier; but Davies's claim as it stands is anachronistic.

Secondly, while W. D. Davies accepts the presence of these commandments in Acts 15, he follows the dominant interpretation in assuming both that Paul did not know the Decree and that he did not regard even the substance of the Noachide Commandments as '*in any sense* normative'.[97] The reason for the former assumption is the usual answer that the Decree is not mentioned in Gal 2 and 1 Cor 8–10, where one might have expected it.

---

[94]Cf. e.g. Tertullian, *Pud.* 12; *Apol.* 9; Eusebius, *Eccl. Hist.* 5.1.26; *Ps.-Clem. Rec.* 1.30; 4.36; *Hom.* 7.4, 8; 8.19; *Didascalia* 24; also *Qur'an* 5.3; 2.173; 6.145; 16.115. On the influence of the Decree, see further Böckenhoff 1903; Resch 1905; Six 1912; K. Müller 1998:200–10; also Tomson 1990:178–9 (citing Flusser/Safrai, Harnack, et al.).

[95]See also Callan 1993:296–7, who suggests that in Luke's view the Apostolic Decree spells out the laws that apply to Gentile 'God-fearers'; on his interpretation they correspond to those commandments in Lev 17–18 whose infringement leads to extirpation. Bauckham 1995 offers the somewhat more precise observation that the laws found in Acts 15 are those that in Lev 17–18 apply to the alien 'in the midst of' (בתוך) Israel; outside these two chapters, Pentateuchal laws with this qualification occur only in Lev 16.29; Num 15.14–16, 29; 19.10 (Bauckham 1995:461).

[96]W. D. Davies 1980:113ff. (a work first published in 1948).

[97]W. D. Davies 1980:119 (ital. mine); similarly e.g. Simon 1981:437: 'Paul would certainly have objected to such a document.'

This second point merits further comment. It may be noted that while the Noachide Commandments (or their pre-rabbinic equivalent) are admittedly not *sufficient* to account for Paul's ethics, it is worth considering if in substance they may not after all be *necessary*. That is to say, in practice *more* than the laws for resident aliens is binding for Paul (e.g. what he calls the 'law of Christ'), but certainly *no less*.

From that perspective, Paul may well fail to mention the Decree in Gal 2 because its meaning indeed 'contributed nothing' (Gal 2.6) to the Gentile mission: nothing, that is, beyond the moral demands that pertain to it in any case, and which Paul takes for granted and consistently upholds, even in Galatians (5.19–21, 23b). In 1 Corinthians 5–10 in particular, Paul's practical exhortation clearly parallels the halakhic concerns of Acts 15; indeed M. Simon has poignantly argued that these chapters 'represent a sort of commentary on the Decree'.[98] Even if that position is difficult to prove outright, it is possible to trace the influence of pertinent Old Testament passages like Lev 18–20 throughout these chapters, as a number of scholars have shown.[99]

Among recent writers, Peter Tomson and Alan Segal have also stressed the importance of halakhic reasoning for Paul's ethics in general, and the proximity to the Noachide Commandments in particular. In the case of 1 Cor 8–10, where numerous scholars have assumed Paul's condoning of idol food, Tomson suggests instead that the Apostle's criterion for idolatry is related to the halakhic principle of conscious intention (מחשבה = συνείδησις: 10.25–9; 8.7–12), which came to prominence especially in legal issues pertaining to idolatry.[100] Contrary to widespread scholarly opinion, then, idol food is certainly *not* a simply matter of indifference for Paul;[101] what is at issue is instead one's idolatrous intention. Like certain more lenient Rabbis, and unlike Rabbi Eliezer (p. 158 and

[98]Simon 1981:429–30; also Hurd 1965:257–60 and others cited by him. (As we saw in n. 97, Simon thinks that Paul would have accepted the Decree at most for reasons of expediency; see also Simon 1986:334–5.)

[99]E.g. Rosner 1994; cf. p. 148 and n. 10 above.

[100]Tomson 1990:208–16; cf. Bockmuehl 1991. While the specific halakhic term at issue is attested primarily in rabbinic texts later than the time of Paul, the use of συνείδησις in this sense of conscious moral *intention* is clearly documented, e.g. in Sir 42.18 *v. l.*; Josephus, *Ant.* 16.4.2 §103, 16.7.4 §212; cf. also Acts 23.1; 1 Tim 1.5, 19 etc.; *1 Clem.* 1.3.

[101]Note, above all, 1 Cor 10.14. This point is now forcefully documented in the important work of Cheung 1999, whatever one makes of his doubtful comments about 'Western secular materialism' as the cause of the widespread misinterpretation. Cheung's position provides an important corrective to the exaggerated stress on ambiguity in Newton 1998: however muddled Corinthian sentiments on this issue clearly must have been, Paul's own halakhic priorities with regard to idolatry are not in doubt.

n. 53 above), Paul would assume that the unspecified intention of Gentiles is *not* towards idolatry. Only if one explicitly says, 'This has been offered in sacrifice' (1 Cor 10.28), is one's συνείδησις assumed to be specifically idolatrous.

Soteriologically and theologically, the coming of Christ means for Paul that the Law has lost its defining covenantal function and instead exercises a primarily deictic or prophetic role.[102] From now on, covenant membership in the elect people of God is defined in christo-logical and 'Abrahamic' rather than Sinaitic terms (Gal 3–4; Rom 4). However, it is the covenant's terms of membership, not its moral and spiritual intention, which the coming of Christ opens up: in the very fact of messianic fulfilment lie both the reformation of the covenant relationship and the continuity of its substance and purpose (see already Jer 31; Ezek 36). For the realm of practical morality, therefore, Paul seems quite content to draw on the existing Old Testament as written for 'our' discipline and instruction (εἰς τὴν ἡμετέραν διδασκαλίαν, Rom 15.4; εἰς νουθεσίαν ἡμῶν, 1 Cor 10.11).[103] This suggests that the Scriptures retain their moral force even for Gentile conduct, although clearly that force derives from those laws about idolatry, sexual morality, robbery, lawcourts (note 1 Cor 6.1–6) etc. *which in fact apply to Gentiles.* In spite of Paul's own profuse polemic against the Law, numerous examples indicate that the Pentateuch, especially passages like Lev 18–20, actually continues to play a substantive role in the formulation of his ethics (cf. p. 148 above).[104]

It is worth commenting briefly on the fact that Paul never mentions the law of the torn limb or prohibits blood consumption. This might seem at first sight to cast doubt on the thesis here advanced, and would indeed require further discussion. Nevertheless, there is good reason to think that the omission may not be very significant, and perhaps even accidental. Given the consistent practice of Judaism and of the ancient Church in both East and West, the burden of proof seems to lie pretty squarely with those who would argue that Paul blithely tolerated Christian consumption of blood. (It is not irrelevant in this regard that Paul's eucharistic language, like that of Luke, studiously avoids the notion of 'drinking Christ's blood'.[105])

---

[102]Cf. Bockmuehl 1990:148–56, and others cited there.

[103]See further 1 Cor 4.6; 9.9–10; 2 Tim 3.16, etc.; and cf. Rosner 1994.

[104]It is interesting to compare Bauckham 1999:149, who writes, 'For our purposes what is especially important is that in his thought about this aspect of the law – the law as in some sense a permanent standard of the righteousness God requires of human life – Paul has largely taken over the Jewish Christian interpretation of the law which we find in James and which derives in part from the teaching of Jesus.'

[105]See 1 Cor 10.16; 11.25; contrast Matt 26.27–28 par. Mark 14.23–24, and especially John 6.53–55. Cf. further W. D. Davies 1980:245–7.

Conversely, however, the problem of blood consumption is in fact rarely mentioned even in contemporary Jewish texts.[106] In practice, even pagan slaughter routinely drained meat of its blood.

Even if black pudding (*sanguiculus*) was readily available at certain specialist butchers (*botularii*),[107] the actual consumption of meat with blood was untypical even among pagans, and easily avoidable for Jews. Ostensibly, the Jewish problem in the Diaspora was less that meat without blood was unavailable, but that so much of it was sacrificed before coming to market. The religiously or culturally fastidious, however, might well object to it simply on the grounds that it was Gentile. As E. P. Sanders writes with reference to contemporary documents from Ephesus and Sardis,

At least some of the time in some cities, meat could be bought in the market which was from suitable animals, which had no blood, and which had not been offered to an idol .... A reasonable Jewish citizenry in a city with reasonable merchants ... could have found acceptable meat.... The problem could be remedied. Pagans could be required to make available food which Jews could eat....

The second possibility is that ... Jews were reluctant to eat Gentile food, especially meat, just because it was Gentile. The objection, that is, may not have been technical – 'it has blood in it' – but vague and traditional – 'our family has never eaten Gentile meat'.[108]

All of this goes some way towards explaining why, in Paul's *ad hoc* correspondence as in the writings of other diaspora Jews, the danger of blood consumption was likely to be a less pressing concern than sexual misconduct and idol meat. For Paul as for early Christian literature generally, then, idolatry (perhaps including arrogance, greed and blasphemy) and sexual immorality are probably the most fundamental of all moral concerns.[109]

One final point on Paul's halakhah. What position did he take on the moral authority of the Torah? For present purposes, I follow W. D. Davies and others in supporting the so-called 'status quo' theory on Paul's view about the validity of the Torah.[110] The apostle

[106]So rightly E. P. Sanders 1990a:278–9; Barclay 1996:434. Even the concerns expressed in *Jos. Asen.* 8.5 and Philo, *Spec. Leg.* 4.122–3 (and in the πνικτῶν of Acts 15.20, 29) are in fact surprisingly rare.

[107]See e.g. Corbier 1989:233. I am grateful to Dr. Justin Meggitt for drawing my attention to this valuable study.

[108]Sanders 1990a:279.

[109]On the link between pagan idolatry and sexual immorality, see e.g. Wisd 14.12–31 and Rom 1.23–27 and p. 155, n. 38 above. Justin, *Dial.* 34–35, in agreement with Trypho, makes abstention from idol meat a touchstone of orthodoxy, e.g. *vis-à-vis* the Gnostics.

[110]See W. D. Davies 1980:69–74; Tomson 1990:237 and *passim*; also cf. Stendahl 1976 and Gaston 1987. The classic statement on the failure of Paul's 'status quo' theory is that of Albert Schweitzer 1931:193–9; cf. Wechsler 1991:269–72.

himself in 1 Corinthians 7.17–20 makes clear that his 'rule for all the churches' is for Jews to keep the Torah (indeed Gal 5.3, too, may mean they are obliged to do so)[111] and for Gentiles to keep what pertains to them – and only that. In either case, what matters are the applicable commandments of God.[112] From the *halakhic* perspective on Paul, Michael Wyschogrod makes a highly apposite point when he states somewhat provocatively, 'The distinction that needs to be made, therefore, is not between the law before Christ and after Christ, but the law for Jews and for Gentiles.'[113]

Two objections to this view must be addressed. First, the 'status quo' argument might be thought to come to grief on Paul's desire to be 'all things to all people' (1 Cor 9.19–23).[114] Here, it seems, the apostle merrily dispenses with the special laws of Judaism if that helps him to win a few more Gentiles, and keeps them if it helps to win Jews. Nevertheless, the central issue of the larger context should be kept in view. Quite possibly, the passage means no more than what 1 Cor 8 and 10 also say: Paul has come to follow a lenient halakhah on the Gentiles' supposedly idolatrous intention, and therefore to give them the benefit of the doubt as far as that more liberal tradition allows.[115] When he eats with conservative Jews, on the other hand, he is prepared to accommodate himself to their stricter parameters of observance. Thus, 'not being under the law' means that while Paul himself does not affirm the narrowly ethnic type of halakhah, he can happily adapt to it and operate within it, if thereby he can win some of his stricter compatriots.

A second objection is implicit in the argument of Alan Segal. While stressing the significance of Noachide Commandments for Paul's ethics,[116] he suggests that by halakhically retreating to the level of the Noachide Laws, Paul denies the saving significance of special laws *even for Jews*.[117] It is not clear that either a retreat or a denial of this kind necessarily follows. What *does* follow, however, is another, unintentional consequence of almost equally serious

---

[111]See Tomson 1990:68, 88–9.

[112]This is why it makes little sense to speak of Paul's 'abolition' or 'rejection' of the food laws and with them the entire Torah, *pars pro toto*, and thereby making his definitive break with Judaism (so again recently Heil 1994:304 and *passim*; cf. the critique in Muller 1996).

[113]Wyschogrod 1988:187; cf. his important programmatic essay of 1993. That the problem of Pauline ethics is fundamentally that of 'Jewish ethics for Gentiles' is also identified by Carras 1990.

[114]Cf. Richardson 1980; Tomson 1990:274–81; also Bockmuehl 1991.

[115]Thus Tomson 1990:276.

[116]A. F. Segal 1990:187–223.

[117]A. F. Segal 1990:200.

implications: *Paul's view that Gentiles are saved as Gentiles begins in practice to look as though Jews are not saved as Jews* – and as though the Jewish special laws are no longer required of Jews. Such an appearance will have been fuelled by the altercation at Antioch (Gal 2.11–14), and would in due course naturally lead to the charge of apostasy, as Segal rightly concludes and as Acts 21.21 independently confirms.[118]

Different Jewish perspectives, we suggested earlier, regarded Gentiles as either damned outright, saved as righteous Gentiles, or saved as converted Jews. Paul gets into trouble not because for him the Gentiles are saved without conversion, nor because of his Noachide halakhah for them. His problem, and his ultimate undoing in Jewish eyes, lies in the attempt to forge a united body of Jewish and Gentile Christians in a fellowship of equals, in which the former continue to live by the whole Torah and the latter merely by the Noachide laws.[119] With Paul's principle of the strong accommodating the weak, there is no a priori reason why such a vision of the church might not have worked. Nevertheless, Paul's opponents and the evidence of Acts 21 are proof that Jews of the stricter persuasion (soon to be embodied by R. Eliezer) would have understood Paul as teaching Jews to abandon their ancestral halakhah, including circumcision. It was apparently on these grounds that the Jerusalem church expressed its doubts about Paul, possibly refusing his offering from the Gentile churches,[120] and left him to be arrested.

Conclusion

Various other early Christian texts would benefit from examination in this context, including passages in the Pastoral Epistles (1 Tim 1.9–10), 1 Peter (4.3) and the book of Revelation (e.g. 2.14, 20; 9.20–21; 21.8, 15), but also in Tertullian and the Pseudo-Clementines (see e.g. n. 94 above). But for present purposes it is time to conclude.

The doctrine of the Noachide Commandments is a rabbinic development of the biblical laws about resident aliens. In its

---

[118]A. F. Segal 1990:202, 223 and *passim* (though, oddly, he never discusses Acts 21.21); cf. Barclay 1996:394–5.

[119]Cf. in this regard the halakhic relevance of Eph 2.11–22, a passage which W. D. Davies 1980:113 uses to good effect.

[120]Thus e.g. Dunn 1977:256–7; note also Rom 15.31 and the silence of Acts on the subject. On balance, however, a more positive construal seems preferable, not least in view of Acts 24.17. The funds were perhaps used at least in part to pay for the costly sacrifices of certain Christian Nazirites (Acts 21.24; cf. Georgi 1992:125–6 and see pp. 42–3 above).

explicitly developed form it does not predate the second century, but the underlying ideas are clearly present in literary sources of the Second Temple period.

To be sure, the Noachide Commandments are not the *theological* key to New Testament ethics: that should instead be sought in christology and the teaching and example of Jesus. But the cumulative argument here presented shows that these legal constructs and their predecessors provide an essential clue to the specific *rationale and content* of early Christian ethics, as well as its criteria of selection in the use of Old Testament laws. During the transition from Jewish to Gentile Christianity, the laws for resident aliens established the hermeneutical parameters within which to appropriate the moral teaching and example of Jesus for a worldwide church. In practical and political terms, Jewish concepts of a universal law for Gentiles proved to be indispensable for the development of Christian ethics.

Part Three

The Development of Public Ethics

8

THE BEGINNING OF CHRISTIAN PUBLIC ETHICS

FROM LUKE TO ARISTIDES AND *DIOGNETUS*

Christianity's rapid march from legal toleration to becoming the official religion of the Roman Empire took place entirely in the fourth century, well after the period we are primarily considering in this book. In fact, of course, Christians had occasion to think about the public communication of their faith a good deal earlier than that. In this penultimate chapter, we shall review the circumstances contributing to the beginning of 'public' Christian ethics before turning to a closer examination of this theme in two second-century case studies, Aristides of Athens and the *Epistle to Diognetus*.

Three Beginnings

The Beginning of 'Christianity'

One rarely stops to consider the significance of the fact that the New Testament refers to 'Christians' only three times, and never as a self-designation. If Luke is to be believed, that term (Χριστιανοί) first came into use around a decade after Jesus' death and resurrection (Acts 11.27; cf. 26.28; 1 Pet 4.16). Having most likely originated within the Roman imperial administration of Syria,[1] this nomenclature soon served to reinforce the fledgling Christian movement's emerging public identity within the Graeco-Roman setting. While the ongoing internal Jewish debate over Christianity seems to have concerned sectarian groupings like the 'Nazarenes' (see already Acts 24.5),[2] within the wider Graeco-Roman public sphere the followers of the new movement came to be recognizable as Χριστιανοί, 'Christians' – a group that may at first have appeared Jewish, like the analogously named 'Herodians', but which before long took on a distinct public image of its own.

For the first two centuries, the Christian population of the Empire remained very small both in absolute terms and in relation to the much larger Jewish community.[3] Nevertheless, and even if the

---

[1]See recently J. Taylor 1994; Hengel & Schwemer 1997:230; 1998:350–1 and cf. p. 49 above.
[2]For the problems associated with this name, cf. e.g. Pritz 1988.
[3]See recently Hopkins 1998:195, 212–16 and *passim*. Stark 1996:49–71 overstates his otherwise intriguing proposal that Christianity was rather more 'Jewish', and its mission to the Jews rather more successful, than has usually been supposed.

evidence is initially sporadic and regional, a clear change in the Roman perception of Christianity can be documented in several stages, by examples ranging from Claudius (when there is no evidence of a separate public identity) to Trajan (when it seems that Gentile Christians at any rate are no longer being mistaken for Jews). First, in describing the disturbances in the Jewish community at Rome in AD 47–48, the second-century historian Suetonius relies on sources that see the problem in internal Jewish disputes, instigated by an otherwise unknown 'Chrestus'. The official Roman response on that occasion was Claudius's expulsion of (some) Jews from Rome (*Claudius* 25.4; cf. also Acts 18.2). The likelihood that this account implies Jewish messianic disputes about 'Christ' has been argued frequently, if perhaps still rather inconclusively.[4] It is, at any rate, significant that from the official point of view this matter involved no one outside the *Jewish* community: the category of 'Christians', if relevant, had as yet no public profile in Rome.

Regardless of the precise circumstances underlying Suetonius's brief account, the Roman view of that incident seems comparable to what we find in the account of another, if less serious, quarrel in the Jewish community of Corinth three years later (Acts 18.12–17). That incident, recorded from Luke's Christian perspective, shows a formal charge against Paul's mission being brought by his Jewish opponents before the new proconsul Gallio, recently arrived from Rome. Gallio's handling of the incident is characteristic of Roman perspectives at this time: Christians were perceived as of no distinct import for public order, as an internal Jewish phenomenon to be dealt with by the Jewish community itself (18.14–15).[5]

Both these episodes, therefore, illustrate that until at least the mid-first century AD Christianity was from the Roman perspective not a publicly identifiable entity, even in the Eastern Empire. Instead, it still sheltered anonymously under the public umbrella of 'Judaism', being in equal measure affected by the dangers and the benefits of that identification. Our examples may also, incidentally, suggest a more plausible context for the New Testament's relative silence on Christianity's public self-presentation and social ethics – more plausible, that is, than the widely held notion that their intense millenarian eschatology left Christians unconcerned about their

---

[4]Chrestos was a common slave name, which in Hellenistic Greek was liable to be pronounced 'Christos'. If Suetonius had understood his source to mean Jesus of Nazareth, a religious leader who had been dead for quite a long time, one might have expected to see this acknowledged, as in Tacitus, *Annals* 15.44.3–4. See also Mottershead 1986:149–57.

[5]The Roman legal framework for Gallio's decision is discussed most recently by Winter 1999.

relationship with the present world. Far from being preoccupied with otherworldly concerns, Christianity in the first several decades of its existence defined itself primarily *vis-à-vis* other *Jewish* groupings within Palestine and the Diaspora; its attitude to the state and society remained largely implicit, and in essentials indistinguishable from that of the mother faith. Concerted hostility was at most sporadic and predominantly Jewish, as the accounts in Acts and Paul's letters show.

By the latter part of Nero's reign, however, Christians had begun, at first locally and sporadically, to become the specific focus of Roman attention and animosity. The obvious illustration of this is usually seen in Nero's cold-blooded accusation and persecution of Christians in his attempt to pin on them the blame for the fire of Rome. In that instance at least, it is Christians rather than Jews who are singled out as culprits in their own right, as the subject of officially organized Roman opprobrium. Regardless of the precise historical setting, however, one should be careful not to over-interpret this move. From all appearances it would appear that Christians merely served as a convenient scapegoat for an increasingly hot-tempered and unpredictable tyrant: it is by no means clear from Tacitus's account that they were officially charged with specific religious or political offences. One must certainly allow for the possibility that Tacitus may reflect a second-century rather than a first-century view when he comments that 'the pernicious superstition' of Christianity had broken out 'even in Rome itself, where all the world's horrible and shameful things collect and find a keen following'.[6] Ruthless and harrowing as Nero's action must have been in its effect on the church at Rome (cf. also *1 Clem.* 6.1), it was probably a despot's temporary and local expedient that did not establish an official policy. Pliny's evident uncertainty in dealing with Christians in Asia Minor half a century later (see below) suggests that on this occasion the emperor may simply have capitalized on an emerging, but still vague, public prejudice against Christianity as a distasteful and odiously un-Roman phenomenon. This, of course, was a view to which more articulate adversaries like Fronto and Celsus were soon to give eloquent expression.

All the same, even if the Neronian persecution may represent less weighty evidence of a clear Christian public profile than is sometimes supposed, three roughly contemporary New Testament texts do seem to confirm the trend towards Christianity's increasingly distinct

---

[6]Tacitus, *Annals* 15.44; cf. Suetonius, *Nero* 16.2, who similarly speaks of a *superstitio nova ac malefica.*

identity and perceived threat to public order in various localities. First, concerted *pagan* opposition to Christianity seems to be assumed in addition to Jewish opposition in Paul's letter to the Roman colony of Philippi in Macedonia, most likely composed in Rome not long after AD 62: Christian loyalties have implicitly emerged as incompatible with the religious and civic obligations incumbent on a colony of Rome.[7] More explicit, if less clearly datable, is the suggestion in 1 Peter 4.14, 16 that persecution in Asia Minor is directed specifically against 'Christians', as those associated with the 'name of Christ'. For the Syrian context, finally, it is also important to note that persecution specifically by 'Gentiles' is explicitly in view in Matt 10.18 (contrast Mark 13.9).

It is sometimes thought that persecution under Domitian lies behind the New Testament book of Revelation (cf. also *1 Clem.* 1.1; 7.1). But even if the evidence could be equally compatible with an earlier date, the letters and visions of Revelation do imply that Christianity *per se* is now the object of pagan and no longer just of Jewish hostility.[8] This impression is confirmed in the letters of Ignatius and Polycarp under Trajan, as well as in the emergence of Christian Apologists in the time of Hadrian, beginning perhaps with Quadratus and Aristides.

Only after the turn of the century do we see the first signs that hitherto local and *ad hoc* responses are beginning to beg for more systematic definition of a central Roman policy on Christianity. Although invariably antagonistic, this policy did not by any means result in systematic and permanent persecution, as is still sometimes assumed. Instead, times and places of spectacular violence and martyrdom merely punctuated two centuries during which Christianity experienced wide-ranging popular expressions of an underlying public antagonism. On the Roman side the most famous, if tentative, record of this groping towards a formal policy is of course Pliny the Younger's correspondence with Trajan about the 'Christian problem' in the province of Asia (*Ep.* 10.96).

Perhaps understandably, this brief caricature of public attitudes to Christianity has concentrated on the rather slender evidence of *official* persecution. This is due in large part to the nature of our first- and second-century sources. Leaving aside martyrs' Acts and apologetic texts, the surviving evidence of attitudes to Christianity is

---

[7]See Bockmuehl 1997:97–8, 232–5 on Phil 1.27–30; 3.20. Cf. Acts 16 and possibly already 1 Thess 2.14.

[8]See e.g. Rev 13.17–18 and cf. recently Slater 1998.

scant and predominantly literary, while popular indicators of public opinion wholly elude us.[9]

The Beginning of Christian Apologetic Discourse

Our main interest here is not of course the question of persecution. Nor even are we concerned to present a detailed account of 'the Christians as the Romans saw them', as that has been ably done by others.[10] What matters for us is to note that by the time the apostolic age was drawing to a close, Christianity was beginning to appear, in its own as well as in Jewish and to some extent in Roman eyes, as a distinct social entity with its own public 'image'. While its Jewish roots initially allowed it in many cases and places to escape being singled out for official scrutiny, 'Christianity' and 'the Christians' were entering Roman popular and administrative consciousness. In political and experiential fact, and before long in their own rhetoric, Christians were fast becoming a kind of 'third race' distinct from Jews and Gentiles,[11] with its own characteristic beliefs and practices.

This deceptively familiar development in turn had wide-ranging consequences. Unless a given community is prepared to opt out altogether from meaningful participation in the wider society, a public image nourished by mystique, intrigue and suspicion sooner or later requires the development of a rudimentary apologetic discourse. Such discourse was required at the very least for purposes of internal reassurance, but also as part of the forging of a Christian identity *vis-à-vis* both Jewish and pagan detractors. These two external apologetic 'fronts' were engaged in very different ways, and the Christian–Jewish debates are already well established by the time the New Testament draws to a close.[12] Christianity's public engagement with pagan society, on the other hand, took some considerable time to get out of the starting blocks.

It is certainly true that, as the book of Revelation shows, the early church encompassed apocalyptic circles that deliberately chose *not* to engage Graeco-Roman society in the terms of rational dialogue but primarily in those of defiance, admonishing their fellow believers to

[9]Lucian's *Peregrinus* may be a partial exception.
[10]E.g. Wilken 1980, 1984; cf. Fox 1986.
[11]See already Aristides (fourth race alongside barbarians, Greeks and Jews) and *Diogn.* 5.17, both discussed below (p. 202 and n. 77); also the *Kerygma Petrou* 2. Cf. recently Kinzig 1994:145–71.
[12]Note, for example, B. Lindars' classic treatment (1961) of New Testament 'apologetics' purely in terms of the apostolic handling of the Old Testament in the proof from prophecy. See further Horbury 1998a.

live out the Christian life and bear the consequences. (Indeed it may well be precisely the Pauline policy of 'constructive engagement' which, in the history of its effects a generation later, incurred the ire of the Apocalypse against the social success of Paul's own churches.[13]) What is more, the number of surviving Christian apocalypses and martyrs' Acts suggests that this reaction was probably not just that of a small minority, but of harassed believers in a good many parts of the Empire. Ignatius of Antioch, writing on his way to martyrdom in Rome, has very little to say on our subject: the church's interaction with the secular powers seems so highly polarized and antipathetic as to be mutually exclusive.[14] A similar perspective of separation from the world prevails in most other writings of the Apostolic Fathers, even if there are occasional exceptions[15] and if their attitude never develops into a full-blown political counter-ideology.[16] The Apostolic Fathers' consistency in this matter, across a wide geographical area, is itself an indication of the relatively undeveloped interest in public ethics in many Christian circles at the beginning of the second century.[17] Even among the subsequent Apologists one still encounters writers like Tatian, who presents his *Oratio ad Graecos* in the form of a defiant farewell to Greek and Roman culture.[18]

---

[13]Cf. the argument of Taeger 1998. See also Venetz 1989 on the contrast between the political philosophy of Romans and that of Revelation.

[14]See e.g. *Magn.* 5.1; *Rom.* 7.1; but cf. also note 15 below.

[15]2 *Clem.* 13.1 urges Christians to please even outsiders by their righteousness, lest God's name be blasphemed (cf. Ezra 5.9; Isa 52.5; Rom 2.24; 1 Tim 6.1; 2 Pet 2.2). Similar concern resembling NT advice about good conduct among pagans is found in Ignatius, *Trall.* 8.2 and Polycarp, *Phil.* 10.2 (citing 1 Pet 2.12); Ignatius, *Eph.* 10.1–2 commends prayers for the repentance of all humanity as well as evangelistic teaching through Christian works of humility, gentleness and forbearance. Note also van Unnik 1980.

[16]Indeed these marks of polarization can in some cases co-exist with a note of pragmatism, for instance concerning law and property (Hermas, *Sim* 1.1.5; 8.9.1); domestic arrangements, including slavery (cf. *1 Clem.* 1.3; Ignatius, *Pol.* 4.3; Polycarp, *Phil.* 4.2–3); and even the state (1 Clem 1.3; 60.4 – 61.2). Cf. Carleton Paget 1997:201–3. In principle, however, Barnard 1978:372 is right to conclude that the Apostolic Fathers are not interested in engaging their pagan surroundings. Their prior concerns include internal schism (*1 Clem.*), catechetical and liturgical order (*Did.*), the problem of a Christian repentance (*Hermas*), unity and authority in the church (Ignatius), the sin of avarice (Polycarp) and the Christian interpretation of the Old Testament (*Barnabas*). At the same time, Brent 1998 suggests that Ignatius's view of his own impending martyrdom is deliberately construed as a counterpart to the sacrifices of the imperial cult.

[17]Cf. Carleton Paget 1997:194.

[18]Tertullian seems at times not far behind, e.g. in his famous antithesis of 'Athens vs. Jerusalem' (*De Praescriptione* 7), or when he extols the abiding apologetic force of martyrdom in his notorious dictum *semen est sanguis Christianorum* ('the blood of Christians is seed', *Apol.* 50.13). See further Grant 1988a:10–13 on Tatian. At the same time, Kurt Aland suggests that the extreme stance of the book of Revelation appears to have remained a solitary exception (1979:81). See further p. 191 below.

Early Christianity's very diverse views of its place in the world are themselves a subject well worth grappling with.[19] Here, however, my aim is to take note of that more explicit engagement with Christianity's public identity which the second century increasingly also produced, especially in the work of the Apologists. Theirs, to be sure, was no less a discourse of defiance, no less a denial of paganism in the name of truth.[20] But the Apologists chose to exercise their resistance by adding to the martyrs' unshakeable counter-assertion of Christ the denunciation of paganism's falsehoods in the terms of its own highest intellectual and moral standards.

At the same time, it would be mistaken to assume that apologetics emerged merely as a pragmatic political necessity – responding to the confrontation by pitting Christ's claims on divinity against Caesar's, as it were. In fact, the New Testament antecedents suggest that, even from Christianity's own theological and confessional point of view, the public 'defence and confirmation of the gospel' (Phil 1.7) is at the very heart of what it means to believe in Christian truth.

Significantly, this is a conviction shared in equal measure by martyrs and Apologists: Christian doctrine inherently required a reasoned resistance to the rival theological and political claims of the Empire. That is to say, martyrs and Apologists alike defended Christians *as Christians*, a legitimate new 'third race' worthy of public respect. The confession of the martyrs became inescapably public when confronted with the test case of public sacrifice to the emperor: their simple *Christianus sum* is at once a public acknowledgement of the charge and a public defence in the form of a decisive repudiation of the idols.[21]

The extant writings of the Christian spokesmen suggest that their public discourse about these convictions was neither an open-ended 'dialogue' nor on the other hand a radical withdrawal, whether of the militant or the quietistic kind. Instead, the Apologists manifest a constructive and sometimes staggeringly optimistic engagement with the world. Christian public discourse arose from the conviction that the incarnation, death and resurrection of the divine Logos made

---

[19]See e.g. recently Dassmann 1992; Cf. Rahner 1961:21–39; Marucci 1992; K. Aland 1979.

[20]The dialectical nature of the early Christian view of the state is nicely presented in H. Rahner 1961:21–39. At least in the second century, it could easily be extended to Christianity's public engagement more generally: we do not yet find the ease of public identification with the philosophical tradition that comes to the fore in Clement of Alexandria.

[21]So e.g. Tertullian on the meaning of martyrdom in *Scorp.* 3.2. See Wendebourg 1987:302; and cf. Hopkins 1998:185–6, who suggests that the term 'Christian' frequently functioned more as a 'persuasive' and 'hopeful' category.

faith in Christ both intelligible and communicable as the fulfilment of all that was good and true in human life and aspiration.

The Beginning of Christian 'Public Ethics'

The emergence of Christian public discourse concerns us here in its specific corollary in the realm of ethics. The Apologists were concerned to defend Christianity against pagan detractors[22] not only in the doctrinal, but also in the moral realm. That is to say, these second-century writers engaged in what one might identify as Christian 'public ethics': the explication and defence of Christian morality in terms that were communicable and intelligible within a wider Graeco-Roman moral discourse. What matters for our purposes is the conviction that Christian ethical argument was, at least in principle, a *public* exercise.[23]

The importance of 'public ethics' is further underscored by the observation that in antiquity our nearly ubiquitous modern distinction between domestic and 'public' morality was either unknown or at any rate far less clear. Collective ideals cut across the divide of private and public sphere. Public opinion was in a sense omnipresent – a fact that in itself helped to reinforce the 'apologetic' need for Christians to give an account of themselves and their moral life.[24]

This 'public' nature of the exercise remains an important feature even in cases where the primary audience may have been an internal Christian one. Thus, whether or not Athenagoras's work is a genuine embassy, presented in AD 177 as a plea for toleration before Marcus Aurelius and his son Commodus, is in a sense immaterial to its rhetorical place and purpose. The Apologists expounded and defended Christian ethics (and of course doctrine) in terms that may be equally 'public', and indeed equally necessary, whether it was presented before the emperor or for the reassurance of an internal Christian audience.[25] And just as in the case of the 'Noachide

---

[22]Justin and others clearly also defended Christian ethics on a second apologetic front, that against Judaism. Nevertheless, and for all the heat of their disagreement about the Law, these discussions could take for granted a good many shared Jewish assumptions about a theonomous universal morality.

[23]W. A. Meeks (1990:309–10, 315–16) detects the phenomenon of a 'quasi-public' ethical discourse for internal consumption in Pauline ethics, too.

[24]Cf. Stegemann 1996:104–108, who cites B. M. Malina and G. Alföldy in taking his cue from Jesus' claim to have 'spoken openly to the world' (John 18.20): 'Im Gegensatz zur Moderne, die eine gewisse Trennung von öffentlicher und privater Sphäre, von Kollektiv und Individuum ermöglicht, war in der Antike die öffentliche Meinung allgegenwärtig' (p. 107).

[25]Note also Edwards 1999:313: 'Christianity being both a proselytizing and a divided faith, we might contend that every book which it produces is directed to outsiders, and conversely that in parleying with outsiders one is bound to take a view on certain questions that are disputed in the church.'

Commandments' examined in Chapter 7 above, we must of course retain the important distinction between defensible *explanations* of morality on the one hand and expectations of actual conformity on the other. Christians, like Jews, obviously had no jurisdiction over outsiders during the period in view, and thus their 'public ethics' was limited to advocacy and persuasion.

Our interest in this chapter, then, is in the Apologists' publicly accountable 'defence and confirmation' of Christian ethics, explained either to outsiders or *as if* to outsiders. Of course the early Apologists themselves at times point out, and even pagan observers occasionally admit,[26] that the persuasive force of Christian ethics derives at least as much from practical example as from philosophical argument. So for Aristides, for example, the very inconspicuousness of Christian acts of mercy can become an apologetic *topos* in its own right: Christians live in public and have nothing to hide, but theirs is an unobtrusive case that does not advertise its works of charity.[27] Similarly, it is clear that the early Christians themselves regarded the noble deaths of their martyrs as constituting one of the most powerful apologetic arguments for the truth of Christian faith and practice, not least by analogy to the death of Socrates.[28] What is more, martyrdom was understood by Clement of Alexandria and others as a public manifestation, jointly in word and deed, of the very essence of Christian ethics – the love of God.[29] In this respect, the arguments of the Apologists are only the articulate tip of a vast iceberg of Christian faith, practice and relationships. In what follows, therefore, we must bear in mind that throughout the second and third centuries this silent voice of Christian praxis exercised an unarticulated and largely undocumented moral witness whose overall significance and influence easily dwarfs that of a handful of educated spokesmen.[30]

Overview

We will begin with a brief survey of New Testament starting points for a Christian public ethics; some of these texts were encountered in

---

[26]See e.g. Galen trans. in Walzer 1949:15. For a more recent appraisal of the Arabic text, see Gero 1990.

[27]Aristides, *Apol* 16.2. Cf. Matt 6.1–4.

[28]See Wendebourg 1987:300–1, citing numerous references; cf. Baumeister 1995.

[29]*Strom.* 4.13.1–2; 4.73.3. See also Wendebourg 1987:301–2. Similarly, compare the accounts of Aqiba's martyrdom in rabbinic literature; cf. p. 240 below.

[30]Wilken 1984:92 writes, 'Through Christian practice, Christian morality, the early Christian movement made its first bid for acceptance within the Greco-Roman world.' Cf. e.g. Walsh & Gottlieb 1992:29–34.

earlier chapters. The main part of this chapter will examine the lines of approach to public ethics in Aristides of Athens and the *Epistle to Diognetus*.

New Testament Antecedents

To set the stage for our examination of the second century, it will be useful to remind ourselves of some of the evidence for an emerging interest in public ethics even in the pages of the New Testament. To be sure, this evidence is somewhat patchy and sporadic, and the NT writers for the most part are *not* specifically interested in public ethics as an apologetic strategy. That is also why it seems appropriate in this context not to devote a separate chapter to their handling of it. The problem of a universal ethic is indeed an important one for the NT, as we saw in Chapters 6 and 7. But it is addressed primarily from the perspective of positive revelation, and its *Sitz im Leben* is largely the instruction of Gentile converts rather than the apologetic or evangelistic explication of Christian morality to pagan observers. Five authors may briefly be singled out.

Matthew

Christian ethics as a fundamental issue in relations with outsiders is in principle already anticipated in the Sermon on the Mount. Thus, Jesus instructs his disciples, 'Let your light so shine before others that they may see your good works and give glory to your Father in heaven' (Matt 5.16). To be sure, Matthew does not greatly develop this theme. The outsiders with whom he seems predominantly concerned are the scribes and Pharisees (e.g. 5.20; 23.2–36); and although his gospel specifically concludes by affirming the world-wide mission to the Gentiles, we have few indications either of a significant Gentile presence in the church he envisages or of any concerted effort to communicate central topics of Christian ethics in publicly accessible terms. It is of course true that we find repeated affirmations of ethics defined in a universal domain rather than in terms of a narrowly confessional prerogative. Just as the heavenly Father 'makes his sun rise on the evil and on the good, and sends rain on the just and on the unjust', so disciples ought to greet and love even their enemies, and their morality should exceed that of both the religious and the irreligious (5.44–47; cf. 5.20). Nevertheless, as we saw in chapter 7, Matthew offers no developed ethical dialogue with Gentile outsiders. Significantly, the same is true for Mark, despite the fact that his gospel does seem to assume a clearly Gentile audience (e.g. 7.3–4, 19).

Luke-Acts

Luke is the only one among the synoptic evangelists to address himself explicitly to the encounter between Christian faith and pagan culture; but even he does so mainly in Acts – and then only in passing, in his account of the early mission to the Gentiles. The passage concerned with the Apostolic Council and Decree (Acts 15) was discussed at some length in chapter 7, and in its overall context the debate reflected there clearly does have implications for the emergence of a Christian public ethics. Nevertheless, that episode (and in all probability its original *Sitz im Leben*) clearly has its primary concern in an inner-Christian discussion not about public ethics but about 'convert ethics'. The issue, as we saw above, is about how Gentile *believers* must live in order to be saved (Acts 15.1 and *passim*). In other words, we are dealing not with the explication of Christian ethics to outsiders, but with a decision about what constitutes ethics for (Gentile) *insiders*. While it is therefore an invaluable resource in assessing the NT rationale for a universal ethic, the actual rhetorical intent of Acts 15 in a church composed of Jews and Gentiles is not that of 'public ethics'.

One or two other passages in Luke-Acts are marginally more pertinent for our present purposes. In particular, the accounts of Paul's preaching in Lystra and in Athens are perhaps the only ones that offer some hints of what in Luke's view an explication of Christian ethics to pagan outsiders might look like. At Lystra, Paul and Barnabas concisely summarize one aspect of the gospel's moral impact on pagan culture in Asia Minor:

Friends, why are you doing this? We are mortals just like you, and we bring you good news, that you should turn from these worthless things to the living God, who made the heaven and the earth and the sea and all that is in them. In past generations he allowed all the nations to follow their own ways; yet he has not left himself without a witness in doing good – giving you rains from heaven and fruitful seasons, and filling you with food and your hearts with joy. (Acts 14.15–17, NRSV)

While one should certainly not read too much into this brief paragraph, it is significant that we already find here *in nuce* several affirmations which recur in a more fully developed form in the second-century material to be examined below. They are:

1 Pagan gods are dead, pagan sacrifices and superstitions are 'vain' (μάταιος).
2 They must be abandoned if truth is to be recognized.
3 Human beings must instead turn to the Creator, the living God (ἐπὶ θεὸν ζῶντα)
4 His character of goodness (ἀγαθουργῶν: both redemptive and exemplary) is attested in his works since creation.

This is of course only a minimal outline, closely comparable to well-established traditions of Jewish Hellenistic ethics (see Chapters 5–7 above) – and in this form not even concerned to communicate specifically *Christian* ethics. Nevertheless, it plausibly recounts one of the earliest Christian attempts to communicate to a Hellenistic audience something of the essential building blocks of a theonomous, Judaeo-Christian ethic. A similar passage occurs as part of Paul's famous speech at Athens in Acts 17. Here, the Creator is proclaimed as the one 'unknown' to the Athenians (17.23–24), whom all nations can and should search after.

Since we are God's offspring, we ought not to think that the deity is like gold, or silver, or stone, an image formed by the art and imagination of mortals. While God has overlooked the times of human ignorance, now he commands all people everywhere to repent, because he has fixed a day on which he will have the world judged in righteousness by a man whom he has appointed, and of this he has given assurance to all by raising him from the dead.

This passage is less obviously related to our question about ethics. Nevertheless, it resembles the earlier one in asserting that unlike the pagan gods, the true God cannot be imagined or worshipped through idols made by human hands. Unlike Acts 14, however, this text contains an otherwise undeveloped, but *public* moral demand that arises from a distinctly Christian assertion: through Christ and his resurrection, God announces universal judgement and calls for repentance. Other than the denial of pagan religious images, it remains unclear what such repentance might mean in practice: as we saw in chapters 5–6, the primary point in these passages may well be epistemological rather than moral. The possibility of a universal moral appeal does indeed seem to be implied, but neither the verb μετανοέω nor the content of that appeal is here expounded in ways that might be regarded as 'publicly accessible' in our present frame of reference.

One other passage in Acts merits our attention at least in passing, since it confirms Luke's point of view that in the trial and defence of Paul the gospel itself is being publicly tried and defended. On trial before Festus, Paul affirms that of the life, death and resurrection of Christ that 'this has not been done in a corner' (οὐ γάρ ἐστιν ἐν γωνίᾳ πεπραγμένον τοῦτο, Acts 26.26). It is significant, as e.g. A. J. Malherbe has pointed out,[31] that this assertion forms part of a consistently 'public' apologetic concern in Luke-Acts. Significantly, in Luke's view the imprisoned Paul's apologetic efforts incorporate a rudimentary attempt to expound Christian ethics to Festus's predecessor, Felix, including the principles of 'righteousness and self-control (ἐγκράτεια, cf. Gal 5.23) and the future judgement' (Acts 24.25). Since Felix is described as married to a Jewish wife and already well-acquainted with the Christian message (24.22, 24), it may be questioned to what extent this really qualifies as 'public' ethics in the broader Roman context addressed by the second-century Apologists. But at least since the apostles' remarkably Socratic-sounding reply in 4.29, Luke has left little doubt about his intention in the narrative of Acts: the Christian witness to the ends of the earth (cf. 1.8) comprises the publicly accessible communication of Christian faith and life as public truth.

Paul

There is, as Chapters 6–7 suggested, a good deal of material relevant to a public ethic in the writings of St. Paul – not least in his engagement with social and rhetorical conventions. Themes similar to those found in Acts and many Hellenistic Jewish passages recur in a number of Pauline texts like Romans 1.19–27 (cf. also 1 Thess 1.9–10), which seem to take for granted a universal call to abandon the inherently irrational and inescapably immoral worship of the creature in place of the true worship of the one Creator. In particular, we noted that the logic of Rom 1.19–27 runs in the following form, which may be compared with that observed for the two passages just cited from Acts:

1. God's existence and invisible power are revealed in creation and can be known by observing the created order (1.19–20).
2. The pagans thus knew about God and should have given him the glory. They are without excuse.
3. Instead they perverted the natural order to make idols out of created things, and treat them as gods.
4. Idolatry leads to shameless and abominable immorality, which is itself an instance of worshipping the creature instead of the creator.

Once again, this analysis of the passage makes it clear that while in certain contexts the argument might well prove pertinent to questions of public ethics, its rhetorical intention here is primarily an indictment of pagan *idolatry*, and only in that connection of

---

[31]See Malherbe 1986a.

immorality. For the context of Romans, at any rate, a positive exposition of universal ethics is neither stated nor, arguably, implied.

A number of other Pauline passages do appeal to universal principles, not in order to formulate public ethics but to strengthen a moral argument directed at *Christians*. These texts include 1 Cor 5.1 and 11.14, 1 Thess 4.11–12, Phil 4.8 and probably Rom 13.1–7. All of these were previously discussed in Chapter 6, and will in a general sense serve as background to the discussion below: while they do not address our subject directly, they arguably contribute to an understanding of the wider context in which Christian public ethics were formulated and developed.

1 Peter

The remainder of the New Testament addresses our subject to an even more limited extent. While the sapiential exhortations in the Letter of James are of interest as a genre whose moral rhetoric derives at least in part from traditions and sources outside the written Scriptures, a more explicit sensitivity to the issue of Christianity's public moral stance can be noted in 1 Peter. The author of this document clearly does have a concern for the civic profile of Christianity in a pagan world. To be sure, he makes no attempt to formulate his own ethics or apologetics in such a way as to persuade outsiders. His readers, however, are explicitly urged to develop a constant apologetic readiness (ἕτοιμοι ἀεὶ πρὸς ἀπολογίαν) towards their pagan accusers, to be able to account for their hope with gentleness and reverence (3.15–16). The mode and the aim of such persuasion seem at the same time to be primarily in the realm of practical conduct (ἀναστροφή), and in that sense comparable to those of Matt 5.16: the persuasive force of the Christian message lies in the quiet testimony of *visible* faithfulness, be it on the part of Christians in the world generally (2.12), of women's domestic witness to unbelieving husbands (3.1–2), or specifically *vis-à-vis* pagan persecutors (3.16).

The assumption throughout is that Christian moral behaviour carries its own *inherently* persuasive force: its strength lies not perhaps in the force of argument so much as in the fact that God himself desires that right conduct should 'silence the ignorance of the foolish' (2.15; cf. 2.12; 3.1–2; cf. 4.4) and shame the pagan adversaries (3.16; NB divine passive). The writer takes for granted that the message implied in Christian conduct is indeed universally intelligible and carries apologetic weight. This conviction serves as a rudimentary platform for his instructions about Christian public ethics.

1 Peter, then, is pertinent to our subject in two ways. First, it establishes as a topic of importance the public credibility and justification of Christian conduct, and explicitly stresses the need for apologetic witness.[32] But secondly, its approach points to an understanding of public moral persuasion as achieved primarily in Christian *praxis*, rather than through philosophical or rhetorical argument. Although most of the second-century writers discussed in this chapter do endorse an explicitly rational approach to public moral persuasion, the precedent of 1 Peter and possibly a few other NT texts (cf. 1 Thess 4.11–12; 1 Tim 3.7; Matt 5.16) is a vital pointer to the ongoing role of *praxis* as an indispensable pillar of early Christianity's public moral profile. Appeal to Christian conduct is widespread in the second century, both among the Apologists and among martyrs and others who eschew formal argument.

Revelation

Lastly, another brief word on the book of Revelation. In many ways it is of course true that this vision contains a host of material relevant to our exercise. There are numerous impassioned warnings against pagan idolatry in all its forms, and not least in specific application to the politically charged spheres of public religion, power and commerce. In that sense, to speak of the 'political thought' of the book of Revelation is highly appropriate, and a number of recent treatments have rightly exploited this theme.[33]

Nevertheless, the book's genre as an early Christian apocalypse makes it only obliquely concerned with the subject here at hand. Like many of the martyrs' Acts, the Apostolic Fathers and other Christian apocalyptic texts, Revelation's stance constitutes an emphatic counterpoint to those whose vision of Christianity included constructive participation in Graeco-Roman public life[34] – including, by extension, the Apologists. In the place of direct rational engagement, it offers only a protest call to non-co-operation with the power structures of the pagan world. Revelation posits resistance and radical witness in the place of public moral persuasion. To be sure – and this is often overlooked in recent interpretations – the writer's vision of the other side of Armageddon is indeed an emphatically 'public' one, a vision of a new Jerusalem which attracts not

[32]Cf. similarly 1 Cor 14.24; Col 4.6; 1 Thess 4.12; 1 Tim 3.7. See further Goppelt 1972; van Unnik 1980.

[33]Cf. e.g. O'Donovan 1986; Bauckham 1991; Kerner 1998:78–107; Söding 1999.

[34]See recently Räisänen 1995:161–2, 164 and *passim*; cf. p. 182 above.

only the worshippers but the wealth and power of the nations (21.24, 26), and from which nonetheless all uncleanness and immorality are excluded (21.8, 27; 22.15). This is where apocalyptic and apologetic presuppositions need not be mutually exclusive, as perhaps Tertullian illustrates most clearly. For our purposes, however, the specific concern of a publicly accessible exposition of Christian ethics is here not just absent, but seemingly avoided. Revelation, and other voices like it, must accompany our examination of early Christian public ethics as silent witnesses. They are a salutary reminder that a politics without prophetic resistance will inevitably lose much of its justification and Christian authenticity. Both engagement and disengagement are needed, even if our treatment here necessarily concentrates on the former.[35]

General Observations on the New Testament

Our brief New Testament survey has produced fairly slim pickings for the subject at hand. Perhaps one might argue the inclusion of a number of additional texts. Doubtless, too, there is room for disagreement about the assessment of several of the sources I have classified as less directly relevant to the issue of 'public ethics'. In all this, one is inevitably compelled to choose one or another out of numerous possible definitions of the kind of 'public' that early Christianity might be envisaged as addressing. Is a given text concerned, either directly or indirectly, with 'public opinion' or only with the public arbiters of power? Does it address the pagan world of first- or second-century Roman imperial culture in a general, abstracted sense or merely the respective power brokers in a particular locality? These and other questions, most of which are equally valid for Jewish apologetic works, like the *Epistle of Aristeas*

---

[35]It is worth noting what has perhaps remained implicit in our earlier discussions, viz. that a similar split over the issue of cultural engagement vs. disengagement existed in Judaism at this time. Philo and Josephus, and before them writings like the *Epistle of Aristeas* and in their own way even the *Sibylline Oracles*, represent a form of Hellenistic Judaism that affirmed the public defensibility of the Jewish faith. By contrast, early rabbinic (and before it Pharisaic and Essene) Judaism came to reject this kind of apologetics. Although the Mishnah commends that one should 'know how to answer Epicurus' (i.e. the unbeliever, whether Jewish or Gentile: *m. 'Abot* 2.14; cf. *m. Sanh.* 10.1), and even though one finds occasional anecdotes about rabbis conversing with Gentiles, these discussions are invariably conducted on the rabbi's terms and the punchlines achieved at the pagan's expense. Any apologetic purpose remains purely internal. It is probably not accidental that rabbinic Judaism preserved none of the ancient Jewish apologetic writings. Despite certain halakhic and midrashic traditions in common with rabbinic Judaism (note also S. Belkin on the medieval *Midrash Tadshe*, cited in Stemberger 1996:346), the first Jew after Josephus to mention Philo by name is Azariah dei Rossi in 1573. See more generally Horbury 1998a and Krauss/Horbury 1996.

or Josephus's *Against Apion*, are clearly relevant and will continue to occupy us in the second-century Christian writers. Nevertheless, the fact remains that the New Testament writers make few overt attempts to persuade their pagan contemporaries about the nature and truth of Christian morality. Occasional efforts to define a profile of Christian behaviour within the *polis* and empire do emerge; but the pagan world as such is only fleetingly addressed, and what social ethics we find tends to be concentrated at the level of *ekklésia* and *oikos*.[36]

All that being said, the relative absence of public ethics from the NT ought to be unsurprising, given its social context. In spite of periodic claims to the contrary,[37] it remains the case that the vast majority of early Christians would have belonged to a class whose place in society was defined predominantly by their relationships within the *household* rather than in relation to the 'public' forum of city or empire. Within the New Testament, even the spiritual or material leadership of the small Christian communities dotted around the Mediterranean would only rarely have included people in a position to persuade, influence or benefit those who, even locally, exercised power.[38] Christians at this stage normally played no part either in the conduct of government or in the public forums of philosophy and oratory. In this sense, the development of a 'public ethics' could not really begin until the gradual emergence of a Christian intelligentsia who were both able and concerned to formulate a more 'public' discourse about morality. And yet, this very delay throws into stark relief Luke's seminal account of Paul's mission in Acts, which anticipates by at least half a century the increasing importance which a direct interaction with both government and the instruments of classical *paideia* would play for the public face of the Christian mission from the second century onward.

What we must retain from this survey, however, is that the second- and third-century question of a publicly accessible defence

---

[36]Cf. Meeks 1993:37–51.

[37]E.g. Winter 1988, 1994.

[38]Cf. Meeks 1993:46: 'By and large the persons who played the part of patrons to the Christian groups ... were not regularly engaged in the governance of the polis or in the liturgies by which the wealthiest citizens were required to support civic amenities while enhancing their own power and prestige.' It is possible that Christian slaves or freedmen were employed in the imperial civil service in Rome (cf. Bockmuehl 1997:269–70 on Phil 4.22 with Rom 16.10–11). Erastus, city treasurer at Corinth (Rom 16.23), is often argued to have been a person of influence (e.g. Theissen 1982:75–83; Clarke 1993:46–56; Murphy-O'Connor 1996:269–70; contrast recently Meggitt 1996 *against* the identification of Erastus with the Roman *aedilis* of that name known from a Corinthian inscription).

and exposition of Christian ethics is already implicitly acknowledged in the New Testament itself. Moreover, even some of the arguments offered in the second century can be traced *in nuce* in the first. This is in fact true not only for many of the questions posed and the answers given, but also for the rhetorical fronts on which the early church defined its position. Notoriously ambiguous and permeable as these fronts undoubtedly were, it is clear that Christians of the first as of the second century found themselves having to account for their moral teaching (as of course for their theology) *vis-à-vis* at least three different groups of critics: (i) Pagans, (ii) Jews and (iii) 'heretics', above all perhaps of the Gnostic variety. Especially the latter two rhetorical fronts addressed internal as well as external dissent: much of the early *adversus Iudaeos* and *adversus haereses* literature is manifestly engaged in an exercise of self-definition, boundary marking and damage control against an enemy who may well be within as much as without. All three polemical and apologetic fronts are already evident, in all their ambiguity, in the New Testament; indeed several of its authors address themselves to more than one. What is more, it is easy to see how at certain times and places the implied adversarial 'public', whether in ethical or in theological discourse, might well be Jewish (e.g. Matthew; Hebrews; cf. Justin, *Dial.*; Aristo of Pella; *Jason and Papiscus*) or even heretical (e.g. Jude, 1–3 John, 1–2 Tim.; cf. Irenaeus) rather than principally pagan (as perhaps in Luke-Acts and most of the Apologists).

Public Ethics in the Second Century

Having been anticipated by Luke and perhaps one or two other New Testament writers, the task of explaining the new faith to Gentile inquirers and critics was more clearly recognized and taken up in the second century. In the last decades of the first century, 1 Peter had encouraged readiness to give an account of the Christian hope, while Luke had set out to offer Theophilus a rationally defensible, 'accurate' and 'orderly' account (ἀκριβῶς καθεξῆς Luke 1.3), including such reference to 'convincing proofs' (ἐν πολλοῖς τεκμηρίοις, Acts 1.3) as seemed appropriate. In the same way the *Epistle to Diognetus*, dating perhaps from the mid-second century,[39] addresses its inquirer as follows (1.1):

I see, most excellent Diognetus, that you are very eager to understand the religion of the Christians, and that you are making careful and accurate inquiry about them

---

[39]See below for the date of *Diognetus*.

(πάνυ σαφῶς καὶ ἐπιμελῶς πυνθανόμενον περὶ αὐτῶν): what God they trust and how they worship him; that they all disregard the world (τόν τε κόσμον ὑπερορῶσι) and despise death; that they neither take account of those whom the Greeks regard as gods, nor observe the superstition of the Jews; what is the affection (φιλοστοργίαν) which they have for one another; and, finally, why this new people and practice (γένος ἢ ἐπιτήδευμα) has come to life now rather than long ago. I gladly welcome your eagerness, and I ask of God, who enables us both to speak and to hear, that he may grant me to speak in such a way that you may be built up by what you hear.

Neither the New Testament authors nor their successors were content to ignore the slanders of the persecutors and of public opinion. False accusations could not simply be ignored, but invited refutation; the church's public image was not an indifferent concern.[40] For second-century Christians, public perception of the truth about Christianity mattered. And as in the famous paradigm case of Socrates, the public defence of that truth called for rational argument.

In practice, much of this argument concerned questions of philosophical anthropology and cosmology, with a good deal of emphasis placed on the defence of Christian beliefs rather than practices. Some of the most common apologetic *topoi* include monotheism, the proof of Christ from prophecy, the critique of contradictory views among the pagan philosophers, and the refutation of idolatry as well as specific pagan religious beliefs and practices. While this allowed considerable scope for ethical matters, the following will of necessity be a somewhat eclectic account.

We shall begin with a brief survey of approaches to public ethics in a variety of second-century apologetic writings, before turning to a closer examination of Aristides and *Diognetus*. Formally, four basic genres of second-century apologetic writings may be distinguished for convenience.[41]

1. The forensic defence of Christianity, usually tolerant and cosmopolitan in style, is a formal, but invariably unsuccessful petition (a *libellus*) to the emperor to receive an official reply (*subscriptio*) that would resolve the precarious legal status of Christians.[42] This is the *Apologia* proper, as composed by Quadratus, Aristides of Athens, Justin, Miltiades, Melito of Sardis, Apollinaris of Hierapolis and Athenagoras (the *Embassy*, πρεσβεία: technically probably also a *libellus*, if authentic[43]). An important

[40]So rightly Barnard 1978:37.
[41]For the identification of Christian apologetic as a genre, see e.g. Scholten 1993; note also Fredouille 1992, 1995; Edwards (forthcoming) would also appear relevant.
[42]See e.g. Kinzig 1989:302–3 and *passim*; C. Bammel 1993:310–11.
[43]Cf. Kinzig 1989:304–6. For the question of authenticity, cf. further Barnard 1984; Runia 1992; Markschies 1997; Pilhofer 1999b.

Jewish precedent is Philo's *Legatio ad Gaium*.[44] By the late second century, Christian writers began to create apologies as literary fictions (e.g. Tertullian's *Apologeticum*; some scholars would include Athenagoras under this heading[45]).

2. The more general speech or tractate 'To the Greeks' (πρὸς τοὺς Ἕλληνας) tends to have a more explicitly 'public' character and appeal, and may relate most easily to the patterns found in Hellenistic Jewish literature, as well as in apostolic speeches in Acts and in documents like the *Kerygma Petrou* and the *Pseudo-Clementine Recognitions*. However, since they may also include anti-pagan invective and ridicule (e.g. Tatian, Miltiades, Hermias), one wonders if they were ever effectively used in any properly secular forum. Some works are dedicated to individuals (e.g. Theophilus *Against Autolycus*; *Epistle to Diognetus*).

3. Somewhat unusually in apologetic literature directed at pagans,[46] Minucius Felix cast his treatise in the form of a *dialogue*.[47]

4. Lastly, there are apologetic and polemical works against *Judaism*, which fall outside our present remit and could be further subdivided in terms of literary form. They include such texts as Aristo of Pella's *Jason and Papiscus*, Melito of Sardis, Justin's *Dialogue with Trypho*, and Tertullian's *Adversus Iudaeos*.

The development of the genre was determined in part by internal needs and circumstantial considerations, such as the relatively peaceful political conditions and open intellectual climate under the Antonine emperors in the middle decades of the second century.[48] More specifically, the stage for the earliest second-century apologies may have been set by the imperial rescript reportedly sent by the Emperor Hadrian to Minucius Fundanus, proconsul of Asia, instructing him to condemn no one without proper indictment and a well-founded accusation.[49] The real significance of this document

[44]Cf. Frend 1983:56–7: Philo shows an 'innate loyalty to the empire by praising Augustus, in something like messianic terms, as the one who had brought peace and harmony to mankind by ending the prevailing internecine divisions between city and city and nation and nation'.

[45]See on this subject the cautious remarks of Kinzig 1989:304–6; Schoedel 1989:57–9.

[46]Contrast e.g. Justin Martyr and Ariston of Pella with their Christian–Jewish dialogues.

[47]See, however, Speyer 1989 for the view that this treatise is wholly fictional.

[48]Cf. e.g. Grant 1988b:34 and *passim*; C. Bammel 1993:295–6.

[49]Cf. Eusebius, *Eccl. Hist.* 4.9.1–3; Justin, *1 Apol.* 68.6–10. See further Keresztes 1979:287–92. Kinzig 1989:302–3 and *passim* sees in the recurrent motif of appeals to the emperor an indication that the works of the second-century Apologists are themselves composed as petitions (*libelli*/ὑπομνήματα) for precisely such an imperial rescript. He views their disappearance as due to the publication of universal anti-Christian rescripts, which rendered further appeals pointless (p. 316). See also Kinzig 1989:302 n. 29 for further literature on the rescripts.

has been widely contested. Nevertheless, something like this sort of official acceptance of due process, together with Christianity's increasingly visible emancipation from Judaism (not least since the Bar Kokhba revolt), might help to explain why Apologists like Quadratus and Aristides appeared around the time of Hadrian rather than, say, under Vespasian or Domitian.

Two hundred years earlier, the very idea of a public or universal ethic had still been in substantial dispute, as local cultures around the Mediterranean successively found themselves subdued by the might of Rome.[50] W. A. Meeks has aptly pointed out the significance of the gradual (and not unproblematic) redefinition of a citizen's *public* identity, from the local city state to Rome as the world empire, the universal polis.[51]

By the mid-second century, it had become far more possible to think of the Mediterranean as 'ours' (*mare nostrum*) and to consider the *pax Romana* as administering a world empire of converging political and cultural values, at least in the urban centres. Philosophy, too, was ceasing to be the private domain of exclusive intellectual elites in the academies of Athens and Alexandria. Instead, through its widespread dissemination in oratory and public lectures (such as those of the Cynics, of Dio Chrysostom or of Aelius Aristides,[52] middle-Platonic cosmology and Stoic moral philosophy had attracted a following among a much wider public, with leading exponents eventually ranging from slaves like Epictetus to emperors like Marcus Aurelius. In this sense, a 'public' moral discourse was for the first time becoming accessible and interesting to a wider literate or semi-literate audience around the Empire.[53]

The mission and expansion of Christianity, therefore, also benefited from an intellectual climate in which it was both possible and indeed expected to argue the defence of moral and philosophical truth claims on the large canvas of a universal discourse. It is true that in arguing for the greater antiquity of their tradition or the superior asceticism of its adherents, the arguments of a Jewish Josephus or a Christian Justin capitalize on that Graeco-Roman mixture of awe and dismay at the dark secrets harboured by Oriental

---

[50]In 156/155 BC, Carneades of Athens lectured in Rome on two successive days. On the first, he argued for an ideal of universal justice; but on the second day he refuted all his earlier arguments by asserting that government is solely based on power, and that great nations like Rome rule by robbery of others. See Meeks 1986:31. He cites Cicero, *Rep.* 3 and Capelle 1932.

[51]Meeks 1986:23–8.

[52]Cf. Meeks 1986:63.

[53]For the relatively broad social importance of 'public ethics' cf. also p. 229 below.

cultures far older than that of Greece and Rome.[54] But for all the growing popularity of Oriental mysteries, and the undoubted amazement at the grandeur of pyramids or ascetic stunts told of Syrian hermits and Indian Brahmins, *in Tiberim defluxit Orontes*[55] was not an altogether comfortable thought to the educated; and by the later second century, excessive asceticism had begun to be widely viewed as morally subversive rather than edifying.[56] What was popularly known of Christianity appeared suspect and unsavoury in terms of both politics and morality. The Apologists, however, wished to create an image of the new faith as socially presentable, and of its ethics as beneficial rather than threatening to public welfare.

At the same time, the greater visibility of Christianity also brought it public enemies. Tacitus (c. 55–117) and even Aelius Aristeides (c. 117–87) still dismiss Christianity with brief throwaway comments; Lucian of Samosata (c. 125–90) says little more, and evidently knows Christianity only from a distance.[57] Pliny's concern under Trajan to define an official policy towards this *prava superstitio* was probably a fairly localized exception. Once the pagans started taking Christian claims seriously enough to dispute them, however, their reaction in itself documents the changing public face of the church.

In this sense, therefore, the genre of the Christian *apologia* also came in time to be substantially affected by the gathering intellectual opposition to Christianity that was mounted by various pagan critics including Fronto and Celsus, beginning in the mid-second century.[58]

For our present investigation, it is significant that the accusations of Fronto and Celsus tend, apart from cursory jibes, to side-step Christian *individual* ethics in order to concentrate on Christianity's

---

[54]However, see also Celsus (*C. Cels.* 1.14–15) on the *palaios logos*, the religious tradition of antiquity which he accuses Christians of abandoning. Cf. Stroumsa 1998a:86–7, and more generally Pilhofer 1990.

[55]Juvenal, *Sat.* 3.62: *iam pridem Syrus in Tiberim defluxit Orontes* , i.e. 'the Syrian river Orontes has long since poured into the (Roman) Tiber'. For similar sentiments, cf. Tacitus, *Ann.* 15.44.4.

[56]See e.g. Francis 1995, especially ch. 3. Note further the argument that from the Christian perspective virginity and celibate widowhood were not primarily anti-sexual, but affirmative of an independent status of women: cf. S. L. Davies 1980; Judge 1984a:770; Sivan 1993. Interestingly, a parallel development of resistance to ascetic practices may be attested in parts of rabbinic Judaism at this time; cf. further Fraade 1986. Note Tertullian's defence of asceticism as not an attack on creation but an offering of humility (*De Cultu Feminarum* 2.9.36–8).

[57]We could add the passing objections voiced by Epictetus, Marcus Aurelius and even Galen's otherwise more balanced view; Justin also mentions the Stoic critic Crescens in 2 Apol. 3. See Barnes 1991:231–43; also, more generally, Benko 1980.

[58]For the date of Fronto and similar anti-Christian arguments in the late 150s, see e.g. C. Bammel, 1993:308–9.

attitude to the state, including public office and military service. As a result, their charge against Christianity as arrogantly anti-social meant that the earlier apologetic dichotomies of pagan corruption versus Christian virtue needed to give way to more sophisticated reflection on Christianity's contribution to society. Tatian's impassioned advocacy of the radical 'Barbarian alternative' proved to be a precarious and ultimately unworkable foundation for a public Christian discourse on morality, and found no prominent apologetic heirs. Celsus's powerful and well-aimed attack on Christian irrationality, secrecy and asceticism could not go unanswered without serious detriment to the church's political integrity.

While this chapter treats only a segment of second-century public ethics, it is worth sketching the overall context in which that segment should be located. It is now generally thought unlikely that the majority of the second-century Apologists wrote specifically to meet the pagan backlash by men like Fronto and Celsus.[59] Nevertheless, the relevant sources can be naturally divided into those whose perspective is effectively 'pre-critical' and those who can be seen in one way or another to have begun responding to specific pagan criticism. The latter begins to emerge in Justin, Theophilus and especially Athenagoras[60] and is then perhaps best exemplified in the different approaches of Tertullian, Clement and of course Origen.[61]

Especially at Alexandria, Christian theology almost imperceptibly became an ascendant school of thought within the larger enterprise of philosophical ethics, which it would in time subsume and assimilate. The dividing wall between ethics as public and universal on the one hand and as ecclesial and confessional on the other was becoming less clear, both philosophically and politically. It is perhaps Clement of Alexandria who constitutes the end of one era and the beginning of another: he is a Christian Stoic philosopher concerned to defend a Christian *modus vivendi* within in the given social order, if necessary by internalizing some of Christianity's primitive ascetic and eschatological radicalism.

The boundary lines between 'public' and 'in-house' formulations of Christian ethics began in the third century to become increasingly porous and indistinct, as Christian theology and Hellenistic philosophy, and with them theological and philosophical ethics, developed an ever closer affinity. Following Clement, it is probably

---

[59]Cf. e.g. R. J. Hauck 1986.
[60]Cf. Barnes 1991:234.
[61]Cf. e.g. Kinzig 1989:317, who sees in Tertullian both the climax and the close of early Christian apologetics; and see more generally the magisterial work of Fredouille 1972.

Origen whose extensive and important reply to Celsus marks the definitive transition in the conduct of Christian public ethics. This new departure might in itself be thought a measure of the success of the earlier Apologists; more likely, perhaps, it indicates the extent to which they had correctly understood and anticipated the changing philosophical mood of the times. In any case the third-century writers show how, well before the Edict of Milan, Christian ethics in the public sphere was coming to be reconceived by many of its cultured practitioners. From now on, Christian moral discourse was not so much a defensible and indeed categorically superior *alternative* to that of pagan *paideia*, but rather the superior exercise of the *same* philosophical discipline.[62] Neo-Platonism allowed a convenient re-conception of Christian ethics as related to a graduated mystical progress towards God – a move that happily suited the philosophical *Zeitgeist*.[63]

Within just one generation, the initially imperceptible transformation of Christianity's relationship with Graeco-Roman culture began to gather pace in unprecedented ways. The head of the Alexandrian academy was now a suitable and desirable presence at court.[64] What is more, the persecutions under Decius in the middle of the century paradoxically left his successor's imperial palace in Rome populated with record numbers of Christians.[65] Hints of future toleration,[66] as well as of the state's co-operation with church authorities,[67] began to appear.

The new Christian attitude to society and culture might seem to be a reasonable consequence of earlier ideas about the eternal witness of the *Logos spermatikos*.[68] At the same time, the concomitant loss of the earlier counter-cultural rhetoric may go some way to explain the apparent ease and optimism with which, only a century later, Alexandrian training could in the person of Eusebius go on to compose symphonic designs of the classical culture's *praeparatio*

---

[62]Cf. P. Brown 1992:123. But note Steiner 1989 on Tertullian's more troubled, dialectical perspective.

[63]Cf. e.g. Osborn 1976:80–3 on Clement of Alexandria and the *Sentences* of Sextus; note also Armstrong 1967:227–8 and *passim* on Plotinus' views about the integration of virtue and intelligence, or mysticism and moral progress.

[64]See Eusebius, *Eccl. Hist.* 6.21.3–4; cf. 6.34–6 on Origen's correspondence with an inquiring emperor, Philip the Arab (AD 244–9).

[65]Eusebius, *Eccl. Hist.* 7.10.3. Note already Tertullian's warning in *Ad Scapulam* (AD 213) that systematic persecution of Christians would decimate the governor's own entourage; cf. Barnes 1991:236.

[66]*Eccl. Hist.* 7.13.9, 12–14.

[67]*Eccl. Hist.* 7.30.18–20.

[68]E.g. Justin, 1 *Apol.* 46; 2 *Apol.* 10.13; Irenaeus, *Haer.* 3.16.6; cf. 3.18.1; 4.33.4.

evangelica, and hymn the birth of Christian Empire. Well before then, however, and arguably since Clement, the Alexandrian synthesis of Christianity and culture began to show signs of surrendering the task of cultural criticism, and the formulation of a distinctive vision of public ethics, to marginal and heretical groups, including eventually the Montanists, Donatists and Circumcellions.[69]

<h2 style="text-align:center">The Earliest Apologists</h2>

The first Apologist is generally held to have been Quadratus, whom Eusebius reports to have presented his embassy on behalf of the Christians during the emperor Hadrian's visit to Athens in the year 125/26. Unfortunately, no more than a brief paragraph of Quadratus's work survives (Eusebius, *Eccl. Hist.* 4.3.1–2), none of it particularly pertinent to our inquiry; and we are in no position to identify the aim or occasion of his work.[70] Scholars have in the past attempted to attribute to find other fragments of Quadratus in various documents from the Pseudo-Clementines to the *Epistle to Diognetus*, but it is now widely accepted that the most honest assessment must be to admit ignorance of his other work.

The same fragmentary pattern unfortunately pertains to several other early Apologists, whose surviving utterances are of limited value for the question of public ethics. Some would wish to include among the Apologists the fragmentary *Kerygma Petrou*[71] or certain speeches in the Pseudo-Clementine literature, which do indeed reflect some common themes and arguments encountered in the later apologetic works.[72] But aside from their attestation of the widespread use of such material, these sources remain too uncertain to permit of confident conclusions. Similarly, little or nothing of pertinence to our study survives of the works of Miltiades, Melito or Apollinaris.

Here, we must confine ourselves in the second half of this chapter to a case study of Aristides of Athens and the *Epistle to Diognetus*, as two early examples of Christian public ethics. Both can either be confidently dated before Celsus or at least (in the case of *Diognetus*)

---

[69]Cf. Frend 1983:63–70.

[70]Quadratus's major theme in the extant fragment is somewhat uncharacteristic of the later apologetic *topoi*: he stresses the living proof provided by those whom Jesus healed, some of them surviving to the present time. Among recent treatments see e.g. Beck 1999; Grant 1977, 1992; also P. F. Barton (forthcoming).

[71]See frag. 2 in Clem. Alex., *Strom.* 6.5.39–41.

[72]Compare e.g. *Strom.* 6.5.39 with Aristides, *Apol.* 1.4; *Strom.* 6.5.41 with *Apol.* 2.2; 14.4; 16.4. The base text of the *Pseudo-Clementines* is widely thought to date from the first third of the third century (see e.g. ODCC[3], 365; Hofmann 1999:132).

do not as yet show any self-conscious need to respond to his accusations. We are dealing, therefore, with Christian public moral arguments in a relatively primitive form; later writers became increasingly more sophisticated.[73]

Aristides of Athens

The work of Aristides has been reconstructed from Syriac and Armenian translations as well as two Greek papyri and two chapters of the medieval legendary *Lives of Barlaam and Joasaph*.[74] Although Eusebius believed this apology to have been presented to Hadrian in the mid-120s (see *Eccl. Hist.* 4.3.3), on the basis of the dedication preserved in the Syriac translation it is also often dated to the early part of Antoninus Pius's reign (138–61).[75] At the same time, like a number of other Christian apologies the work of Aristides shows signs of being designed to appeal to a wider public; we cannot be certain that it was ever formally presented to the emperor.[76]

Outline

Aristides mounts a confident critique of the false religious ideas and practices of Barbarians, Greeks and even Jews, in explicit contrast to the life and doctrine of Christians as a 'fourth race' (*Apol.* 2.1–6, 9 and *passim*).[77] Significantly, while the Barbarians worship the four created elements, Greeks are culpable for their worship of immoral and changeable gods in human form. Jews admittedly have an altogether

[73]Cf. e.g. Schoedel 1979:70 on Athenagoras: he 'does not rant (like Tatian); he is not stubborn (like Justin); he is not simple-minded (like Aristides). He is the best informed of the second century Apologists'.

[74]For the textual problems, cf. e.g. Alpigiano 1988:10, 28–9, 38–48; Essig 1986:163–5; Oesterle 1980.

[75]Essig 1986:166, however, considers possible a date *after* Justin, although he agrees that a second-century date during a period relatively free from persecution is most likely (ibid. p. 187). For the earlier date, cf. recently *ODCC*[3], 101; Pilhofer 1999a. Internal arguments (based e.g. on the relatively primitive christology and positive view of the Jews) are notoriously slippery.

[76]A literary fiction has periodically been suggested, e.g. by Essig 1986:187; contrast e.g. Kinzig 1989:303–4.

[77]The Greek text of 2.2 in *Barlaam and Joasaph* has τρία γένη. On this motif, classically identifying Christianity as a *third* race (*tertium genus*), see already *Kerygma Petrou* frag. 2 (Clem. Alex., *Strom.* 6.5.39–41; note earlier Rom 9.25–26; 1 Pet 2.9–10) and cf. Harnack 1924:264–5; Kinzig 1994:147–52 and *passim*. Lieu 1996:169 (and 193 n. 62) points out the similarity with texts like *Sib. Or.* 3.219, 573 and cites L. Baeck and H. Karpp in considering the possible Jewish origin of this phrase. This intriguing suggestion should perhaps be balanced against the derogatory *pagan* use of the term in North Africa in the later second century (Tertullian, *Ad Nationes* 1.8).

superior view of God, and their philanthropy is commendable: they have mercy on the poor, redeem the prisoners, bury the dead and do what is pleasing to God and humanity, according to the tradition of their forefathers (14.3).[78] Nevertheless, their calendrical feasts and observances show that in fact even they fall prey to worshipping angels, i.e. powers lower than God.[79]

All this is set in stark contrast to the life and doctrine of the Christians, who 'alone of all people in the world have discovered truth. For they know God, by whom all things have been created and made, in his only begotten Son and in the Holy Spirit; and they worship none other besides him' (15.1).[80]

In bold and somewhat naïve lines, Aristides already presents the typical range of ideas subsequently developed in the more polished writers. Some of his arguments, like the criticism of pagan idolatry and religious practices, appropriate *topoi* widely used in earlier Jewish critiques of traditional pagan religion; indeed the rejection or allegorization of the immoral deities in the ancient myths had, in Athens, Alexandria and elsewhere, been common fare for several centuries.[81] Theologically and christologically, however, Aristides' relatively glib assertion of Christianity's superiority over paganism takes insufficient account of the repercussions which his frontal attack on Greek religious anthropomorphism might have for his own Christian doctrine of a historical incarnation (e.g. 'the Son of God descended and took flesh in a Hebrew virgin', 2.6).[82] There is much here which in comparison with later second-century writers like Justin and Irenaeus seems callow and half-baked. Even on the rhetorical level, the form and presentation leave something to be desired.[83]

---

[78]Note that the Syriac version appears to offer the more reliable text in ch. 14 on the Jews, as Lieu 1996:169 rightly notes.

[79]*Apol.* 14.4; cf. the *Kerygma Petrou* 2, quoted in Clem. Alex. *Strom.* 6.5.41: 'if the moon is not visible, they do not hold the Sabbath, which is called the first; nor do they hold the new moon, nor the feast of unleavened bread, nor the feast, nor the Great Day [i.e. Yom Kippur]'.

[80]For Aristides' doctrine of God, cf. also van Unnik 1983; van den Broek 1986.

[81]Heraclitus (fl. c. 500 BC) frags. 5, 14–15 had already despised the worship of idols and the rituals of the mystery religions; in the first two Christian centuries, such views had come to be widely echoed by Stoics and Epicureans alike. Cf. Macmullen 1981:77–9 and more generally Buffière 1956; Grant 1957; Pépin 1976:85–214, and others.

[82]For Aristides' view of history, see Alfonsi 1976.

[83]As Athenagoras, Melito and others were well aware, an embassy to the Emperor must begin with generous compliments to his gentleness, mildness and peaceableness, his respect for the law, piety, accessibility and fondness for learning (e.g. Athenagoras, *Leg.* 1.2). Schoedel 1989:56–7 cites Menander the rhetorician, for example, in commending that an embassy (πρεσβευτικὸς λόγος) must be in praise of the king's φιλανθρωπία. See also Grant 1988a:5–9 and Schoedel 1979. Although in their present form the apologies are too long for embassies and may well be literary constructs, Schoedel rightly points out that Athenagoras nevertheless writes as one who is hopeful of a reply (1989:57–9, 74–5 and *passim*).

Public Ethics

It is Aristides' moral arguments that are of primary interest for our study. In this area, too, he speaks of Christian behaviour with the sort of straightforward and untroubled confidence that is particularly characteristic of the early apologetic works. Although he is already concerned to counter the three typical pagan charges of Christian atheism, 'hatred of humanity' and secret cultic orgies (cf. 17.1), it is for him sufficient to assert the self-evidently exemplary moral excellence of the Christian way of life. However one might assess the logical persuasiveness of this argument, for our purposes it is Aristides' selection and presentation of ethical *topoi* which offers a valuable clue to his implicit approach to public ethics. What, in other words, are the moral principles which Aristides felt he could or ought to press even before a pagan audience?

We may conveniently divide the relevant material into three categories:

1. The explicit appeal to general principles assumed to be 'common ground', affirmed in the introduction almost by way of *captatio benevolentiae*;

2. moral criteria employed in the attack on pagan religion, again implicitly taking for granted the assent of any cultured and philosophically astute Graeco-Roman reader;

3. the defence of Christian faith and practice proper, in selective but publicly accessible terms, involving persuasion both by argument and by dint of moral example. The aim here is to engender respect and therefore tolerance, though not necessarily the endorsement of Christian ethics as a universal moral standard.

While categories (1) and (2) are clearly adduced as carrying a self-evident public moral authority, (3) has the more complex function of refuting slanderous allegations of Christian misconduct, publicly explaining certain moral distinctives, and eliciting respect for the Christian way of life as morally commendable.

The structure of Aristides' *Apology* is in effect to examine the truth in the various religions, based on the universal concepts of God and human behaviour outlined in Chapter 1.[84] It is a significant feature of his Christian apologetic that there is no appeal to revelation, but only to arguments drawn from common philosophical and moral logic. The argument ascends from animism and pantheism via polytheism to Jewish (compromised) monotheism and, eventually, true Christian (Trinitarian) monotheism.[85] Monotheism indeed is

[84]Cf. Alpigiano 1988:17.
[85]Note 15.1; and cf. Alpigiano 1988:19.

clearly one of the central themes of this apology – a fact that confirms its continuity with the genre of Jewish apologies.[86]

In his opening remarks (*propositio*) about the nature of God, Aristides claims as his one basic moral concept a kind of abstract reminiscent of the negative Golden Rule: 'the only thing of value is to honour God and not to injure one's fellow human being' (*Apol.* 1.3). In this form, the prominent opening statement of morality is clearly unobjectionable to the popular second-century currents of Stoic and Pythagorean philosophies, and evidently aims to capture the goodwill of a broad potential audience. In his discussion of Christianity as a 'fourth race' after Barbarians, Greeks and Jews, Aristides likewise appears to doff his hat to social and rhetorical convention by observing that the apostolic proclamation of Christ was proffered 'in all gentleness and modesty' (*Apol.* 2.8 S).

While the Barbarians are primarily criticized in familiar Jewish and early Christian theological terms, as worshipping creatures instead of the Creator, Aristides attacks Graeco-Roman religion on a more self-evidently ethical note. The Greeks invented for themselves gods[87] who were adulterers and murderers, envious and jealous, angry and hot-tempered, parricides and fratricides, thieves and robbers (*Apol.* 8.2). By means of their manifestly appalling behaviour, these deities have 'caused people to commit adultery and fornication, robbery and everything evil, ugly and vile. They are the cause of wars, famines, captivity and destitution' (8.6). At the very core of official pagan mythology are deities who have led human beings astray into every form of perversion and abomination, extending to all manner of sexual perversion (8.4; 9.8–9; 17.2 and *passim*), violence and even the sacrifice of children.[88] Throughout the central section of his apology (cf. chapters 9–12), Aristides thus links undisputed moral evils with the very structure of Graeco-Roman religion, drawing on familiar and well-established philosophical critiques of pagan beliefs and practices. Later Apologists were to take up this theme.

Aristides' primary rhetorical aim in all this of course is the denigration of paganism in favour of Judaism (note 14.3) and above all of Christianity. He is thus not in the first instance concerned to

---

[86]Cf. Alpigiano 1988:14–15; Essig 1986:179–80 offers a useful tabular arrangement of parallels between Aristides' doctrinal attributes of God and those in Philo and Josephus; see also Geffcken 1907:83.

[87]A familiar Hellenistic philosophical *topos*, deriving from Euhemerus and other early philosophers. Cf. Nestle 1950.

[88]9.2; cf. 13.4; also e.g. Justin, 2 *Apol.* 12.5; Minucius Felix, *Oct.* 30.3; Tertullian, *Apol.* 9.1–3.

discourse about public morality, but to defend the legitimacy of Christian life and faith. Within that frame of reference, however, he does not shy away from a critique of Graeco-Roman society's official religious morality, and (in chapters 15–17) from asserting the Christian option in such a way as to make its ethics appear admirable by contemporary philosophy's own highest standards.

For Aristides, received apologetic tradition and contemporary philosophical critiques of religion made the link between pagan religion and immorality not only obvious to the community of faith, but also manifestly defensible in the public realm. Graeco-Roman religion, both in popular practice and even in its canonical texts, paradoxically compromised and undermined the highest values that even right-thinking and noble-minded pagans might embrace. Any thoughtful person could see that the morality everywhere implicit in pagan religion constitutes an attack on the good of humanity: a god who, like Zeus and all his pantheon, commits adultery, immorality, homosexuality or parricide, is worse than a demon (Aristides, *Apol.* 9.6–7, 8–9).[89] 'Can this be a god?' asks Aristides about the thieving and greedy Hermes (10.3–4). (The educated pagan's reply, one suspects, might resemble what the first-century Alexandrian Heraclitus said about Homer: the myths may only be read allegorically, or not at all.[90]) Further examples of Aristides' rhetoric could be multiplied.[91]

Humans invariably imitate their gods, and it is significant that Aristides' statements about public morality are inseparable from his critique of Graeco-Roman religion. A similar paradigmatic linkage of theology and morality is repeatedly encountered in other Apologists, not least in Justin.[92]

The subjects treated up to this point are of course largely adopted from the conventional stock-in-trade of Jewish and Christian apologetic, drawing on popular philosophical assumptions and quite possibly even on existing manuals or collections of pagan arguments

---

[89]Cf. Theophilus, who similarly attacks the immorality of the gods as praised in pagan poets: they are promiscuous and practise bestiality, thirst for human blood and eat human flesh (*Ad Autol.* 3.8).

[90]Heraclitus pointedly says of Homer: πάντα ἠσέβησε, εἰ μηδὲν ἠλληγόρησεν (1.1). It is interesting to note the hermeneutical common ground that pagans, Christians and Greek-speaking Jews shared in the allegorical interpretation of Moses, of Homer and even of Virgil (a papyrus fragment of *Aeneid* 4.9 turned up at Masada). See also Alexander 1998 and Horbury 1999:157–62 and *passim*; also cf. n. 81 above.

[91]Also in reference to the Egyptian gods (12.1–9), whose increasingly respected status in this period is reflected in their being discussed here in connection with the Greek rather than the Barbarian gods.

[92]E.g. Justin, *1 Apol.* 21.4–5; *2 Apol.* 12.5–6.

and sources.[93] One could rightly argue, moreover, that the conventional moral *topoi* Aristides highlights are almost exclusively in the realm of *individual* morality rather than of the wider social and legal structures in the *polis* or empire. Indeed, in this respect it might be urged that the differences between Aristides and the Apostolic Fathers or the NT are negligible, pertaining to genre and style rather than substance.

Is Aristides therefore in any meaningful sense concerned with 'public' and political ethics, any more than the earlier Christian writers were? Much of what we have discussed under the heading of 'public ethics' so far is admittedly concerned with the universal application of a domestic morality pertaining to individuals and households. Nevertheless, Aristides does manifest a somewhat more explicitly 'public' moral concern in buttressing his critique of pagan religion by an appeal to the Greek laws:

> For if their laws are just, then their gods must be unjust, since they transgress these laws by murdering each other and committing sorcery, adultery, robbery and theft, and sleeping with males, in addition to all their other misdeeds. But if these gods acted justly, then the Greek laws must be unjust. (13.8)

Given his overall argument, Aristides' comment on the Greek laws here evidently takes for granted the basic soundness of the Graeco-Roman legal infrastructure. The laws of the Greeks are assumed to be valid – and it is precisely these laws which show that their gods must be villains. This assumption of the essential goodness of the political order is remarkably consistent among second-century authors who all the while denounce the unjust persecution of Christians.[94] It is a point of view that has important antecedents in the political ethics both of Judaism (e.g. *m. 'Abot* 3.2; Josephus, *Ag. Ap.* 2.6 §77) and of the New Testament (e.g. Rom 13). Although Greeks in general are assumed to imitate the immorality of their gods, the government of Rome nevertheless enjoys a divine sanction to ensure public order, and its laws are thought sufficiently fair and just to warrant loyalty and submission to the authorities. Without wishing to read too much into a passing comment, this statement does point to a seedbed of Jewish and Christian political thought with significant potential for Christianity's ability, in the aftermath of Celsus's attack, to formulate a credible and consistent position on matters of public ethics.[95]

---

[93]Büchsel 1950:540. The *topoi* addressed can be readily attested not only in Jewish sources but also in the influential Stoic philosophers of the time: see e.g. Malherbe 1986b:144–61.

[94]Cf. H. Rahner 1961:22–35.

[95]It is, however, worth noting the occasional commendation of virtuous *pagan* examples in a few early texts, e.g. *1 Clem.* 55.1 (on which see Salzmann 1994).

Aristides turns at last to Jews and Christians. His arguments from now on fall into the third category sketched above: he extols the virtuous example of Jews, and above all of Christians, as evidently worthy of Roman respect and recognition.

It is particularly interesting to observe the parallels between Jewish (14) and Christian (15) philanthropy, even though the depiction of the equivalent Christian virtues is clearly more abundant and generous. Aristides' unusually favourable view of Judaism has sometimes been thought to imply his use of a Jewish source in chapters 1–14,[96] but this seems on balance an unwarranted postulate. Instead, it is logically consistent with the flow of the overall argument about monotheism (see above); similarly, the charge against Judaism is the unexpected but rhetorically polished one of having corrupted pure monotheism. At any rate, the superiority of Judaism over paganism is that the latter imitates the sordid practices of its corrupt and immoral gods, whereas Jews (and presumably Christians too) 'imitate God in the love they have for human beings', in compassion for the poor, freeing prisoners, burying the dead and the like.[97]

Once again, the moral criteria here discussed are assumed to be readily apparent as commendable and exceptionally virtuous, even if not universally mandatory. In other words, while the *critique* of Barbarian and Greek religion addresses that which is morally reprehensible, the *positive* construct of Christian practice attempts to show the latter to be not merely legitimate but admirable. Nevertheless, we shall see that the content of the passage remains thoroughly Christian and substantially reflects the sorts of Jewish and Christian ethical summaries we discussed in the earlier chapters of this volume.

Rhetorically, as much as this concluding section of his apology seems to score its decisive points on the superiority of Christian *behaviour*, the argument of Aristides is not primarily that of a simple moralist. Instead, as for all the second-century Apologists, superior practice for Aristides is always a function of superior belief, and moral arguments remain logically subsidiary evidence supporting the case for monotheism *vis-à-vis* polytheism.[98] As 1.3 suggests and as we saw above, the argument at each stage is concerned with the

---

[96]E.g. Geffcken 1907:82–3; O'Ceallaigh 1958:245ff. Although widely dismissed, a more sympathetic reconsideration of O'Ceallaigh's thesis is in Essig 1986:181–2, 185.

[97]So the (longer) Syriac version of 14.3. Marmorstein 1950:113 rightly notes the points of contact with the Tannaitic doctrine of the *imitatio Dei*.

[98]Cf. Alpigiano 1988:15–16. Note Aristides 16.1, and the same logic in Rom 1.19–32 and Wisd 13–14.

proper *worship of God* and its practical expression in human life. In 15.1–2, the proof that Christians have discovered the truth about God is similarly developed in terms of their moral behaviour.

The long catalogue of Christian virtues in chapter 15 could, as we saw, be examined from a variety of perspectives. It is generally based on an eclectic use of traditional Christian and Jewish building blocks, including a number of legal summaries of the kind we encountered in earlier chapters, but also reference to evangelical works of mercy (Matt 25.35–36) and respect for the dead.

Aristides arguably manages to steer clear of the Christian fideism that came to be so derided by Celsus and Galen.[99] Nevertheless, he does not shy away from identifying his collection of Christian moral precepts very explicitly as 'commandments' (ἐντολαί) of Christ, which are 'engraved in the hearts' of believers (cf. Gal 6.2; Rom 2.15? Jer 31?) and which they 'keep' (φυλάττουσι).[100] As with other Apologists, there is also no attempt to play down the importance for ethics of Christianity's explicitly *eschatological* orientation. Christians observe the laws of Christ because they expect (προσδοκῶντες) 'the resurrection of the dead and the life of the world to come' (cf. 16.3 S; 1 Thess 1.9–10).

The concise opening paragraph of moral principles (15.2–3) is very closely constructed around such traditional Jewish and early Christian formulations. Cast descriptively in the present tense and the third person plural, it begins with a clear paraphrase of elements taken from the Decalogue (οὐ μοιχεύουσιν, οὐ πορνεύουσιν, οὐ ψευδομαρτυροῦσιν, οὐκ ἐπιθυμοῦσι τὰ ἀλλότρια, τιμῶσι πατέρα καὶ μητέρα) followed by the simplified love commandment of Lev 19.18 (τοὺς πλήσιον φιλοῦσι) and the familiar *topos* of just judgement (δίκαια κρινοῦσιν),[101] the negative Golden Rule and finally two further motifs from the Sermon on the Mount: reconciliation with

---

[99] Origen, *C. Cels.* 1.9; cf. 3.44. Galen, *On the Anatomy of Hippocrates* (Arabic text translated in Walzer 1949:15). Wilken 1984:77–8 observes, however, that by the time Galen and Celsus raised these accusations, Christian thinkers like Justin, Athenagoras and others had already begun to answer them. Note, however, Dihle's attempt (1976:325–8) to link the changing Christian political views with the increasing institutionalisation of the church itself. Cf. also Stroumsa 1998a:85, who sees in Galen and Marcus Aurelius the first leading pagans to recognize in Christianity a new and distinct 'philosophical' and religious entity.

[100] Similarly 15.8: τὰ προστάγματα τοῦ θεοῦ ἀσφαλῶς φυλάττουσι. Note that Theophilus of Antioch goes on to link these commandments more specifically to the Decalogue (described as the 'holy law') and the Golden Rule: *Ad Autol.* 2.34–5; also 3.9 (the Decalogue and the commandments of justice in the Pentateuch).

[101] Cf. its use in the Noachide Commandments and in early Christian sources; see e.g. *m. 'Abot* 1.8; 2.5; 1 Cor 6.1–6; and cf. pp. 159, 169 above.

adversaries (cf. Matt 5.23–25; Rom 12.18) and kindness to enemies (cf. Matt 5.44–45; Rom 12.14, 17, 20).[102]

This compact summary is then followed by a paragraph more specifically concerned to expound Christian sexual ethics (15.4), in evident rebuttal of the pagan accusations of incest and promiscuity[103] and in keeping with the prominence of sexual matters in related Jewish expositions.[104] The praiseworthy sexual modesty and purity of Christian men and especially of women is once again rooted in eschatological hope (ἔλπιδος γὰρ μεγάλης ἀντέχονται τῆς μελλούσης), although unlike other writers Aristides does not develop it in an obviously ascetic direction.

Alpigiano points out that several of the Christian virtues seem deliberately formulated in contradistinction to the corresponding pagan vices which Aristides discussed in chapters 3–13;[105] and this is particularly true of the area of sexual ethics. The purity of Christians (15.2, 4) is evidently set in contrast to the adulterous and homosexual practices of the Greeks (9.7–9; 10.7–8; 11.3–5; note 17.2). It is true that this theme is here associated with the prominent Stoic virtue of ἐγκράτεια.[106] But although this came to be much favoured by radical Christian ascetics like Tatian (Iren. *Haer.* 1.28.1), Aristides here favours not a subversive asceticism but self-control, specifically *vis-à-vis* illicit sexual unions and impurity (ἀπὸ πάσης συνουσίας ἀνόμου καὶ ἀκαθαρσίας, 15.4).

Several other subjects of relevance in Aristides' list are worth mentioning at least briefly. The first is slavery (15.4). As already in the NT (e.g. Phlm; Col 4.1), it is clear that some Christians keep slaves – though the ἐὰν ἔχωσιν may imply that it is not the norm.[107] Even when they have slaves, Christians treat them as 'brothers' without distinction (cf. Phlm 16). There is no mention of manumission here,[108] but this is characteristic of early Christian as

---

[102]Cf. also 17.3S on patient suffering of injustice at pagan hands.

[103]See already Apuleius, *Metamorphoses* 9.14; Fronto in Minucius Felix, *Oct.* 8.3 – 9.6.

[104]Note the lack of such a corollary in the discussion of Jews in ch. 14.

[105]Alpigiano 1988:20.

[106]Cf. in the NT Acts 24.25; 1 Cor 7.9; 9.25; Gal 5.23; Tit 1.8; 2 Pet 1.6.

[107]Athenagoras, *Leg.* 35, seems to imply that it is more common: 'some have few and some have many'. Cf. further Schäfke 1979:534–5, who also (p. 539) offers the interesting suggestion that it may have been precisely the equality of slaves within the church which diluted any felt urgency to achieve any wholesale change in the social order. On the widely attested phenomenon of slave ownership among non-elite circles, see recently Meggitt 1998:129–31, with extensive references.

[108]On attitudes to manumission in early Christianity, see Harrill 1995; it is also worth noting that for all its manifest flaws and frequent wretchedness, slavery did function in many cases as an instrument of welfare policy. The relative silence on the institution of slavery in the New Testament and the early Fathers understandably strikes post-nineteenth-century readers

of Stoic texts that affirm the equality of slaves, and need not be especially significant. Indeed, what is at issue is not slavery as such but the treatment of dependants (note the explicit inclusion of 'children').

More interesting, however, is the evident *apologetic* intent of this brief section on domestic dependants. Alpigiano 1988:21 rightly notes the unexpected use of ἀλλὰ καί (as opposed to δέ) to introduce this topic, which indicates the implicit denial of a contrary view of Christian behaviour.[109] The polemical thrust is almost certainly directed against pagan misunderstanding and derision of the Christian custom of relating to each other as ἀδελφοί.[110] Aristides' point is that Christians do not exploit their dependants, whether children or slaves. Instead, they treat them kindly, persuade them to become Christians, and consider them brothers and sisters when they have come to faith. The weak are not abused; nor is their treatment as 'brothers' a cloak for depravity of the kind against which Aristides defends the Christians (note 15.5 οὐ γὰρ κατὰ σάρκα).

Chapter 15 closes with a description of the corporate life of Christians and of their public-spirited charitable concern. They do not worship foreign gods; they are humble, forbearing, modest and honest, and love one another. They care for widows, protect orphans from oppression (so 15.5 S; cf. Gk. συνδιασῴζουσιν), and generously provide for the needy according to their means.

Aristides then illustrates this love and concern for social welfare through a series of four examples, each of which is introduced by a conditional clause.[111] These examples concern (a) hospitality to strangers (15.5); (b) burial of the poor; (c) collections to pay for the needs and, if possible, the freedom of Christians imprisoned for their faith (15.6); and (d) sacrificial provision for slaves and the poor, if necessary by means of fasting (15.7).[112]

---

as morally dubious and embarrassing. A balanced assessment of this problem, however, is certain to remain beyond our grasp as long as scholars base their *Sachkritik* on easy correlations of ancient Roman with early modern slavery (cf. e.g. recently Barclay 1997:119–26). Bartchy 1992:73 issues the salutary warning, 'For the most part knowledge of slavery as practiced in the New World in the 17th–19th centuries has hindered more than helped achieving an appropriate, historical understanding of social-economic life in the Mediterranean world of the 1st century' (p. 73). Cf. also O'Donovan 1996:264.

[109]ἀλλὰ καί in this context means 'but actually', 'but rather'; cf. Bockmuehl 1997:113–14 on Phil 2.4; Louw & Nida 1989:§91.11.

[110]Cf. e.g. Lucian, *Peregr.* 13; Minucius Felix, *Oct.* 9.2, Tertullian, *Apol.* 39.2.

[111]ἐάν, εἰ; a participial clause is used for the prisoners.

[112]The Greek at this point has a problematic addition emended by Alpigiano 1988:120 to read, 'they think it right to forgo their own pleasure inasmuch as these people are called to joy' – οἰόμενοι αὐτοὶ <μὴ> εὐφρονᾶσθαι, ὡς ἐκείνους ἐπ᾽ εὐφρασία<ν> κεκλῆσθαι; cf. Hermas, *Sim.* 5.3.7.

It is significant that, apart from the reference to 'the condemned for the sake of Christ' (ἕνεκεν τοῦ ὀνόματος τοῦ Χριστοῦ κατακεκριμένου), all the examples of social charity are kept in *general* terms, probably implying that the beneficiaries are not merely Christians. Whether or not this is specifically implied here, Christian charity to outsiders is a theme that has solid early support[113] and finds useful apologetic application.

The concluding paragraph resumes the general description of the life and worship of Christians, and finally relates this specifically to their joy at Christian births and deaths alike (15.8–10).

Aristides' description of Christian ethics formally ends with 15.10 (NB S has 'law'). He goes on in chapter 16 to introduce various other aspects of the Christian life which are concerned, not so much to expound central principles of Christian ethics, but to depict the church's public profile in the best possible light. His comments here link their prayer and conduct to their knowledge of the truth (16.1–2; ὄντως οὖν οὗτοι εὗρον τὴν ἀλήθειαν) and stress their charity done in secret (16.3 S, cf. Matt 6.1–4).

The Syriac version at this stage adds the dramatic claim that the world is sustained by the intercessions of the Christians (16.7). Christian prayer for the world (16.4) is a theme anticipated in the intercession for secular *rulers* affirmed in Judaism (e.g. Josephus, *Ag. Ap.* 2.6 §77), in the NT (e.g. 1 Tim 2.2) and in the Apostolic Fathers, especially in *1 Clem.* 60.4 – 61.3 (and cf. Pol., *Phil.* 12.3).[114]

---

[113]Aside from plentiful evidence in the Jesus tradition, other New Testament antecedents include Gal 6.10; Rom 12.17–21.

[114]On this much-discussed passage from *1 Clement*, see the balanced assessment of Ziegler & Brunner 1992, who argue that the text has political implications but not a primary political intention. It is of course true that *1 Clement* manifests a post-apostolic attempt to preserve a Christian *modus vivendi* within the social and political structures of imperial Rome: and thus there are clear elements of accommodation to the hierarchies and synergies of what is often summarily and dismissively dubbed the 'status quo' (cf. e.g. Wengst 1987:106–18; Welborn 1992:1059; Horrell 1996:272–80). Just as under more recent totalitarian regimes, however, Christians and others after AD 70 understood only too well the fate of communities that embarked on a direct confrontation course with 'the system'. To achieve a measure of pragmatic accommodation without surrendering vital theological commitments was, for both Jews and Christians, not a 'soft option', but frequently the only means of survival with integrity. *1 Clement* must be read against this background, not that of the late-modern academy's armchair revisionism. It is extraordinary how contemporary political fashions prevent many scholars from seeing in this sort of text anything more than the terminal bourgeois rot of the pristine gospel of egalitarian deconstruction. A harassed minority's yearning for a 'quiet and godly life', as the least bad setting of corporate practical discipleship in the present evil age, is always bound to appear distasteful to an establishment of cultured despisers who have drunk deep at the fountains of suspicion on the *rive gauche*. Reduced to a discourse about power, however, the logic of the early Christian vision becomes wholly

In this form of prayer for the *world*, however, Aristides is the first to use this motif.[115] While the possibility of a secondary interpolation into the Syrian text cannot be ruled out, it seems on balance more likely that the Greek text abbreviates.[116] We must note in any case that similar claims occur in other second-century apologetic writings, including *Diognetus* (see below) and, more specifically, Apollinaris of Hierapolis, who is the first to appeal to the successful intercession of Christian soldiers as saving the Twelfth Legion on the Danube from certain demise by a miraculous rainstorm in AD 176.[117] Clearly both Christian prayer and praxis are here viewed as inherently contributing to the common good.[118]

In closing, Aristides commends to the emperor that he should read the Christian Scriptures and thus find the truth of these arguments confirmed (16.6; cf. 2.7: an intriguingly early defence of unrestricted public access to the Bible![119]) Somewhat surprisingly, the *Apology* concludes with an eschatologically motivated exhortation to worship the true God in view of the future judgement and the life to come.

Conclusion

Several themes stand out in Aristides' contribution to Christian thought about what we are here calling 'public' ethics. First, he

---

unintelligible in its own terms – especially when that deconstruction serves as the postmodern reader's definitive analytical tool.

Theophilus, likewise, sets the dominical commandment of the love of all people in the context of the prayer for the authorities (*Ad Autol.* 3.14, citing Isa 66). By the time of Tertullian (hardly an apologist for the political 'status quo'!), this has become more specific: the Christian prayer for the Emperors includes *vitam illis prolixam, imperium securum, domum tutam, exercitus fortes, senatum fidelem, populum probum, orbem quietum* (*Apol.* 30.19; cf. already Athenagoras, *Leg.* 3.2). He acknowledges that when the empire is shaken, Christians suffer too (31.3); but by their prayer for the continuation of the empire they hold up the coming of the eschatological catastrophe, and thus contribute to the continued existence of Rome (32.1–3; cf. 2 Thess 2.6–7).

[115]Cf. Geffcken 1907:92.

[116]cf. Alpigiano 1988:22, 183.

[117]Eusebius, *Eccl. Hist.* 5.5.4. Tertullian similarly appeals to this famous episode in *Apol.* 5.6; 35.9; cf. Origen, *C. Cels.* 8.68–9. See Grant 1988a:4; and more generally Justin, *2 Apol.* 7.1; *Ep. Diogn.* 6.7; Tertullian, *Apol.* 39.2; cf. 46.2.

[118]Munier 1988:46 suggests that liturgical prayer for the authorities was one of the most significant political expressions of Christian loyalty. It is certainly true that Jewish prayer and even sacrifice on behalf of the emperor functioned in this way; see above, p. 212.

[119]Cf. already Acts 17.11; John 5.39. Note, however, that the Syriac text of Aristides 17.1 does limit this openness by acknowledging that the Christian sacred books contain words difficult to expound, except in practice – a viewpoint evidently shared by the author of 2 Peter 3.16.

confirms and establishes a principle whose antecedents we already encountered in certain New Testament writers and, *mutatis mutandis*, in Judaism: the truth and accountability of Christian life and praxis are matters that cannot remain in isolation from the life of the world at large, and which indeed require public exposition and defence.

In this respect Aristides, along with the other early Apologists, sets the stage for all subsequent consideration of this matter in terms of both form and substance. Formally, he pursues the publicly accessible discussion of Christian ethics from the three points of view outlined above: (a) pithy universalizing summary statements of Christianity designed to capture the goodwill of pagan observers; (b) the critique of pagan religion by selectively appealing to some of pagan philosophy's own highest moral criteria; and (c) an exposition of Christian moral conviction and practice in recognizably 'respectable' terms so as to refute slander, evoke toleration and respect and, if possible, to encourage interested inquiry. If the extant text of 16.1, 6 is reliable, Aristides is, moreover, the first Christian writer publicly to introduce the claim that Christian prayer and praxis are beneficial for the world at large – a theme picked up by several later Apologists.[120]

Beyond this, we must of course recognize the limited scope of Aristides' own particular enterprise, which may also be understood in terms of three concerns closely related to the general ones we have established. His purpose is, firstly, to claim the formal validity and accountability of monotheistic Christian ethics in the forum of public moral discourse. Next, he intends to refute false allegations and turn outsiders' criticisms back on pagan polytheistic religion and morality itself. And thirdly, he aims to establish a public space of toleration – and, if possible, of admiration – for Christian faith and practice.

This, therefore, is 'public' ethics in the restricted sense that it asserts and maps out a place for Christian ethics in the public domain, with the aim of moral toleration and commendation. In so doing, however, it nevertheless sets the stage for Christianity's much more explicit moral engagement with society in subsequent centuries. Aristides' open critique of pagan morality and defence of

---

[120]Cf. e.g. Justin, *2 Apol.* 7.1; *Ep. Diogn.* 6.7 and Tertullian, *Apol.* 39.2 on the public benefit of Christian intercession; also Tertullian, *Apol.* 40.13ff. on Christian presence in the world. On Christian prayer for the world, see further Aristides 17.2. At the same time, it is worth noting Brennecke's interesting suggestion (1992:221) that Aristides, like other second- and third-century Christian writers, appears to assume that the Great Commission of Matt 28.19 applies only within the confines of the Empire.

Christian ethics already signals a future Christian voice in Graeco-Roman public moral discourse.

The *Epistle to Diognetus*

If the date of Aristides is occasionally disputed, this is more consistently true for the so-called *Epistle to Diognetus*, an anonymous treatise (not really a letter) addressed to an otherwise unknown inquirer about Christianity (cf. 1.1, cited earlier).[121] While the final chapters (11–12) are generally agreed to be a later addition from a different author, a good case can be made for the early date of the bulk of the document (chapters 1–10). Virtually everyone nowadays would agree on a date of *Diognetus* prior to AD 250. What is more, the relative absence of a personal christology,[122] liturgy,[123] ecclesiology and a canon of Scripture, along with the stereotypical but still relatively naïve development of standard apologetic *topoi*, render a date in the later second century plausible to many. One proposal has been the period of the Antonine or Severan emperors (with chapters 11–12 dating perhaps from c. 190),[124] an impression which might be confirmed if in fact the 'Diognetus' in view, albeit fictitiously, is the emperor Marcus Aurelius' tutor in philosophy and art.[125]

Nevertheless, the date remains difficult to pin down, and there is nothing to rule out a date rather closer to Hadrian.[126] Several intriguing additional considerations support at least the possibility of an early date, even if they are admittedly tenuous. First, *Diognetus* roundly criticizes Old Testament laws and their observance by Jews (3.1–4.5) in a way that is somewhat reminiscent of the *Epistle of Barnabas*. The argument reflects the sort of decisive alienation from Judaism that one might expect in the aftermath of the Bar Kokhba revolt, but without as

---

[121]Marrou 1965:242–3 tabulates proposed dates ranging from before AD 70 (because 3.5 supposedly assumes an active sacrificial cult) all the way to its first editor Henricus Stephanus in 1592.

[122]Jesus Christ is never mentioned by name. But see e.g. 7.4; 8.11 – 9.3, on his role in soteriology.

[123]But note chapters 11–12, which have been thought more comparable to Hippolytus and Melito.

[124]See e.g. Norelli 1991:61–4; cf. Brändle 1995; Baumeister 1988.

[125]Cf. Marcus Aurelius, *Meditations* 1.6. Grant 1992, however, doubts even a fictional correlation.

[126]*Pace* Wengst 1984:308 (cf. 1999:172), who excludes a date as early as AD 150 on the grounds that *Diognetus* seems too familiar with standard apologetic (and 'protreptic') argument, and primarily concerned to find an attractive form of presenting them. Baumeister 1988:108–10 similarly denies that *Diognetus* could represent an earlier form of Christian apologetic; but his own argument that 'martyr' terminology was widespread in Christian texts from AD 160 makes its absence from *Diognetus* all the more striking. Grant 1992, Brändle 1995 and others also discount an early date. Lindemann 1979:339 is among those who would allow for a date in the mid-second century; cf. also Weima 1997:303; Jefford 1996:159–69.

yet any obvious awareness of the views of Marcion or indeed of Gnosticism more broadly.[127] What is more, the author's explicit critique of Jewish feasts (4.1, 5) betrays no knowledge of the Quartodeciman paschal dispute, which after AD 154 took hold in Rome between Polycarp of Smyrna and Pope Anicetus.[128] Similarly, *Diognetus* makes no reply to the pagan accusations of Christian incest and promiscuity, even though these remained part of the standard repertoire of Christian Apologists for some time.[129] When compared to Clement, it is precisely the lack of apologetic sophistication in the *Epistle to Diognetus* that casts doubt on the view of it as the product of an educated late second-century Alexandrian writer.[130] Half a century earlier, the attempt to dress relatively commonplace apologetic positions in rhetorically polished garb still makes sense; and given the events of recent memory in Palestine under Hadrian, the adoption of standard anti-Jewish rhetoric is also not out of place. But at a time when the polemic advanced by Fronto and Celsus, Lucian and Galen began to have a wider impact, *Diognetus'* blithe political innocence would be more difficult to imagine in one so gifted with rhetorical flair.[131]

No certainty is possible, but a number of indications favour composition around the middle of the second century,[132] at the hands of a socially privileged and educated author who worked perhaps in Rome or Alexandria.[133]

[127]*Pace* Wengst 1984:302–3, who sees a close connection with Marcion in *Diognetus*'s critique of Jewish sacrifices and affirmations of God's goodness, patience, absence of wrath (on which note similarly Aristides, *Apol.* 1.5; Athenagoras, *Leg.* 21.1) sending of his Son, etc. Simone Pétrement 1966 even suggested Valentinus as the author of *Diognetus*. More general connections with Gnosticism are proposed by Brändle 1975:62–4. But all such arguments run up against the writer's unquestionably positive view of God as Creator and Redeemer (4.2; 7.2; 8.2, 7; 10.2). Cf. further Lindemann 1979:349–50, who views *Diognetus* as wholly independent of Gnosticism.

[128]For this observation, see Perrini 1986:9–10. Note that even 12.9 speaks unself-consciously of 'the Lord's Passover'.

[129]*Pace* Wengst 345 n. 44, who regards this as an argument for a late date.

[130]So e.g. Baumeister 1988, Brändle 1995, Marrou 1965. I have been unable to consult Nautin (forthcoming).

[131]See also R. L. Wilken's comment cited in n. 99 above.

[132]Cf. e.g. Barnard 1978:384; Lindemann 1979:348; contrast e.g. Brändle 1975:21 and Marrou 1965:260–5, who date the work closer to the time of Clement of Alexandria's *Protrepticus* (Marrou 266–7 in fact proposes Clement's teacher Pantaenus as the likely author). Wengst 1984:308–9 argues that the date must be between the end of the second century and the time of Constantine.

[133]The author must almost certainly be seen as a socially advantaged intellectual with a basic philosophical awareness and sound rhetorical training. Cf. e.g. Wengst 1984:304–5, 344–5 n. 40. One wonders at the same time whether, in his eagerness to stress the author's socially privi-leged status, Wengst underrates the possibility that *Diognetus* may not itself be a product of the elite. Might it not constitute an expression of Christianity's second-century apologetic and evangelistic effort to *reach* the upper classes, in which up to this point it had been relatively underrepresented? Cf. in this regard B. Aland 1983:12 and *passim*.

Diognetus is presented as its author's answer to questions about the God of the Christians, their mutual charity, and the reasons why this supposedly universal faith only appeared so very recently (1.1). Following conventional apologetic argument familiar from Aristides and Jewish writers, *Diognetus* begins with a peremptory dismissal of pagan and Jewish religion (Chapters 2–4) before offering a somewhat fuller exposé of the Christian faith in the garb of a superior philosophy, which the addressee is invited to embrace (Chapters 5–10). Despite the lack of any explicit mention of Jesus Christ, the theology of this treatise focuses on the sovereignty of the one God and his work of vicarious redemption through his Son.

For our purposes, it is of considerable significance that *Diognetus*, even more than Aristides, views Christian life and worship as demonstrating most clearly the truth and attractiveness of the new faith. For this author, Christians serve neither the absurdly flawed gods of the Greeks (2.10; 3.3) nor the similarly ludicrous and cringing rituals which the Jews offer to the one true God – as if he needed them (3.2–4).

The author's attack on pagan idolatry in chapter 2 is a long-established apologetic commonplace found also in Jewish texts. His pronounced critique of Judaism, however, (3–4) goes beyond that of Aristides. Thus, he blames the Jews not only for a somewhat inferior theology (treating God as though he needed sacrifices and the like; cf. 3.3), but also as offering a worship marked by a folly analogous to that of the pagans. Specifically, he attacks the supposed irrationality of circumcision as well as Sabbath observance and other calendrical peculiarities.[134] Christians, by contrast, offer their life, 'publicly' lived in the world, as their form of religion.[135] As in Justin, it is Christian praxis itself that provides one of the strongest 'public' arguments for the moral and theological truth of Christianity.[136]

More powerfully and more cleverly than Aristides, therefore, *Diognetus* develops the motif of Christians as a distinct people, a

---

[134]Although in doing so he remains well within the generalities of standard Graeco-Roman critiques of Judaism, it is nonetheless interesting that his criticism centres on the 'boundary markers' which Jews themselves not infrequently stressed as distinctive, and which had played a significant part in the 'Judaizing' disputes in the Pauline churches.

[135]The structure of the argument in 4.6ff.; 6.4, 10 makes it very clear that the Christians' life is itself their form of religion (cf. Wengst 1984:290).

[136]For examples see Aristides 15–17, Justin, *1 Apol.* 14–17, Athenagoras, *Leg.* 31–3, *Diogn.* 5–6. Cf. Kühneweg 1988:112–20, who also cites Goodspeed 1914. Note p. 113: 'Ist also die Praxis ein so wesentliches Element des Christentums, kann sie auch als Argument für seine Wahrheit dienen.' Because human nature knows the distinction between good and evil, the quality of Christian morality is in principle accessible even to pagans – even if persuasion is required (Justin, *1 Apol.* 12.11; cf. Kühneweg 1988:114).

tertium genus in a very specific sense. Their separate identity is not straightforwardly counter-cultural; instead, it arises from the fact that while the Christians are in every way actively and responsibly resident in the world, their ultimate loyalties belong elsewhere.

On this view, Christians are not separated from society by their dwelling places, their speech, culture, or superior knowledge (5.1–2). Instead, in an image reminiscent of New Testament images like the 'salt of the earth' (Matt 5.13) or the ubiquitous apostolic 'fragrance' of the knowledge of God (2 Cor 2.14–15; cf. further Phil 2.15), *Diognetus* describes the Christian presence in the world like that of the soul in a body (6.1), i.e. presumably as dispersed throughout the body and in some sense maintaining it.[137]

This intriguing notion must be understood in the context of contemporary Stoic and Platonic ideas, according to which the cosmos may be understood as a body in which the divine spirit is dispersed. But *Diognetus*'s highly unusual and, one suspects, potentially provocative departure from its philosophical precedent resides in the fact that whereas Stoicism viewed the world soul as divine and eternal, here the historical, human entity of Christians is substituted for the transcendental and pantheistic one implied in writers like Seneca.[138] Like the world soul, Christians can be described as 'sustaining' the world, 'holding it together' (συνέχουσιν τὸν κόσμον, 6.7).

For *Diognetus* as for 1 Peter, the Christians are πάροικοι, 'aliens'[139] – strangers to a world they inhabit but which is not their home. Like St Paul (e.g. Phil 3.20[140]), the author uses the language of citizenship to indicate that Christians have their true home in heaven (5.9): in the world they are at once citizens of the earthly state (5.5)[141] and yet strangers in it; they have their residence in it, but their home elsewhere (6.3, 8). Theirs is a discriminating presence in the world,

---

[137]For the church as 'dispersed' (σπείρω) throughout the world, cf. also Irenaeus, *Haer.* 3.11.8.

[138]See Seneca, *Ep.* 65.24; cf. further Brändle 1975:156–7. For this innovative use of the concept of 'world soul' cf. further Norelli 1991:152, following Marrou. (Contrast the passionate, not to say pathetic, critique of Marrou by Joly 1973:210–20: he views it as a commonplace formulation rather than an expression of genius, meaning almost anything one wants it to mean.)

[139]*Diogn.* 5.5; 1 Pet 2.11; cf. Eph 2.19; Heb 11.13; Philo, *Conf.* 77–8.

[140]On the 'Paulinism' of *Diognetus* see e.g. Lindemann 1979 and Noormann 1997 (the latter also in criticism of Wengst's more sceptical position).

[141]Wengst 1984:344–5 is probably right to note the implications of this talk of 'citizenship' for the writer's own social status. This suggestion must, however, be tempered in view of the Pauline antecedent in Phil 1.27; 3.20 (on which cf. n. 7 above). Compare also the slightly different idea of 'citizens of the world' found e.g. in Philo, *Opif.* 142–3 on Adam (also Rom 4.13; Sir 44.21 on Abraham!) and in Epictetus 3.24.66. Justin lays stress on the fact that Christians are in fact the most faithful of citizens, *1 Apol.* 12.1.

refusing its social orders any ultimate allegiance while contributing constructively to human welfare within them.[142] Wengst, by contrast, misreads the sense of political ambivalence in terms of a de-eschatologized and internalized isolation from the world.[143] Such an assessment does not do justice to *Diognetus* any more than to the comparable affirmations about otherworldly citizenship in the NT or in Philo. While this document manifests few specifically millenarian or apocalyptic points of view (but note e.g. 10.7–8), it nevertheless retains clear eschatological expectations (6.8; 7.6; 10.2).

As Brändle 1975 rightly suggests,[144] therefore, the central thrust of *Diognetus's* statement about the public role of Christianity in the world is best understood *theologically*, rather than in terms of received clichés of popular Hellenistic philosophy. This applies to 6.1, 7 as well, where Platonic influence does not suffice to explain the notion of Christians preserving the world. Instead, Christians are dispersed throughout the world like salt or light,[145] giving flavour and sustenance to the whole without being lost in it. *Diognetus* echoes something of the Johannine and Pauline dialectic *vis-à-vis* both the world and the heavenly kingdom.[146]

Jewish writings offer numerous parallels to the notion that the world is created and sustained only for the presence of God's people within it.[147] The same idea became popular in earliest Christianity and was used by several of the early Apologists[148] – so much so that Celsus came to mock the Christians for claiming that 'all things were made for our sake' (Origen, *C. Cels.* 4.23).[149] Related to this is the

---

[142]Cf. similarly Noormann 1997:228, who speaks of 'einer grundsätzlichen Nicht-Zugehörigkeit zur Welt bei gleichzeitiger positiver Zuordnung auf die Welt hin'.

[143]*Pace* Wengst 1984:300, 344 n. 38. While Brändle 1975:79–99 may exaggerate his insistence on the importance of eschatology for ethics, Wengst ignores what is in fact there. His comparison with Paul's ὡς μή in 1 Cor 7.29–31 (p. 299) is indeed highly relevant, but it overstates the supposed contrast with *Diogn*. Cf. further Noormann 1997:210–17, 227 for similar criticisms.

[144]Brändle 1975:148, 150, 154.

[145]Cf. the discussion in Brändle 1975:161–2.

[146]Brändle 1975:168–9, 211–12, 217–21 and *passim* rightly suggests that *Diognetus* combines a quasi-Johannine view of 'the world' (note κόσμος in 1.1; 6.3–5, 7; 10.7; but also 10.2) with a quasi-Pauline view of 'the flesh' (5.8; 6.5–6).

[147]Note e.g. Gen 18.23–32; *As. Mos.* 1.12; *2 Apoc. Bar.* 15.7 (cf. 21.24); 4 Ezra 6.55–59; 7.10–11; cf. Hermas, *Vis.* 1.1.6; later rabbinic attestations of this idea include *Gen. Rab.* 66.2; *Pesiq. R.* 28.2; and *Midr. Ps.* 2.13–14; 25.9; 109.4; 137.3 (cf. further references cited in Str-B, 4.852–3).

[148]Note *Gos. Thom.* 12; Hermas, *Vis.* 2.4.1; Justin, *2 Apol.* 7; a more sophisticated version appears in Clem. Alex., *Quis Dives Salvetur* 36.

[149]Together with several related themes, including those of salt, rain and springs of water, the Syrian church father Aphrahat also developed this theme, as J. B. Bauer 1963 showed; cf. Brändle 1975:163–5. Cf. Minnerath 1973:28–9 on this theme of what he calls 'Christiano-centrism'; also pp. 29–32 on the related idea of Christians preserving the world.

idea, not uncommon in the Apologists (including Aristides), that the prayer and presence of Christians is what preserves the world ahead of the judgement to come.[150] Without showing obvious dependence on any one source, *Diognetus* 6.7 may well draw on this same tradition.[151]

Diognetus does not of course proffer a systematic 'public ethics'. Nevertheless, in its dialectical vision of heavenly citizenship and life in the world, this document takes up and develops a tradition of Christian political thought that begins with Jesus (Mark 12.14 par.) and Paul (Phil 3.20) and progresses via Origen[152] to its initial culmination in Augustine's *City of God*.[153] And even at this early stage, the public moral dimension of that political tradition is highly significant – not least because it facilitates a perspective which does not straightforwardly identify the world either as the domain of the Evil One or as the kingdom of God. Instead, the world here remains the stage for the drama of redemption, a drama that requires an engagement of both love and resistance: Christians oppose the pleasures of the world, and yet love those who hate them as a result of that opposition (6.5–6).

On this view, then, Christians are not culturally isolationist but shape their lives as ordinary citizens in accordance with the language and dress, food, customs and laws of the countries in which they live (5.1–5). Their exercise of citizenship genuinely and deliberately pertains to the particular localities in which they find themselves ('as each one's lot is cast', 5.4) – a sentiment not unlike that commended to Jewish exiles as early as the book of Jeremiah (Jer 29.7).[154] Indeed, *Diognetus* goes one step further and makes the extraordinary claim that Christians are positively *forbidden* to desert their ministry as the sustainers of the world (6.10; cf. 6.6).[155] There are obvious philosophical parallels to this idea (e.g. Plato, *Apology*

---

[150]Cf. Aristides, *Apol.* 16.1, 6 (most clearly in the Syriac text); Justin, *1 Apol.* 45.1; *2 Apol.* 7.1; *Dial.* 39.2. See pp. 212–13 above.

[151]Brändle 1975:158–9 also draws the interesting connection of θεοσέβεια ('religion, godliness') in 6.4 with 4.6 (and cf. 10.7), suggesting that the secret of the Christians' religion is the fact that through it they participate in the mystery of God, i.e. his ministry to the world. *Pace* Wengst 346 n. 72, who denies any Jewish background or eschatological connection to the idea of Christians sustaining the world, and sees here a 'triumphalistic tendency'.

[152]Cf. Rahner 1961:39 on *C. Cels.* 8.74.

[153]See e.g. Bockmuehl 1995:83–7 on the effective history of the New Testament theme of 'citizenship'.

[154]For the application of this early Christian view of citizenship to the practice of euergetism and philanthropy, see e.g. Winter 1994; Pearson 1997b; Chadwick 1992 explores the wider aspects of civic virtue and culture. See also p. 128 and n. 53 above.

[155]*Pace* e.g. Marrou 1965:137, 144, who suspects the prohibition is of suicide; cf. Norelli 1991:154–5.

28d–29a), but it is probably inadequate to reduce this supposed divine 'command' simply to a philosophical commonplace. Both biblical Testaments offer plenty of antecedents for the idea that the people of God in exile should maintain their distinct lifestyle and identity without shutting themselves off from the world around them – i.e. to embrace dispersion while resisting dissolution.[156]

The application and development of this biblically grounded 'diaspora principle' of a dialectical citizenship is *Diognetus*'s main contribution to public ethics. And while it is difficult to be certain that our author predates Celsus, we may nevertheless suggest that his primitive and skeletal political theory already points towards the path adopted by the later Apologists in their reply to the great pagan counter-apologist.

Actual ethical particulars, however, remain skeletal, unexceptional, and easily summarized; in this respect at least, Wengst is right to speak of a 'mysterious paleness' of the author's ethics.[157] To some extent, this invites Celsus's criticism that Christians have nothing new or distinctive to offer in the area of morality;[158] by the author's own admission, indeed, Christian piety (θεοσέβεια) remains hidden (6.4). Christians participate in conventional family life but do not expose new-born children;[159] they openly share their board but not their marriage bed.[160] They do not live according to the flesh (5.8); instead, they love those who hate them and bless those who curse them (5.11, 15). Their basic principle is to love their neighbour and imitate God, for 'those who take up a neighbour's burden and wish

---

[156]See e.g. Jer 29.7; 1 Pet 1.1; 2.12; Phil 2.15–16; 1 Thess 4.11–12, etc.

[157]Wengst 1984:344 n. 35; cf. Rizzi 1989:290. At the same time, it is worth pondering the possible relevance to second-century ethics of G. T. Burke's observation about doctrine: viz., that Celsus's relatively *monochrome* impression of Christianity casts further doubt on W. Bauer's classic model of heretical pre-eminence in the second century (Burke 1984). Note, however, Wolfgang Speyer's argument (1994) that significant parallels to Caecilius's accusations against Christians in Minucius Felix can in fact be identified in Epiphanius's description of *Gnostic* practices (and e.g. in Irenaeus's Carpocratians). For Speyer, this is evidence that the difference between heresy and orthodoxy was in the second century imperceptible to outsiders, and that Bauer's perspective can probably be confirmed at least for Egyptian groups. Birger A. Pearson (e.g. 1997a:178–85) offers the more nuanced observation that the Egyptian heretics invariably received their Christian texts from diverse but non-Gnostic Christian groups, and their own writings tacitly concede that they are a ('spiritual') minority among the ('psychic') non-Gnostic majority.

[158]See below, p. 225.

[159]*Diogn.* 5.6; cf. *Didache* 2.2; Justin, *1 Apol.* 27.1; Tertullian, *Apol.* 9.6–8.

[160]If κοιτήν rather than κοινήν is to be read, with the majority of interpreters. This could be an indirect response to the pagan charge of promiscuity. According to Theophilus (*Ad Autolycum* 3.6), Plato proposed that wives were to be held in common (*Republic*, 5.7, 457c–d; not Book 1, as Theophilus says) and Epicurus condoned incest, even though Solon explicitly legislated against all this.

to use resources to help another person's lack, by supplying to people in need what they themselves have received from God, become a god to those who receive them: they are imitators of God' (*Diogn.* 10.6).[161]

Conclusion

We have seen that the rise of Christian apologetics is the necessary corollary of Christianity's emergence as an increasingly distinct third entity apart from both Jews and Gentiles. The development of the new 'public ethics' is best understood against the same background: while many of the basic building blocks are familiar from Jewish and to some extent from pagan philosophical texts, an identifiably Christian perspective does begin to surface in the early Apologists.

In this chapter we have concentrated on Aristides and the *Epistle to Diognetus* as two case studies in early Christian public ethics. A fuller treatment of second-century writers up to and including Clement and Tertullian would be highly desirable in this connection, but must await another occasion. All we can usefully offer here are a few interim conclusions about strengths and weaknesses of these early approaches.

Undoubtedly, one of the abiding strengths of these early texts, as of others like them, is their robustly *theological* approach to the rational defence of Christianity. This point seems commonplace, not to say trivial, to readers familiar with 1,800 years of subsequent Christian engagement with the classical tradition. Such a course of action, however, was by no means as obvious in the second century as in the twenty-first. Aristides, *Diognetus* and others took up the challenge bequeathed to them by apostolic proto-Apologists like Luke, to provide a publicly accountable defence of Christian faith and praxis. Despite its manifest failure in the political realm,[162] the argument for constructive rational engagement as pioneered by the early Apologists was both an important theological resource for the wider church in its struggle for self-definition and a decisive vote

---

[161]Cf. also p. 208 above on Jewish views of *imitatio Dei*.

[162]This is widely recognized; see e.g. Grant 1988a:14. At the same time, Averil Cameron rightly dismisses the equally widespread assumption that the Christian apologetic discourse failed altogether to have any public effect (so e.g. B. Aland 1983:18–19): 'Since it is commonly asserted that the Christian Apologists of the period wrote only for the converted and that pagans were hardly touched by Christian teachings, it is obviously a problem to explain how any increase in numbers took place at all' (Cameron 1991:44–5). Barnes 1991:236 goes so far as to suggest that it was precisely the success and influence of the Apologists' work which meant that apologetics in the second-century style were no longer needed in the third.

against the sort of cultural isolation advocated by Tatian and certain apocalyptic circles. As Robert Grant writes,

Apologetic influence within the churches was more important, for Christian teachers could make use of their approaches to politics, morality, and culture. Above all, they provided structures for philosophical theology, especially significant before the rise of the Christian school at Alexandria. Their ideas when reflected and corrected by men like Irenaeus passed into the mainstream of Christian thought.[163]

Although in many ways unsophisticated in outlook, both Aristides and *Diognetus* already embrace an explicitly *philosophical* critique of pagan religion, judging it by the standards of pagan philosophy's own highest moral criteria. As we saw, their accounts are perhaps short on distinctive moral innovations; and this is a point to which we shall return briefly in a moment. But their primary achievement is to set down a clear marker, a claim that Christian ethics has a place in the public domain, showing it to be not only publicly tolerable but also commendable and even attractive. In both theology and ethics, therefore, the early Apologists strike a pioneering blow for the rational articulation and defence of Christian faith: Christian moral truth, for them as previously for Luke, is public truth. This belief both validated and indeed necessitated the extensive process of appropriation and transformation of Hellenistic philosophical theology that was to be played out over the next two centuries.[164]

The first contribution of the early Apologists to Christian public ethics, therefore, is their commitment to a critical engagement and critique of pagan morality on accessible terms. Beyond this, perhaps the most abiding achievement of *Diognetus* in the realm of ethics is the active development of the 'dual citizenship' motif from the dominical teaching about God and Caesar and other New Testament antecedents – a theme which is frequent in other Apologies and also became a basic staple of the martyrs' Acts.[165]

Finally, however, our conclusion cannot fail to acknowledge that these early Apologists also contributed to the development of Christian public ethics in important *negative* respects, through

---

[163]Grant 1988a:14–15.

[164]See e.g. Pannenberg 1959:15–16 and *passim* (and Ritter 1997 for a recent account of the extensive secondary literature on this study); cf. also Chadwick 1966.

[165]See e.g. Justin, *1 Apol.* 17: Christians pay taxes to the best of their ability, 'as Christ taught us'; they worship God alone but render joyful obedience to the emperor in everything else, and pray for him. Theophilus 1.11: Christians honour the emperor not by worshipping him but thinking well of him, being subject to him and praying for him. On prayer for the emperor, see n. 114 above and cf. e.g. Speratus in *Acts of the Scillitan Martyrs* 6 (ed. Musurillo, pp. 86–7).

several glaring weaknesses. Their account of Christian morality, perhaps especially inasmuch as it is more widely characteristic of mid-century Christian discourse, still manifests a notable naïveté. Indeed, it could be said to have prepared the ground for the sort of concerted pagan attack on Christianity that was about to be launched by the likes of Fronto and Celsus.

In many ways, the rhetoric of Aristides and *Diognetus* runs into the open knife of Christianity's critics precisely in its insufficiently self-critical awareness of some of its own philosophical and political weaknesses, and its inability to anticipate detractors. Justin Martyr, by contrast, is rather more alert, for example in asking Trypho whether he too believes that 'we eat people' (*Dial.* 10.1). Similarly, he is well aware of the allegations of Oedipodean promiscuity and Thyestian feasts, and confronts them explicitly.[166] By the time of Athenagoras, Apologists have become painfully alert to these charges,[167] and Clement of Alexandria of course represents a far more suave and sophisticated attempt to harness the classical tradition of *paideia*.

It was all very well to castigate pagan immorality as a convenient foil to the unassailable, if perhaps (as Celsus retorted) undistinguished, purity of Christian virtue. But as Athenagoras and Tertullian began to realize, such a polarizing approach could in the end turn out to be seriously counterproductive. The more Christian discourse stressed the contrast between church and society, the more it would simply reinforce the pagan charge that Christians were irrational, ill-educated and secretive mystery-mongers, anti-cultural separatists whose loyalty to their insalubrious founder (a γοητής, charlatan) led them to ignore the common good of humanity in favour of setting up their own private society.[168]

---

[166]1 *Apol.* 12.2; cf. Theophilus, *Ad Autol.* 3.4; Tertullian, *Apol.* 31.3 and of course Minucius Felix, *Oct.* 9 and *passim*.

[167]See *Leg.* 3 and *passim*.

[168]So e.g. Celsus in Origen, *C. Cels.* 8.2. Minucius Felix's pagan critic famously calls the Christians 'a people sulking and shunning the light, silent in public but garrulous in corners' (*Oct.* 8.4; cf. 5.4; 12.5; cf. further Tertullian, *Apol.* 31.3; 42). Similarly, Celsus pokes fun at Christianity's appeal to uneducated yokels who keep to themselves and remain silent in public (Origen, *C. Cels.* 3.55). Cf. J. A. Francis 1995:160: 'For Celsus, the Christians' deliberate xenophobia and separatism were symptomatic of their desire to create a society distinct from that which surrounded them.' Herein may lie another reason why the early Fathers, like their pagan contemporaries (cf. Burnyeat 1994), never quite developed the notion of universal 'human rights'.

At the same time, Christianity's social inclusiveness as well as its attention to the private sphere were distinctive achievements that could be turned to good rhetorical effect too, as Averil Cameron points out (1991:8, 111–12, 146–7, 149, 185–6). See in this respect Origen's retort against Celsus that Stoicism was a form of spiritual aristocracy more interested in the upper classes: *C. Cels.* 7.60.

Pagans, too, moreover, valued religion and piety (εὐσέβεια, *pietas*) highly, and understandably resisted and resented wholesale attacks on their ancestral religion, whether on philosophical or on moral grounds.[169] The official cult was part of the social glue of the empire, and to ridicule the popular religion (rather than politely to allegorize, as the philosophers did) was an attack on the very fabric of society. Just as the author of *Diognetus* takes pride in Christians refusing to participate in the public life and service of society (5.4–5, 9), so it is precisely here that Minucius Felix's critic Caecilius objects.[170] In this respect, then, both Aristides and *Diognetus* are characteristic of the earlier Apologists, who had not yet self-consciously come to terms with how Roman society was in fact beginning to view them. Christians, as R. L. Wilken puts it, 'were seen as religious fanatics, self-righteous outsiders, arrogant innovators, who thought that only their beliefs were true.'[171]

Similarly, we noted a certain lack of distinctively Christian moral characteristics in both the writers we examined. This would turn out to be another of Celsus' points of attack, as when he protests that Christians have nothing new to say about morality.[172] On the one hand, this had certain advantages: it was of course precisely the fact of shared ethical convictions that made moral debate even possible.

In their moral and social teaching Christians came very near to pagans: Clement presupposes Christian support and acceptance of the prevailing political order when he likens the Christian's feelings toward God to those of the citizen toward a good ruler [*Paed.* 9.87], and Christians and pagans alike preached domestic virtue and sexual continence [cf. Plutarch, *Conjug. Praec.*]. It is just this area of ambiguity or overlap that allows persuasion.[173]

Christians admittedly did not develop a moral *system* of their own. They did, however, adopt a number of distinctive and socially costly *practices* – even if many of these (along with most of their moral taboos)[174] are clearly inherited from Jewish Christianity. Thus, Dassmann rightly lists the emphasis on mercy, humility, love of

---

[169]Note the reply of the Roman official in the *Acts of the Scillitan Martyrs* 3, 5 (ed. Musurillo, pp. 86–7): 'We too are a religious people [*et nos religiosi sumus*] ... If you begin to malign our religious rites ... I shall not listen to you.' Cf. further Stroumsa 1998a:84–5 and *passim* on the religion of Celsus and its misapprehension by Origen.

[170]Minucius Felix, *Oct.* 10.1–2; 12.5–7. Tertullian tends to turn this accusation into a virtue (*Apol.* 38.3).

[171]Wilken 1984:63 (cf. 64–6); and see Walsh & Gottlieb 1992:25–7.

[172]Origen, *C. Cels.* 1.4; 2.5; Origen would appear to concede this point when he replies that it is unsurprising: Christians indeed introduce no new ethics.

[173]Cameron 1991:40–41.

[174]Cf. Meeks 1993:122–3.

neighbour and enemy, non-violence, a pronounced marriage and family ethos (marital faithfulness of both sexes and prohibition of divorce, abortion and infanticide – principles that were compromised only on pain of excommunication), as well as care for the sick.[175]

We should certainly bear in mind, of course, that Christian praxis even in these areas could be assumed to overlap in part with pagan ideals of 'domestic' virtue, and therefore to carry a measure of inherent moral persuasion. So, for example, the very fact that the Apologists appeal to the Christian rejection of abortion and infanticide must imply that high-minded pagans could be assumed to see this as morally commendable, even if popular practice clearly did not conform to it.[176] In imperial times many pagans, too, shared the concern for ascetic and moral excellence.[177] Nevertheless, as even the pagan critic Lucian of Samosata concedes,[178] Christian philanthropy was certainly one vital and publicly visible hallmark of the new faith. The sociologist Rodney Stark has recently shown that in the urban poverty, squalor and social dislocation of the second and third centuries, the public impact of Christian charity was very considerable indeed.[179]

By the end of the second century, Christians had begun to articulate much more specifically the substance and rationale of their 'public' praxis. Aside from the principles just mentioned, examples include the widely practised avoidance of public feasts and banquets, games and other spectacles such as races, gladiatorial combat and

---

[175]See e.g. Dassmann 1992:204–7. On the other hand, Dassmann also rightly points out (1996:157) on the subject of marriage that many lower-class Christians, especially slaves, living in relationships of cohabitation or dependency, may in practice have had little chance to contribute to the formation of a culturally distinctive lifestyle. The latter would almost presuppose the case of entire Christian *oikoi*. On a related point, Schäfke 1979:518 stresses that slaves and other lower-class Christians may often have had no real alternative to concubinage (albeit monogamous). Nevertheless, it is worth noting Hippolytus's concern (*Apost. Trad.* 16) that converts living in concubinage should either marry their partners or separate.

[176]Apologetic literature is bound to appeal to principles that are calculated to meet with consent. See Mayer-Maly 1979 on the practice of exposing infants. There were evidently exceptions to pagan popular practice on this front: Dr Justin Meggitt draws my attention to the elaborate burial of an apparently cherished hydrocephalous infant of 10–11 months from Roman Britain, born to cosmopolitan parents (documented in A. Taylor 1993: 201–2, 208). Nevertheless, overall there must have been very significant interference with natural birth rates, given e.g. the large preponderance of men over women in the Roman world (see Stark 1996:97–9). On Christian and pagan attitudes to birth control, abortion and infanticide, cf. further Stark 1996:118–25.

[177]*Pace* Walsh & Gottlieb 1992:29 with the notion that the pagan mystery and redeemer cults lacked moral content; they would appear to contradict this idea themselves on p. 30.

[178]Lucian, *Pereg.* 13.

[179]Stark 1996:161 and *passim*; and note similarly Pearson 1997b:207–13.

the theatre – in many of which Christians saw complicity to bloodshed and adultery.[180] There is strong evidence that Christians avoided not only all explicit idolatry, including of course the public sacrifice to the emperor, but also (in keeping with Acts 15, as we saw in Chapter 7) the consumption of meat sacrificed to idols.[181] They shunned, and their converts generally abandoned, professions such as soldiers, sculptors, teachers, astrologers, magicians, public officials with the right to execute, bordello keepers and prostitutes; similarly drivers and keepers of race chariots, trainers or competitors in games or gladiatorial contests.[182] (It is also clear that, at least by the time of Tertullian, some of these prohibitions – e.g. of military service – must have been less consistently followed.[183]) The attitude toward public baths is predominantly one of rejection – although it may be that, like some other topics cited, this attitude is in some cases a function of social class.[184]

It is significant for the argument of this book that many of the Apologists' (and not merely Tertullian's) views on Christian public behaviour are (despite certain Stoic sympathies) more closely analogous to those found in rabbinic halakhah of the Tannaitic period.[185] Just as Christians and Jews were subject to analogous pagan accusations about their attitude to public life and public service,[186] so their responses to pagan culture were impelled by jointly inherited notions of universal morality. Just as much of Christian ethics emerged out of Jewish ethics for Gentiles, therefore, so the beginning of Christian public ethics may be understood as part of that same *Wirkungsgeschichte* of Jewish public ethics.

(Partly in view of these parallels with Judaism, it is interesting that

[180]Note Athenagoras, *Leg.* 35; Theophilus, *Ad Autol.* 3.15; Tatian, *Or.* 23; Minucius Felix, *Oct.* 30.6, 37.11; as well as Tertullian's *Apol.* 9.5 and of course his De *spectaculis*; also Canon 2 of the Council of Elvira (c. 306). Cf. Schäfke 1979:502–11.

[181]See also the documentation in Schäfke 1979:495–502.

[182]On the subject of the forbidden professions, see especially Hippolytus, *Apostolic Tradition* 16; Tertullian, *De Idol.* 4–5, 8, etc. Many of the relevant texts are usefully presented in Guyot & Klein 1994:98–121 and nn. See also e.g. Minnerath 1973:195–6; Schäfke 1979:540.

[183]On the attitude to Christian service in the Roman army, see the treatments by Harnack 1981, Rordorf 1969, Riesner 1991 and Brennecke 1997. See also n. 117 above.

[184]Cf. Minnerath 1973:182–4; Schäfke 1979:506–8.

[185]See the interesting documentation in Bergmann 1908:11–23; also Synek 1998 on the quasi-rabbinic mixture of halakhah and haggadah in the legal development of the *Apostolic Constitutions*. Note the contrast with the flavour of Clement's far more urbane and philosophical approach in the *Paedagogus* (especially books 2–3; see e.g. Dassmann 1996:148–55). On the subject of Tertullian's ethics, see more generally Brandt 1928; Fredouille 1972.

[186]See, for example, Tacitus's charge of misanthropy against both Jews (*Hist.* 5.5) and Christians (*Ann.* 15.44.4).

Christians, unlike the rabbis, did not generally run their own schools. As Dassmann also points out (1992; 1996:145), those who did send their children to schools were, it seems, prepared to put up with the thoroughly pagan syllabus – though not to become teachers.[187] Therein may lie another reason for the relative ease and conviction with which many of the Fathers came at the end of the second century to embrace the classical tradition of *paideia*.)

As the subsequent course of Christian apologetic discourse shows, the development of a more sophisticated Christian public discourse about ethics can be described to some extent as the result of ongoing dialogue on topics like these between the Apologists and the cultured opponents of Christianity – a dialogue whose very continuity is eloquent testimony to the fact that both sides had come to take each other seriously.[188] To quote Wilken once more, 'Christianity became the kind of religion it did because it had critics like Celsus, Porphyry and Julian.'[189] This statement applies equally to the question of Christianity's public discourse about ethics. Thus, the charge that Christianity in fact had nothing distinctive to contribute in the sphere of ethics would lead in the next generation to Clement's refined and circumspect comments about the nature of Christian character and public demeanour.[190] In this sense, Aristides and *Diognetus* were early pioneers in a dialogue that even now has lost none of its urgency.

---

[187]Note Tertullian's telling comment that students can more easily preserve an inner reservation and detachment at school (*Idol.* 10.24–30) – he concedes that teachers will find this far more difficult. In his view, this is why there are no mathematicians and astrologers in the church (*Idol.* 9.24, with reference to 1 Cor 1.20).

[188]Cf. Wilken 1984:135 (on Porphyry), 199.

[189]Wilken 1984:205.

[190]In this respect one would need to modify Barbara Aland's assertion (1983:19) that the apologetic appeal to Christian ethics failed because pagan observers could see no more than a stubborn willingness and ability to suffer. (Regardless of success or failure, it is clearly the case that Justin and others not only understood praxis as an essential element of Christian faith, but in fact used it as an argument for the truth of Christianity: so rightly Kühneweg 1988:113.) The apologetic function of praxis is well attested in both Old and New Testaments, e.g. Deut 4.6; Ezra 5.9; Matt 5.16; 1 Pet 2.12; see also n. 15 above.

Clement of Alexandria expounds the idea of a distinctive Christian character as developed from the example of the Lord himself, but applied in a courtesy diffused throughout every detail of life: the Christian is frugal, humble, unselfish, generous, cheerful. This character even shows in one's gait when walking, in mealtime manners and ordinary social contacts – and yet it remains natural and unrestrained. See Clem. Alex., *Paed.* 1.99; cf. Chadwick, 1966:42–3; and see P. Brown 1992:121–2, who sees in such perspectives the Christian upper-class endorsement of classical *paideia*.

9

JEWISH AND CHRISTIAN PUBLIC ETHICS IN THE EARLY ROMAN EMPIRE

We turn in this concluding chapter from a historical to a more synthetic study of some of the issues affecting Jewish and Christian public ethics in the Graeco-Roman context. Among the issues defining the limits of corporate tolerance in Christianity and Judaism are matters of morality and lifestyle. In this context, it can be revealing to examine the distinctive characteristics of how Jews and Christians explained and justified that morality in public discourse. By 'public' discourse, I mean (as in Chapter 8) that which is carried on in terms relevant and accessible to outsiders, within the early imperial environment of pluralistic paganism. Such public dialogue may be real or only notional, just as apologetics may be for internal as well as external dialogue; indeed the difference between internal and external need not always be clear.[1] Ethics for present purposes is 'public' regardless of whether its communication to outsiders is intended to be persuasive, reassuring, or straightforwardly explanatory.

Before going on to look at some of the substantive questions on this subject, it is worth considering briefly the social *Sitz im Leben* of such public discourse. It must be admitted from the outset that for both Judaism and Christianity, deliberate thought about public ethics probably always remained a fringe activity on the part of a social and intellectual elite. What is more, Jewish life and practice at least in the larger centres like Palestine, Alexandria or Antioch was a sufficiently established reality on the ground to make popular preoccupation with this subject the exception rather than the rule.

Nevertheless, it would be erroneous to conclude that the subject of public moral discourse is therefore only of marginal interest for our subject.[2] There are in fact a number of points worth raising in reply. First, smaller diaspora communities throughout the empire would almost constantly have had to face the problem of justifying the Jewish way of life in terms intelligible to a hostile or indifferent

---

[1] It is an intriguing but undeniable phenomenon that a good deal of Christian evangelism at the same time serves an apologetic purpose for believers, almost regardless of their social standing. (Conversely, apologetics may of course also be evangelistic in effect.) Cf. also Baumgarten 1998:45 and 57 n. 70 on the Habad movement.

[2] See also above, p. 197.

majority. The same consideration must have been true in *all* cases for the fledgling Gentile Christian churches.

But even for the larger communities it is clearly the case that apologetic efforts were periodically needed: 3 Maccabees and Philo's mission to Gaius demonstrate this for Alexandria, as Josephus arguably does for Rome (and perhaps for Jerusalem). Periodic imperial chicaneries in the province of Judaea and elsewhere would make the satisfactory public justification of Jewish customs and practices a matter of concern not just for an elite but for entire communities. A variety of other indicators show that apologetic concerns, including those relating to morality, were at times not just of academic interest, but a matter of life and death and the very essence of Jewishness. Additional examples of this can be found to range all the way from the book of Daniel (3–6) and the Maccabean revolt (1 Macc 1.45–48) to the Bar Kokhba War and beyond. The widespread interest in such matters further recurs in the didactic stereotype of rabbis in dialogue or dispute with Gentiles;[3] and the need for it appears in the echoes, in Juvenal and other writers,[4] of widespread popular bigotry against Jews. Finally, funerary inscriptions can provide another useful gauge of the public self-portrayal at least of the middle and upper classes; and here it is significant to note the many cases of eulogies in self-consciously popular Gentile terms of praise.[5]

Many of these arguments about the Jewish need for public ethics apply *a fortiori* to Christianity, which at no time in the first three centuries of our era enjoyed the civil and religious rights pertaining to an ancestral *religio licita*. The public face of Christian morality was a constant concern, as the pages of the New Testament, along with subsequent public opprobrium and persecution, make very clear.

The Problem of Halakhah in Jewish and Christian Ethics

Before going on to comment specifically on the main topics of public ethics, it is necessary to offer a few more *general*, comparative observations on the nature of Jewish and early Christian morality.

1. Ancient *Jewish* ethics in the broadest sense cannot properly be

---

[3]Note the frequent colloquies between Rabbi (Yehudah ha-Nasi) and 'Antoninus' (Caracalla?): on this see Krauss 1910; Stemberger 1979:367–75. Similarly, one finds numerous encounters between rabbis and Roman matrons or pagan inquirers, e.g. in the tractate '*Abodah Zarah* in both the Mishnah and the Talmud (see below, p. 235).

[4]Juvenal, *Satires* 14.96–106; Tacitus, *Histories* 5.1–13; *Annals* 15.44.

[5]Cf. Horbury 1994.

understood without reference to the concept of halakhah. True, there are significant Graeco-Roman philosophical influences on the form and presentation especially of diaspora ethical texts. Jewish Hellenistic virtue and vice lists do owe a great deal to Stoicism and to the shape of popular Graeco-Roman philosophy.[6] But as we have seen throughout this book, that influence does not explain the *selection criteria* for how much of pagan morality is included – and what is left out. At the end of the day, mainstream authors are rarely, if ever, prepared to step outside recognized principles of binding halakhah, whether these are based on the written Torah, on tradition, or on both. That much, I suspect, is largely uncontroversial.

2. On the *Christian* side, however, we run into difficulty as soon as we attempt to say anything comparative. The basic rationale of Christian ethics is generally assumed to be both straightforward and yet manifestly distinctive. In particular, the New Testament authors do of course share a highly theological approach to ethics and often explicitly ground their appeals on christology, pneumatology and eschatology. Their view of Jewish law as a source of moral authority often comes across as ambivalent: despite a certain undeniable overlap in substance, explicit appeals to Jewish law are extremely rare in these writers. What is more, both Paul and the Jesus of the Gospels frequently appear to criticize aspects of the Torah itself or at least of conventional Torah observance.

Most commonly, therefore, textbooks of ethics assume a straightforward shift from Torah to Christ, from halakhah to aggadah, and so on.[7] While a growing number of scholars writers would allow varying degrees of influence of the Torah even on Paul's ethical teaching, it is still very widely assumed that the Torah *qua law* no longer has any normative place in the canonical writings of the New Testament. (Matthew and James are sometimes allowed as partial exceptions.)

Nevertheless, the substantive *specificity* of the New Testament approach to ethics must still somehow be accounted for. The single most important reason for this, I would submit, is neither christology nor pneumatology nor eschatology, whether of the realized or the millenarian kind. These matters by themselves might perhaps *contribute* to a distinctively Christian outlook; and it is of course true that the teaching and example of Christ are both

[6]See e.g. recently Feldman 1993:201–31 on Jewish use of the cardinal virtues.
[7]See e.g. Vielhauer 1979:220; J. A. Sanders 1975:373–4; W. D. Davies 1980:147–76 and *passim*. Cf. above, pp. 148–50.

foundational to Christian faith and not infrequently serve as a significant ethical motif.[8] But they do not *ipso facto* explain the New Testament's remarkable neglect or indeed outright antipathy towards what both Paul and 4QMMT appear to call the 'works of the law'[9]: circumcision, *Kashrut, Toharot,* and sacrificial regulations. Jewish Christianity presumably had all or much of the eschatology and messianology without being critical of the commandments whose observance shows Jews to be Jewish.

Similarly, no-one nowadays would dispute the influence of *Hellenistic* patterns of moral instruction on the formulation of early Christian ethics. However, just as the use made of such material by Jewish authors is not indiscriminate but ultimately governed by halakhic criteria, so also it will not do to ignore the fundamental rationale behind its appearance in Christian ethical texts. The Apostle Paul and others are in fact highly *selective* and specific in their adoption of Hellenistic moral principles, as e.g. John Barclay has shown for Galatians.[10] And once again, the *teaching and example* of Jesus do seem to contribute significantly to those Christian selection criteria. Nevertheless, christology, pneumatology or eschatology seem to supply only the theological frame of reference, but have relatively little specific bearing on the matter of selection. Paul's Corinthian and Galatian correspondence offers eloquent testimony to the fact that the instruction to 'walk in the Spirit' could, by itself, mean alarmingly different things to different people.

If, therefore, christology alone fails to account sufficiently for the concrete substance and character of New Testament ethics, another explanation must be sought. It has been the argument of this book that the most plausible alternative consists in the *Gentile audience* that is envisaged in most or all of the New Testament writings. In Chapter 7 above, I attempted to demonstrate that the New Testament authors make very substantial use of a traditional *halakhah for Gentiles,* which can be traced from the Pentateuchal laws for resident aliens all the way to the rabbinic Noachide Commandments. Ever since the Levitical Holiness Code and the

---

[8]Messianism itself can arguably function as a catalyst in the development of a sectarian outlook: cf. e.g. Baumgarten 1998. For the imitation of Christ in Pauline ethics, see e.g. Fowl 1990; M. Thompson 1991; and cf. Bockmuehl 1997:121–5.

[9]See Gal 2.15; 3.2, 5, 10, 12; 4QMMT C 29. On the possible connection between the two, see Dunn 1997 and Abegg 1999.

[10]Barclay 1988:170–7 and *passim.* On the need for discrimination, see also H. D. Betz 1988:200–1.

prophets, these views had concentrated on the prohibitions of idolatry, sexual immorality, and blood offences.

Certain elements of Jewish halakhah in New Testament ethics were discussed in Parts I and II of this book; a fuller treatment must here be left for another occasion. For now, these short comments may suffice to alert us to the legitimacy and likely usefulness of a *comparative halakhic approach* to Jewish and early Christian ethics.

With this in mind, the next two sections of this chapter briefly address the substance of Jewish and Christian public ethics.

Jewish Public Ethics

I should like here for the sake of convenience to divide the material into (1) sources clearly intended for an internal Jewish audience and (2) sources intended for an external or quasi-external audience.

1. Internal Discourse

We have no space to rehearse the relevant texts, many of which are familiar from Chapter 7. The sources cover what might be called Jewish 'international' law. I mean of course the halakhah for Gentiles, i.e. texts which in effect relate to the Noachide Commandments. In addition to the relevant biblical texts and the standard rabbinic passages on the 'Seven Commandments',[11] an important early text is the book of *Jubilees* (7.20), where the Noachide doctrine is directly alluded to. This passage is particularly significant as it shows that Gentile morality was a long-standing concern even in narrowly sectarian circles.

Moving on a little to somewhat more 'extrovert' literature, the most important sources include the *Letter of Aristeas*, Wisdom 14.12–31, the *Sibylline Oracles* 3–5, and Pseudo-Phocylides.[12] Scholars are now generally convinced that despite their adoption of secular Graeco-Roman literary *forms*, these documents are written by Jews and for Jews. At the same time, each one gives the appearance of being concerned with a minimum morality which,

---

[11]T. *'Abod. Zar.* 8.4; other Tannaitic texts include *b. Sanh.* 56a bottom [*baraita*]; *Mek.* Baḥodesh, Yitro 5 (R. Simeon b. Eleazar; ed. Horovitz/Rabin, p. 221); *Sifre Deut.* 343 (Deut 33.2; ed. Finkelstein, p. 396) cf. further *b. 'Abod. Zar.* 2b bottom; *Gen. Rab.* 34.8, etc. and see the discussion in Chapter 7 above.

[12]Cf. e.g. *Sib. Or.* 3.36–45, 185–91, 235–45, 373–80, 593–6, 732–40, 758 ('the Immortal in the starry heaven will put in effect a common law for people throughout the whole earth'), 762–6; 4.30–4; 5.165–74, 386–93, 430–1. See also 12.110–12; and *Letter of Aristeas* 131–6, 168–9, 171 and *passim*.

although addressed in the first instance to Jews, commends itself in principle even to Gentiles. Most (although not all) of the material also concerns matters that fall broadly within the categories expected in a Noachide context: idolatry, sexual ethics, violence, property and blood offences.[13]

Two other examples of 'internal' ethics for Gentiles may be mentioned in passing. The first issue relates to the larger topic of *'abodah zarah*, i.e. pagan idolatry (lit. 'foreign worship'). Scholars have devoted considerable effort to the ancient debates about purchasing olive oil and other materials from potentially idolatrous Gentiles.[14] Does one assume with R. Eliezer ben Hyrcanus that the unspecified moral intention of Gentiles is always idolatrous, or not?[15] Opinions differed, but the issue clearly illustrates interest in how one should expect Gentiles to behave.

The second example is the issue of Gentile sabbath observance. This concerns halakhic questions about Gentiles ploughing fields in *Eretz Israel* on a sabbath, and could be said to comprise many of the classic controversies and traditions which eventually led to the doctrine of the 'Shabbes Goy': the Gentile may rightly do work for himself on the Sabbath which is forbidden to the Jew – even if the Jew thereby benefits.[16]

A special subset of inner-Jewish concern about Gentile ethics are those texts which speak to an internal audience about injustices and atrocities committed by pagan enemies or overlords. This is of course a commonplace concern whose antecedents are well attested in Scripture (Amos 1–2 etc.). The moral tenor of these is not prescriptive so much as plaintive: even Gentiles are subject to certain universal norms of justice and should have known better. Examples from the Second Temple and Tannaitic periods include 1–3 Maccabees, the campaigns of Holofernes in Judith, *Psalms of Solomon, 2 Baruch* and several other apocalypses. Rabbinic passages about the bloodiness of the Bar Kokhba revolt imply a similar

---

[13]Some might wish to include in this category Jewish Testamentary literature, especially the *Testaments of the Twelve Patriarchs*. However, despite their identifiable Hellenistic moral tone these documents do not in fact concern themselves in any sense with *Gentiles*, who indeed are almost always dismissed as morally irrelevant. E.g. *Test. Dan* 5.5, 8; *Test. Naph.* 4.1; but see *Test. Sim.* 7.2, a Christian interpolation. Cf. p. 156 above.

[14]See e.g. E. P. Sanders 1990a:272–83; Tomson 1990:168–76.

[15]M. Ḥul. 2.7; see p. 158 above. Compare the opinion in the Dead Sea *War Scroll* that clean animals may not be sold to Gentiles lest they sacrifice them to idols (CD 12.8).

[16]Cf. in this regard Katz 1989. We must leave aside here the disputed issue of the halakhah strictly concerned with Jewish behaviour toward Gentiles, e.g. respecting business dealings and the charging of usury etc. Like the testamentary literature, this material is not strictly concerned with *Gentile* behaviour.

perspective. The same is true of legends of martyrdom from Shadrach, Meshach and Abednego via the Maccabean revolt to Rabbi Aqiba. It would also be worth exploring the attitudes toward the governmental policies of imperial Rome implied in the legends about R. Shim'on ben Yoḥai and rabbinic visitors to Rome.

2. 'Public' Discourse

In addition to the frequently halakhic discussion intended for an internal audience, however, there is also the apologetic approach directed towards an *external* or quasi-external audience. In these contexts, public ethics are propounded in terms intelligible to outsiders, and intended either to persuade outsiders or to encourage insiders about the moral excellence or indeed superiority of the Jewish way of life.

The obvious examples of this perspective include a good deal of ethical material in Philo and Josephus; perhaps it is worth especially singling out Philo's *Legatio ad Gaium* and the *Hypothetica*; in Josephus the most obvious section is perhaps the summary of the Law in *Ag. Ap.* 2.16–30 §157–219. Despite their stylized character, they reflect an engagement with genuine public challenges, including on the subject of Jewish morality. It is interesting to note the practical *Sitz im Leben* of embassies to Roman authorities on behalf of endangered Jewish communities. Such appeals to the government stress the role of Jews as followers of an ancient and venerable religion, and as exemplary citizens whose way of life is outstanding and praiseworthy even by Roman standards. (This line of argument almost suggests a kind of Kantian constraint in public ethics: 'we Jews live the kind of life which deserves universal respect, and which is beneficial for humanity as a whole'.)

Rabbinic literature offers mainly an internal perspective on public ethics, which has rather more to say about Jewish dealings with Gentiles than about how Gentile society ought to behave. Nevertheless, we do get the occasional glimpse of an 'internal moral apologetic'. A reflection of *public* dialogue about morality may well be found in some of the popular tales of encounter between famous rabbis and their Gentile interlocutors. Borrowing a phrase from *m. 'Abot* (2.14), one might call these the '*el Epikuros*' stories. Perhaps the most famous example is Hillel's encounter with the non-proselyte Gentile who wants to learn the Torah while standing on one leg. Hillel replies by commending the Golden Rule[17] (once again a reply which, in another context, might have pleased Immanuel Kant).

---

[17]*'Abot R. Nat.* B 29 (ed. Schechter, pp. 61–2); *b. Šab.* 31a. See also Rabban Gamaliel and Proclus in *m. 'Abod. Zar.* 3.4.

Characteristics of the Christian Approach

A treatment of early Christian public ethics is also subject to the distinction between internal and external discourse about the subject. On the one hand, most of New Testament ethics is 'extrovert' in that it addresses Gentiles to whom the Torah does not apply in its entirety. Terms of reference are frequently taken from the familiar Jewish halakhah for Gentiles.

On the other hand, from the perspective of the authors and their communities, they themselves are the new 'insiders' of the chosen people constituted by God's purposes in Jesus Christ; they are in turn very well aware of community boundaries and of the difference between themselves and the outside world, designated variously as 'Gentiles', 'the world', 'those outside', 'unbelievers', etc. (sometimes even 'the Jews'). Christians *were* once 'Gentiles' (1 Cor 12.2) and 'aliens' (Eph 2.19), but are so no longer, having converted from the service of idols to the living God (1 Thess 1.9) and thus become part of the chosen people. New Testament moral instruction, therefore, is formulated as ethics *for insiders*, and it spells out ethical principles characteristic of self-conscious insiders. In that sense, therefore, New Testament ethics shows signs of being both 'public' or universal and yet internal.

The difference between Christian ethics and a universal morality explicable to outsiders is not always clear. In general, the substance of Christian public ethics follows the Jewish pattern of ethics for Gentiles. The difference is that now there is a distinction not between Torah for insiders and Noachide Commandments for outsiders, but between the largely Jewish moral assessment of outsiders (Rom 1.18–32; 13.1–7; 1 Thess 1.9–10; Eph 4.17–24, etc.) and an internal re-formulation of the halakhah for Gentiles in light of the person and work of Christ (NB Rom 12–15) and of his parousia (1 Cor 7; 1 Thess 4).

As a result, therefore, Christian *public* ethics properly speaking is remarkably similar to Jewish public ethics. This is true especially for its negative or critical function: the very Jewishness of early Christianity's criteria of sin and evil has often been pointed out.[18] The wickedness of pagans and yet the usefulness of the restraining secular orders of Caesar, *polis* and *oikos* are all reiterated in traditional Jewish terms. Positively, we find in numerous New Testament authors[19] the familiar desire to present the Christian way

[18]See e.g. Meeks 1993:122–3.
[19]E.g. Matthew (5.16; 23.1–12), Luke-Acts (Luke 19.8; Acts 2.44–47), Paul (1 Thess 4.11–12; Rom 13; Phil 2.15–16); 1 Tim 2.1–2; 3.7; Tit 2.10; 3.2; 1 Pet 2.13.

of life publicly as blameless, concerned for the welfare of others, and morally superior to paganism. The difference here is that even in their public demeanour, Christians are also motivated by the teaching and example of Christ. It is worth noting that while New Testament vice lists are almost entirely conventional (Jewish Hellenistic and/or Stoic), there is a good deal of conceptual and theological innovation in the lists of *virtues* (cf. p. 138 above).

The same pattern continues in the second century with the writings of the Apologists. Aristides, Justin Martyr, Origen and others portray Christianity as actively sponsoring the welfare of all humanity, and thus even of the empire. Opponents accused Christianity of undermining the Empire by their supposed atheism, secret immorality and failure to render public service. In reply to this, the Christian writers followed the cue of the Lucan and Pauline corpus of the New Testament in arguing the public respectability of Christianity, indeed its benefit to society as a whole. Most famously, as we saw in Chapter 8, the *Epistle to Diognetus* affirms about Christians,

Every foreign country is their native land, and every native land is a foreign country. They marry as all do; they beget children, but they do not destroy their offspring. They have a common table but not a common bed. They are in the flesh, but do not live after the flesh. ... They love all people, and are persecuted by all. ... They are poor and make many rich. ... They are abused and give blessing. ... To put it shortly: what the soul is in the body, that the Christians are in the world. ... Christians are in the world, but are not of the world. ... Christians are confined in the world as in a prison, and yet they are the preservers of the world' (5–6).[20]

The impressiveness, if not the persuasive force, of such arguments of public ethics can be documented by occasional pagan acknowledgements, on the part of Pliny the Younger, Galen, and others.[21]

One other issue is worth bearing in mind before we conclude. The lines of distinction between insiders and outsiders are somewhat blurred on the question of whether *Jews* are insiders or outsiders. This problem arises in Matthew and Paul and becomes painfully obvious in the Johannine Corpus. Acts 21 specifically identifies the cause of opposition to Paul as significantly related to his attitude towards the *halakhah*: he is accused of teaching Diaspora Jews to forsake Moses (ἀποστασίαν διδάσκεις ἀπὸ Μωϋσέως), circumcision and 'the customs' (μηδὲ τοῖς ἔθεσιν περιπατεῖν). But even beyond this, we know that tensions between Palestinian Jewish Christians

---

[20]See p. 218 above; cf. Origen, *C. Cels.* 8.73–5; Wilken 1984:118–19, 124–5.
[21]E.g. Pliny, *Epistles* 10.96; Galen in Eusebius, *Eccl. Hist.* 5.28.15.

and Jews sometimes centred on halakhic disputes. Thus, in the year 62, James the Just was on a Sadducean initiative executed by stoning, supposedly as a transgressor of the law.[22] The Talmud further records an intriguing discussion at Sepphoris, between Eliezer ben Hyrcanus and Jacob of Sikhnin, concerning Jesus' supposed halakhah on the tithe of prostitutes.[23]

More specifically, the Gospel of Matthew morally indicts a doctrinally 'inside', but politically hostile majority of Jewish Pharisees on numerous occasions for 'hypocrisy' and failing to practise what they preach. Jews appear as persecutors in the Gospels and in Paul; several later Christian sources complain against the injustice of Jewish persecution of Christians in the Bar Kokhba revolt (Justin Martyr, Jerome, Eusebius;[24] cf. the *Apocalypse of Peter*[25]). The injustice of enemies was a theme of public morality for both Jews and Jewish Christians, and it was met with denunciation and sometimes martyrdom. But while martyrdom for Jews was evidence of the general wickedness of pagans, for Christians it could initially be due either to pagan or to Jewish hard-heartedness.

Conclusion

Similarities of substance between the Jewish and Christian approaches abound, as we have also seen in several of the earlier chapters in this book. There is very significant agreement between Jewish and Christian public ethics on the practical substance of a halakhah for non-converting Gentiles. Closer examination shows, moreover, that the same Jewish halakhah for Gentiles also sheds light on a good deal of *internal* Christian ethics. Even in the second century, some Christians explicitly acknowledged that their understanding of natural law was shared with Judaism.[26] What, then, were the *distinctive* emphases in their respective public ethics?

Specifically Christian contributions to public moral discourse were perhaps not many, as we saw in Chapter 8. Nevertheless, they include a greater apologetic emphasis on the exemplary lifestyle of Christianity, with a comparatively greater stress on Christian concern for the social welfare of outsiders. This was perhaps partly

[22]See Josephus, *Ant.* 20.9.1 §200.
[23]See *t. Ḥul.* 2.24; *Qoh. Rab.* 1.1.8; *b. 'Abod. Zar.* 16b–17a.
[24]Note on this subject Horbury 1982, 1998b.
[25]Note e.g. Hills 1991 and Bauckham 1998b.
[26]Irenaeus states unambiguously, *naturalia omnia praecepta communia sunt nobis et illis* (*Haer.* 4.13.4). For Tertullian, the Torah and the Prophets merely reformed the *lex naturalis*, which was already given to Adam (*Adv. Iud.* 2).

through pragmatic necessity, and partly by explicit appeal to the person of Jesus.

Christians at least in the first two centuries also took a strong public stance in favour of pacifism, non-retaliation, and refusal of military service, sometimes at considerable cost to themselves. Intolerance of public norms led to denunciation and often martyrdom. Christian resistance in the early centuries was consistently non-violent. Martyrdom soon came to be viewed not nationally, on behalf of the Jewish people, but as occurring for and through Christ. It is here that the teaching and example of Jesus had a powerful impact on Christian public ethics.

Perhaps the greatest social difference lies in the fact that despite periodic pogroms and endemic anti-Semitism, Judaism's presence on the Graeco-Roman scene was that of an established ethnic group with civic rights and privileges. Christianity, by contrast, was a newcomer on the scene and had no obvious claims to being a *religio licita*. This necessitated a significant difference in the apologetic approach to matters of morality. As we find in sources as early as the second century BC, Jewish apologists could afford to stress the ancient and venerable origin of their religion, its exalted ethical standards and achievements predating and excelling Homer and the great philosophers.

Many of the church fathers were fully aware of the force of this argument from antiquity. They, too, therefore, attempted to mount such a case based on their claim to be the true heirs of the Old Testament, not just theologically but in terms of moral probity as well. For Christians, this argument served the threefold apologetic purpose of reassuring insiders, silencing pagan detractors and, more problematically, establishing the legitimacy of Christianity *vis-à-vis* Judaism.[27] From the perspective of Christian–Jewish ethical polemics, a particularly interesting reflection of the debate about Old Testament Law may be present in the *baraita* about the removal of the Decalogue from the daily liturgy. This was said to be due to *Minim* who claimed that only the Ten Commandments were spoken to Moses at Sinai.[28]

At the same time, however, early Christianity was a clearly recent and non-ethnic voluntary association, which therefore could not straightforwardly appeal to the venerable antiquity of its moral teaching. Instead, while still paradoxically claiming to be the true

[27]See Simon 1986:146–55 and *passim*; also Pilhofer 1990 and Simonetti 1994, *passim*.

[28]See Urbach 1990, who wrongly rejects the link with early Christian claims. Geza Vermes 1968 points out the similarity of the argument of Stephen in Acts 7.53 (cf. Acts 7.38; Gal 3.19) with that of the *Minim*. Furthermore, as early as *Barn.* 4.7–8; Justin, *Dial.* 19–20; *Ps.-Clem. Rec.* 35–6 one finds the argument that the laws given after the Golden Calf incident (and hence after the Decalogue) served only the inferior purpose of preventing Israel's idolatry.

heirs to the Old Testament, Christians also began to bank on the idea of progress and innovation. The apologists stressed that they were the new chosen people from all nations, the 'third race' whose moral probity and unselfish love surpassed both Jew and Gentile.[29] This argument, which has its roots in the New Testament itself and its first clear occurrence in the *Kerygma Petrou*,[30] could be said to underlie much of the public self-definition of early Christianity, in terms not only of theology but also of moral argument. In this mode of discourse, the visible distinctiveness of Christian moral praxis is publicly linked with the novelty of the gospel.

This means that while the apologists do appeal to Christianity's inherent attractiveness and persuasiveness,[31] the explicit and implied moral parameters continue all the while to be determined by the Christian revelation. In view of its eschatological horizon, Christian ethics must therefore be inescapably *dialectical*, never content either to subordinate creation to redemption or vice versa. It is for this reason that the early church's developing public moral discourse necessarily, if sometimes uneasily, comprised both engagement and withdrawal, the apologetic voice as much as the apocalyptic. Each needs the other to remain a valid witness to the truth of the gospel.

At the end of the day, of course, this same tacit epistemological priority of revelation over 'universal' rationality was held in common by Jews and Christians alike. All true wisdom corresponds to the law of God: it was this conviction which defined – and defines – both the scope and the limits of their public ethics. We have seen in this book that ancient Jews and Christians shared an ethical heritage that claimed to express no mere sectarian preference, but rather God's truth for the world. It is not without a deep symbolic irony, then, that for both Jews and Christians their public witness to that truth could be said to find its clearest and most eloquent expression in the acts of their martyrs. The same categorical resistance to the lie of idolatry is embodied, *mutatis mutandis*, in Aqiba's dying confession of אחד, '[the Lord is] One',[32] and in the words *Christianus sum*, 'I am a Christian'.[33]

[29]For the Christian idea of innovation and progress see the in-depth study by Kinzig 1994.

[30]Fragment 2, quoted in Clem. Alex., *Strom.* 6.5.39–41. See e.g. Schneemelcher 1992:2.39 and Paulsen 1997, who sees this document as illustrating the transition from the literature of Christian origins to the patristic and apologetic literature. Cf. also Stanton 1992:94–7.

[31]See e.g. the *Letter to Diognetus*, cited above; and cf. Aristides, *Apology* 15–16; Justin, *1 Apol.* 16, 65; *Dial.* 110; Tertullian, *Apol.* 39.1–6.

[32]Deut 6.4: see *b. Ber.* 61b.

[33]See e.g. *Mart. Pol.* 10.1; *Acts of the Scillitan Martyrs* 9–10, 13; Justin, *2 Apol.* 2; *Martyrdom of Justin* 3–4; Eusebius, *Eccl. Hist.* 5.1.19–20 and *passim* (martyrs of Lyons and Vienne). Translations of these texts are conveniently collected in Stevenson 1957:18–43.

BIBLIOGRAPHY

Abegg, Martin G. 1999. '4QMMT C 27, 31 and "Works Righteousness"'. *DSD* 6:139–47.

Abrahams, Israel. 1917, 1924. *Studies in Pharisaism and the Gospels*. 2 vols. London: Macmillan.

Adamson, James B. 1989. *James: The Man and His Message*. Grand Rapids: Eerdmans.

Aharoni, Yohanan. 1979. *The Land of the Bible: A Historical Geography*. Trans. & ed. A. F. Rainey. Second edn. London: Burns & Oates.

Aland, Barbara. 1983. 'Christentum, Bildung und römische Oberschicht: Zum "Octavius" des Minucius Felix'. In *Platonismus und Christentum: Festschrift für Heinrich Dörrie*, 11–30. JAC Supplement 10. Ed. H.-D. Blume & F. Mann. Münster: Aschendorffsche Verlagsbuchhandlung.

Aland, Kurt. 1979. 'Das Verhältnis von Kirche und Staat in der Frühzeit'. *ANRW* II 23.1:60–246.

Alexander, Philip S. 1974. 'The Toponymy of the Targumim with Special Reference to the Table of Nations and the Borders of the Holy Land'. Oxford: D. Phil. dissertation.

Alexander, Philip S. 1982. 'Notes on the "Imago Mundi" of the Book of Jubilees'. *JJS* 33:197–213.

Alexander, Philip S. 1997. 'Jesus and the Golden Rule'. In *Hillel and Jesus: Comparative Studies of Two Major Religious Leaders*, 363–88. Ed. J. H. Charlesworth & L. L. Johns. Philadelphia: Fortress Press.

Alexander, Philip S. 1998. '"Homer the Prophet of All" and "Moses our Teacher": Late Antique Exegesis of the Homeric Epics and of the Torah of Moses'. In *The Use of Books in the Ancient World*, 127–42. Ed. L. V. Rutgers et al. Leuven: Peeters.

Alfonsi, L. 1976. 'La teologia della storia nell'Apologia di Aristide'. *Augustinianum* 16:37–40.

Allison, Dale C. 1998. *Jesus of Nazareth: Millenarian Prophet*. Minneapolis: Fortress Press.

Alon, Gedaliahu. 1996. 'The Halacha in the Teaching of the Twelve Apostles'. In *The Didache in Modern Research*, 165–94. Ed. J. A. Draper. AGJU 37. Leiden: Brill. [=ET of original Hebrew in *Studies in Jewish History in the Times of the Second Temple, the Mishna, and the Talmud* ([Tel Aviv]: Histadrut/Kibbutz ha-Me'uchad, 1967), 1:274–94.]

Alpigiano, Carlotta. 1988. *Aristide di Atene: Apologia*. Biblioteca Patristica 11. Florence: Nardini.

Anderson, H. 1985. '4 Maccabees: A New Translation and Introduction'. In *OTP* 2:531–64.

Anderson, R. Dean, Jr. 1996. *Ancient Rhetorical Theory and Paul*. CBET 18. Kampen: Kok Pharos.

Arkes, Hadley. 1992. 'That "Nature Herself Has Placed in Our Ears a Power of Judging": Some Reflections on the "Naturalism" of Cicero'. In *Natural Law Theory: Contemporary Essays*, 245–77. Ed. R. P. George. Oxford: Clarendon Press.

Armstrong, A. H. 1967. 'Plotinus'. In *The Cambridge History of Later Greek and Early Medieval Philosophy*, 193–268. Ed. A. H. Armstrong. Cambridge: Cambridge University Press.

Attridge, H. 1985. 'Fragments of Pseudo-Greek Poets: A New Translation and Introduction'. In *OTP* 2:821–30.

Aune, David E. 1995. 'Human Nature and Ethics in Hellenistic Philosophical Traditions and Paul: Some Issues and Problems'. In *Paul in His Hellenistic Context*, 291–313. Ed. T. Engberg-Pedersen. Minneapolis: Fortress.

Aune, David E. 1996. 'Zwei Modelle der menschlichen Natur bei Paulus'. *TQ* 176:28–39.

Austgen, Robert J. 1969. *Natural Motivation in the Pauline Epistles*. Second edn. Notre Dame: University of Notre Dame Press.

Avigad, Nahman. 1971. 'The Burial-Vault of a Nazirite Family on Mount Scopus'. *IEJ* 21:185–200 + pl. 33–43.

Avi-Yonah, Michael. 1966. *The Holy Land from the Persian to the Arab Conquests (536 BC to AD 640): A Historical Geography*. Grand Rapids: Baker.

Avi-Yonah, Michael. 1976. *Gazetteer of Roman Palestine*. Qedem 5. Jerusalem: Institute of Archaeology/CARTA.

Baker, William R. 1995. *Personal Speech-Ethics in the Epistle of James*. WUNT 2:68. Tübingen: Mohr (Siebeck).

Balch, David L. 1981. *Let Wives be Submissive: The Domestic Code in 1 Peter*. SBLMS 26. Chico: Scholars Press.

Balsdon, J. P. V. D. 1962. *Roman Women: Their History and Habits*. London: Bodley Head.

Bammel, Caroline. 1993. 'Die erste lateinische Rede gegen die Christen'. *ZKG* 104:295–311.

Bammel, Ernst. 1984. 'Romans 13'. In *Jesus and the Politics of His Day*, 365–83. Ed. E. Bammel & C. F. D. Moule. Cambridge: Cambridge University Press.

Barclay, John M. G. 1988. *Obeying the Truth: A Study of Paul's Ethics in Galatians*. SNTW. Edinburgh: T&T Clark.

Barclay, John M. G. 1993. 'Conflict in Thessalonica'. *CBQ* 55:512–30.

Barclay, John M. G. 1996. *Jews in the Mediterranean Diaspora from Alexander to Trajan (323 BCE – 117 CE)*. Edinburgh: T&T Clark.

Barclay, John M. G. 1997. *Colossians and Philemon*. NT Guides. Sheffield: Sheffield Academic Press.

Barnard, Leslie William. 1978. 'Apologetik: I. Alte Kirche'. *TRE* 3: 371–411.

Barnard, Leslie William. 1984. 'The Authenticity of Athenagoras' *De resurrectione*'. *Studia patristica* 15.1:39–49.

Barnes, Timothy. 1991. 'Pagan Perceptions of Christianity'. In *Early Christianity: Origins and Evolution to AD 600. In Honour of W. H. C. Frend*, 231–43. Edited by Ian Hazlett. London: SPCK.

Barr, James. 1990. 'Biblical Law and the Question of Natural Theology'. In *The Law in the Bible and in its Environment*, 1–22. Ed. T. Veijola. Publications of the Finnish Exegetical Society 51. Helsinki: Finnish Exegetical Society; Göttingen: Vandenhoeck & Ruprecht.

Barr, James. 1993. *Biblical Faith and Natural Theology*. Oxford: Clarendon Press.

Barrett, C. K. 1963. 'Cephas and Corinth'. In *Abraham unser Vater: Juden und Christen im Gespräch über die Bibel. Festschrift für Otto Michel zum 60. Geburtstag*, 1–12. Ed. O. Betz et al. AGJU 5. Leiden/Cologne: Brill. [=Repr. in *Essays on Paul*, 28–39. London: SPCK.]

Barrett, C. K. 1987. 'The Apostolic Decree of Acts 15.29'. *AusBR* 35:50–59.

Barrett, C. K. 1997. 'Christocentricity at Antioch'. In *Jesus Christus als die Mitte der Schrift: Studien zur Hermeneutik des Evangeliums*, 303–39. BZNW 86. Ed. C. Landmesser et al. Berlin/New York: de Gruyter.

Barrett, C. K. 1998. *A Critical and Exegetical Commentary on the Acts of the Apostles*. Vol. 2. Edinburgh: T&T Clark.

Bartchy, S. Scott. 1992. 'Slavery (Greco-Roman)'. *ABD* 6:65–73.

Barton, John. 1979. 'Natural Law and Poetic Justice in the Old Testament'. *JTS* N. S. 30:1–14.

Barton, John. 1980. *Amos's Oracles against the Nations*. SOTSMS 6. Cambridge: Cambridge University Press.

Barton, John. 1998. *Ethics and the Old Testament*. London: SCM Press.

Barton, John. 1999. 'Virtue in the Bible'. *Studies in Christian Ethics* 12:12–22.

Barton, P. F. (Forthcoming). 'Quadratus, der Apologet'. In *ANRW* II 27.2.

Barton, Stephen C. 1994. *Discipleship and Family Ties in Mark and Matthew*. SNTSMS 80. Cambridge: Cambridge University Press.

Basser, Herbert W. 1993. 'Let the Dead Bury Their Dead'. In *Approaches to Ancient Judaism*, NS vol. 5, pp. 79–96. Ed. H. Basser & S. Fishbane. Atlanta: Scholars Press.

Bauckham, Richard. 1991. 'The Economic Critique of Rome in Revelation 18'. In *Images of Empire*, 47–90. Ed. L. Alexander. JSOTSup 122. Sheffield: Sheffield Academic Press.

Bauckham, Richard. 1995. 'James and the Jerusalem Church'. In *The Book of Acts in Its Palestinian Setting*, 415–80. Ed. R. Bauckham. Grand Rapids: Eerdmans; Carlisle: Paternoster Press.

Bauckham, Richard. 1996. 'James and the Gentiles (Acts 15.13–21)'. In *History Literature, and Society in the Book of Acts*, 154–84. Ed. B. Witherington. Cambridge: Cambridge University Press.

Bauckham, Richard. 1997. 'Anna of the Tribe of Asher (Luke 2:36–38)'. *RB* 104:161–91.

Bauckham, Richard J. 1998a. 'The Scrupulous Priest and the Good Samaritan: Jesus' Parabolic Interpretation of the Law of Moses'. *NTS* 44:475–89.

Bauckham, Richard J. 1998b. 'Jews and Jewish Christians in the Land of Israel at the Time of the Bar Kokhba War, With Special Reference to the *Apocalypse of Peter*'. In *Tolerance and Intolerance in Early Judaism and Christianity*, 228–38. Ed. G. N. Stanton & G. G. Stroumsa. Cambridge: Cambridge University Press.

Bauckham, Richard 1999. *James: Wisdom of James, Disciple of Jesus the Sage*. London/New York: Routledge.

Bauer, J. B. 1963. 'An Diognet VI'. *VC* 17:207–10.

Baumeister, Theofried. 1988. 'Zur Datierung der Schrift an Diognet'. *VC* 42:105–11.

Baumeister, Theofried. 1995. 'Das Martyrium als Thema frühchristlicher apologetischer Literatur'. In *Martyrium in Multidisciplinary Perspective: Memorial Louis Reekmans*, 323–32. Ed. M. Lamberigts & P. van Deun. BETL 117. Leuven: University Press/Peeters.

Baumgarten, Albert I. 1996. 'Ḥaṭṭa't sacrifices'. *RB* 103:337–42.

Baumgarten, Albert I. 1998. 'The Pursuit of the Millennium in Early Judaism'. In *Tolerance and Intolerance in Early Judaism and Christianity*, 38–60. Ed. G. N. Stanton & G. G. Stroumsa. Cambridge: Cambridge University Press.

Beare, Francis Wright. 1981. *The Gospel According to Matthew: A Commentary*. Oxford: Blackwell.

Beck, Marcus. 1999. 'Quadratus'. *LACL*[2], 529.

Bellah, Robert N., et al. 1985. *Habits of the Heart: Individualism and Commitment in American Life*. Berkeley: University of California Press.

Bengel, Johann Albrecht. 1855. *Gnomon Novi Testamenti*. Ed. M. E. Bengel & J. Steudel. 3rd edn. London: Nutt, Williams & Norgate; Cambridge: Macmillan.

Benko, Stephen. 1980. 'Pagan Criticism of Christianity during the First Two Centuries A.D.' *ANRW* II 23.2:1054–1118.

Berger, Klaus. 1972. *Die Gesetzesauslegung Jesu*, vol. 1. WMANT 40. Neukirchen-Vluyn: Neukirchener.

Berger, Klaus. 1989. *Die Weisheitsschrift aus der Kairoer Geniza*. Tübingen: Francke.

Berger, Klaus. 1996. 'Jesus als Nasoräer/Nasiräer'. *NovT* 38:323–35.

Bergmann, J. 1908. *Jüdische Apologetik im neutestamentlichen Zeitalter*. Berlin: Reimer.

Bernheim, Pierre-Antoine. 1997. *James, Brother of Jesus*. Trans. J. Bowden. London: SCM Press.

Betz, Hans Dieter. 1972. *Der Apostel Paulus und die sokratische Tradition: Eine exegetische Untersuchung zu seiner Apologie 2. Korinther 10–13*. BHT 45. Tübingen: Mohr (Siebeck).

Betz, Hans Dieter. 1979. *Galatians: A Commentary on Paul's Letter to the Churches in Galatia*. Hermeneia. Philadelphia: Fortress Press.

Betz, Hans Dieter. 1988. 'Das Problem der Grundlagen der paulinischen Ethik (Röm 12,1–2)'. *ZTK* 85:199–218.

Bickerman, E. J. 1938. *Institutions des Séleucides*. Paris: Geuthner.

Bing, J. Daniel. 1992. 'Cilicia'. *ABD* 1:1022–4.

Black, Matthew. 1971. *An Aramaic Approach to the Gospels and Acts*. Third edn. Oxford: Clarendon Press.

Blomberg, Craig L. 1992. *Matthew*. NAC 22. Nashville: Broadman.

Blomberg, Craig L. 1984. 'The Law in Luke-Acts'. *JSNT* 22:53–80. [=Repr. in *The Synoptic Gospels*, ed. C. A. Evans & S. E. Porter, The Biblical Seminar 31 (Sheffield: Sheffield Academic Press, 1995), 240–67.]

Bloom, Allan. 1987. *The Closing of the American Mind*. New York: Simon & Schuster.

Blum, Wilhelm, trans. & ed. 1981. *Byzantinische Fürstenspiegel: Agapetos, Theophylakt von Ochrid, Thomas Magister*. Bibliothek der griechischen Literatur 14. Stuttgart: Hiersemann.

Bockmuehl, Markus. 1990. *Revelation and Mystery in Ancient Judaism and Pauline Christianity*. WUNT 2:36. Tübingen: Mohr (Siebeck). [=Repr. Grand Rapids: Eerdmans, 1997.]

Bockmuehl, Markus. 1991. Review of Peter J. Tomson, *Paul and the Jewish Law: Halakha in the Letters of the Apostle to the Gentiles*, CRINT 3.1 (Assen/Maastricht: Van Gorcum; Minneapolis: Fortress Press, 1990). *JTS* NS 42:682–8.

Bockmuehl, Markus. 1997. *The Epistle to the Philippians*. BNTC. London: A&C Black.

Bockmuehl, Markus. 1999. Review of Jürgen Wehnert, *Die Reinheit des 'christlichen Gottesvolkes' aus Juden und Heiden*, FRLANT 173 (Göttingen: Vandenhoeck & Ruprecht, 1997). *JTS* NS 50:260–8.

Bockmuehl, Markus. Forthcoming. '1 Thessalonians 2.14–16 and the Church in Jerusalem'. In Proceedings of the XVI Colloquio Paolino, Rome 1999. Ed. M. D. Hooker. Monograph Series 'Benedictina'. Rome: Abbey of St Paul outside the Walls.

Böckenhoff, Karl. 1903. *Das apostolische Speisegesetz in den ersten fünf Jahrhunderten: Ein Beitrag zum Verständnis der quasi-*

levitischen Satzungen in älteren kirchlichen Rechtsquellen. Paderborn: Schöningh.

Boertien, Maas. 1971. *Nazir (Nasiräer): Text, Übersetzung und Erklärung samt einem textkritischen Anhang.* Die Mischna III.4. Berlin/New York: de Gruyter.

Bolkestein, Hendrik. 1939. *Wohltätigkeit und Armenpflege im vorchristlichen Altertum: Ein Beitrag zum Problem "Moral und Gesellschaft".* Utrecht: Oosthoek.

Bonhoeffer, Dietrich. 1955. *Ethics.* Trans. N. H. Smith. London: SCM Press.

Booth, Roger P. 1986. *Jesus and the Laws of Purity: Tradition History and Legal History in Mark 7.* JSNTSup 13. Sheffield: JSOT Press.

Borgen, Peder. 1988. 'Catalogues of Vices, the Apostolic Decree, and the Jerusalem Meeting'. In *The Social World of Formative Christianity and Judaism,* 126–41. Ed. J. Neusner et al. Philadelphia: Fortress Press.

Bornkamm, Günther. 1968. 'Ehescheidung und Wiederverheiratung im Neuen Testament'. In *Geschichte und Glaube* 1 [= *Gesammelte Aufsätze* 3], 56–9. BEvT 48. Munich: Kaiser.

Böttrich, Christfried. 1992. *Weltweisheit, Menschheitsethik, Urkult: Studien zum slavischen Henochbuch.* WUNT 2:50. Tübingen: Mohr (Siebeck).

Bovon, François. 1996. *Das Evangelium nach Lukas.* Vol. 2. EKKNT 3. Zurich: Benziger; Neukirchen-Vluyn: Neukirchener.

Brändle, Rudolf. 1975. *Die Ethik der 'Schrift an Diognet': Eine Wiederaufnahme paulinischer und johanneischer Theologie am Ende des zweiten Jahrhunderts,* ATANT 64. Zurich: Theologischer Verlag.

Brändle, Rudolf. 1995. 'Diognet'. *LTK*[3] 3: 238–9.

Brandon, S. G. F. 1967. *Jesus and the Zealots: A Study of the Political Factor in Primitive Christianity.* Manchester: Manchester University Press.

Brandt, Theodor. 1929 [cover 1928]. *Tertullians Ethik: Zur Erfassung der systematischen Grundanschauung.* Gütersloh: Bertelsmann.

Brennecke, Hanns C. 1992. 'Ecclesia est in re publica, id est in imperio Romano (Optatus III 3): Das Christentum in der Gesellschaft an der Wende zum "Konstantinischen Zeitalter" '. *JBT* 7: 209–39.

Brennecke, Hanns C. 1997. '"An fidelis ad militam converti possit?" [Tertullian, de idolatria 19,1]: Frühchristliches Bekenntnis und Militärdienst im Widerspruch?' In *Die Weltlichkeit des Glaubens in der Alten Kirche: Festschrift für Ulrich Wickert zum siebzigsten Geburtstag,* 45–100. Ed. D. Wyrwa et al. BZNW 85. Berlin/New York: de Gruyter.

Brent, Allen. 1998. 'Ignatius of Antioch and the Imperial Cult'. *VC* 52:30–58.

Brin, Gershon. 1994. *Studies in Biblical Law. From the Hebrew Bible to the Dead Sea Scrolls.* JSOTSup 176. Sheffield: Sheffield Academic Press.

Brin, Gershon. 1997. 'Divorce at Qumran'. In *Legal Texts and Legal Issues: Proceedings of the Second Meeting of the International Organization for Qumran Studies, Cambridge 1995. Published in Honour of Joseph M. Baumgarten*, 231–44. Ed. M. Bernstein et al. STDJ 23. Leiden: Brill.

Broer, Ingo. 1986. 'Anmerkungen zum Gesetzesverständnis des Matthäus'. In *Das Gesetz im Neuen Testament*, 128–45. Ed. K. Kertelge. QD 108. Freiburg: Herder.

Broer, Ingo. 1992. 'Jesus und das Gesetz: Anmerkungen zur Geschichte des Problems und zur Frage der Sündenvergebung durch den historischen Jesus'. In *Jesus und das jüdische Gesetz*, 61–104. Ed. I. Broer. Stuttgart: Kohlhammer.

Brown, John Pairman. 1993. 'From Hesiod to Jesus: Laws of Human Nature in the Ancient World'. *NovT* 35:313–43.

Brown, Peter. 1992. *Power and Persuasion in Late Antiquity: Towards a Christian Empire.* Madison: University of Wisconsin Press.

Brown, Raymond E. and Meier, John P. 1983. *Antioch and Rome.* New York: Paulist Press.

Bubmann, Peter. 1993. 'Naturrecht und christliche Ethik'. *ZEE* 37:267–80.

Büchsel, F. 1950. 'Apologetik'. *RAC* 1: 533–45.

Buffière, Félix. 1956. *Les Mythes d'Homère et la Pensée Grecque.* Paris: Belles Lettres.

Bultmann, Christoph. 1992. *Der Fremde im antiken Juda. Eine Untersuchung zum sozialen Typenbegriff 'ger' und seinem Bedeutungswandel in der alttestamentlichen Gesetzgebung.* FRLANT 153. Göttingen: Vandenhoeck & Ruprecht.

Bultmann, Rudolf. 1963. *History of the Synoptic Tradition.* Translated by J. Marsh. Rev. edn. Oxford: Blackwell.

Burke, Gary T. 1984. 'Walter Bauer and Celsus: The Shape of Late Second-Century Christianity'. *SecCent* 4:1–7.

Burnyeat, M. F. 1994. 'Did the Ancient Greeks Have the Concept of Human Rights?' (Russian, with English summary.) *Hyperboreus: Studia Classica* 1:19–27. [ET in *Polis* (Swansea/York: The Society for Greek Political Thought) 13 (1994) 1–11.]

Callan, Terrance. 1993. 'The Background to the Apostolic Decree (Acts 15.20, 29; 21:25)'. *CBQ* 55:284–97.

Cameron, Averil. 1991. *Christianity and the Rhetoric of Empire: The Development of Christian Discourse.* Sather Classical Lectures 55. Berkeley: University of California Press.

Capelle, Wilhelm. 1932. 'Griechische Ethik und römischer Imperialismus'. *Klio* 25:86–113.

Carleton Paget, James. 1997. 'The Vision of the Church in the Apostolic Fathers'. In *A Vision for the Church*, 193–206. Ed. M. Bockmuehl & M. B. Thompson. Edinburgh: T&T Clark.

Carras, George P. 1990. 'Jewish Ethics and Gentile Converts: Remarks on 1 Thes 4,3–8'. In *The Thessalonian Correspondence*, 305–15. Ed. R. F. Collins. BETL 87. Leuven: Leuven University Press.

Carrington, Philip. 1940. *The Primitive Christian Catechism*. Cambridge: Cambridge University Press.

Casey, P. M. 1988. 'Culture and Historicity: The Plucking of the Grain'. *NTS* 34:1–23.

Casey, Maurice. 1998. *Aramaic Sources of Mark's Gospel*. SNTSMS 102. Cambridge: Cambridge University Press.

Cassidy, Richard J., and Scharper, Philip J., eds. 1983. *Political Issues in Luke-Acts*. Maryknoll: Orbis.

Catastini, Alessandro. 1987. '4QSam^a 1: Samuele il "Nazireo" '. *Henoch* 9: 161–95.

Catchpole, David R. 1977. 'Paul, James and the Apostolic Decree'. *NTS* 23:428–44.

Chadwick, Henry. 1966. *Early Christian Thought and the Classical Tradition: Studies in Justin, Clement, and Origen*. Oxford: Clarendon Press.

Chadwick, Henry. 1992. 'Humanität'. *RAC* 16:663–711.

Charles, J. Daryl. 1997. *Virtue amidst Vice: The Catalog of Virtues in 2 Peter 1*. JSNTSup 150. Sheffield: Sheffield Academic Press.

Charlesworth, James H. 1988. *Jesus within Judaism*. London: SPCK.

Cheung, Alex T. 1999. *Idol Food in Corinth: An Examination of Paul's Approach in the Light of its Background in Ancient Judaism and Legacy in Early Christianity*. JSNTSup 176. Sheffield: Sheffield Academic Press.

Chilton, Bruce. 1987. *God in Strength*. Sheffield: Sheffield Academic Press.

Chilton, Bruce. 1992. *The Temple of Jesus: His Sacrificial Program Within a Cultural History of Sacrifice*. University Park: Pennsylvania State University Press.

Chilton, Bruce. 1997a. 'E. P. Sanders and the Question of Jesus and Purity'. In Chilton & Evans 1997:221–30.

Chilton, Bruce. 1997b. 'A Generative Exegesis of Mark 7:1–23'. In Chilton & Evans 1997:297–315.

Chilton, Bruce. 1998. 'The Brother of Jesus and the Interpretation of Scripture'. In *The Use of Books in the Ancient World*, 29–48. Ed. L. V. Rutgers et al. CBET 22. Leuven: Peeters.

Chilton, Bruce, and Evans, Craig A. 1997. *Jesus in Context: Temple, Purity, and Restoration*. AGFU 39. Leiden: Brill.

Cimok, Fatih, ed. 1995. *Antioch Mosaics*. Istanbul: A Turizm Yayinlari.

Clarke, Andrew D. 1993. *Secular and Christian Leadership in Corinth: A Socio-Historical and Exegetical Study of 1 Corinthians 1–6*. AGJU 18. Leiden/New York: Brill.

Classen, C. Joachim. 1991. 'Paulus und die antike Rhetorik'. *ZNW* 82:1–33.

Classen, C. Joachim. 1993. 'St. Paul's Epistles and Ancient Greek and Roman Rhetoric'. In *Rhetoric and the New Testament: Essays from the 1992 Heidelberg Conference*, 265–91. JSNTSup 90. Ed. S. E. Porter & T. H. Olbricht. Sheffield: Sheffield Academic Press.

Clements, R. E. 1965. *Prophecy and Covenant*. SBT 43. London: SCM Press.

Clines, David J. A. 1974. 'The Tree of Knowledge and the Law of Yahweh (Psalm XIX)'. *VT* 24:8–14.

Cohen, Boaz. 1966. *Jewish and Roman Law: A Comparative Study*, vol. 1. New York: Jewish Theological Seminary of America.

Cohen, Naomi G. 1992. 'Taryag and the Noahide Commandments'. *JJS* 43:46–57.

Cohen, Shaye J. D. 1989. 'Crossing the Boundary and Becoming a Jew'. *HTR* 82:13–33.

Collins, John J. 1998. 'Natural Theology and Biblical Tradition: The Case of Hellenistic Judaism'. *CBQ* 60:1–15.

Cooper, Alan. 1994. 'Creation, Philosophy and Spirituality: Aspects of Jewish Interpretation of Psalm 19'. In *Pursuing the Text: Studies in Honor of Ben Zion Wacholder on the Occasion of his Seventieth Birthday*, 15–33. Ed. J. C. Reeves & J. Kampen. JSOTSup 184. Sheffield: Sheffield Academic Press.

Corbier, Mireille. 1989. 'The Ambiguous Status of Meat in Ancient Rome'. *Food and Foodways* 3:223–64.

Corrington, Gail Paterson. 1991. 'The "Headless Woman": Paul and the Language of the Body in 1 Cor 11:2–16'. *Perspectives in Religious Studies* 18:223–32.

Craigie, Peter C. 1983. *Psalms 1–50*. WBC 19. Waco: Word.

Crouch, James E. 1972. *The Origin and Intention of the Colossian Haustafel*. FRLANT 109. Göttingen: Vandenhoeck & Ruprecht.

Crouzel, Henri. 1971. *L'Église Primitive Face au Divorce: Du premier au cinquième siècle*. Théologie Historique 13. Paris: Beauchesne.

Dalman, Gustav. 1922. *Jesus-Jeschua*. Leipzig: Hinrichs. [ET *Jesus-Jeshua: Studies in the Gospels*, trans. P. P. Levertoff (London: SPCK, 1929).]

Dalman, Gustav. 1924. *Orte und Wege Jesu*. BFCT 2:1. Gütersloh: Mohn.

Dalrymple, William. 1997. *From the Holy Mountain: A Journey in the Shadow of Byzantium*. London: HarperCollins.

Danby, Herbert, trans. 1933. *The Mishnah*. Oxford: Oxford University Press.

250 JEWISH LAW IN GENTILE CHURCHES

Danker, Frederick. 1982. *Benefactor: Epigraphic Study of a Graeco-Roman and New Testament Semantic Field*. St. Louis: Clayton.

Dassmann, Ernst. 1992. 'Weltflucht oder Weltverantwortung: Zum Selbstverständnis frühchristlicher Gemeinden und zu ihrer Stellung in der spätantiken Gesellschaft'. *JBT* 7:189–208.

Dassmann, Ernst. 1996. 'Klemens von Alexandrien und eine christliche Familienkultur in nicht-christlicher Umwelt'. In *Christlicher Glaube als Lebensstil*, 145–58. Ed. R. Englert et al. Stuttgart: Kohlhammer.

Daube, David. 1956. *The New Testament and Rabbinic Judaism*. London: Athlone Press.

Daube, David. 1981. *Ancient Jewish Law: Three Inaugural Lectures*. Leiden: Brill.

Dautzenberg, Gerhard. 1986. 'Gesetzeskritik und Gesetzesgehorsam in der Jesustradition'. In *Das Gesetz im Neuen Testament*, 46–70. Ed. K. Kertelge. QD 108. Freiburg: Herder.

Dautzenberg, Gerhard. 1998. 'Markus und das Gesetz: Überlegungen zur gleichnamigen Untersuchung von Heikki Sariola'. *BZ* 42:91–5.

Davies, G. I. 1992. *Hosea*. NCB Commentary. Grand Rapids: Eerdmans; London: Marshall Pickering.

Davies, Margaret. 1995. 'Work and Slavery in the New Testament: Impoverishments of Traditions'. In *The Bible in Ethics*, 315–47. Ed. J. W. Rogerson et al. JSOTSup 207. Sheffield: JSOT Press.

Davies, Stevan L. 1980. *Revolt of the Widows: The Social World of the Apocryphal Acts*. Carbondale: Southern Illinois University Press; London: Feffer & Simons.

Davies, W. D. 1952. *Torah in the Messianic Age and/or the Age to Come*. JBLMS 7. Philadelphia: SBL.

Davies, W. D. 1972. 'The Moral Teaching of the Early Church'. In *The Use of the Old Testament in the New and Other Essays: Studies in Honor of William Franklin Stinespring*, 310–32. Ed. James M. Frend. Durham, NC: Duke University Press.

Davies, W. D. 1974. *The Gospel and the Land: Early Christianity and Jewish Territorial Doctrine*. Berkeley/London: University of California Press.

Davies, W. D. 1980. *Paul and Rabbinic Judaism: Some Rabbinic Elements in Pauline Theology*. Third edn. Philadelphia: Fortress Press.

Davies, W. D. 1982. *The Territorial Dimension of Judaism*. Berkeley etc.: University of California Press.

Davies, W. D., & Allison, Dale C. 1988, 1991, 1997. *A Critical and Exegetical Commentary on the Gospel According to Saint Matthew*. 3 vols. Edinburgh: T&T Clark.

Davis, George B. 1999. 'True and False Boasting in 2 Cor 10–13'. Cambridge: Ph.D. dissertation.

de Lacey, D. R. 1992. 'In Search of a Pharisee'. *TynBul* 43:353–72.

Derrett, J. Duncan M. 1970. *Law in the New Testament*. London: Darton, Longman & Todd.

Derrett, J. Duncan M. 1982. 'Law and Society in Jesus's World'. ANRW II 25.1:477–564.

Derrett, J. Duncan M. 1983. 'Bechuqey hagoyim: Damascus Document 9:1 again'. *RevQ* 11:409–15.

Derrett, J. Duncan M. 1985. 'Two "Harsh" Sayings of Christ Explained'. *Downside Review* 103:218–29. [Repr. in idem, *Studies in the New Testament*, vol. 5 (Leiden: Brill, 1989), 71–82.]

Diestel, L. 1869. *Geschichte des Alten Testaments in der christlichen Kirche*. Jena: Mauke's Verlag.

Dihle, Albrecht. 1976. 'Antikes und Unantikes in der frühchristlichen Staatstheorie'. In *Assimilation et résistance à la culture Gréco-Romaine dans le monde Ancien: Travaux du VIe Congrès International d'Etudes Classiques*, 323–32. Ed. D. M. Pippidi. Bucharest: Editura Academiei; Paris: Belles Lettres.

Dodd, C. H. 1951. *Gospel and Law*. Cambridge: Cambridge University Press.

Dodd, C. H. 1953. 'Natural Law in the New Testament'. In *New Testament Studies*, 129–43. Manchester: Manchester University Press.

Doering, Lutz. 1999. *Schabbat: Sabbathalacha und -praxis im antiken Judentum und Urchristentum*. TSAJ 78. Tübingen: Mohr Siebeck.

Downey, Glanville. 1952. 'Greek and Latin Inscriptions'. In *Antioch on-the-Orontes*, vol. 2: *The Excavations 1933–1936*, 148–65. Ed. R. Stillwell. Princeton: Princeton University Press; London: Oxford University Press; The Hague: Martinus Nijhoff.

Downey, Glanville. 1961. *A History of Antioch in Syria: From Seleucus to the Arab Conquest*. Princeton: Princeton University Press.

Drijvers, Han J. W. 1984. 'Athleten des Geistes: Zur politischen Rolle der syrischen Asketen und Gnostiker'. In *Religionstheorie und Politische Theologie*, vol. 2: *Gnosis und Politik*, 109–20. Ed. J. Taubes. Munich: Fink; Paderborn: Schöningh.

Dunn, James D. G. 1977. *Unity and Diversity in the New Testament: An Inquiry into the Character of Earliest Christianity*. London: SCM Press.

Dunn, James D G. 1983. 'The Incident at Antioch (Gal 2:11–18)'. *JSNT* 18:3–57.

Dunn, James D. G. 1990. *Jesus, Paul and the Law*. London: SCM Press.

Dunn, James D. G. 1993. *The Epistle to the Galatians*. BNTC. London: A&C Black.

Dunn, James D. G. 1997. '4QMMT and Galatians'. *NTS* 43:147–53.

Edwards, M. J. 1999. Review of B. Bernard & J. Doré (eds.), *Les Apologistes chrétiens et la culture grecque*, Théologie Historique 105 (Paris: Beauchesne, 1998). *JTS* NS 50:311–14.

Edwards, M. J. Forthcoming. 'Aristides and the Beginning of Christian Apologetic'. *ANRW* II 27.2.

Eisenman, Robert H. 1997. *James, the Brother of Jesus*. London: Faber.

Engberg-Pedersen, Troels. 1995. 'Stoicism in Philippians'. In *Paul in His Hellenistic Context*, 256–90. Ed. T. Engberg-Pedersen. Edinburg: T&T Clark, Minneapolis: Fortress Press.

Eshel, Esther. 1997. '4Q414 Fragment 2: Purification of a Corpse-Contaminated Person'. In *Legal Texts and Legal Issues: Proceedings of the Second Meeting of the International Organization for Qumran Studies, Cambridge 1995. Published in Honour of Joseph M. Baumgarten*, 3–10. STDJ 23. Ed. M. Bernstein et al. Leiden: Brill.

Eshel, Hanan, and Greenhut, Zvi. 1993. 'Ḥiam el-Sagha, A Cemetery of the Qumran Type, Judaean Desert'. *RB* 100:252–9.

Esler, Philip S. 1987. *Community and Gospel in Luke-Acts: The Social and Political Motivations of Lucan Theology*. SNTSMS 57. Cambridge: Cambridge University Press.

Esler, Philip S. 1998. *Galatians*. New Testament Readings. London/New York: Routledge.

Essig, Klaus-Gunther. 1986. 'Erwägungen zum geschichtlichen Ort der Apologie des Aristides'. *ZKG* 97:163–88.

Evans, Craig A. 1997. ' "Who Touched Me?" Jesus and the Ritually Impure'. In Chilton & Evans 1997:353–76.

Fallon, F. 1985. 'Eupolemus: A New Translation and Introduction'. In *The Old Testament Pseudepigrapha*, 2:861–72. Ed. J. H. Charlesworth. Garden City: Doubleday.

Feil, Ernst. 1985. *The Theology of Dietrich Bonhoeffer*. Trans. M. Rumscheidt. Philadelphia: Fortress Press.

Feissel, Denis. 1985. 'Deux listes de quartiers d'Antioche astreints au creusement d'un canal (73–74 après J.-C.)'. *Syria* 62:77–103.

Feldman, Louis H. 1993. *Jew and Gentile in the Ancient World: Attitudes and Interactions from Alexander to Justinian*. Princeton: Princeton University Press'. In *Das Gesetz im Neuen Testament*, 71–87. Ed. K. Kertelge. QD 108. Freiburg, etc.: Herder.

Fiedler, Peter. 1986. 'Die Tora bei Jesus und in der Jesusüberlieferung'. In *Das Gesetz im Neuen Testament*, 71–87. Ed. K. Kertelge. QD 108. Freiburg etc.: Herder.

Finkelstein, Louis. 1923. 'The Book of Jubilees and the Rabbinic Halaka'. *HTR* 16:39–61.

Finsterbusch, Karin. 1996. *Die Thora als Lebensweisung für Heiden-*

christen: Studien zur Bedeutung der Thora für die paulinische Ethik.
SUNT 20. Göttingen: Vandenhoeck & Ruprecht.

Fitzmyer, Joseph A. 1981a. 'The Matthean Divorce Texts and Some New Palestinian Evidence'. In *To Advance the Gospel: New Testament Essays*, 79–111. New York: Crossroad.

Fitzmyer, Joseph A. 1981b. *The Gospel According to Luke: Introduction, Translation, and Notes.* Vol. 1. AB 28. Garden City: Doubleday.

Fitzmyer, Joseph A. 1993. *Romans: A New Translation with Introduction and Commentary.* AB 33. New York: Doubleday.

Fitzmyer, Joseph A. 1998. *The Acts of the Apostles: A New Translation with Introduction and Commentary.* AB 31. New York: Doubleday.

Flückiger, Felix. 1954. *Geschichte des Naturrechtes,* vol. 1: *Altertum und Frühmittelalter.* Zollikon/Zürich: Evangelischer Verlag.

Flusser, David and Safrai, Shmuel. 1986. 'Das Aposteldekret und die Noachitischen Gebote'. In *"Wer Tora vermehrt, mehrt Leben": Festgabe für Heinz Kremers zum 60. Geburtstag,* 173–92. Ed. E. Brocke & H.-J. Barkenings. Neukirchen-Vluyn: Neukirchener Verlag.

Forbes, Christopher. 1986. 'Comparison, Self-Praise and Irony: Paul's Boasting and the Conventions of Hellenistic Rhetoric'. *NTS* 32:1–30.

Fowl, Stephen E. 1990. *The Story of Christ in the Ethics of Paul.* JSNTSup 36. Sheffield: JSOT Press.

Fox, Robin Lane. 1986. *Pagans and Christians in the Mediterranean World from the Second Century A. D. to the Conversion of Constantine.* Harmondsworth: Viking.

Fraade, S. D. 1986. 'Ascetical Aspects of Ancient Judaism'. In *Jewish Spirituality from the Bible through the Middle Ages,* 253–88. Ed. A. Green. New York: Crossroad.

Francis, James A. 1995. *Subversive Virtue: Asceticism and Authority in the Second-Century Pagan World.* University Park: Pennsylvania State University Press.

Frankfort, Henri. 1949. *Before Philosophy: The Intellectual Adventure of Ancient Man. An Essay on Speculative Thought in the Ancient Near East.* Harmondsworth: Penguin.

Fredouille, Jean-Claude. 1972. *Tertullien et la conversion de la culture antique.* Paris: Études Augustiniennes.

Fredouille, Jean-Claude. 1992. 'L'apologétique chrétienne antique: Naissance d'un genre littéraire'. *Revue des Études Augustiniennes* 38:219–34.

Fredouille, Jean-Claude. 1995. 'L'apologétique chrétienne antique: métamorphoses d'un genre polymorphe'. *Revue des Études Augustiniennes* 41:201–16.

Frend, W. H. C. 1983. 'Early Christianity and Society: A Jewish Legacy in the Pre-Constantinian Era'. *HTR* 76:53–71.

Freund, Richard A. 1998. 'The Decalogue in Early Judaism and Christianity'. In *The Function of Scripture in Early Jewish and Christian Tradition*, 124–41. Ed. C. A. Evans & J. A. Sanders. JSNTSup 154. Sheffield: Sheffield Academic Press.

Freyne, Séan. 1988. *Galilee, Jesus and the Gospels: Literary Approaches and Historical Investigations*. Philadelphia: Fortress Press.

Friedrich, J., Pöhlmann, J., and Stuhlmacher, P. 1976. 'Zur historischen Situation und Intention von Röm 13,1–7'. *ZTK* 73:131–66.

Fuks, Alexander. 1979–80. 'The Sharing of Property by the Rich with the Poor in Greek Theory and Practice'. *Scripta Classica Israelica* 5:46–63.

Furnish, Victor Paul. 1979. *The Moral Teaching of Paul: Selected Issues*. Nashville: Abingdon.

Gärtner, Bertil E. 1955. *The Areopagus Speech and Natural Revelation*. ASNU 21. Uppsala: Almqvist & Wiksells.

Gail, Anton J., trans. & ed. 1968. *Erasmus von Rotterdam: Fürstenerziehung. Institutio Principis Christiani: Die Erziehung eines christlichen Fürsten*. Paderborn: Schöningh.

Garnsey, Peter, ed. 1980. *Non-Slave Labour in the Greco-Roman World*. Proceedings of the Cambridge Philological Society, Suppl. Vol. 6. Cambridge: Cambridge Philological Society.

Gaston, Lloyd. 1987. *Paul and the Torah*. Vancouver: University of British Columbia Press.

Geffcken, Johannes. 1907. *Zwei griechische Apologeten*. Sammlung wissenschaftlicher Kommentare zu griechischen und römischen Schriftstellern. Leipzig/Berlin: Teubner.

Gehman, Henry S. 1960. 'Natural Law and the Old Testament'. In *Biblical Studies in Memory of H. C. Alleman*, 109–22. Ed. J. M. Myers et al. Gettysburg Theological Studies. Locust Valley: Augustin.

Georgi, Dieter. 1992. *Remembering the Poor: The History of Paul's Collection for Jerusalem*. (Trans. I. Racz.) Nashville: Abingdon Press.

Gero, Stephen. 1990. 'Galen on the Christians: A Reappraisal of the Arabic Evidence'. *Orientalia Christiana Periodica* 56:371–411.

Gese, Hartmut. 1977. *Zur biblischen Theologie*. Munich: Kaiser.

Gilat, Itzchak D. 1984. *Rabbi Eliezer ben Hyrcanus: A Scholar Outcast*. Ramat-Gan: Bar-Ilan University Press.

Gleßmer, Uwe. 1995. *Einleitung in die Targume zum Pentateuch*. TSAJ 48. Tübingen: Mohr (Siebeck).

Glombitza, Otto. 1971. 'Die christologische Aussage des Lukas in seiner Gestaltung der drei Nachfolgeworte Lukas ix, 57–62'. *NovT* 13:14–23.

Gnilka, Joachim. 1986–92. *Das Matthäusevangelium*. HTKNT 1.1–2. Freiburg, etc.: Herder.

Goldberg, Abraham. 1987. 'The Tosefta – Companion to the Mishna'. In *The Literature of the Sages*, 1:283–302. Ed. S. Safrai. CRINT 2.3. Assen: van Gorcum; Philadelphia: Fortress Press.

Goldenberg, David M. 1996. 'Retroversion to Jesus' *ipsissima verba* and the Vocabulary of Jewish Palestinian Aramaic: the Case of *mata*' and *qarta*' '. *Bib* 77:64–83.

Goldenberg, Robert. 1998. *The Nations That Know Thee Not: Ancient Jewish Attitudes Toward Other Religions*. Washington Square, NY: New York University Press.

Goodenough, E. R. 1935. *By Light, Light: The Mystic Gospel of Hellenistic Judaism*. New Haven: Yale University Press; London: Oxford University Press.

Goodenough, E. R. 1962. *An Introduction to Philo Judaeus*. Second edn. Oxford: Blackwell.

Goodman, Martin. 1990. 'Kosher Olive Oil in Antiquity'. In *A Tribute to Geza Vermes: Essays on Jewish and Christian Literature and History*, 227–45. Ed. P. R. Davies & R. T. White. JSOTSup 100. Sheffield: JSOT Press.

Goodspeed, Edgar J. 1914. *Die ältesten Apologeten: Texte mit kurzen Einleitungen*. Göttingen: Vandenhoeck & Ruprecht.

Goppelt, Leonhard. 1972. 'Prinzipien neutestamentlicher Sozialethik nach dem 1. Petrusbrief'. *Neues Testament und Geschichte: Historisches Geschehen und Deutung im Neuen Testament. Oscar Cullmann zum 70. Geburtstag*, 285–96. Ed. H. Baltensweiler & B. Reicke. Tübingen: Mohr (Siebeck).

Gordis, Robert. 1986. *Judaic Ethics For a Lawless World*. New York: Jewish Theological Seminary of America.

Goulder, Michael D. 1974. *Midrash and Lection in Matthew*. The Speaker's Lectures in Biblical Studies. London: SPCK.

Grainger, John D. 1990. *The Cities of Seleucid Syria*. Oxford: Clarendon Press.

Grant, Robert M. 1957. *The Letter and the Spirit*. London: SPCK.

Grant, Robert M. 1977. 'Quadratus, the First Christian Apologist'. In *A Tribute to Arthur Vööbus: Studies in Early Christian Literature and its Environment, Primarily in the Syrian East*, 177–83. Ed. R. H. Fischer. Chicago: Lutheran School of Theology.

Grant, Robert M. 1978. *Early Christianity and Society*. London: Collins.

Grant, Robert M. 1988a. 'Five Apologists and Marcus Aurelius'. *VC* 42:1–17.

Grant, Robert M. 1988b. *Greek Apologists of the Second Century*. Philadelphia: Westminster Press.

Grant, Robert M. 1992. 'Quadratus'. *ABD* 5:582–83.

Green, H. Benedict. 1975. *The Gospel According to Matthew in the*

Revised Standard Version: Introduction and Commentary. NCB. Oxford: Oxford University Press.

Greenfield, Jonas C. 1980. 'The Genesis Apocryphon – Observations on Some Words and Phrases'. In *Studies in Hebrew and Semitic Languages: Dedicated to the Memory of Prof. Eduard Yechezkel Kutscher*, xxxii–xxxix. Ed. G. B. Sarfatti et al. Ramat-Gan: Bar-Ilan University.

Greidanus, Sidney. 1985. 'The Universal Dimension of Law in the Hebrew Scriptures'. *Studies in Religion* 14:39–51.

Guttmann, Michael. 1927. *Das Judentum und seine Umwelt: Eine Darstellung der religiösen und rechtlichen Beziehungen zwischen Juden und Nichtjuden mit besonderer Berücksichtigung der talmudisch-rabbinischen Quellen*. Berlin: Philo.

Guyot, Peter, & Klein, Richard, eds. 1994. *Das Frühe Christentum bis zum Ende der Verfolgungen*. Vol. 2: *Die Christen in der heidnischen Gesellschaft*. Texte zur Forschung 62. Darmstadt: Wissenschaftliche Buchgesellschaft.

Hachlili, Rachel. 1992. 'Burials'. *ABD* 1:785–94.

Hachlili, Rachel. 1993. 'Burial Practices at Qumran'. *RevQ* 16:247–64.

Hadot, P. 1972. 'Fürstenspiegel'. Trans. J. Engemann. *RAC* 8:555–632.

Haenchen, Ernst. 1968. *Die Apostelgeschichte*. KEKNT 3. 6th edn. Göttingen: Vandenhoeck & Ruprecht.

Hahn, F., & Müller, P. 1998. 'Der Jakobusbrief'. *TRu* 63:1–73.

Hands, Arthur Robinson. 1968. *Charities and Social Aid in Greece and Rome*. London: Thames & Hudson.

Ha-Parchi, Estori. 1897–9. *Caftor va-pherach: Contient toutes les lois religieuses concernant la Terre-Sainte, la topographie de tout le pays et ses divisions, etc.* (Hebr.). Ed. A. M. Luncz. 2 vols. Jerusalem: Luncz.

Harnack, Adolf von. 1924. *Die Mission und Ausbreitung des Christentums in den ersten drei Jahrhunderten*. Fourth edn. Leipzig: Hinrichs.

Harrill, J. Albert. 1995. *The Manumission of Slaves in Early Christianity*. HUT 32. Tübingen: Mohr (Siebeck).

Harris, J. Rendel. 1916, 1920. *Testimonies*. 2 vols. Cambridge: Cambridge University Press.

Hauck, F., & Schulz, S. 1968. 'πόρνη, κτλ'. *TDNT* 6:579–95.

Hauck, Robert J. 1986. 'Omnes contra Celsum?' *SecCent* 5:211–25.

Hays, Richard B. 1996. *The Moral Vision of the New Testament: A Contemporary Introduction to New Testament Ethics*. Edinburgh: T&T Clark.

Hayward, C.T.R. 1989. 'The Date of Targum Pseudo-Jonathan: Some Comments'. *JJS* 40:7–30.

Heckel, Ulrich. 1993. *Kraft in Schwachheit: Untersuchungen zu 2. Kor 10–13*. WUNT 2:56. Tübingen: Mohr (Siebeck).

Heil, Christoph. 1994. *Die Ablehnung der Speisegebote durch Paulus: Zur*

Frage nach der Stellung des Apostels zum Gesetz. BBB 96. Weinheim: Beltz Athenäum.

Heinemann, Isaak. 1927. 'Die Lehre vom ungeschriebenen Gesetz im jüdischen Schrifttum'. *HUCA* 4:149–71.

Heinemann, Isaak. 1959. *Taʿamê ha-Miṣvot be-Sifrut Yisraʾel*, vol. 1. 'Obadiah' Series. Jerusalem: Histadrut.

Hemer, Colin J. 1989. *The Book of Acts in the Setting of Hellenistic History.* WUNT 49. Tübingen: Mohr (Siebeck).

Hempel, Charlotte. 1998. *The Laws of the Damascus Document: Sources, Tradition and Redaction.* STDJ 29. Leiden: Brill.

Hengel, Martin. 1973. *Judentum und Hellenismus.* Second edn. Tübingen: Mohr (Siebeck). [ET *Judaism and Hellenism: Studies in their Encounter in Palestine During the Early Hellenistic Period,* 2 vols. in 1, trans. J. Bowden (London: SCM Press, 1974).]

Hengel, Martin. 1974. *Property and Riches in the Early Church.* Trans. J. Bowden. London: SCM Press.

Hengel, Martin. 1989. *The Zealots: Investigations into the Jewish Freedom Movement in the Period from Herod I until 70* A.D. Edinburgh: T&T Clark.

Hengel, Martin. 1996. *The Charismatic Leader and his Followers.* Trans. J. C. G. Greig; ed. J. Riches. Second edn. Edinburgh: T&T Clark. [First English edn. 1981; originally published as *Nachfolge und Charisma: eine exegetisch-religionsgeschichtliche Studie zu Mt. 8,21f. und Jesu Ruf in die Nachfolge* (Berlin: Töpelmann, 1968).]

Hengel, Martin. 2000. 'Ἰουδαία in der geographischen Liste Apg 2,9–11 und Syrien als "Grossjudäa"'. *RHPR* 80:51–68.

Hengel, Martin, & Schwemer, Anna Maria. 1997. *Paul Between Damascus and Antioch.* Trans. J. Bowden. London: SCM.

Hengel, Martin, & Schwemer, Anna Maria. 1998. *Paulus zwischen Damaskus und Antiochien.* WUNT 108. Tübingen: Mohr (Siebeck).

Herr, Theodor. 1976. *Naturrecht aus der kritischen Sicht des Neuen Testamentes.* Abhandlungen zur Sozialethik 11. Munich: Schöningh.

Hill, Craig C. 1992. *Hellenists and Hebrews: Reappraising Division Within the Earliest Church.* Minneapolis: Fortress Press.

Hills, Julian V. 1991. 'Parables, Pretenders, and Prophecies: Translation and Interpretation in the *Apocalypse of Peter* 2'. *RB* 98:560–73.

Hiltbrunner, Otto. 1994. 'Humanitas (φιλανθρωπία)'. *RAC* 16:711–52.

Hirzel, Rudolf. 1900. *ΑΓΡΑΦΟΣ ΝΟΜΟΣ.* Abhandlungen der philologisch-historischen Classe der Königl. Sächsischen Gesellschaft der Wissenschaften 20.1. Leipzig: Teubner.

Hodgson, Robert. 1976. 'Die Quellen der paulinischen Ethik'. Heidelberg: Dr. theol. dissertation.

Hoffmann, David. 1885. *Der Schulchan-Aruch und die Rabbinen über das Verhältniß der Juden zu Andersgläubigen*. Berlin: Verlag der Expedition der 'Jüdischen Presse'.

Hofmann, Johannes. 1999. 'Ps.-Clementinische Literatur'. *LACL*², 132–3.

Holladay, Carl R. 1992. 'Eupolemus'. *ABD* 2:671–2.

Holmberg, Bengt. 1998. 'Jewish *Versus* Christian Identity in the Early Church?' *RB* 105:397–425.

Holtz, Traugott. 1981. 'Zur Frage der inhaltlichen Weisungen bei Paulus'. *TLZ* 106:386–400. [ET in Rosner 1995:51–71.]

Holtz, Traugott. 1986. 'Der antiochenische Zwischenfall (Galater 2.11–14)'. *NTS* 32:344–61.

Hooker, M. D. 1967. *The Son of Man in Mark*. London: SPCK.

Hooker, M. D. 1991. *The Gospel According to St Mark*. BNTC. London: A&C Black.

Hooker, M. D. 1997. *The Signs of a Prophet: The Prophetic Actions of Jesus*. London: SCM Press.

Hopkins, Keith. 1998. 'Christian Number and Its Implications'. *JECS* 6:185–226.

Horbury, William. 1979. 'Paul and Judaism'. *ExpTim* 90:116–18.

Horbury, William. 1985. 'Extirpation and Excommunication'. *VT* 35:13–38. [Repr. in Horbury 1998a:43–67.]

Horbury, William. 1986. 'The Twelve and the Phylarchs'. *NTS* 32:503–27.

Horbury, William. 1988. 'Old Testament Interpretation in the Writings of the Church Fathers'. In *Mikra: Text, Translation, Reading and Interpretation of the Hebrew Bible in Ancient Judaism and Early Christianity*, 727–87. Ed. M. J. Mulder. CRINT 2.1. Assen/Maastricht: van Gorcum; Philadelphia: Fortress Press.

Horbury, William. 1994. 'Jewish Inscriptions and Jewish Literature in Egypt, with Special Reference to Ecclesiasticus'. In *Studies in Early Jewish Epigraphy*, 9–43. Ed. J. W. van Henten & P. W. van der Horst. AGJU 21. Leiden: Brill.

Horbury, William. 1997. 'Septuagintal and New Testament Conceptions of the Church'. In *A Vision for the Church: Studies in Early Christian Ecclesiology in Honour of J. P. M. Sweet*, 1–17. Ed. M. Bockmuehl & M. B. Thompson. Edinburgh: T&T Clark.

Horbury, William. 1998a. *Jews and Christians in Contact and Controversy*. Edinburgh: T&T Clark.

Horbury, William. 1998b. 'Early Christians on Synagogue Prayer and Imprecation.' In *Tolerance and Intolerance in Early Judaism and Christianity*, 296–317. Ed. G. N. Stanton & G. G. Stroumsa. Cambridge: Cambridge University Press.

Horbury, William. 1999. 'Der Tempel bei Vergil und im herodianischen Judentum'. In *Gemeinde ohne Tempel – Community without Temple: Zur Substituierung und Transformation des Jerusalemer Tempels und seines Kults im Alten Testament, antiken Judentum und frühen Christentum*, 149–68. Ed. B. Ego et al. WUNT 118. Tübingen: Mohr (Siebeck).

Horbury, William. Forthcoming. 'Pappus and Lulianus in Jewish Resistance to Rome'. In the Proceedings of the 1998 Congress of the European Association for Jewish Studies at Toledo. Ed. A. Saénz-Badillos.

Horn, Friedrich W. 1997. 'Paulus, das Nasiräat und die Nasiräer'. *NovT* 39:117–37.

Horrell, David G. 1996. *The Social Ethos of the Corinthian Correspondence: Interests and Ideology from 1 Corinthians to 1 Clement*. SNTW. Edinburgh: T&T Clark.

Horsley, Richard A. 1978. 'The Law of Nature in Philo and Cicero'. *HTR* 71:35–60.

Horst, Friedrich. 1961. 'Naturrecht und Altes Testament'. In *Gottes Recht: Studien zum Alten Testament*, 235–59. Ed. H. W. Wolff. Munich: Kaiser [=*EvT* 10 (1950–1) 253–73].

Houston, W. J. 1982. Review of J. Barton 1980. *JTS* N. S. 33:216–17.

Hurd, John Coolidge. 1965. *The Origin of 1 Corinthians*. London: SPCK.

Ilan, Tal. 1992. 'New Ossuary Inscriptions from Jerusalem'. *Scripta Classica Israelica* 11:149–59.

Jefford, Clayton N. 1996. *Reading the Apostolic Fathers: An Introduction*. Peabody: Hendrickson.

Jeremias, Joachim. 1967. 'Die älteste Schicht der Menschensohn-Logien'. *ZNW* 58:159–72.

Jeremias, Joachim. 1971. *New Testament Theology*, vol. 1: *The Proclamation of Jesus*. Trans. J. Bowden. New Testament Library. London: SCM Press.

Jewett, Robert. 1971. 'The Agitators and the Galatian Congregations'. *NTS* 17:198–212.

Jewett, Robert. 1986. *The Thessalonian Correspondence*. Philadelphia: Fortress Press.

Johnson, Alan F. 1982. 'Is There a Biblical Warrant for Natural-Law Theories?' *JETS* 25:185–99.

Jolowicz, H. F. 1952. *Historical Introduction to the Study of Roman Law*. Second edn. Cambridge: Cambridge University Press.

Joly, Robert. 1973. *Christianisme et Philosophie: Études sur Justin et les Apologistes Grecs du Deuxième Siècle*. Brussels: Editions de l'Université de Bruxelles.

Judge, Edwin A. 1984a. 'Gesellschaft/Gesellschaft und Christentum: III. NT; IV. Alte Kirche'. *TRE* 14:764–9, 769–73.

Judge, Edwin Arthur. 1984b. 'Cultural Conformity and Innovation in Paul: Some Clues from Contemporary Documents'. *TynBul* 35:3–24.

Käsemann, Ernst. 1942. 'Die Legitimität des Apostels'. *ZNW* 41: 33–71.

Kallai, Zecharia. 1983. 'The Reality of the Land and the Bible'. In *Das Land Israel in biblischer Zeit: Jerusalem-Symposium 1981 der Hebräischen Universität und der Georg-August-Universität*, 76–90. Ed. G. Strecker. GTA 25. Göttingen: Vandenhoeck & Ruprecht.

Katz, Jacob. 1989. *The Shabbes Goy: A Study in Halakhic Flexibility*. Philadelphia/New York: Jewish Publication Society.

Kaufman, Stephen A. 1994. 'Dating the Language of the Palestinian Targums and their Use in the Study of First Century CE Texts'. In *The Aramaic Bible: Targums in their Historical Context*, 118–41. Ed. D. R. G. Beattie & M. J. McNamara. JSOTSup 166. Sheffield: JSOT Press.

Kaufman, Stephen A. 1997. 'On Methodology in the Study of the Targums and their Chronology'. In *New Testament Text and Language*, 267–74. Ed. S. E. Porter & Craig A. Evans. Biblical Seminar 44. Sheffield: Sheffield Academic Press.

Kee, H. C. 1983. 'Testaments of the Twelve Patriarchs: A New Translation and Introduction'. In *OTP* 1:775–828.

Kennedy, G. A. 1984. *New Testament Interpretation through Rhetorical Criticism*. Chapel Hill: University of North Carolina Press.

Keresztes, Paul. 1979. 'The Imperial Roman Government and the Christian Church: I. From Nero to the Severi'. *ANRW* II 23.1:247–315.

Kerner, Jürgen. 1998. *Die Ethik der Johannes-Apokalypse im Vergleich mit der des 4. Esra: Ein Beitrag zum Verhältnis von Apokalyptik und Ethik*. BZNW 94. Berlin: de Gruyter.

Kieffer, René. 1982. *Foi et justification à Antioche: Interprétation d'un conflit (Ga 2,14–21)*. LD 111. Paris: Cerf.

Kinzig, Wolfram. 1989. 'Der "Sitz im Leben" der Apologie in der Alten Kirche'. *ZKG* 100:291–317.

Kinzig, Wolfram. 1994. *Novitas Christiana: Die Idee des Fortschritts in der Alten Kirche bis Eusebius*. Forschungen zur Kirchen- und Dogmengeschichte 58. Göttingen: Vandenhoeck & Ruprecht.

Klawans, Jonathan. 1995. 'Notions of Gentile Impurity in Ancient Judaism'. *AJS Review* 20:285–312.

Klawans, Jonathan. 1997. 'The Impurity of Immorality in Ancient Judaism'. *JJS* 48:1–16.

Klawans, Jonathan. 1998. 'Idolatry, Incest, and Impurity: Moral Defilement in Ancient Judaism'. *JSJ* 29:391–415.

Klein, Gottlieb. 1909. *Der älteste christliche Katechismus und die jüdische Propaganda-Literatur*. Berlin: Reimer.

Klemm, Hans G. 1969. 'Das Wort von der Selbstbestattung der Toten: Beobachtungen zur Auslegungsgeschichte von Mt 8:22 Par'. *NTS* 16:60–75.

Kloft, Hans, ed. 1988. *Sozialmassnahmen und Fürsorge: Zur Eigenart antiker Sozialpolitik*. Grazer Beiträge, Supplement 3. Graz/Horn: Berger.

Kloner, Amos, and Gat, Yosef. 1982. 'Burial Caves in the Region of East Talpiyot' (Hebr.). *Atiqot* 8: 74–6, 171–2.

Knights, Chris H. 1993. ' "The Story of Zosimus" or "The History of the Rechabites"?' *JSJ* 24:235–45.

Knights, Chris H. 1997. 'A Century of Research into the Story/Apocalypse of Zosimus and/or the History of the Rechabites'. *JSP* 15:53–66.

Knox, Wilfred L. 1925. *St Paul and the Church of Jerusalem*. Cambridge: Cambridge University Press.

Koester, Helmut. 1968. 'ΝΟΜΟΣ ΦΥΣΕΩΣ: The Concept of Natural Law in Greek Thought'. In *Religions in Antiquity: Essays in Memory of Erwin Ramsdell Goodenough*, 521–41. Ed. J. Neusner et al. Leiden: Brill.

Koester, Helmut. 1974. 'φύσις κτλ'. *TDNT* 9:251–77.

Koet, Bart J. 1996. 'Why Did Paul Shave His Hair (Acts 18,18)? Nazirate and Temple in the Book of Acts'. In *The Centrality of Jerusalem: Historical Perspectives*, 128–42. Ed. M. Poorthuis & Ch. Safrai. Kampen: Kok Pharos.

Kötting, Bernhard. 1953. 'Das Wirken der ersten Styliten in der Öffentlichkeit: Missions- und Erbauungspredigt'. *ZMR* 37:187–97 [=Repr. in idem, *Ecclesia Peregrinans, das Gottesvolk unterwegs: Gesammelte Aufsätze*, 1:3–14, Münsterische Beiträge zur Theologie 54 (Münster: Aschendorff, 1988)].

Kötting, Bernhard. 1957. 'Digamus'. *RAC* 3:1016–24.

Kötting, Bernhard. 1988. *Die Bewertung der Wiederverheiratung (der zweiten Ehe) in der Antike und in der frühen Kirche*. Rheinisch-Westfälische Akademie der Wissenschaften, Vorträge G 292. Opladen: Westdeutscher Verlag.

Kolb, Frank. 1996. 'Antiochia in der frühen Kaiserzeit'. In *Geschichte—Tradition—Reflexion: Festschrift für Martin Hengel zum 70. Geburtstag*, 2:97–118. Ed. H. Cancik et al. Tübingen: Mohr (Siebeck).

Konstan, David. 1995. 'Patrons and Friends'. *CP* 90:328–42.

Kraeling, Carl H. 1932. 'The Jewish Community at Antioch'. *JBL* 51:130–60.

Kraus, Hans-Joachim. 1978. *Psalmen*, vol. 2. BKAT 15.2. Fifth edn. Neukirchen-Vluyn: Neukirchener.

Krauss, Samuel. 1903. 'Les Préceptes des Noachides'. *REJ* 47:32–40.

Krauss, Samuel. 1910. *Antoninus und Rabbi*. Vienna: Israelitisch-theologische Lehranstalt.

Krauss, Samuel. 1995. *The Jewish Christian Controversy*, vol. 1: *From the Earliest Times to 1789*. Ed. & rev. W. Horbury. TSAJ 56. Tübingen: Mohr (Siebeck).

Küchler, Max. 1979. *Frühjüdische Weisheitstraditionen: Zum Fortgang weisheitlichen Denkens im Bereich des frühjüdischen Jahweglaubens.* OBO 26. Fribourg: Universitätsverlag; Göttingen: Vandenhoeck & Ruprecht.

Kühneweg, U. 1988. 'Die griechischen Apologeten und die Ethik'. *VC* 42:112–20.

Lassus, Jean. 1977. 'La ville d'Antioche à l'époque romaine d'après l'archéologie'. *ANRW* 2.8:54–102.

Lassus, Jean. 1984. 'Sur les Maisons d'Antioche'. In *Apamée de Syrie. Bilan des recherches archéologiques 1973–1979: Aspects de l'architecture domestique d'Apamée*, 361–75. Fouilles d'Apamée de Syrie: Miscellanea, Fasc. 13. Ed. J. Balty. Brussels: Centre Belge de recherches archéologiques à Apamée de Syrie.

Lemcio, Eugene E. 1991. *The Past of Jesus in the Gospels.* Cambridge: Cambridge University Press.

Levenson, Jon D. 1987. 'The Sources of Torah: Psalm 119 and the Modes of Revelation in Second Temple Judaism'. In *Ancient Israelite Religion: Essays in Honor of Frank Moore Cross*, 559–74. Ed. P. D. Miller et al. Philadelphia: Fortress Press.

Levi, Doro. 1944. 'Aion'. *Hesperia* 13:269–314.

Levy, Ernst. 1949. 'Natural Law in Roman Thought'. *Studia et Documenta Historiae et Iuris* 15:1–23.

Lieu, Judith M. 1996. *Image and Reality: The Jews in the World of the Christians in the Second Century.* SNTW. Edinburgh: T&T Clark.

Lim, Timothy H. 1992. 'The Chronology of the Flood Story in a Qumran Text (4Q252)'. *JJS* 43:288–98.

Lindars, Barnabas. 1961. *New Testament Apologetic: The Doctrinal Significance of the Old Testament Quotations.* London: SCM Press.

Lindars, Barnabas. 1983. *Jesus Son of Man.* London: SPCK.

Lindemann, Andreas. 1979. 'Paulinische Theologie im Brief an Diognet'. In *Kerygma und Logos: Beiträge zu den geistesgeschichtlichen Beziehungen zwischen Antike und Christentum. Festschrift für Carl Andresen zum 70. Geburtstag*, 337–50. Ed. A. M. Ritter. Göttingen: Vandenhoeck & Ruprecht.

Lindenberger, J. M. 1985. 'Ahiqar: A New Translation and Introduction'. *OTP* 2:479–507.

Litfin, A. Duane. 1994. *St. Paul's Theology of Proclamation: 1 Corinthians 1–4 and Graeco-Roman Rhetoric.* SNTSMS 79. Cambridge: Cambridge University Press.

Loewe, Raphael. 1966. 'Potentialities and Limitations of Universalism in the *Halakhah*'. In *Studies in Rationalism, Judaism & Universalism*, 115–50. Ed. R. Loewe. London: Routledge & Kegan Paul; New York: Humanities.

Lohse, Eduard. 1989. 'Die Berufung auf das Gewissen in der paulinischen Ethik'. In *Neues Testament und Ethik: Für Rudolf Schnackenburg*, 207–19. Ed. H. Merklein. Freiburg: Herder.

Lombardi, Gabrio. 1946. *Ricerche in Tema di Ius Gentium*. Milan: Giuffrè.

Lombardi, Gabrio. 1947. *Sul Concetto di Ius Gentium*. Rome: Istituto di Diritto Romano.

Longenecker, Bruce W. 1998. *The Triumph of Abraham's God: The Transformation of Identity in Galatians*. Edinburgh: T&T Clark.

Louw, Johannes P., and Nida, Eugene A. 1989. *Greek-English Lexicon of the New Testament: Based on Semantic Domains*. Second edn. New York: United Bible Societies.

Lull, D. J. 1986. 'The Servant-Benefactor as a Model of Greatness (Luke 22.24–30)'. *NovT* 28:289–305.

Luz, Ulrich. 1985, 1990. *Das Evangelium nach Matthäus*. EKKNT 1.1–2 Zurich: Benziger; Neukirchen-Vluyn: Neukirchener.

Lyonnet, S. 1967. ' "Lex naturalis" quid praecipiat secundum S. Paulum et antiquam Patrum traditionem'. *Verbum Domini* 45:150–61.

Maccoby, Hyam. 1997. 'The Corpse in the Tent'. *JSJ* 28:195–209.

MacIntyre, Alasdair. 1981. *After Virtue: A Study in Moral Theory*. London: Duckworth.

Macmullen, Ramsay. 1981. *Paganism in the Roman Empire*. New Haven/London: Yale University Press.

Malherbe, Abraham J. 1986a. ' "Not in a Corner": Early Christian Apologetic in Acts 26:26'. *SecCent* 5:193–210.

Malherbe, Abraham J. 1986b. *Moral Exhortation: A Greco-Roman Sourcebook*. LEC 4. Philadelphia: Westminster Press.

Malina, Bruce J. 1981. *The New Testament World: Insights from Cultural Anthropology*. Atlanta: John Knox Press.

Marcic, René. 1964. 'Sklaverei als "Beweis" gegen Naturrecht und Naturrechtslehre'. *Österreichische Zeitscrift für öffentliches Recht* 14:181–95.

Markschies, Christoph. 1997. 'Athenagoras von Athen'. *Der Neue Pauly*, 2:167.

Marmorstein, A. 1950. *Studies in Jewish Theology*. Ed. J. Rabbinowitz and M. S. Lew. London, etc.: Oxford University Press.

Marrou, Henri Irénée. 1965. *A Diognète: Introduction, édition critique, traduction et commentaire*. SC 33bis. Second edn. Paris: Cerf.

Marshall, Peter. 1987. *Enmity in Corinth: Social Conventions in Paul's Relations with the Corinthians*. WUNT 2:23. Tübingen: Mohr (Siebeck).

Martens, John W. 1992. 'Unwritten Law in Philo: A Response to Naomi G. Cohen'. *JJS* 43:38–45.

Martens, John W. 1994a. 'Romans 2.14–16: A Stoic Reading'. *NTS* 40:55–67.

Martens, John. 1994b. 'Nomos Empsychos in Philo and Clement of Alexandria'. In *Hellenization Revisited: Shaping a Christian Response Within the Greco-Roman World*, 323–38. Ed. W. F. Helleman. Lanham: University Press of America.

Marucci, Corrado. 1992. 'Die Haltung der neutestamentlichen Schriftsteller gegenüber dem römischen Reich'. *ZKT* 114:317–26.

Maschi, Carlo Alberto. 1937. *La concezione naturalistica del diritto e degli istituti giuridici romani*. Milan: Vita e pensiero.

Matera, Frank J. 1996. *New Testament Ethics: The Legacies of Jesus and Paul*. Louisville: Westminster John Knox.

Mayer-Maly, Theo. 1971. 'Gemeinwohl und Naturrecht bei Cicero'. In *Das neue Cicerobild*, 371–87. Ed. K. Büchner. Wege der Forschung 27. Darmstadt: Wissenschaftliche Buchgesellschaft.

Mayer-Maly, Theo. 1979. 'Kinderaussetzung'. *KlPauly*, 3:214.

McCane, Byron R. 1990. '"Let the Dead Bury Their Own Dead": Secondary Burial and Matt 8:21–22'. *HTR* 83:31–43.

McKnight, Scot. 1999. *A New Vision for Israel: The Teachings of Jesus in National Context*. Grand Rapids/Cambridge: Eerdmans.

McNamara, Martin, trans. 1995. *Targum Neofiti I: Numbers*. And Clarke, E. G., trans. *Targum Pseudo-Jonathan: Numbers*. The Aramaic Bible 4. Edinburgh: T&T Clark.

Meeks, Wayne A. 1986. *The Moral World of the First Christians*. Philadelphia: Westminster Press.

Meeks, Wayne A. 1990. 'The Circle of Reference in Pauline Morality'. In *Greeks, Romans, and Christians: Essays in Honor of Abraham J. Malherbe*, 305–17. Ed. D. L. Balch et al. Minneapolis: Fortress.

Meeks, Wayne A. 1993. *The Origins of Christian Morality: The First Two Centuries*. New Haven/London: Yale University Press.

Meeks, Wayne A., and Wilken, Robert L. 1978. *Jews and Christians in Antioch in the First Four Centuries of the Common Era*. Missoula: Scholars Press.

Meggitt, Justin J. 1996. 'The Social Status of Erastus (Rom. 16:23)'. *NovT* 38:218–23.

Meggitt, Justin J. 1998. *Paul, Poverty and Survival*. SNTW. Edinburgh: T&T Clark.

Merkel, Helmut. 1984. 'The Opposition between Jesus and Judaism'. In *Jesus and the Politics of His Day*, 129–44. Ed. E. Bammel & C. F. D. Moule. Cambridge: Cambridge University Press.

Metzger, Bruce M. 1975. *A Textual Commentary on the Greek New Testament*. Second edn. London/New York: United Bible Societies.

Meyer, Ben F. 1979. *The Aims of Jesus*. London: SCM.

Meyers, Eric M. 1971. *Jewish Ossuaries: Reburial and Rebirth. Secondary Burials in their Ancient Near Eastern Setting.* BibOr 24. Rome: Biblical Institute.

Milgrom, Jacob. 1997. 'The Blood Taboo'. *BRev* 13:21, 46.

Millar, Fergus. 1993. *The Roman Near East: 31 BC – AD 337.* Cambridge/London: Harvard University Press.

Millard, Matthias. 1995. 'Die rabbinischen noachidischen Gebote und das biblische Gebot Gottes an Noah: Ein Beitrag zur Methodendiskussion'. *WD* 23:71–90.

Millett, Paul C. 1996. 'Labour'. *OCD³*, 809–10.

Mimouni, Simon C. 1998. 'Les Nazoréens: Recherche étymologique et historique'. *RB* 105:208–62.

Minnerath, R. 1973. *Les chrétiens et le monde (Iᵉʳ et IIᵉ siècles).* Paris: Lecoffre.

Mottershead, J. 1986. *Suetonius: Claudius.* Bristol: Bristol Classical Press.

Müller, Klaus. 1993. 'Gottes Gebot für die Menschheit: Die Noachidische Tora als rabbinische Gestalt universaler Ethik'. *Kirche und Israel* 8:133–43.

Müller, Klaus. 1998. *Tora für die Völker: Die noachidischen Gebote und Ansätze zu ihrer Rezeption im Christentum.* Studien zu jüdischem Volk und christlicher Gemeinde 15. Second edn. Berlin: Institut Kirche und Judentum.

Muller, Earl C. 1996. Review of Heil 1994. *CBQ* 58:753–4.

Munier, Charles. 1988. 'Les doctrines politiques de l'Église ancienne'. *RevScRel* 62:42–53.

Murphy-O'Connor, Jerome. 1990. '1 Corinthians'. *NJBC,* 798–815.

Murphy-O'Connor, Jerome. 1996. *Paul: A Critical Life.* New York/Oxford: Oxford University Press.

Musurillo, Herbert, ed. 1972. *The Acts of the Christian Martyrs.* Oxford: Clarendon Press.

Nautin, P. Forthcoming. 'L'Épître à Diognète: Révision'. *ANRW* II 27.2.

Neaman, Pinchas. 1971–72. *Encyclopedia of Talmudical Geography.* 2 vols. Tel Aviv: Ts'ats'ik.

Nembach, Ulrich. 1970. 'Ehescheidung nach AT und jüdischem Recht'. *TZ* 26:161–71.

Nestle, W. 1950. 'Aufklärung'. *RAC* 1:938–54.

Neubauer, Adolphe. 1868. *La Géographie du Talmud.* Paris: Michel Lévy.

Neusner, Jacob. 1973. *Eliezer ben Hyrcanus: The Tradition and the Man.* SJLA 4. 2 vols. Leiden: Brill.

Neusner, Jacob. 1998. *From Scripture to 70: The Pre-Rabbinic Beginnings of the Halakah.* South Florida Studies in the History of Judaism 192. Atlanta: Scholars Press.

Newton, Derek. 1998. *Deity and Diet: The Dilemma of Sacrificial Food at Corinth*. JSNTSup 169. Sheffield: Sheffield Academic Press.

Neyrey, Jerome, ed. 1991. *The Social World of Luke-Acts: Models for Interpretation*. Peabody: Hendrickson.

Nicholas, Barry. 1962. *An Introduction to Roman Law*. Oxford: Clarendon Press.

Nicholas, Barry. 1996. 'Law of Nature'. OCD^3, 835.

Niebuhr, Karl-Wilhelm. 1987. *Gesetz und Paränese: Katechismusartige Weisungsreihen in der frühjüdischen Literatur*. WUNT 2:28. Tübingen: Mohr (Siebeck).

Niebuhr, Karl-Wilhelm. 1998. 'Der Jakobusbrief im Licht frühjüdischer Diasporabriefe'. *NTS* 44:420–43.

Nolland, John. 1993. *Luke 9:21–18:34*. WBC 35B. Dallas: Word.

Noormann, Rolf. 1997. 'Himmelsbürger auf Erden: Anmerkungen zum Weltverhältnis und zum "Paulinismus" des Auctor ad Diognetum'. In *Die Weltlichkeit des Glaubens in der Alten Kirche: Festschrift für Ulrich Wickert zum siebzigsten Geburtstag*, 199–229. Ed. D. Wyrwa et al. BZNW 85. Berlin/New York: de Gruyter.

Norelli, Enrico. 1991. *A Diogneto: Introduzione, traduzione e note*. Milan: Edizioni Paoline.

Norris, Frederick W. 1990. 'Antioch as Religious Center: I. Paganism before Constantine'. *ANRW* II 18.4:2322–79.

Norris, Frederick W. 1991. 'Artifacts from Antioch'. In *Social History of the Matthean Community*, 248–58. Ed. D. Balch. Minneapolis: Fortress Press.

Novak, David. 1983. *The Image of the Non-Jew in Judaism: An Historical and Constructive Study of the Noahide Laws*. Toronto Studies in Theology 14. New York/Toronto: Mellen.

Novak, David. 1992. *Jewish Social Ethics*. New York/Oxford: Oxford University Press.

Novak, David. 1998. *Natural Law in Judaism*. Cambridge: Cambridge University Press.

O'Ceallaigh, G. C. 1958. ' "Marcianus" Aristides, On the Worship of God'. *HTR* 51:227–54.

O'Donovan, Oliver M. T. 1986. 'The Political Thought of the Book of Revelation'. *TynBul* 37:61–94.

O'Donovan, Oliver. 1994. *Resurrection and Moral Order*. Second edn. Leicester: Apollos.

O'Donovan, Oliver. 1996. *The Desire of the Nations: Rediscovering the Roots of Political Theology*. Cambridge: Cambridge University Press.

Oakes, Edward T. 1999. 'Nature as Law and Gift'. (Review of D. Novak, *Natural Law in Judaism* [Cambridge: Cambridge University Press, 1998].) *First Things* 93:44–51.

Oesterle, Hans-Joachim. 1980. 'Textkritische Bemerkungen zur "Apologie" des Aristides von Athen'. *ZDMG* 130:15–23.

Osborn, Eric. 1976. *Ethical Patterns in Early Christian Thought.* Cambridge: Cambridge University Press.

Painter, John. 1997. *Just James: The Brother of Jesus in History and Tradition.* Columbia: University of South Carolina Press.

Pannenberg, Wolfhart. 1959. 'Die Aufnahme des philosophischen Gottesbegriffs als dogmatisches Problem der frühchristlichen Theologie'. *ZKG* 70:1–45 [=repr. in idem, *Grundfragen systematischer Theologie: Gesammelte Aufsätze* (Göttingen: Vandenhoeck & Ruprecht, 1967), 296–346; ET 'The Appropriation of the Philosophical Concept of God as a Dogmatic Problem of Early Christian Theology', in *Basic Questions in Theology*, trans. G. H. Kehm, vol. 2 (London: SCM Press, 1971), 119–83.]

Pannenberg, Wolfhart. 1993. *Toward a Theology of Nature: Essays on Science and Faith.* Oxford: Blackwell.

Patte, Daniel. 1987. *The Gospel According to Matthew: A Structural Commentary on Matthew's Faith.* Philadelphia: Fortress Press.

Paulsen, Henning. 1997. 'Das Kerygma Petri und die urchristliche Apologetik'. In *Zur Literatur und Geschichte des frühen Christentums: Gesammelte Aufsätze*, 173–209. WUNT 99. Tübingen: Mohr (Siebeck).

Pearson, Birger A. 1997a. 'Unity and Diversity in the Early Church as a Social Phenomenon'. In *The Emergence of the Christian Religion: Essays on Early Christianity*, 169–85. Harrisburg: Trinity Press International.

Pearson, Birger A. 1997b. 'Philanthropy in the Greco-Roman World and in Early Christianity'. In *The Emergence of the Christian Religion: Essays on Early Christianity*, 186–213. Harrisburg: Trinity Press International.

Pelikan, Jaroslav. 1993. *Christianity and Classical Culture: The Metamorphosis of Natural Theology in the Christian Encounter with Hellenism.* The Gifford Lectures 1992–3. New Haven/London: Yale University Press.

Pendergraft, Mary. 1992. ' "Thou Shalt Not Eat the Hyena": A Note on "Barnabas" Epistle 10.7'. *VC* 46:75–9.

Pépin, Jean. 1976. *Mythe et Allégorie: Les origines grecques et les contestations judéo-chrétiennes.* Second edn. Paris: Études Augustiniennes.

Perles, F. 1919–20. 'Zwei Übersetzungsfehler im Text der Evangelien', *ZNW* 19:96.

Perrini, Matteo. 1986. *A Diogneto: Alle sorgenti dell'esistenza cristiana.* Brescia: La Scuola.

Pétrement, Simone. 1966. 'Valentin est-il l'auteur de l'épître à Diognète?' *RHPR* 46:34–62.

Pilch, John J., & Malina, Bruce J. 1993. *Biblical Social Values and their Meaning: A Handbook.* Peabody: Hendrickson.

Pilhofer, Peter. 1990. *Presbyteron kreitton: Der Altersbeweis der jüdischen und christlichen Apologeten und seine Vorgeschichte.* WUNT 2:39. Tübingen: Mohr (Siebeck).

Pilhofer, Peter. 1999a. 'Aristides'. *LACL²*, 51.

Pilhofer, Peter. 1999b. 'Athenagoras'. *LACL²*, 63–4.

Plummer, Alfred. 1909. *An Exegetical Commentary on the Gospel According to S. Matthew.* ICC. Edinburgh: T&T Clark.

Pohlenz, Max. 1949. 'Paulus und die Stoa'. *ZNW* 42:69–104.

Pratscher, Wilhelm. 1987. *Der Herrenbruder Jakobus und die Jakobustradition.* FRLANT 139. Göttingen: Vandenhoeck & Ruprecht.

Pritz, Ray. 1988. *Nazarene Jewish Christianity: From the End of the New Testament Period until its Disappearance in the Fourth Century.* Jerusalem: Magnes; Leiden: Brill.

Procopé, John. 1991. 'Höflichkeit'. *RAC* 15:930–86.

Qimron, Elisha. 1992. 'Celibacy in the Dead Sea Scrolls and the Two Kinds of Sectarians'. In *The Madrid Qumran Congress,* 1:287–94. Ed. J. T. Barrera & L. V. Montaner. Leiden: Brill; Madrid: Complutense.

Qimron, Elisha. 1994. 'The Halakha'. In *Qumran Cave 4: V. Miqṣat Maʿase ha-Torah,* 123–77. Ed. E. Qimron & J. Strugnell. DJD 10. Oxford: Clarendon Press.

Rahner, Hugo. 1961. *Kirche und Staat im frühen Christentum.* Munich: Kösel.

Räisänen, Heikki. 1992. *Jesus, Paul and Torah: Collected Essays.* Translated by D. E. Orton. JSNTSS 43. Sheffield: Sheffield Academic Press.

Räisänen, Heikki. 1995. 'The Clash Between Christian Styles of Life in the Book of Revelation'. In *Mighty Minorities? Minorities in Early Christianity—Positions and Strategies: Essays in Honour of Jacob Jervell on his 70th Birthday 21 May 1995,* 151–66. Ed. D. Hellholm et al. Oslo: Scandinavian University Press.

Rajak, Tessa. 1992. 'The Jewish Community and Its Boundaries'. In *The Jews Among Pagans and Christians in the Roman Empire,* 9–28. Ed. J. Lieu et al. London/New York: Routledge.

Reinmuth, Eckart. 1985. *Geist und Gesetz: Studien zu Voraussetzungen und Inhalt der paulinischen Paränese.* Theologische Arbeiten 44. Berlin: Evangelische Verlagsanstalt.

Resch, Gotthold. 1905. *Das Aposteldecret nach seiner ausserkanonischen Textgestalt.* TU 28.3 (NS 13.3). Leipzig: Hinrichs.

Richardson, Peter. 1980. 'Pauline Inconsistency: 1 Corinthians 9:19-23 and Galatians 2:11–14'. *NTS* 26:347–62.

Ricken, Friedo. 1994. 'Naturrecht I: Altkirchliche, mittelalterliche und römisch-katholische Interpretationen'. *TRE* 24:132–53.

Riesner, Rainer. 1991. 'Militia Christi und Militia Caesaris: Tertullian und Clemens Alexandrinus als paradigmatische Positionen in der alten

Kirche'. In *Gott lieben und seine Gebote halten/Loving God and Keeping His Commandments: In memoriam Klaus Bockmühl*, 49–72. Ed. M. Bockmuehl & H. Burkhardt. Giessen/Basle: Brunnen.

Riesner, Rainer. 1994. *Die Frühzeit des Apostels Paulus: Studien zur Chronologie, Missionsstrategie und Theologie.* WUNT 71. Tübingen: Mohr Siebeck. [ET *Paul's Early Period: Chronology, Mission Strategy, Theology,* trans. D. Stott (Grand Rapids: Eerdmans, 1998).]

Ritter, Adolf Martin. 1997. 'Ulrich Wickert, Wolfhart Pannenberg und das Problem der "Hellenisierung des Christentums" '. In *Die Weltlichkeit des Glaubens in der Alten Kirche: Festschrift für Ulrich Wickert zum siebzigsten Geburtstag,* 303–18. Ed. D. Wyrwa et al. BZNW 85. Berlin/New York: de Gruyter.

Rizzi, Marco. 1989. *La Questione dell'unita dell'Ad Diognetum.* Studia patristica Mediolanensia 16. Milan: Vita e pensiero.

Rodd, C. S. 1972. 'Shall Not the Judge of All the Earth Do What is Just? (Gen. xviii. 25)' *ExpTim* 83:137–9.

Roldanus, Johannes. 1987. 'Références patristiques au "chrétien-étranger" dans les trois premiers siècles'. *Cahiers de Biblica Patristica* 1: 27–52.

Rordorf, Willi. 1969. 'Tertullians Beurteilung des Soldatenstandes'. *VC* 23:105–41.

Rosenthal, Franz. 1959. Review of N. Avigad and Y. Yadin, A *Genesis Apocryphon* (Jerusalem: Magnes, 1956). *JNES* 18:82–4.

Rosner, Brian S. 1994. *Paul, Scripture and Ethics: A Study of 1 Corinthians 5–7.* AGJU 22. Leiden: Brill Press [=Repr. Grand Rapids: Baker, 1999].

Rosner, Brian S., ed. 1995. *Understanding Paul's Ethics: Twentieth Century Approaches.* Grand Rapids: Eerdmans; Carlisle: Paternoster Press.

Rüger, Hans Peter. 1991. *Die Weisheitsschrift aus der Kairoer Geniza: Text, Übersetzung und philologischer Kommentar.* WUNT 53. Tübingen: Mohr (Siebeck).

Runia, David T. 1992. '*Verba Philonica*, and the Authenticity of the *De resurrectione* Attributed to Athenagoras'. *VC* 46:313–27.

Sacchi, Alessandro. 1973. 'La Legge Naturale nella lettera ai Romani'. *Atti della XXII Settimana Biblica Italiana,* 375–89.

Safrai, Shmuel. 1983. 'The Land of Israel in Tannaitic Halacha'. In *Das Land Israel in biblischer Zeit: Jerusalem-Symposium 1981 der Hebräischen Universität und der Georg-August-Universität,* 201–15. Ed. G. Strecker. GTA 25. Göttingen: Vandenhoeck & Ruprecht.

Sahlin, Harald. 1970. 'Die drei Kardinalsünden und das neue Testament'. *ST* 24: 93–112.

Saldarini, Anthony J. 1992. 'Pharisees'. *ABD* 5: 289–303.

Saller, Richard P. 1982. *Personal Patronage under the Early Empire.* Cambridge: Cambridge University Press.

Salzmann, Jörg Christian. 1994. 'Vorbildliche Heiden: Überlegungen zum 1. Clemensbrief 55,1'. In *Die Heiden: Juden, Christen und das Problem des Fremden*, 317–24. WUNT 70. Tübingen: Mohr (Siebeck).

Sampley, John Paul. 1980. *Pauline Partnership in Christ: Christian Community and Commitment in Light of Roman Law*. Philadelphia: Fortress Press.

Sanders, E. P. 1985. *Jesus and Judaism*. London: SCM Press.

Sanders, E. P. 1990a. *Jewish Law from Jesus to the Mishnah: Five Studies*. London: SCM Press; Philadelphia: Trinity Press International.

Sanders, E. P. 1990b. 'When is a Law a Law? The Case of Jesus and Paul'. In *Religion and Law*, 139–58. Edited by E. B. Firmage et al. Winona Lake: Eisenbrauns.

Sanders, E. P. 1990c. 'Jewish Association with Gentiles and Galatians 2:11–14'. In *The Conversation Continues: Studies in Paul & John in Honor of J. Louis Martyn*, 170–88. Ed. R. T. Fortna & B. R. Gaventa. Nashville: Abingdon Press.

Sanders, E. P. 1993. *The Historical Figure of Jesus*. London: Allen Lane/Penguin.

Sanders, James A. 1975. 'Torah and Christ'. *Int* 29:372–90.

Sariola, Heikki. 1990. *Markus und das Gesetz: Eine redaktionskritische Untersuchung*. Helsinki: Suomalainen Tiedeakatemia.

Savage, Timothy B. 1996. *Power through Weakness. Paul's Understanding of the Christian Ministry in 2 Corinthians*. SNTSMS 86. Cambridge: Cambridge University Press.

Schaeder, Hans Heinrich. 1942. 'Ναζαρηνός, Ναζωραῖος'. *TDNT* 4:879–84.

Schäfer, Peter. 1998. 'From Jerusalem the Great to Alexandria the Small: The Relationship between Palestine and Egypt in the Graeco-Roman Period'. In *The Talmud Yerushalmi and Graeco-Roman Culture*. Ed. P. Schäfer et al. TSAJ 71. Tübingen: Mohr (Siebeck).

Schäfke, Werner. 1979. 'Frühchristlicher Widerstand'. *ANRW* II 23.1:460–723.

Schelkle, Karl Hermann. 1978. 'Arbeit III: Neues Testament'. *TRE* 3: 622–4.

Schenk, Alexander, Graf von Stauffenberg. 1931. *Die römische Kaisergeschichte bei Malalas: Griechischer Text der Bücher IX–XII und Untersuchungen*. Stuttgart: Kohlhammer.

Schiffman, Lawrence H. 1975. *The Halakhah at Qumran*. SJLA 16. Leiden: Brill, 1975.

Schlatter, Adolf. 1893. *Zur Topographie und Geschichte Palästinas*. Calw/Stuttgart: Vereinsbuchhandlung.

Schlatter, Adolf. 1925. *Geschichte Israels von Alexander dem Großen bis Hadrian*. Third edn. Stuttgart: Calwer.

Schlatter, Adolf. 1929. *Der Evangelist Matthäus: Seine Sprache, sein Ziel, seine Selbständigkeit*. Stuttgart: Calwer.

Schnackenburg, Rudolf. 1986, 1988. *Die sittliche Botschaft des Neuen Testaments*. 2 vols. Second edn. Freiburg: Herder.

Schneemelcher, Wilhelm, ed. 1991, 1992. *New Testament Apocrypha*. 2 vols. Rev. edn. of the Collection initiated by E. Hennecke. ET ed. R. McL. Wilson. Cambridge: Clarke; Louisville: Westminster/John Knox Press.

Schniewind, Julius. 1960. *Das Evangelium nach Matthäus*. NTD 2. Ninth edn. Göttingen: Vandenhoeck & Ruprecht.

Schoedel, William R. 1979. 'In Praise of the King: A Rhetorical Pattern in Athenagoras'. In *Disciplina Nostra: Essays in Memory of Robert F. Evans*, 69–90. Edited by Donald F. Winslow. Patristic Monograph Series 6. Cambridge, MA: Philadelphia Patristic Foundation.

Schoedel, William R. 1989. 'Apologetic Literature and Ambassadorial Activities'. *HTR* 82:55–78.

Scholem, Gershom. 1971. *The Messianic Idea in Judaism*. New York: Schocken.

Scholten, Clemens. 1993. 'Apologeten, frühkirchliche'. *LTK*[3] 1:832–4.

Schrage, Wolfgang. 1988. *The Ethics of the New Testament*. Trans. D. E. Green. Philadelphia: Fortress Press.

Schrage, Wolfgang. 1991, 1995. *Der erste Brief an die Korinther*. Vols. 1–2. EKKNT 7.1–2. Zurich: Benziger; Neukirchen-Vluyn: Neukirchener.

Schrot, Gerhard. 1979. 'Incestus'. *KlPauly*, 5:1386–7.

Schürer, Emil. 1890. *A History of the Jewish People in the Time of Jesus Christ*. Trans. J. Macpherson. 5 vols. Edinburgh: T&T Clark.

Schürer, Emil. 1973, 1979, 1986, 1987. *The History of the Jewish People in the Age of Jesus Christ (175 B.C. – A.D. 135)*. Rev. & ed. G. Vermes et al. 3 vols. in 4. Edinburgh: T&T Clark. [Schürer/Vermes]

Schürmann, Heinz. 1994. *Das Lukasevangelium*. Vol. 2. THKNT 3. Freiburg: Herder.

Schwartz, Daniel R. 1996. 'Temple or City: What did Hellenistic Jews See in Jerusalem?' In *The Centrality of Jerusalem: Historical Perspectives*, 114–27. Ed. M. Poorthuis & Ch. Safrai. Kampen: Kok Pharos.

Schwartz, Daniel R. 1998. 'The Other in 1 and 2 Maccabees'. In *Tolerance and Intolerance in Early Judaism and Christianity*, 30–7. Ed. G. N. Stanton & G. G. Stroumsa. Cambridge: Cambridge University Press.

Schweitzer, Albert. 1931. *The Mysticism of Paul the Apostle*. Trans. W. Montgomery. London: A&C Black.

Schweizer, Eduard. 1960. '"Er wird Nazoräer heißen": Zu Mc 1,24; Mt 2,23'. In *Judentum–Urchristentum–Kirche: Festschrift für Joachim Jeremias*, 90–3. Ed. W. Eltester. BZNW 26. Berlin: Töpelmann. [Repr. in idem, *Neotestamentica: Deutsche und Englische Aufsätze 1951–1963* (Zürich: Theologischer Verlag, 1963), 51–5.]

Schweizer, Eduard. 1976. *Good News According to Matthew*. London: SPCK.

Schwemer, Anna Maria. 1998. 'Paulus in Antiochien'. *BZ* 42:161–80.

Scott, James M. 1995. *Paul and the Nations: The Old Testament and Jewish Background of Paul's Mission to the Nations with Special Reference to the Destination of Galatians*. WUNT 84. Tübingen: Mohr (Siebeck).

Seccombe, David. 1982. *Possessions and the Poor in Luke-Acts*. SNTU B6. Linz: Fuchs.

Seeberg, Alfred. 1903. *Der Katechismus der Urchristenheit*. Leipzig: Deichert. [=Repr. Munich: Kaiser, 1966; ET of pp. 1–22 in Rosner 1995:155–75.]

Segal, Alan F. 1990. *Paul the Convert: The Apostolate and Apostasy of Paul the Pharisee*. New Haven/London: Yale University Press.

Segal, Alan F. 1995. 'Universalism in Judaism and Christianity'. In *Paul in His Hellenistic Context*, 1–29. Ed. T. Engberg-Pedersen. Minneapolis: Fortress Press.

Segal, Ben-Zion, and Levi, Gershon, eds. 1990. *The Ten Commandments in History and Tradition*. Publications of the Perry Foundation for Biblical Research. Jerusalem: Magnes.

Seifrid, Mark A. 1998. 'Natural Revelation and the Purpose of the Law in Romans'. *TynBul* 49:115–29.

Selwyn, Edward Gordon. 1947. *The First Epistle of St. Peter*. Second edn. London: Macmillan.

Sevenster, J. N. 1961. *Paul and Seneca*. NovTSup 4. Leiden: Brill.

Sigal, Philip. 1986. *The Halakhah of Jesus of Nazareth According to the Gospel of Matthew*. Lanham: University Press of America.

Simon, Marcel. 1981. 'The Apostolic Decree and its Setting in the Ancient Church'. In *Le Christianisme antique et son contexte religieux: Scripta Varia Volume II*, 414–37. WUNT 23. Tübingen: Mohr (Siebeck).

Simon, Marcel. 1986. *Verus Israel: A Study of the Relations Between Christians and Jews in the Roman Empire (135–425)*. Trans. H. McKeating. The Littman Library. Oxford: Oxford University Press.

Simonetti, Manlio. 1994. *Biblical Interpretation in the Early Church: An Historical Introduction to Patristic Exegesis*. Trans. J. A. Hughes; ed. A. Bergquist & M. Bockmuehl. Edinburgh: T&T Clark.

Singer, Bruno. 1983. 'Fürstenspiegel'. *TRE* 11:707–11.

Sivan, Hagith. 1993. 'On Hymens and Holiness in Late Antiquity: Opposition to Aristocratic Female Asceticism at Rome'. *JAC* 36:81–93.

Six, Karl. 1912. *Das Aposteldekret (Act 15,28, 29): Seine Entstehung und Geltung in den ersten vier Jahrhunderten*. Veröffentlichungen des biblisch-patristischen Seminars zu Innsbruck 5. Innsbruck: Rauch.

Slater, Thomas B. 1998. 'On the Social Setting of the Revelation to John'. *NTS* 44:232–56.

Slingerland, Dixon. 1986. 'The Nature of Nomos (Law) within the Testaments of the Twelve Patriarchs'. *JBL* 105:39–48.

Smend, Rudolf. 1983. 'Das uneroberte Land'. In *Das Land Israel in biblischer Zeit: Jerusalem-Symposium 1981 der Hebräischen Universität und der Georg-August-Universität*, 91–102. Ed. G. Strecker. GTA 25. Göttingen: Vandenhoeck & Ruprecht.

Smith, Morton. 1987. *Palestinian Parties and Politics that Shaped the Old Testament*. Second edn. London: SCM Press.

Söding, Thomas. 1999. 'Heilig, heilig, heilig: Zur politischen Theologie der Johannes-Apokalypse'. *ZTK* 96:49–76.

Soggin, J. Alberto. 1990. 'Krieg: II. Altes Testament'. *TRE* 20:19–25.

Speyer, Wolfgang. 1963. 'Zu den Vorwürfen der Heiden gegen die Christen'. *JAC* 6: 129–35 [=repr. in idem, *Frühes Christentum im antiken Strahlungsfeld: Ausgewählte Aufsätze*, 7–13, 493. WUNT 50. Tübingen: Mohr Siebeck, 1989].

Speyer, Wolfgang. 1989b. 'Octavius, der Dialog des Minucius Felix: Fiktion oder historische Wirklichkeit?' In *Frühes Christentum im antiken Strahlungsfeld: Ausgewählte Aufsätze*, 14–20. WUNT 50. Tübingen: Mohr (Siebeck).

Spidlík, Tomas. 1990. 'Stylites'. *Dictionnaire de Spiritualité*, 14:1267–75.

Stacey, David. 1990. *Prophetic Drama in the Old Testament*. London: Epworth Press.

Stanton, Graham. 1992. 'Aspects of Early Christian and Jewish Worship: Pliny and the *Kerygma Petrou*'. In *Worship, Theology and Ministry in the Early Church: Essays in Honor of Ralph P. Martin*, 84–98. Ed. M. J. Wilkins & T. Paige. JSNTSup 87. Sheffield: Sheffield Academic Press.

Stark, Rodney. 1996. *The Rise of Christianity: A Sociologist Reconsiders History*. Princeton: Princeton University Press.

Stegemann, Ekkehard. 1996. '"Ich habe öffentlich zur Welt gesprochen": Jesus und die Öffentlichkeit'. *JBT* 11:103–21.

Stein, D. 1974. 'The Development of the Notion of *Naturalis Ratio*'. In *Daube Noster: Essays in Legal History for David Daube*, 305–16. Ed. A. Watson. Edinburgh/London: Scottish Academic Press.

Steiner, Heinrich. 1989. *Das Verhältnis Tertullians zur antiken Paideia*. Studien zur Theologie und Geschichte 3. St. Ottilien: EOS Verlag.

Stemberger, Günter. 1979. 'Die Beurteilung Roms in der rabbinischen Literatur'. *ANRW* II 19.2:338–96.

Stemberger, Günter. 1983. 'Die Bedeutung des "Landes Israel" in der rabbinischen Tradition'. *Kairos* 25:176–99.

Stemberger, Günter. 1996. *Introduction to the Talmud and Midrash*. Trans. & ed. M. Bockmuehl. Second edn. Edinburgh: T&T Clark.

Stendahl, Krister. 1976. *Paul among Jews and Gentiles and Other Essays*. Philadelphia: Fortress Press.

Stevenson, J., ed. 1957. *A New Eusebius: Documents Illustrative of the History of the Church to* A.D. *337*. London: SPCK.

Stipp, Hermann-Josef. 1995. 'Simson, der Nasiräer'. *VT* 45:337–69.

Strack, Hermann L. & Billerbeck, Paul. 1922–61. *Kommentar zum Neuen Testament aus Talmud und Midrasch*. 7 vols. Munich: Beck.

Stroumsa, Guy G. 1998a. 'Celsus, Origen and the Nature of Religion'. In *Discorsi di Verità: Paganesimo, Giudaismo e Cristianesimo a confronto nel* Contro Celso *di Origene. Atti del II Convegno del Gruppo Italiano di Ricerca su 'Origene e la Tradizione Alessandrina'*, 81–94. Ed. L. Perrone. Studia Ephemeridis Augustinianum 61. Rome: Estratto/Institutum Patristicum Augustinianum. [=repr. in Stroumsa 1999:44–56].

Stroumsa, Guy G. 1998b. 'Tertullian on Idolatry and the Limits of Intolerance'. In *Tolerance and Intolerance in Early Judaism and Christianity*, 173–84. Ed. G. N. Stanton & G. G. Stroumsa. Cambridge: University Press [=repr. in Stroumsa 1999:100–9].

Stroumsa, Guy G. 1999. *Barbarian Philosophy: The Religious Revolution of Early Christianity*. WUNT 112. Tübingen: Mohr (Siebeck).

Sussmann, J. 1981. 'The Inscription in the Synagogue at Reḥob'. In *Ancient Synagogues Revealed*, 146–53. Jerusalem: Israel Exploration Society.

Sussmann, Ya'akov. 1994. 'The History of the Halakha and the Dead Sea Scrolls: Preliminary Talmudic Observations on Miqṣat Ma'ase ha-Torah (4QMMT)'. In *Qumran Cave 4: V. Miqṣat Ma'ase ha-Torah*, 179–200. Ed. E. Qimron & J. Strugnell. DJD 10. Oxford: Clarendon Press.

Swanson, Dwight D. 1995. *The Temple Scroll and the Bible: The Methodology of 11QT*. STDJ 14. Leiden: Brill.

Synek, Eva M. 1998. 'Die Apostolischen Konstitutionen – ein "christlicher Talmud" aus dem 4. Jh'. *Bib* 79:27–56.

Taatz, Irene. 1991. *Frühjüdische Briefe: Die paulinischen Briefe im Rahmen der offiziellen religiösen Briefe des Frühjudentums*. NTOA 16. Fribourg: Universitätsverlag; Göttingen: Vandenhoeck & Ruprecht.

Taeger, Jens-W. 1998. 'Begründetes Schweigen: Paulus und paulinische Tradition in der Johannesapokalypse'. In *Paulus, Apostel Jesu Christi: Festschrift für Günter Klein zum 70. Geburtstag*, 187–204. Ed. M. Trowitzsch. Tübingen: Mohr (Siebeck).

Taylor, Alison. 1993. 'A Roman Lead Coffin with Pipeclay Figurines from Arrington, Cambridgeshire'. *Britannia* 24:191–225.

Taylor, Justin B. 1994. 'Why Were the Disciples First Called "Christians" at Antioch (Acts 11,26)?' *RB* 101:75–94.

Taylor, Justin. 1998. 'Why Did Paul Persecute the Church?' In *Tolerance and Intolerance in Early Judaism and Christianity*, 99–120. Ed. G. N. Stanton & G. G. Stroumsa. Cambridge: Cambridge University Press.

Taylor, Nicholas. 1992. *Paul, Antioch and Jerusalem: A Study in Relationships and Authority in Earliest Christianity.* JSNTSup 66. Sheffield: JSOT Press.

Theissen, Gerd. 1982. *The Social Setting of Pauline Christianity: Essays on Corinth.* Trans. J. H. Schutz. Edinburgh: T&T Clark.

Theissen, Gerd. 1992. *The Gospels in Context: Social and Political History in the Synoptic Tradition.* Trans. L. M. Maloney. Edinburgh: T&T Clark.

Thomas, Johannes. 1992. *Der jüdische Phokylides: Formgeschichtliche Zugänge zu Pseudo-Phokylides und Vergleich mit der neutestamentlichen Paränese.* NTOA 23. Fribourg: Universitätsverlag; Göttingen: Vandenhoeck & Ruprecht.

Thompson, Cynthia L. 1988. 'Hairstyles, Head-coverings, and St. Paul: Portraits from Roman Corinth'. *BA* 51:99–115.

Thompson, Michael B. 1991. *Clothed with Christ: The Example and Teaching of Jesus in Romans 12.1–15.13.* JSNTSup 59. Sheffield: Sheffield Academic Press.

Thrall, Margaret E. 1980. 'Super-Apostles, Servants of Christ, and Servants of Satan'. *JSNT* 6: 42–57.

Thyen, Hartwig. 1955. *Der Stil der jüdisch-hellenistischen Homilie.* FRLANT 65. Göttingen: Vandenhoeck & Ruprecht.

Tomson, Peter J. 1988. 'Zavim 5:12 – Reflections on Dating Mishnaic Halakhah'. In *History and Form: Dutch Studies in the Mishnah*, 53–69. Edited by A. Kuyt & N. A. van Uchelen. Amsterdam: University of Amsterdam.

Tomson, Peter J. 1990. *Paul and the Jewish Law: Halakha in the Letters of the Apostle to the Gentiles.* CRINT 3:1. Assen/Maastricht: Van Gorcum; Minneapolis: Fortress Press.

Treidler, Hans. 1975. 'Amanos'. *Der Kleine Pauly*, 1:287–8.

Tsevat, Matitiahu. 1992. 'Was Samuel a Nazirite?' In *"Sha'arei Talmon": Studies in the Bible, Qumran and the Ancient Near East, presented to Shemaryahu Talmon*, 199–204. Ed. M. Fishbane. Winona Lake: Eisenbrauns.

Ulrich, Eugene Charles, Jr. 1978. *The Qumran Text of Samuel and Josephus.* HSM 19. Missoula: Scholars Press.

Urbach, Ephraim E. 1987. *The Sages: Their Concepts and Beliefs.* Trans. I. Abrahams. Cambridge, MA/London: Harvard University Press.

Urbach, Ephraim E. 1990. 'The Decalogue in Jewish Worship'. In *The Ten Commandments in History and Tradition*, 166–81. Ed. B.-Z. Segal & G. Levi. Jerusalem: Magnes.

van den Broek, Roelof. 1988. 'Eugnostus and Aristides on the Ineffable God'. In *Knowledge of God in the Graeco-Roman World*, 202–18. Ed. R. van den Broek et al. Études préliminaires aux Religions orientales dans l'Empire Romain 112. Leiden: Brill. [Repr. in idem, *Studies in Gnosticism and Alexandrian Christianity*, NHS 39 (Leiden: Brill, 1996), 22–41.]

van der Horst, P. W. 1985. 'Pseudo-Phocylides'. In *OTP*, 2:565–82.

van Houten, Christiana. 1991. *The Alien in Israelite Law*. JSOTSup 107. Sheffield: Sheffield Academic Press.

van Unnik, W. C. 1954. 'The Teaching of Good Works in 1 Peter'. *NTS* 1:92–110.

van Unnik, W. C. 1975. 'Lob und Strafe durch die Obrigkeit: Hellenistisches zu Röm. 13,3–4'. In *Jesus und Paulus: Festschrift für Werner Georg Kümmel zum 70. Geburtstag*, 334–43. Ed. E. E. Ellis & E. Grässer. Göttingen: Vandenhoeck & Ruprecht.

van Unnik, W. C. 1980. 'Die Rücksicht auf die Reaktion der Nicht-Christen als Motiv in der altchristlichen Paränese'. In *Sparsa Collecta: The Collected Essays of W. C. van Unnik*, 2:307–22. NovTSup 30. Leiden: Brill.

van Unnik, W. C. 1983. 'Die Gotteslehre bei Aristides und in gnostischen Schriften'. In *Sparsa Collecta: The Collected Essays of W. C. van Unnik*, 3:106–13. NovTSup 31. Leiden: Brill.

van Zyl, D. H. 1986. 'Cicero and the Law of Nature'. *South African Law Journal* 103:55–68.

Veltri, Giuseppe. 1992. 'Mittelalterliche Nachahmung weisheitlicher Texte: Datierung und Herkunft der sog. "Weisheitsschrift aus der Kairoer Geniza" '. *TRu* 57:405–30.

Venetz, Hermann-Josef. 1989. 'Zwischen Unterwerfung und Verweigerung: Widersprüchliches im Neuen Testament? Zu Röm und Offb'. In *Prophetie und Widerstand*, 142–65. Ed V. Eid. Theologie zur Zeit 5. Düsseldorf: Patmos-Verlag.

Vermes, Geza. 1983. *Jesus the Jew*. Second edn. London: SCM Press.

Vermes, Geza. 1968. 'The Decalogue and the Minim'. In *In Memoriam Paul Kahle*, 232–40. Ed. M. Black & G. Fohrer. BZAW 103. Berlin: Töpelmann [=Repr. in *Post-Biblical Jewish Studies*, SJLA 8 (Leiden: Brill, 1975), 37–49].

Vielhauer, Philipp. 1979. 'Paulus und das Alte Testament'. In *Oikodome: Aufsätze zum Neuen Testament*, 2:196–228. Ed. G. Klein. TBü 65. Munich: Kaiser.

Vögtle, Anton. 1936. *Die Tugend- und Lasterkataloge im Neuen Testament*. NTAbh 16:4–5. Münster: Aschendorff.

Voigt, Moritz. 1966 [=1856–76]. *Das Ius Naturale, Aequum et Bonum und Ius Gentium der Römer*. 4 vols. Aalen: Scientia.

von Rad, Gerhard. 1957. *Theologie des Alten Testaments*, vol. 1. Munich: Kaiser.

von Rad, Gerhard. 1970. *Weisheit in Israel*. Neukirchen-Vluyn: Neukirchener.

Waage, Dorothy. 1952. *Antioch on-the-Orontes*, vol. 4.2: *Greek, Roman, Byzantine and Crusaders' Coins*. Princeton: Princeton University Press; London: Oxford University Press; The Hague: Martinus Nijhoff.

Wagner, H. 1978. *Studien zur allgemeinen Rechtslehre des Gaius: Ius gentium und ius naturale in ihrem Verhältnis zum ius civile*. Studia Amstelodamensia ad Epigraphicam, Ius Antiquum et Papyrologicam Pertinentia 15. Zutphen: Terra.

Waldstein, W. 1988. 'Bemerkungen zum ius naturale bei den klassischen Juristen'. *Zeitschrift der Savigny-Stiftung für Rechtsgeschichte* (Romanistische Abteilung) 105:702–11.

Waldstein, Wolfgang. 1983. 'Naturrecht bei den klassischen römischen Juristen'. In *Das Naturrechtsdenken heute und morgen: Gedächtnisschrift für René Marcic*, 239–53. Ed. D. Mayer-Maly & P. M. Simons. Berlin: Duncker & Humblot.

Waldstein, Wolfgang. 1994. 'Ius naturale im nachklassischen römischen Recht und bei Justinian'. *Zeitschrift der Savigny-Stiftung für Rechtsgeschichte* (Romanistische Abteilung) 111:1–65.

Wallace, Richard, and Williams, Wynne. 1998. *The Three Worlds of Paul of Tarsus*. London: Routledge.

Walsh, Joseph J., and Gottlieb, Gunther. 1992. 'Zur Christenfrage im zweiten Jahrhundert'. In *Christen und Heiden in Staat und Gesellschaft des zweiten bis vierten Jahrhunderts: Gedanken und Thesen zu einem schwierigen Verhältnis*, 3–86. Edited by G. Gottlieb & P. Barceló. Schriften der Philosophischen Fakultäten der Universität Augsburg 44: Historisch-sozialwissenschaftliche Reihe. Munich: Vögel.

Waltke, Bruce K. 1979. 'Abomination'. *ISBE* 1:13–14.

Walzer, Richard. 1949. *Galen on Jews and Christians*. London: Oxford University Press.

Watson, Duane F. 1995. 'Rhetorical Criticism of the Pauline Epistles Since 1975'. *CRBS* 3:219–48.

Wechsler, Andreas. 1991. *Geschichtsbild und Apostelstreit: Eine forschungsgeschichtliche und exegetische Studie über den antiochenischen Zwischenfall (Gal 2,11–14)*. BZNW 62. Berlin/New York: de Gruyter.

Wedderburn, A. J. M. 1993. 'The "Apostolic Decree": Tradition & Redaction'. *NovT* 35:362–89.

Wehnert, Jürgen. 1997. *Die Reinheit des 'christlichen Gottesvolkes' aus Juden und Heiden: Studien zum historischen und theologischen Hintergrund des sogenannten Aposteldekrets*. FRLANT 173. Göttingen: Vandenhoeck & Ruprecht.

Weima, Jeffrey A. D. 1997. 'Diognetus, Epistle to'. *DLNT*, 302–4.

Weinfeld, Moshe. 1983. 'The Extent of the Promised Land – the Status of Transjordan'. In *Das Land Israel in biblischer Zeit: Jerusalem-Symposium 1981 der Hebräischen Universität und der Georg-August-Universität*, 59–75. Ed. G. Strecker. GTA 25. Göttingen: Vandenhoeck & Ruprecht.

Weinfeld, Moshe. 1993. *The Promise of the Land: The Inheritance of the Land of Canaan by the Israelites*. Taubman Lectures in Jewish Studies 3. Berkeley: University of California Press.

Weiss, E. 1917. 'Ius gentium'. *PW* 10:1218–31.

Welborn, Laurence L. 1992. 'Clement, First Epistle of'. *ABD* 1:1055–60.

Wellhausen, Julius. 1905. *Prolegomena zur Geschichte Israels*. Sixth edn. Berlin: Reimer.

Wendebourg, Dorothea. 1987. 'Das Martyrium in der alten Kirche als ethisches Problem'. *ZKG* 98:295–320.

Wengst, Klaus. 1984. *Didache (Apostellehre), Barnabasbrief, Zweiter Klemensbrief, Schrift an Diognet*. Schriften des Urchristentums 2. Darmstadt: Wissenschaftliche Buchgesellschaft.

Wengst, Klaus. 1987. *Pax Romana and the Peace of Jesus Christ*. Trans. J. Bowden. London: SCM Press.

Wengst, Klaus. 1999. 'Diognetbrief'. *LACL*², 172–3.

Wenham, G. J. 1984. 'Matthew and Divorce: An Old Crux Revisited'. *JSNT* 22:95–107.

Wenham, G. J. 1986. 'The Syntax of Matthew 19.9'. *JSNT* 28:17–23.

Westerholm, Stephen. 1986–7. 'On Fulfilling the Whole Law (Gal 5:14)'. *SEÅ* 51/52:229–37.

Wibbing, Siegfried. 1959. *Die Tugend- und Lasterkataloge im Neuen Testament*. BZNW 25. Berlin: Töpelmann.

Wilken, Robert L. 1984. *The Christians as the Romans Saw Them*. New Haven: Yale University Press.

Winkel, L. C. 1993. 'Einige Bemerkungen über ius naturale und ius gentium'. In *Ars Boni et Aequi: Festschrift für Wolfgang Waldstein zum 65. Geburtstag*, 443–9. Ed. M. J. Schermaier & Z. Végh. Stuttgart: Steiner.

Winter, Bruce W. 1988. 'The Public Honouring of Christian Benefactors'. *JSNT* 34:87–103.

Winter, Bruce W. 1994. *Seek the Welfare of the City: Christians as Benefactors and Citizens*. Grand Rapids: Eerdmans; Carlisle: Paternoster Press.

Winter, Bruce W. 1999. 'Gallio's Ruling on the Legal Status of Early Christianity (Acts 18:14–15)'. *TynBul* 50:213–24.

Wischmeyer, Oda. 1996. 'Physis und Ktisis bei Paulus: Die paulinische Rede von Schöpfung und Natur'. *ZTK* 93:352–75.

Witherington, Ben. 1993. 'Not so Idle Thoughts about *eidolothuton'*. *TynBul* 44:237–54.

Witherington, Ben. 1998. *The Acts of the Apostles: A Socio-Rhetorical Commentary*. Grand Rapids: Eerdmans.

Wolfson, H. A. 1947. *Philo: Foundations of Religious Philosophy in Judaism, Christianity, and Islam*. Structure and Growth of Philosophic Systems from Plato to Spinoza 2. 2 vols. Cambridge, MA: Harvard University Press.

Wright, N. T. 1996. *Jesus and the Victory of God*. Minneapolis: Fortress Press.

Wyschogrod, Michael. 1988. 'A Jewish Postscript'. In *Encountering Jesus: A Debate on Christology*, 179–87. Ed. S. T. Davis. Atlanta: John Knox Press.

Wyschogrod, Michael. 1993. 'Christianity and Mosaic Law'. *Pro Ecclesia* 2:451–9.

Yadin, Yigael. 1983. *The Temple Scroll*. 3 vols. Jerusalem: Israel Exploration Society.

Ziegler, Adolf, & Brunner, Gerbert. 1993. 'Die Frage nach einer politischen Absicht des Ersten Klemensbriefes'. *ANRW* II 27.1:55–76.

Ziesler, John. 1989. *Paul's Letter to the Romans*. TPI New Testament Commentaries. London: SCM Press; Philadelphia: Trinity Press International.

Zimmerli, Walther. 1963. *Das Gesetz und die Propheten: Zum Verständnis des Alten Testaments*. Göttingen: Vandenhoeck & Ruprecht.

Zissu, Boaz. 1998. '"Qumran Type" Graves in Jerusalem: Archaeological Evidence of an Essene Community?' *DSD* 5:158–71.

Zissu, Boaz. 1999. 'Odd Tomb Out: Has Jerusalem's Essene Cemetery Been Found?' *BAR* 25.2:50–5, 62.

LIST OF FIRST PUBLICATIONS

Earlier versions of several chapters appeared in the following publications.

Chapter 1
'Halakhah and Ethics in the Jesus Tradition', in *Early Christian Thought in its Jewish Context*, ed. J. Barclay & J. Sweet (Cambridge: Cambridge University Press, 1996), 264–78.

Chapter 2
'Matthew 5.32; 19.9 in the Light of Pre-Rabbinic Halakhah', *NTS* 35 (1989) 291–5.

Chapter 3
'"Let the Dead Bury their Dead" (Matt. 8:22/Luke 9:62): Jesus and the Halakhah', *JTS* NS 49 (1998) 553–81.

Chapter 4
'Antioch and James the Just', in *James the Just and Christian Origins*, ed. B. Chilton & C. A. Evans, NTSup 98 (Leiden: Brill, 1999), 155–98.

Chapter 5
'Natural Law in Second Temple Judaism', *VT* 45 (1995) 17–44.

Chapter 7
'The Noachide Commandments and New Testament Ethics: With Special Reference to Acts 15 and Pauline Halakhah', *RB* 102 (1995) 72–101.

Chapter 9
'Jewish and Christian Public Ethics in the Early Roman Empire', in *Tolerance and Intolerance in Early Judaism and Early Christianity*, ed. G. N. Stanton & G. G. Stroumsa (Cambridge: Cambridge University Press, 1998), 342–55.

INDEX OF ANCIENT SOURCES

Books of the Old and New Testaments are in (English) canonical order; all others in alphabetical order. Most passing or unspecific references have been omitted.

1. THE BIBLE
1.1. Hebrew Old Testament

Genesis

1.1	108
1.27	6, 104
1–3	96
1–11	87, 89, 90, 150–52
2.16	160
2.16–17	89, 150, 151
2.24	6, 120
3.5	151
3.14	151
4	151
4.10	90
6.5	90
6.11	151
6.11–13	90
6.13	151
9	152, 156, 166
9.1–17	90
9.4–5	166
9.4–6	151
9.20–27	151
10	79
11	151
11.4	90, 151
15.18	62
17	152
18.23–32	219
18.25	92
20.3–4	91
20.9	91
23.4–20	29
26.5	155
32.32	152
34	151
34.7	91
35.22	19, 20
38	151
47.29–30	29
49.4	18, 19
49.13	62
49.26	37, 44
49.29–30	29

Exodus

12.43	153
12.43–49	153
12.49	165
18	91
18.20	29
18.27	39
19.15	46
20	148
20.1	152
20.2	152
20.10	153
20.12	5
20.17	9
20.19	152
21–23	91
23.9	153
23.12	153
23.31	62
24.7	vii
29.37	11
31.14	13
34.15–16	155

Leviticus

11.22	43
11.31–35	4
16.29	167
17.8–9	153
17.10–15	166
17.15	153
17–18	78, 87, 165, 167
17–26	153
18	151, 153
18.8	135
18.20	18, 21
18.22	130
18.26	130
18–20	148, 153, 155, 168, 169
19	160
19.10	153

19.17	9
19.18	153, 209
19.34	153, 165
20	153
20.2–5	153
20.10	19
20.11	20, 135
21.1	31
21.2–3	29
21.6	37
21.7	18
21.11	29, 31
21.11–12	24
21.13–15	18, 21
21.15	18
23.22	153
24	166
24.10–16	153
24.17–22	166
24.22	165
25.6–7	153
25.25–26	153
25.47–55	153
26.19	66

Numbers

5.11–31	38
5.13–14	18, 21
5.20	18, 21
6.1–21	38
6.2	45
6.3–4	41
6.4	41
6.5	43, 46
6.6	24, 29, 31
6.8	37, 46
6.9–12	42
6.11	38
6.14	38
6.16	38
6.18–21	44
9.14	165
13.21	62, 68

1.2 Deuterocanonical Books (Apocrypha)

1.3. New Testament

2. JEWISH LITERATURE
2.1 Qumran

2.2 Philo of Alexandria

2.3 Flavius Josephus

2.4 Other Texts of the Second Temple Period

2.5. Texts of the Rabbinic Period

3. EARLY CHRISTIAN LITERATURE

4. OTHER ANCIENT SOURCES

INDEX OF MODERN AUTHORS

INDEX OF SUBJECTS